# International Perspectives on Socio-Economic Development in the Era of Globalization

Saurabh Sen
*Sunbeam College for Women, India*

Anshuman Bhattacharya
*Sunbeam College for Women, India*

Ruchi Sen
*Sunbeam College for Women, India*

A volume in the Advances in Electronic Government, Digital Divide, and Regional Development (AEGDDRD) Book Series

BUSINESS SCIENCE Reference
An Imprint of IGI Global

Published in the United States of America by
Business Science Reference (an imprint of IGI Global)
701 E. Chocolate Avenue
Hershey PA, USA 17033
Tel: 717-533-8845
Fax: 717-533-8661
E-mail: cust@igi-global.com
Web site: http://www.igi-global.com



Library of Congress Cataloging-in-Publication Data

Names: Sen, Saurabh, 1978- editor.
Title: International perspectives on socio-economic development in the era of globalization / Saurabh Sen, Anshuman Bhattacharya, and Ruchi Sen, editors.
Description: Hershey : Business Science Reference, 2016. | Includes bibliographical references and index.
Identifiers: LCCN 2015046860| ISBN 9781466699083 (hardcover : alk. paper) | ISBN 9781466699090 (ebook)
Subjects: LCSH: Economic development--India. | Human capital--India. | Social change--India. | India--Economic policy--21st century. | Globalization--India.
Classification: LCC HC435.3 .I658 2016 | DDC 338.954--dc23 LC record available at http://lccn.loc.gov/2015046860

This book is published in the IGI Global book series Advances in Electronic Government, Digital Divide, and Regional Development (AEGDDRD) (ISSN: 2326-9103; eISSN: 2326-9111)

British Cataloguing in Publication Data
A Cataloguing in Publication record for this book is available from the British Library.



For electronic access to this publication, please contact: eresources@igi-global.com.

# Advances in Electronic Government, Digital Divide, and Regional Development (AEGDDRD) Book Series

Zaigham Mahmood
*University of Derby, UK & North West University, South Africa*

ISSN: 2326-9103
EISSN: 2326-9111

Mission

The successful use of digital technologies (including social media and mobile technologies) to provide public services and foster economic development has become an objective for governments around the world. The development towards electronic government (or e-government) not only affects the efficiency and effectiveness of public services, but also has the potential to transform the nature of government interactions with its citizens. Current research and practice on the adoption of electronic/digital government and the implementation in organizations around the world aims to emphasize the extensiveness of this growing field.

**The Advances in Electronic Government, Digital Divide & Regional Development (AEGDDRD)** book series aims to publish authored, edited and case books encompassing the current and innovative research and practice discussing all aspects of electronic government development, implementation and adoption as well the effective use of the emerging technologies (including social media and mobile technologies) for a more effective electronic governance (or e-governance).

Coverage

- Adoption of Innovation with Respect to E-Government
- Knowledge Divide, Digital Divide
- ICT within Government and Public Sectors
- ICT Infrastructure and Adoption for E-Government Provision
- Emerging Technologies within the Public Sector
- Case Studies and Practical Approaches to E-Government and E-Governance
- Current Research and Emerging Trends in E-Government Development
- Public Information Management, Regional Planning, Rural Development
- Electronic Government, Digital Democracy, Digital Government
- E-Government in Developing Countries and Technology Adoption

IGI Global is currently accepting manuscripts for publication within this series. To submit a proposal for a volume in this series, please contact our Acquisition Editors at Acquisitions@igi-global.com or visit: http://www.igi-global.com/publish/.

The Advances in Electronic Government, Digital Divide, and Regional Development (AEGDDRD) Book Series (ISSN 2326-9103) is published by IGI Global, 701 E. Chocolate Avenue, Hershey, PA 17033-1240, USA, www.igi-global.com. This series is composed of titles available for purchase individually; each title is edited to be contextually exclusive from any other title within the series. For pricing and ordering information please visit http://www.igi-global.com/book-series/advances-electronic-government-digital-divide/37153. Postmaster: Send all address changes to above address. 

## Titles in this Series

*For a list of additional titles in this series, please visit: www.igi-global.com*

*Comparative Political and Economic Perspectives on the MENA Region*
M. Mustafa Erdoğdu (Marmara University, Turkey) and Bryan Christiansen (PryMarke, LLC, USA)
Information Science Reference • copyright 2016 • 386pp • H/C (ISBN: 9781466696013) • US $205.00 (our price)

*Handbook of Research on Entrepreneurial Success and its Impact on Regional Development*
Luísa Carvalho (Universidade Aberta, Portugal & CEFAGE, Universidade de Évora, Portugal)
Information Science Reference • copyright 2016 • 878pp • H/C (ISBN: 9781466695672) • US $430.00 (our price)

*Trends, Prospects, and Challenges in Asian E-Governance*
Inderjeet Singh Sodhi (St. Wilfred's P.G. College, India)
Information Science Reference • copyright 2016 • 410pp • H/C (ISBN: 9781466695368) • US $190.00 (our price)

*Handbook of Research on Comparative Approaches to the Digital Age Revolution in Europe and the Americas*
Brasilina Passarelli (School of Communications and Arts, University of São Paulo, Brazil) Joseph Straubhaar (The University of Texas at Austin, USA) and Aurora Cuevas-Cerveró (Complutense University of Madrid, Spain)
Information Science Reference • copyright 2016 • 530pp • H/C (ISBN: 9781466687400) • US $325.00 (our price)

*Cloud Computing Technologies for Connected Government*
Zaigham Mahmood (University of Derby, UK & North West University, South Africa)
Information Science Reference • copyright 2016 • 416pp • H/C (ISBN: 9781466686298) • US $195.00 (our price)

*Promoting Social Change and Democracy through Information Technology*
Vikas Kumar (Asia-Pacific Institute of Management, India) and Jakob Svensson (Uppsala University, Sweden)
Information Science Reference • copyright 2015 • 326pp • H/C (ISBN: 9781466685024) • US $195.00 (our price)

*Digital Solutions for Contemporary Democracy and Government*
Kelvin Joseph Bwalya (University of Botswana, Botswana) and Stephen Mutula (University of Kwa Zulu Natal, South Africa)
Information Science Reference • copyright 2015 • 426pp • H/C (ISBN: 9781466684300) • US $200.00 (our price)

*Cases on Grassroots Campaigns for Community Empowerment and Social Change*
Rebecca Nthogo Lekoko (University of Botswana, Botswana)
Information Science Reference • copyright 2015 • 378pp • H/C (ISBN: 9781466685680) • US $175.00 (our price)

IGI GLOBAL
DISSEMINATOR OF KNOWLEDGE
www.igi-global.com

701 E. Chocolate Ave., Hershey, PA 17033
Order online at www.igi-global.com or call 717-533-8845 x100
To place a standing order for titles released in this series, contact: cust@igi-global.com
Mon-Fri 8:00 am - 5:00 pm (est) or fax 24 hours a day 717-533-8661

# Table of Contents

# Detailed Table of Contents



This chapter aims to analyze the roles of human capital and competency in global business, thus explaining the theoretical and practical overviews of human capital and competency; the significance of human capital in global business; and the significance of competency in global business. The accomplishment of human capital and competency is vital for modern organizations that seek to serve suppliers and customers, increase business performance, reinforce competitiveness, and acquire regular success in global business. Thus, it is necessary for modern organizations to analyze their human capital and competency applications, create a strategic plan to constantly explore their functional advancements, and immediately respond to human capital and competency needs of customers. The chapter argues that applying human capital and competency has the potential to enhance organizational performance and achieve strategic goals in the information age.



Marketing plays a vital role to develop the tourism and encourage the tourists to visit the destination and involve the people to enhance their socio economic condition as well. The purpose of this study is to explore three research questions about marketing strategies, about marketing tools and integrated promotional strategies in general and in this particular destination. This study aims to analyze with the help of a questionnaire of 150 respondents. This present study concentrates on impact of 7Ps on Tourists satisfaction. Collected data has analyzed by regression model. There is a great scope of tourism because every village has unique art, culture, folklore, heritage, and lifestyle and so on. Due to lack of proper marketing practices, tourism has facing different problems to pursue parallel with the main stream entrepreneurs. This study is relevant for balancing the demand and supply of tourism motivational requirement indicators which can offer better tourism service excellence in Bishnupur. It will also play a vital role in terms of the policy implication and to analyze the impact for attaining sustainable tourism development in Bishnupur.

Efficiency of assets management is an absolutely unavoidable issue in accomplishing the wealth maximization objective of business. In India, the changing scenario in the front of demographic, social and cultural made a prominent impact on the growth of pharmaceutical industry. In fact, during the last two decades the changing socio-cultural and business environment of India witnessed a rapid change in various managerial as well as financial applications of the Indian pharma sector. Assets management is no doubt a vital part of the overall strategy for achieving financial objectives of any industry. In this backdrop, the present study empirically investigates the relationship between the efficiency of assets management and profitability of the Indian pharmaceutical industry during the period 1998-99 to 2012-13 and also examines whether its findings conform to the theoretical arguments. Besides this, the paper also tries to make a comparison, in respect of the efficiency of assets management, between multinational and domestic companies in the Indian pharmaceutical industry during the same period to know whether changing socio-cultural and business environment gives an age to domestic companies in respect of assets management or not. The sample size of the study consists of ten pharmaceutical companies by taking five multinational and five domestic companies from the Indian pharmaceutical industry. The issues analyzed in this study have been tackled using relevant statistical tools and techniques.



Over the last couple of decades, the world has witnessed a spectacular increase in the size and number of Transnational Corporations (TNCs). This explosion has resulted in the overseas practices of such companies coming under intense scrutiny, and has highlighted that in most cases, governments lack the resources necessary to ensure TNC compliance to international standards in key areas such as labour rights, environmental pollution, and social justice. As a direct result of the failure of national and international attempts to regulate corporate behaviour, recent years have seen the mushrooming of a number of codes aimed at regulating corporate behaviour, and an increased focus on corporate social responsibility. This chapter will attempt to evaluate the effectiveness of such codes of ethical corporate conduct in the light of available evidence, focusing on the conceptualisation of such regulatory mechanisms, and their relationship to the larger corpus of corporate social, commercial, and ethical interactions. The work will then seek to evaluate the effectiveness of such codes as instruments of privatised governance, particularly through the examination of corporate stakeholder behaviour and recent examples of global best practice.



The concept of Financial Inclusion is not a new one. It has become a catchphrase now and has attracted the global attention in the recent past. Lack of accessible, affordable and appropriate financial services has always been a global problem. It is estimated that about 2.9 billion people around the world do not have access to formal sources of banking and financial services. India is said to live in its villages, a convincing statement, considering that nearly 72% of our population lives there. However, a significant proportion of our 650,000 odd villages does not have a single bank branch to boast of, leaving swathes of the rural population in financial exclusion. RBI has reported that the financial exclusion in India leads to the loss of GDP to the extent of one per cent (RBI, Working Paper Series (DEPR): 8/2011). Financially excluded people, consistently, depend on money lenders even for their day to day needs, borrowing at excessive rates to finally get caught in a debt trap. In addition, people in far-off villages are completely unaware of financial products like insurance, which could protect them in adverse situation. Therefore, financial inclusion is a big necessity for our country as a large chunk of the world's poor resides here. Access to finance by the poor and vulnerable groups is a prerequisite for poverty reduction and social cohesion. Present paper is an attempt to highlight the present efforts of financial inclusion in India its future road map, its challenges etc.



Uttarakhand has immense tourism potential for growth of tourist traffic. With the adverse effect of mass tourism and a growing environmental awareness, ecotourism now represents the fastest growing sub sector of the tourism industry, generating billions of dollars annually. Ecotourism plays an important role in economic, socio- cultural and environmental development of the society. Therefore the present research answers the question as to how does ecotourism affect the local community, economy, culture and the environment. According to the collected data the results of the study indicated that when residents in the community were asked to reveal ecotourism impacts, they assessed the perception of impacts in both negative and positive ways.



Women plays a vital role in business and they are a major resource potential in entrepreneurship. Unfortunately, women entrepreneurs tend to face greater obstacles in access to credit, market knowledge, business needs and by the limits of trade agreements and the constraints of trade policies. Thus, there is a need for more efficient policies for the development of female entrepreneurship. The chapter offer analysis of state of the empowerment of women in the globalization. Then, the analysis of the theoretical foundations is for justifying the role of women as entrepreneur and promoter of gender equality and constraints that they are facing. Then, it is an opportunity to offer a brief overview about women in the socio-economic development in MENA region. Finally, the question is how to create policies for the business sector to promote their empowerment. A SWOT analysis is done to explore challenges and limits and offer some recommendations .This chapter is an opportunity to explore new area about the degree of adaptation of women's entrepreneur to the trade policies rules.

E-government portals are playing an important role in facilitating the citizens' life. The e-government services can be executed by citizens without any time and location constraints, which results in great benefits for them. Therefore, governments should pay a special attention when designing, developing and maintaining their e-government portals. In order to achieve this, they need to follow worldwide e-government portals' best practices that would contribute in the enhancement of the portals' quality. Moreover, such best practices can be used to benchmark or rank the portals by measuring the presence of those best practices. This issue is addressed in this chapter by proposing a measurement based e-government portals' maturity model to help governments identify their portals' maturity stage and also provide guidelines and recommendations to move to an upper stage of maturity.



Both Disinvestment and Privatization process in Public Sector Banks initiated by the then NDA Government came to an end soon after UPA Government took over. The Atal Bihari Vajpayee government had proposed to reduce government holding in state-run banks to 33% but the amendment could not be passed in Parliament as Congress, which was the main Opposition party, blocked the move. Later on Congress party with other partners came to power and even The Ministry of Disinvestment was closed .The recommendations of Disinvestment Commission could not be implemented. For last one decade disinvestment process came to a grinding halt, however, now again there are possibilities that Public Sector Banks may initiate the process again. Privatization process may seem to be a remote possibility at present, however, Disinvestment is on agenda of present government. The Government is now set to reduce shareholding to less than 52% while maintaining ownership but selling additional shares which will infuse more capital to fulfil capital adequacy norms as per Basel III. There are a number of challenges to this process and it is necessary to expedite the process. It is assumed that disinvestment process will make public sector banks more accountable and also efficiency may improve, ultimately pave way for privatization in near future.



Banking sector is considered as a backbone of any economy. It not only transacts money but also helps in promoting trade credit and various social welfare schemes of government. With the changing scenario of business, banking has also undergone a paradigm shift. From manual banking it has shifted to computerized core banking and moving fast towards paperless banking with the use of internet and mobile technology. With the expansion of banking activities, various types of risks associated with banking business have also expanded. To counter them, Basel I guidelines were issued in 1988, the loopholes of which were

The chapter is based on the Self Help Group-Bank linkage Programme in India. The objective of the chapter is to assess the SHGs access to credit under SHG-Bank Linkage Programme, to know the progress of SHG-Bank Linkage Programme in India and to evaluate the impact of SHG-Bank Linkage Programme in India. Finally the chapter ends with suggestions to improve self help group-bank linkage programme and concludes that SHG-Bank Linkage Programme has provided a more favorable environment for enhancing India's potential for greater equitable growth with empowerment while considering the positive signs in their performance.



Investing means using funds to start a venture or acquire part of an existing one in hopes that in time the business will accrue profits for the entrepreneur. Often, entrepreneurs opt to purchase companies' stocks. To be able to select the right – profitable – stocks to buy, one requires knowledge of modern portfolio theory, computational investing, stock brokerage, mutual funds, bonds, value investing, how capital gains are taxed, how to trade stocks and options online, and how to use diversification to allocate online investments.

sector, the finance sector, the media industry, and all other sectors that enable the world to run have had to depend on technology for normal function, and on the internet as a way of associating with the public. For instance, the fact that banks have stayed in the forefront of technological advances has led to significant value addition, and improvement of their products and services offered. Therefore, this paper discusses the use of technology in the finance sector, particularly internet banking in today's world, and the various factors associated with it.



Human resources development is the process of increasing the knowledge, the skills, and the capacities of all the people in a society. In economic terms, it could be described as the accumulation of human capital and its effective investment in the development of an economy. In political terms, human resources development prepares people for adult participation in political processes, particularly as citizens in a democracy. From the social and cultural points of view, the development of human resources helps people to lead fuller and richer lives, less bound by tradition. In short, the processes of human resources development unlock the door to modernization. Education is essential for all and is fundamental to their all-round development, material and spiritual. Education has continued to evolve, diversify and extend its reach and coverage since the dawn of human history. Even Alfred Marshall emphasized the importance of education as a national investment and in his view the most valuable of all capital is that invested in human beings. Every country develops its system of education to express and promote its unique socio-cultural identity and also to meet the growing challenges with the changing times. In this regard, major initiatives/programmes taken by the Central as well as State governments. This paper deals with the changes in our education structure and system after independence of country like increment of literacy rate, growth of educational institution, enrolment ratio of girls, pupil teacher ratio in educational institutions, government's expenditure on education, structural change of education and vocationalisation of education.



Ethics and Social Responsibility in business and government today are very important subjects. These are talked about frequently and addressed in the news when unethical decisions are found. There needs to be an overall intent to be ethical and socially responsible in today's business environment in order to stay successful. Ethics are an individual belief system that consists of knowing what is right and wrong. Ethics can vary person to person. Ethics is in part analyzing decisions, beliefs, and actions. This paper is a study on ethics and social responsibility in today's organizations. This paper will explore the various aspects of how to establish ethics at the workplace, and responsibilities of the organization towards society. It also helps in knowing the importance of ethics and social responsibility in the organization.

# Preface

What does socio-economic development mean? In order to understand this concept, let us begin by defining development. Generally, development is defined as a state in which things are improving. But it is defined in different ways in various contexts, social, political, biological, science and technology, language and literature. In the socio-economic context, development means the improvement of people's lifestyles through improved education, incomes, skills development and employment. It is the process of economic and social transformation based on cultural and environmental factors.

Socio-economic development, therefore, is the process of social and economic development in a society. It is measured with indicators, such as gross domestic product (GDP), life expectancy, literacy and levels of employment.

Social development is a process which results in the transformation of social institutions in a manner which improves the capacity of the society to fulfill its aspirations. It implies a qualitative change in the way the society shapes itself and carries out its activities, such as through more progressive attitudes and behavior by the population, the adoption of more effective processes or more advanced technology. As you see in the illustration below, there is a close relation among environments, ways of living and technology. Economic development is the development of economic wealth of countries or regions for the well-being of their inhabitants. Economic growth is often assumed to indicate the level of economic development. The term "economic growth" refers to the increase (or growth) of a specific measures such as real national income, gross domestic product, or per capita income. The term economic development on the other hand, implies much more. It is the process by which a nation improves the economic, political, and social wellbeing of its people.

Globalization is a process of global economic, political and cultural integration. It has made the world become a small village; the borders have been broken down between countries. It can be seen that, globalization has certain advantages such as economic processes, technological developments, political influences, health systems, social and natural environment factors. It has a lot of benefit on our daily life. Globalization has created a new opportunities for third world countries. Such as, technology transfer hold out promise, greater opportunities to access developed countries markets, growth and improved productivity and living standards. However, it is not true that all effects of this phenomenon are positive. Because, globalization has also brought up new challenges such as, environmental deteriorations, instability in commercial and financial markets, increase inequality across and within nations. Globalization helps developing countries to deal with rest of the world increase their economic growth, solving the poverty problems in their country. In the past, developing countries were not able to tap on the world economy due to trade barriers. They cannot share the same economic growth that developed countries had. However, with globalization the World Bank and International Management encourage developing countries to go through market reforms and radical changes through large loans. Many developing nations began to take steps to open their markets by removing tariffs and free up their economies. The developed countries were able to invest in the developing nations, creating job opportunities for the poor people. For example, rapid growth in India and China has caused world poverty to decrease (blogspot. com.2009). It is clear to see that globalization has made the relationships between developed countries and developing nations stronger, it made each country depend on another country. However, globalization has many economy and trade advantages in the developing countries, we must also note many disadvantages that globalization has created for the poor countries. Globalization increases the inequality between the rich and poor, the benefits of globalization is not universal; the richer are getting rich and the poor are becoming poorer. Many developing countries get benefit from globalization but then again, many of such nations are lag behind. In the past two decades, China and India have grown faster than the already rich nations. However, countries like Africa still have the highest poverty rates, in fact, the rural areas of China which do not tap on global markets also suffer greatly from such high poverty. On the other hand, developed countries set up their companies and industries to the developing nations to take advantages of low wages and this causing pollution in countries with poor regulation of pollution. We can clearly see that education has increased in recent years, because globalization has a catalyst to the jobs that require higher skills set. This demand allowed people to gain higher education. Health and education are basic objectives to improve any nations, and there are strong relationships between economic growth and health and education systems, through growth in economy, living standards and life expectancy for the developing nations certainly get better. With more fortunes poor nations are able to supply good health care services and sanitation to their people. In addition, the government of developing countries can provide more money for health and education to the poor, which led to decrease the rates of illiteracy. This is seen in many developing countries whose illiteracy rate fell down recently. It is a truth that, living standards and life expectancy of developing countries increase through economic gains from globalization. According to the World Bank With globalization, more than 85 percent of the world's population can expect to live for at least sixty years and this is actually twice as long as the average life expectancy 100 years ago.

Development is multi-dimensional phenomenon. The most significant factors for overall development process relate to basic needs like education, availability of food, minimum purchasing power and facilities like safe drinking water, health care infrastructure etc. True development requires government action to improve significant factors of development and to remove barriers against marginalized sections of the society, especially women. Although, economic growth in the sense of expanding gross national product and related variables is one of the most fundamental inputs to the overall development process. The basic objectives of development should focus on the expansion of human capabilities which has been neglected for too long in third world countries.

Economies of third world countries are being considered a mighty signature on world economy. On the eve of such recognition, academicians, researchers and scholars feel their responsibility for framing future polices after contemplating the development in retrospect. This book is a conglomeration of various aspects and issues related to socio-economic development in third world countries especially in post Globalised era, which has utmost significance in achieving the objective of socio-economic development in today's scenario. Some of the most recent developments in the era of socio-economic development have found their place in this volume. A range of socio-economic issues and dimensions have been incorporated in this book.

## ORGANIZATION OF BOOK

The book is organized into 16 chapters. A brief description of each of the chapters follows:

Chapter 1 is a study on ethics and social responsibility in today's organizations. This chapter will explore the various aspects of how to establish ethics at the workplace, and responsibilities of the organization towards society. It also helps in knowing the importance of ethics and social responsibility in the organization.

Chapter 2 is an assessment of financial inclusion in India. It is estimated that about 2.9 billion people around the world do not have access to formal sources of banking and financial services. A significant proportion of our 6,50,000 odd villages does not have a single bank branch to boast of. The RBI has reported that the financial exclusion in India leads to the loss of GDP to the extent of one per cent. Financially excluded people, consistently, depend on money lenders even for their day to day needs, borrowing at excessive rates to finally get caught in a debt trap. Therefore, financial inclusion is a necessity for our country as a large chunk of the world's poor resides here.

Chapter 3 discusses about one of the major cons of globalization, high exploitation of natural resources and environment pollution. If we seriously need a solution to these problems, we need to change the way we design, manufacture, and sell the products. The manufacturing sector must use energy and resources efficiently. 'Green Manufacturing' or sustainable industrial activity is the need of the hour. This chapter focuses on the initiative taken by the industries to make the environment eco-friendly.

Chapter 4 deals with the changes in our education structure and system after independence of country like increment of literacy rate, growth of educational institution, enrolment ratio of girls, pupil teacher ratio in educational institutions, government's expenditure on education, structural change of education and vocationalisation of education.

Chapter 5 is based on the Self Help Group-Bank linkage Programme in India. The objective of the chapter is to assess the SHGs access to credit under SHG-Bank Linkage Programme, to know the progress of SHG-Bank Linkage Programme in India and to evaluate the impact of SHG-Bank Linkage Programme in India. Finally, the paper ends with suggestions to improve self help group-bank linkage programme and concludes that SHG-Bank Linkage Programme has provided a more favorable environment for enhancing India's potential for greater equitable growth with empowerment while considering the positive signs in their performance.

Chapter 6 explains that, most of us did not grow up in a resource starved environment and so the implications of wastefulness have had no direct repercussions on our daily lives. We acknowledge the issue is out there and demonstrate concern for what is being done to improve our collective condition but beyond recycling or an interest in non-toxic HH cleaning products, we simply don't have access to green products or services, let alone do we have an understanding for how to evaluate their functionality or benefit- to us or the environment. In the present study narrows down on one specific area and that is to measure the awareness level of the customers with reference to the green marketing.

Chapter 7 discusses about the prospects of eco tourism in Uttarakhand, India. Ecotourism plays an important role in economic, socio- cultural and environmental development of the society. Therefore the present research answers the question as to how does ecotourism affect the local community, economy, culture and the environment? According to the collected data the results of the study indicated that when residents in the community were asked to reveal ecotourism impacts, they assessed the perception of impacts in both negative and positive ways.

Chapter 8 explains how, with the changing scenario of business, banking has also undergone a paradigm shift. From manual banking it has shifted to computerized core banking and moving fast towards paperless banking with the use of internet and mobile technology. With the expansion of banking activities, various types of risks associated with banking business have also expanded. To counter them, Basel I guidelines were issued in 1988, the loopholes of which were covered in improved guidelines issued in 1996 known as Basel II. The economic slowdown of 2008 revealed that risk containing measures were not enough to enable the banks in absorbing shocks arising from financial and economic stress. Thus, to improve the ability of banks to withstand the economic and financial stress, Basel III guidelines were issued in December 2010.

Chapter 9 empirically investigates the relationship between the efficiency of assets management and profitability of the Indian pharmaceutical industry during the period 1998-99 to 2012-13 and also examines whether its findings conform to the theoretical arguments. Besides this, the paper also tries to make a comparison, in respect of the efficiency of assets management, between multinational and domestic companies in the Indian pharmaceutical industry during the same period to know whether changing socio-cultural and business environment gives an age to domestic companies in respect of assets management or not.

Chapter 10 explains how E-government portals are playing an important role in facilitating the citizens' life. The e-government services can be executed by citizens without any time and location constraints, which results in great benefits for them. Therefore, governments should pay a special attention when designing, developing and maintaining their e-government portals. In order to achieve this, they need to follow worldwide e-government portals' best practices that would contribute in the enhancement of the portals' quality. Moreover, such best practices can be used to benchmark or rank the portals by measuring the presence of those best practices. This issue is addressed in this chapter by proposing a measurement based e-government portals' maturity model to help governments identify their portals' maturity stage and also provide guidelines and recommendations to move to an upper stage of maturity.

Chapter 11 offers analysis of state of the empowerment of women in the globalization. Then, the analysis of the theoretical foundations is for justifying the role of women as entrepreneur and promoter of gender equality and constraints that they are facing. Then, it is an opportunity to offer a brief overview about women in the socio-economic development in MENA region. Finally, the question is how to create policies for the business sector to promote their empowerment.

Chapter 12 aims to analyze the roles of human capital and competency in global business, thus explaining the theoretical and practical overviews of human capital and competency; the significance of human capital in global business; and the significance of competency in global business. The accomplishment of human capital and competency is vital for modern organizations that seek to serve suppliers and customers, increase business performance, reinforce competitiveness, and acquire regular success in global business.

Chapter 13 aims to analyze with the help of a questionnaire of 150 respondents. This present study concentrates on impact of 7Ps on Tourists satisfaction. Collected data has analyzed by regression model. Due to lack of proper marketing practices, tourism has facing different problems to pursue parallel with the main stream entrepreneurs. This study is relevant for balancing the demand and supply of tourism motivational requirement indicators which can offer better tourism service excellence in Bishnupur.

Chapter 14 intends to evaluate the effectiveness of codes of ethical corporate conduct, focusing particularly on their conceptualisation and their relationship to the larger corpus of corporate social, commercial, and ethical interactions in emerging markets. The work will then assess the extent of their leverage globally as instruments of privatised governance; particularly through the examination of corporate stakeholder behaviour and recent examples of global best practice.

Chapter 15 explains how internet has changed overall banking sphere. Over recent years, technological developments in the Information and Communications Technology industry have ensured that the internet has become a significant part of man's way of life. Banks have stayed in the forefront of technological advances has led to significant value addition, and improvement of their products and services offered. Therefore, this paper discusses the use of technology in the finance sector, particularly internet banking in today's world, and the various factors associated with it.

Chapter 16 tells about computational investments. Investing means using funds to start a venture or acquire part of an existing one in hopes that in time the business will accrue profits for the entrepreneur. Often, entrepreneurs opt to purchase companies' stocks. To be able to select the right – profitable – stocks to buy, one requires knowledge of modern portfolio theory, computational investing, stock brokerage, mutual funds, bonds, value investing, how capital gains are taxed, how to trade stocks and options online, and how to use diversification to allocate online investments.

# Chapter 1
# Analyzing the Roles of Human Capital and Competency in Global Business

**Kijpokin Kasemsap**
*Suan Sunandha Rajabhat University, Thailand*

## ABSTRACT

*This chapter aims to analyze the roles of human capital and competency in global business, thus explaining the theoretical and practical overviews of human capital and competency; the significance of human capital in global business; and the significance of competency in global business. The accomplishment of human capital and competency is vital for modern organizations that seek to serve suppliers and customers, increase business performance, reinforce competitiveness, and acquire regular success in global business. Thus, it is necessary for modern organizations to analyze their human capital and competency applications, create a strategic plan to constantly explore their functional advancements, and immediately respond to human capital and competency needs of customers. The chapter argues that applying human capital and competency has the potential to enhance organizational performance and achieve strategic goals in the information age.*

## INTRODUCTION

In the global knowledge economy, organizational employees play the significant roles in firms' competitiveness due to their personal competencies and human capital they constitute for modern organizations (Díaz-Fernández, Lopez-Cabrales, & Valle-Cabrera, 2014). Human capital has turn to be a strategic factor required by advanced and emerging economies (Giordano & Pagano, 2013). Human capital has a positive effect on economic growth (Pablo-Romero & Gómez-Calero, 2013). Human capital is one of the most important factors in economic growth process (Qadri & Waheed, 2014). Human capital is recognized as an organizational resource in the workplace (Möller, Gamerschlag, & Guenther, 2011).

Competency is a human resource element that segregates among high, average, and low performers in the workplace (Deshpande, 2014). Competency refers to an individual's ability to achieve a specific task

DOI: 10.4018/978-1-4666-9908-3.ch001

(Succar, Sher, & Williams, 2013). Competency is about the learning of scripts derived from interactions between individual and environment (Morris, Webb, Fu, & Singhal, 2013). Competency is necessary for the education of practice-based professions (O'Connell, Gardner, & Coyer, 2014). Competency provides a starting point to bridge the gap between the individual and organizational levels of analysis (Salvato & Rerup, 2011).

The strength of this chapter is on the thorough literature consolidation of human capital and competency. The extant literature of human capital and competency provides a contribution to practitioners and researchers by describing a comprehensive view of the functional applications of human capital and competency to appeal to different segments of human capital and competency in order to maximize the business impact of human capital and competency in modern organizations.

## BACKGROUND

Human capital is one of the most frequently researched areas in economic sciences in the last decades (Koziol, Koziol, Wojtowicz, & Pyrek, 2014). Human capital is categorized in the literature as either general or firm-specific and measured as the extent of education and experience (Chowdhury, Schulz, Milner, & Van de Voort, 2014). Díaz-Fernández et al. (2014) stated that competencies specify knowledge and skills required to efficiently perform the job. The conceptual foundation of human capital is based on processes and activities as knowledge and skills obtained from individual learning activities (Harpan & Draghici, 2014). Human capital is captured by individual-level professional education, start-up experience, and learning (Santarelli & Tran, 2013). Human capital is one of the largest assets in the economy and plays an important role for asset pricing (Eiling, 2013).

Several studies have identified employees' competency as the main contribution from individuals to firm's competitiveness (Hayton & McEvoy, 2006; Spencer & Spencer, 1993). The particularity and complexity of competencies turn employees' competency into the source of competitive advantage (Hayton & McEvoy, 2006). Competency is appropriate for practice in stable environments (O'Connell et al., 2014). Competency is the subset of outcomes (Hsieh & Hsu, 2013). Competency focuses on individual's ability to perform activities related to work, life skills, and learning (Anema & McCoy, 2010).

## THE ROLES OF HUMAN CAPITAL AND COMPETENCY IN GLOBAL BUSINESS

This section explains the theoretical and practical overviews of human capital and competency; the significance of human capital in global business; and the significance of competency in global business.

### Overview of Human Capital

Many empirical studies have examined the relationship between firm-level human capital and organizational performance (Crook, Todd, Combs, Woehr, & Ketchen, 2011). Human resource management literature focuses on employee-level human capital and its relationships with individual outcomes and productivity (Ployhart & Moliterno, 2011; Schmidt & Hunter, 1998) and concentrates on the practices that create human capital in the global knowledge economy (Wright & McMahan, 2011). The higher levels of human capital attained through advanced education effectively permit organizational employees to be productive in performing jobs (Feeny & Willcocks, 1998).

Firm-level human capital is a valuable resource which is important for a firm's competitive advantage and performance (Huselid, 1995). Firm-level human capital involves knowledge and skills accumulated by employees through education. Firm-level human capital can be captured by aggregating employee-level human capital (Bingley & Westergaard-Nielsen, 2004; Hitt, Bierman, Shimizu, & Kochhar, 2001). Ployhart et al. (2006) defined firm-level human capital as the aggregate knowledge, skills, and other abilities of a firm's workforce. Firm-level human capital is considered as the productive capacity of its employees (Buchholtz, Ribbens, & Houle, 2003).

Human capital is defined as the combination of the knowledge and skills of people working in the firms (Nahapiet & Goshal, 1998; Subramaniam & Youndt, 2005; Wright & McMahan, 2011). Human capital is considered as a valuable resource that is specific and helps firms sustain their competitive advantage (Chowdhury et al., 2014). Human capital is the most intangible resource of an organization (Black & Boal, 1994; Hitt et al., 2001). Superior human capital attributes such as formal education and experience are found to produce higher firm-level outcomes (Pennings, Lee, & van Witteloostuijn, 1998; Sherer, 1995).

Work experience within a firm is considered as a key contributor to a firm's capabilities (Chena & Huang, 2009; Coff, 2002; Leonard-Barton, 1992). Work experience within a firm is recognized as task-specific based on current job and all previous jobs (Clement, Koonce, & Lopez, 2007). Firms invest in employees that work on core activities that are likely to be needed over time, are required for developing firm-specific skills, and are difficult to monitor (Masters & Miles, 2002). Employees gain task-specific human capital through the performance of specific tasks concerning their current job settings within the firm (Zarutskie, 2010). Task-specific human capital developed with tenure in current job enhances job-specific skills and expertise, but firm-specific human capital based on experience in previous jobs is less applicable to current tasks (Clement et al., 2007; Harris, Kacmar, & Carlson, 2006).

Human capital theory posits that employees with superior human capital such as the higher levels of education and experience will achieve more desirable outcomes by being more productive (Becker, 1964). The resource-based view of firm posits that superior organizational performance can be achieved by possessing resources that are valuable, rare, and inimitable (Barney, 1991; Wernerfelt, 1984). The resource-based view has been used as the basis for describing the relationship between firm-level human capital and organizational performance (Carpenter, Sanders, & Gregersen, 2001).

Human capital is accumulated through education and work experience (Lucas, 1988). The accumulation of human capital is important for economic development (Yanagihara & Lu, 2013). The combination of knowledge capital through research and development (R&D) can strengthen industrial competitiveness (Lin, 2014). To gain the necessary knowledge, industrial organizations should handle external activities from R&D activities (Schildt, Maula, & Keil, 2005).

The uniqueness of human capital refers to the degree to which this is firm-specific, and it is internally developed in the firm (Barney, 1991; Williamson, 1975). Human capital plays an essential role in the employability of knowledge workers (Guo, Xiao, & Yang, 2012). Entrepreneurs' skills for implementing managerial approaches are heterogeneous regarding their human capital endowments (Adner & Helfat, 2003; Davidsson & Honig, 2003). Regional human capital endowment is viewed as one of the major causes of regional economic growth (Cheshire & Margini, 2000; Di Liberto, 2008). Regional human capital endowment is recognized as one of the most achievable determinants of differences and divergences in regional wages, productivity, and income (Faggian & McCann 2009).

Applying knowledge management (KM) practices has a positive impact on the improvement of human capital (Palacios-Marques, Gil-Pechuán, & Lim, 2011). Kasemsap (2014a) indicated that KM, strategic orientation, and organizational innovation are effectively correlated with organizational performance. Knowledge-sharing behavior effectively mediates the positive relationships between organizational learning and organizational innovation and between KM and organizational innovation (Kasemsap, 2014b). Human resource management, organizational learning, and KM capability are favorably related to organizational performance in the global knowledge economy (Kasemsap, 2015a). Using data mining for business intelligence helps modern organizations promote effective KM process (Kasemsap, 2015b).

Human capital helps firms improve productivity (Chowdhury et al., 2014). Individuals' human capital assessed in the first stage of career path is positively related to individuals' performance in the second stage of career path and the value is placed on individuals in the third stage of career path (Harris, Pattie, & McMahan, 2015). Bornay-Barrachina et al. (2012) stated that human capital directly affects organizational innovation. Innovation is an important process of developing and maintaining industrial competitive advantage (Castellacci, 2007).

Firms engaged in R&D activities with the different types of partners are able to alleviate the increasing costs of innovation (Rigby & Zook, 2002) and are more likely to effectively capture the benefits of their innovative effort (Cassiman & Venugelers, 2006). Glaeser and Resseger (2010) stated that the high levels of human capital practically advance the range of knowledge and the level of productivity. The greatest human capital endowment favors the generation and absorption of technology making the rate of technological change faster (Benhabib & Spiegel, 2005; Caselli & Coleman, 2006; Glaeser & Resseger, 2010).

## Overview of Competency

Competency is viewed as the mixture of abilities, skills, and knowledge needed to operate a specific task (Foss, Janken, Langford, & Patton, 2004). Competency represents a common set of standards used for human resource planning, management, and development (Lawler, 1994; Mansfield, 1996). Competency is the knowledge, skills, and ability related to the high job performance such as problem solving, analytical thinking, and leadership (Mirabile, 1997). Competency is an approach to arranging knowledge, know-how, and attitudes (Berio & Harzallah, 2005).

Albanese et al. (2008) indicated that competency is related to behavioral theory focusing on producing desired behaviors. Concerning behavioral theory, all behaviors are learned and the learning process is influenced through the manipulation of environment (Braungart & Braungart, 2003; Vandeveer & Norton, 2005). Competency is the behavioral goal defined by organizational leaders based on business strategy and organizational culture used to guide employees, achieve synergy, improve performance, and generate effective results (Intagliata, Ulrich, & Smallwood, 2000). Competency includes coordination ability, effective monitoring, and feedback (Iyer & Jha, 2006).

Competency is a combination of tacit and explicit knowledge, behavior, and skills that give someone the potential effectiveness of tasks (Draganidis & Mentzas, 2006). Competency is knowledge, skills, and mindset toward effective performance (Dubois, 1998). Competency is manifested by demonstrating the ability to achieve desired outcomes through the performance of skills (LaDuke, 2002). Competency is the measurable human capability required for performance demands (Marrelli, 1998). Competency is the performance standard regarding the ability to accomplish the tasks (Hevey, 1997). Competency is a standardized requirement for an individual to complete a specific job (Brozova & Subrt, 2008).

Competency is the effect of combining and implementing resources toward reaching a strategic objective (Trichet & Leclère, 2003). Competency is a level of expertise with the multifaceted abilities that a person needs to be successful in a field (Stevahn, King, Ghere, & Minnema, 2005). Competency is a complex system of knowledge, skills, and strategies applied to work within a profession in conjunction with suitable emotions, attitudes, and effective self-regulation (Rychen, 2001). Competency guides training programs, enhances reflective practice, and drives accreditation procedures (Ghere, King, Stevahn, & Minnema, 2006; Stevahn et al., 2005).

The American Society of Training and Development's (ASTD) Certified Professional in Learning and Performance (CPLP) program is purported to be based on the ASTD Competency Model, outlining foundational competencies, roles, and the areas of expertise in the field of training and performance improvement (Kwon, Wadholm, & Carmody, 2014). At the base of the ASTD Competency Model, there are the foundational competencies of profession. The foundational competencies include personal, interpersonal, and business and management competencies. At the next level of the ASTD Competency Model, there are the nine areas of expertise (i.e., career planning and talent management, coaching, delivering training, designing training, facilitating organizational change, improving human performance, managing the learning function, managing organizational knowledge, and measuring and evaluating). At the top-most level of the ASTD Competency Model, there are four roles. The four roles of the ASTD Competency Model include learning strategist, business partner, project manager, and professional specialist (Kwon et al., 2014).

Rubrics or scoring tools are assessment tools that help students gain complex competencies (Smit & Birri, 2014). Rubrics are used to align lessons with standards (Burke, 2006) and assure the quality of competence-based assessment. Rubrics help faculties evaluate complex competencies assessed in authentic performance tests such as written compositions, oral presentations, and science projects (Libbee, 2001; Popham, 1997). Osana and Seymour (2004) used rubrics to measure pre-service teachers' critical thinking skills in statistical reasoning. When the goals are complex learning outcomes, classroom assessments in combination with rubrics are recommended (Arter & McTighe, 2001).

There is a positive relationship between team members' competency and organizational performance (Dainty, Cheng, & Moore, 2005). Individuals' competencies are defined as the essential characteristics of individuals that predict an effective performance in the workplace (Spencer & Spencer, 1993) and refer to the type of knowledge, behavior, and skills that employees have and use in their jobs. Competency-based education is recognized as an alternative to a traditional college degree (Ordonez, 2014). An active learning strategy is useful for helping undergraduate students gain competency in global education (Shin, Sok, Hyun, & Kim, 2015).

The five employees' competencies include innovation, adaptation, customer-orientation, results-orientation, and technical expertise (Spencer & Spencer, 1993; Zingheim & Schuster, 2003). The first competency, innovation, means that the employee is able to provide original ideas to improve organizational objectives. The second competency, adaptation, means that the individual effectively works in a variety of situations, with diverse individuals and groups. The adaptation competency is about working with different individuals and broadening knowledge that helps firms modify the base of products and services provided by the firms.

The third competency, customer-orientation, is about helping others to meet a given set of needs. Customer-orientation includes the understanding of diverse, opposing, and changing perspectives of a subject, the knowledge of customers' needs, the purchasing processes of consumers, and the means of communication for the exchange of information between firms and customers. The fourth competency, results-orientation, involves the setting of objectives and priorities to maximize the use of resources and the connection between results obtained and organizational objectives. The fifth competency, technical expertise, is correlated with the learning and personal development through the acquisition of technical and professional skills needed in the workplace (Spencer & Spencer, 1993; Zingheim & Schuster, 2003).

## Significance of Human Capital in Global Business

Most countries still lack a comprehensive measurement of human capital as the most available measures are based on the partial measurement of human capital inputs, such as education, which limits the insight that can be gained from research in areas such as economic growth, productivity, and income inequality (Li, Liu, Li, Fraumeni, & Zhang, 2014). The positive effect of human capital on countries' economic growth has been empirically supported from several studies (Bassanini & Scarpetta, 2002; Glaeser, 1994; Goetz & Hu, 1996). Human capital is a significant factor that determines economic growth across a range of countries (Ang, Madsen, & Islam, 2011; Barro, 2013; Goldin, 2001).

The predictability of asset returns using macroeconomic variables is one of the most important research areas in finance (Ren, Yuan, & Zhang, 2014). From a macroeconomic perspective, human capital is defined as the present value of future labor income and is economically measured in the aggregate (Auerbach, Gokhale, & Kotlikoff, 1994). While human capital directly increases labor efficiency, technological progress both directly and indirectly affects productivity growth (Banerjee & Roy, 2014).

Human capital is viewed as one of the most influential determinants of competitiveness and economic growth (Čadil, Petkovová, & Blatná, 2014). Human capital represents the knowledge and skills that individuals utilize in modern organizations (Dimov & Shepherd, 2005). Human capital can be developed through both education and professional skills contributing to both explicit and tacit knowledge of firm (Teixeira & Tavares-Lehmann, 2014). Human capital is a major factor that promotes investment in technology and has a positive impact on economic growth (Aghion & Howitt, 1998).

Human capital and foreign direct investment (FDI) are considered as the crucial resources of economic growth and development (Ahmed, Cheng, & Messinis, 2011; Mah, 2010; Teixeira & Fortuna, 2010). Human capital is related to the association between FDI and income inequality (Lin, Kim, & Wu, 2013). Human capital is recognized as a vital element of FDI (Mengistu & Adhikary, 2011; Noorbakhsh, Paloni, & Youssef, 2001). Foreign-owned companies are the relevant contributors to human capital formation, affecting the demand and supply of skilled labor (Belderbos, Van Roy, & Duvivier, 2013; Bellak, 2004; Krammer, 2010).

FDI is a particular policy in many countries due to its importance and relevance to policymakers toward economic growth and development (Girma, Gong, & Görg, 2009; Rosell-Martinez & Sanchez-Sellero, 2012; Young & Tavares, 2004). The inflows of FDI financially lead to a shift in labor demand in favor of higher skills (Bruno, Crinò, & Falzoni, 2012; Tomohara & Yokota, 2011). Policy initiatives to reduce income inequality economically empower people to arrange skills building opportunities and accumulate their human capital through the access to educational services (Chani, Jan, Pervaiz, & Chaudhary, 2014). Barney and Wright (1998) explained that the competitiveness of firms will be increased if their human resource perspectives establish a valuable human capital.

There is the significance of certain major counter-intuitive policy instruments to facilitate the evolution of human capital formation and research capacity building (Heitor, Horta, & Mendonça, 2014). R&D perspectives have a positive impact on a country's human capital stock (Pollak, 2013). R&D efforts encompass the deployment of well-organized processes of knowledge creation, production, diffusion, and application (Wang, 2010), toward improved organizational innovation in the various domains of society and business (Higón, Antolín, & Manez, 2011).

Knowledge sources and R&D human capital are the necessary means by which the industrial managers identify and gain access to relevant knowledge (Lin, 2014). The involvement of a firm in R&D activities implies the improvement of business processes in which the stock of knowledge in a firm is increased toward improving its absorptive capacity (Castellani & Zanfei, 2003). The local stock of human capital creates positive externalities for local labor market outcomes (Iranzo & Peri, 2009; Shapiro, 2006; Winters, 2013) and leads to future employment and population growth (Glaeser, Scheinkman, & Shleifer, 1995; Simon, 2004; Simon & Nardinelli, 2002).

Human capital is one of the most substantial resources for high-tech industries (Chen & Chien, 2011). The strategic value of human capital refers to its potential to improve organizational effectiveness, exploit market opportunities, and neutralize business threats (Barney, 1991; Ulrich & Lake, 1991). Human capital formation is the practice of business investment in the future (Stark & Dorn, 2013). Human capital helps firms increase business value, provide an additional business service, and adapt the characteristics of products suitable for customers (Lepak & Snell, 1999).

The level of human capital and the presence of foreign shareholders in small and medium-sized enterprises (SMEs) positively influence internationalization (Cerrato & Piva, 2012). Internationalization is a successful strategy for firms in emerging economies to access and explore vast opportunities at the global level and to build their competitive advantage (Guillen & Garcia-Canal, 2009). Firms have to internationalize in order to enlarge their potential markets and reach the higher levels of efficiency (Calza, Aliane, & Cannavale, 2013). If human capital is correlated with income, then a signaling equilibrium can emerge (Moav & Neeman, 2012). There is a positive association between human capital and career success (Guo et al., 2012). Harvey and Novicevic (2005) indicated that the challenge does not just lie in developing the appropriate competencies to compete in a global context, but in how to transform them into a stock of human capital that affects its competitiveness.

Countries with better institutions are likely to have the greater prosperity, healthier environments, higher quality education establishments, and higher levels of human capital (Jones & Potrafke, 2014). Attracting human capital is the key to the participation of rural areas in national and global economic growth, especially in the global knowledge economy (Olfert, Jelinski, Zikos, & Campbell, 2012). The distribution of human capital plays a powerful role for regional differences in economic growth and welfare (Tano, 2014). The effects of human capital policies become larger as the severity of labor market frictions rises (Chen, Chen, & Wang, 2011).

Cooperation between institutions is considered crucial in order to reach research excellence across countries, to develop their human capital, and to maximize business impact (Pozzi, Bottino, & Persico, 2014). Human capital in firms regarding education, experience, and cognitive skills has a positive impact on firms' productivity (Backman, 2014). An increase in the desire to pursue human capital effectively raises the long-term economic growth rate (Chen, 2012). Human capital and social capital practically influence the level of entrepreneurs' export intentions (Evald, Klyver, & Christensen, 2011).

The positive impacts of employee and career development interventions on organizational process and customer competencies are fully mediated by firm-level human capital (Kim, 2015). A large share of local high-skilled employment does not foster regional concentration of human capital, but improves the employment prospects of less-skilled workers (Schlitte, 2012). Firms should appoint the chief executive officers (CEOs) with different types of human capital in order to manage resource dependencies (Peng,

Sun, & Markóczy, 2015). The high levels of founders' human capital concerning education increase investment in R&D (Honjo, Kato, & Okamuro, 2014).

The impact of human capital is essential for increasing efficiency through international trade shows and FDI flows (Ghosh & Mastromarco, 2013). Regarding socio-economic and environmental data, the impact of FDI on pollution emission is highly dependent on the level of human capital (Lan, Kakinaka, & Huang, 2012). The current situation of weak implementation of environmental supervision and evasion of environmental monitoring can be improved by the promotion of internal and external human capital (Lan & Munro, 2013). Human capital is correlated with innovation outcomes (Kato, Okamuro, & Honjo, 2015).

Human capital theory predicts that individuals or groups who possess the greater levels of knowledge, skills, and other competencies will achieve greater performance outcomes than those who possess lower levels (Ployhart & Moliterno, 2011). The common measures of human capital include the level of education, work experience, and other life experiences (Martin, McNally, & Kay, 2013). Entrepreneurship researchers have studied the positive relationships between human capital and entrepreneurship outcomes at the individual level of analysis (Cassar, 2006), the group level of analysis (Zarutskie, 2010), and the business level of analysis (Colombo & Grilli, 2005).

## Significance of Competency in Global Business

In current competitive environments, characterized by rapid technological change and the increased importance of timing in innovation, acquiring external knowledge and technologies as well as initiating in-house developments have become the critical factors for firms (Berchicci, 2013; Hussinger, 2010). The global economy produces a competitive landscape that becomes more complex and dynamic for firms doing business across borders (Caligiuri & Tarique, 2012).

Many global leadership development programs include talent management and leadership succession programs that include a variety of developmental experiences (Evans, Pucik, & Barsouk, 2002; Gupta & Govindarajan, 2002). The organization-initiated developmental experiences include involvement in global teams (Maznevski & DiStefano, 2000), global travel that encourages learning from colleagues in different countries (Oddou, Mendenhall, & Ritchie, 2000), in-country training (Mendenhall & Stahl, 2000), cross-national mentors (Mezias & Scandura, 2005), global rotational programs (Caligiuri & Di Santo, 2001), formal instructional programs (American Management Association, 2010), and international assignments (Dickmann & Doherty, 2010; Kreng & Huang, 2009; Yan, Guorong, & Hall, 2002).

Dynamic cross-cultural competencies are recognized as competencies related to the cross-cultural knowledge absorption (Kayes, Kayes, & Yamazaki, 2005), the predictors of performance among expatriates (Shaffer, Harrison, Gregersen, Black, & Ferzandi, 2006) and the skills of global leaders (Maznevski & DiStefano, 2000). Dynamic cross-cultural competencies are enhanced through training and development (O'Sullivan, 1999; Shaffer et al., 2006). The three competencies concerning leadership in a global context include the reduced ethnocentrism, cultural flexibility, and tolerance of ambiguity (Caligiuri & Tarique, 2012). Ethnocentrism is an individual's nationalistic self-centeredness, the belief that those from other cultures are inferior (Bizumic, Duckitt, Popadic, Dru, & Krauss, 2009). Ethnocentric individuals interpret and evaluate other's behavior using their own standards and make little effort to modify their own behavior to suit host cultural values (Black, 1990). Ethnocentrism is negatively related to interaction adjustment and contextual performance and positively related to withdrawal cognitions (Shaffer et al., 2006).

Cultural flexibility is considered as the capacity to practically exchange activities appreciated in one's home country with activities in the host country (Shaffer et al., 2006). Cultural flexibility is positively related to cross-cultural adjustment (Shaffer et al., 2006), self-esteem and self-confidence (Mendenhall & Oddou, 1985), adapting to the foreign environments (Black, 1990), and success on foreign assignments (Arthur & Bennett, 1995). Tolerance for ambiguity is the ability to operate ambiguous, new, different, and unstable situations (Caligiuri & Tarique, 2012). People with greater tolerance for ambiguity are more likely to effectively control the stress imposed by uncertain environments and to be more adaptive and receptive to change (Judge, Thoresen, Pucik, & Welbourne, 1999), and promptly changing conditions. Individuals with higher tolerance for ambiguity are better appropriate for positions characterized by ambiguity (Sherrill, 2005).

Focusing on competency involves a major change toward the increased knowledge transfer and higher order thinking skills (HOTS) in modern organizations (Crujeiras & Jiménez-Aleixandre, 2013). Organizational individuals' competencies enable firms to generate profits and maintain their competitive advantage (Subramaniam & Youndt, 2005; Youndt, Subramaniam, & Snell, 2004). Competencies that are not available in the labor market cannot be easily imitated by other companies and provide a strong potential for competitive advantage (Snell, Youndt, & Wright, 1996; Wright & McMahan, 1992). Employees' competencies potentially contribute if they are in line with the firm's strategic objectives (Capelli, 1993; Rodriguez, Patel, Bright, Gregory, & Gowing, 2002).

Competencies such as strategy architect, business knowledge, and human resource technology have positive correlation with organizational performance (Long, 2013). The relationship between organizational strategy and individuals' competency has been analyzed by many researchers, focusing on managerial competency that enhances organizational innovation (Kabanoff & Brown, 2008; Song, Nason, & Di Benedetoo, 2008). The implementation of strategic option prepares various behaviors, skills, and knowledge that employees utilize them in firms (Jackson & Schuler, 1995; Soosay, 2005; Wright & McMahan, 1992). Prospector strategies define the behaviors of individuals that are different to defender strategies (Kabanoff & Brown, 2008; Miles & Snow, 1978; Song et al., 2008).

The catalyst for entry success of the high-tech industry in emerging market has received attention in international business, where many researchers emphasize the influential role of competencies to enhance entry success (Wang & Lestari, 2013). The mechanism of how competencies can drive entry success can be categorized in two main perspectives. The resource-based view suggests that competencies are catalysts to asset accumulation toward sustaining competitive advantage (Verdin & Williamson, 1994), contributes to business value, and acts as a gateway to new markets (Coates & McDermott, 2002; Hamel, 1994), while the industrial organization emphasizes that entry success is influenced by the firm's ability to acquire resources and capabilities (Robinson & McDougall, 2001), which can collect firm's strength and reduce entry barriers (Pehrsson, 2004; Porter, 1980).

Creativity and innovation competencies are considered as the crucial factors for firms to build and sustain a competitive advantage in the fast-changing market environments (Racela, 2014). A source of competitive advantage for multinational enterprise (MNE) is the ability to leverage the competencies of internationally dispersed subsidiaries (Dimitratos, Liouka, & Young, 2014). MNE subsidiaries can play the important roles within the MNE system regarding subsidiary-specific competencies (Rugman, Verbeke, & Nguyen, 2011). Cantwell and Mudambi (2005) distinguished between competence-exploiting subsidiaries and competence-creating subsidiaries. Rugman and Verbeke (2001) defined the characteristics of both competence-exploiting subsidiaries and competence-creating subsidiaries in terms of subsidiary-specific advantages generated as a result of the affiliate's autonomous activities. Rugman and Verbeke (2001) defined subsidiary-specific advantages as idiosyncratic strengths developed by host country managers depending on host country-specific advantages.

Both competence-exploiting subsidiaries and competence-creating subsidiaries include global vision and entrepreneurial MNE networking (Boojihawon, Dimitratos, & Young, 2007), thus generating business value to the stakeholders of the firm (Birkinshaw, 1997). Entrepreneurial competencies derive from an entrepreneurial firm's strategic orientation (Dimitratos et al., 2014). Entrepreneurial competencies are perceived to be the combination of activities and processes, which allow the firm to exploit opportunities and generate business value (Prahalad & Hamel, 1990; Stevenson & Jarillo, 1990; Teece, Pisano, & Shuen, 1997).

The relationship between organizational strategy and competencies is required to be analyzed by practitioners and researchers in details (Díaz-Fernández et al., 2014). There is a relationship between the various characteristics and the behaviors of employees (Hughes, 2003; Hunter, Bernhardt, Hughes, & Skuratowicz, 2001; Soosay, 2005). Competency helps firms achieve an improved performance, emphasizing the precision, orientation, and involvement that make organizational employees a source of competitive advantage (Hayton & McEvoy, 2006). Hervas-Oliver et al. (2014) indicated that SMEs conducting a process innovation strategy rely on the acquisition of external sources of knowledge in order to complement their weak internal innovative capabilities.

## FUTURE RESEARCH DIRECTIONS

The strength of this chapter is on the thorough literature consolidation of human capital and competency. The extant literature of human capital and competency provides a contribution to practitioners and researchers by describing a comprehensive view of the functional applications of human capital and competency to appeal to different segments of human capital and competency in order to maximize the business impact of human capital and competency in global business. The classification of the extant literature in the domains of human capital and competency will provide the potential opportunities for future research. Future research direction should broaden the perspectives in the implementation of human capital and competency to be utilized in the global knowledge economy.

Practitioners and researchers should recognize the suitability of a more multidisciplinary approach toward research activities in implementing human capital and competency in terms of KM-related variables (i.e., knowledge-sharing behavior, knowledge creation, organizational learning, learning orientation, and motivation to learn). It will be useful to bring additional disciplines together (i.e., strategic management, marketing, finance, and human resources) to support a more holistic examination of human capital and competency in order to combine or transfer existing theories and approaches to inquiry in this area.

## CONCLUSION

This chapter aimed to analyze the roles of human capital and competency in global business, thus explaining the theoretical and practical overviews of human capital and competency; the significance of human capital in global business; and the significance of competency in global business. Firms should implement both human capital (in terms of firm-level human capital and employee-level human capital) and competency recognized as the influential organizational assets for producing high-technology goods and services in order to obtain sustainable competitive advantage in the global knowledge economy.

The combination of human capital and competency is crucial for modern business to achieve better organizational performance. Organizations that embed the practices of human capital and competency across a range of human resource management activities effectively create and develop a boundary spanning culture connecting with various organizational disciplines in the global knowledge economy. Knowledge-intensive industries regularly seek to improve positive relationships between forms of human capital and modes of competency. The ability of executives and managers to handle human capital is considerably significant in order to improve individuals' competency in modern organizations.

The accomplishment of human capital and competency is vital for modern organizations that seek to serve suppliers and customers, increase business performance, reinforce competitiveness, and acquire regular success in global business. Thus, it is necessary for modern organizations to analyze their human capital and competency applications, create a strategic plan to constantly explore their functional advancements, and immediately respond to human capital and competency needs of customers. Applying human capital and competency in global business has the potential to increase organizational performance and gain sustainable competitive advantage in the era of globalization.

## REFERENCES

Adner, R., & Helfat, C. E. (2003). Corporate effects and dynamic managerial capabilities. *Strategic Management Journal*, *24*(10), 1011–1025. doi:10.1002/smj.331

Aghion, P., & Howitt, P. (1998). *Endogenous growth theory*. Cambridge, MA: MIT Press.

Ahmed, A. D., Cheng, E., & Messinis, G. (2011). The role of exports, FDI and imports in development: Evidence from Sub-Saharan African countries. *Applied Economics*, *43*(26), 3719–3731. doi:10.1080/00036841003705303

Albanese, M. A., Mejicano, G., Mullan, P., Kokotailo, P., & Gruppen, L. (2008). Defining characteristics of educational competencies. *Medical Education*, *42*(3), 248–255. doi:10.1111/j.1365-2923.2007.02996.x PMID:18275412

American Management Association. (2010). *Developing successful global leaders: A global study of challenges and opportunities*. New York, NY: American Management Association.

Anema, M. G., & McCoy, J. (2010). *Competency-based nursing education: Guide to achieving outstanding learner outcomes*. New York, NY: Springer–Verlag.

Ang, J. B., Madsen, J. B., & Rabiul Islam, M. (2011). The effects of human capital composition on technological convergence. *Journal of Macroeconomics*, *33*(3), 465–476. doi:10.1016/j.jmacro.2011.03.001

Arter, J. A., & McTighe, J. (2001). *Scoring rubrics in the classroom: Using performance criteria for assessing and improving student performance*. Thousand Oaks, CA: Corwin Press.

Arthur, W. Jr, & Bennett, W. Jr. (1995). The international assignee: The relative importance of factors perceived to contribute to success. *Personnel Psychology*, *48*(1), 99–114. doi:10.1111/j.1744-6570.1995.tb01748.x

Auerbach, A. J., Gokhale, J., & Kotlikoff, L. J. (1994). Generational accounting: A meaningful way to assess generational policy. *The Journal of Economic Perspectives*, *8*(1), 74–94. doi:10.1257/jep.8.1.73

Backman, M. (2014). Human capital in firms and regions: Impact on firm productivity. *Papers in Regional Science*, *93*(3), 557–575. doi:10.1111/pirs.12005

Banerjee, R., & Roy, S. S. (2014). Human capital, technological progress and trade: What explains India's long run growth? *Journal of Asian Economics*, *30*, 15–31. doi:10.1016/j.asieco.2013.12.003

Barney, J. B. (1991). Firm resources and sustained competitive advantage. *Journal of Management*, *17*(1), 99–120. doi:10.1177/014920639101700108

Barney, J. B., & Wright, P. M. (1988). On becoming the strategic partner: The role of human resources in gaining competitive advantage. *Human Resource Management*, *37*(1), 31–46. doi:10.1002/(SICI)1099-050X(199821)37:1<31::AID-HRM4>3.0.CO;2-W

Barro, R. J. (2013). Education and economic growth. *Annals of Economics and Finance*, *14*(2), 301–328.

Bassanini, A., & Scarpetta, S. (2002). Does human capital matter for growth in OECD countries? A pooled mean-group approach. *Economics Letters*, *74*(3), 399–405. doi:10.1016/S0165-1765(01)00569-9

Becker, G. (1964). *Human capital: A theoretical and empirical analysis, with special reference to education*. New York, NY: Columbia University Press.

Belderbos, R., Van Roy, V., & Duvivier, F. (2013). International and domestic technology transfers and productivity growth: Firm level evidence. *Industrial and Corporate Change*, *22*(1), 1–32. doi:10.1093/icc/dts012

Bellak, C. (2004). How domestic and foreign firms differ and why does it matter? *Journal of Economic Surveys*, *18*(4), 483–514. doi:10.1111/j.0950-0804.2004.00228.x

Benhabib, J., & Spiegel, M. (2005). Human capital and technology diffusion. In P. Aghion & S. Durlauf (Eds.), *Handbook of economic growth* (pp. 935–966). Amsterdam, The Netherlands: Elsevier.

Berchicci, L. (2013). Towards an open R&D system: Internal R&D investment, external knowledge acquisition and innovative performance. *Research Policy*, *42*(1), 117–127. doi:10.1016/j.respol.2012.04.017

Berio, G., & Harzallah, M. (2005). Knowledge management for competence management. *Journal of Universal Knowledge Management*, *0*(1), 21–28.

Bingley, P., & Westergaard-Nielsen, N. (2004). Personnel policy and profit. *Journal of Business Research*, *57*(5), 557–563. doi:10.1016/S0148-2963(02)00321-1

Birkinshaw, J. (1997). Entrepreneurship in multinational corporations: The characteristics of subsidiary initiative. *Strategic Management Journal*, *18*(3), 207–229. doi:10.1002/(SICI)1097-0266(199703)18:3<207::AID-SMJ864>3.0.CO;2-Q

Bizumic, B., Duckitt, J., Popadic, D., Dru, V., & Krauss, S. (2009). A cross-cultural investigation into a reconceptualization of ethnocentrism. *European Journal of Social Psychology*, *39*(6), 871–899. doi:10.1002/ejsp.589

Black, J. A., & Boal, K. B. (1994). Strategic resources: Traits, configurations and paths to sustainable competitive advantage. *Strategic Management Journal*, *15*(S2), 131–148. doi:10.1002/smj.4250151009

Black, S. (1990). The relationship of personal characteristics with the adjustment of Japanese. *Management International Review*, *30*(2), 119–134.

Boojihawon, D. K., Dimitratos, P., & Young, S. (2007). Characteristics and influences of multinational subsidiary entrepreneurial culture: The case of the advertising sector. *International Business Review*, *16*(5), 549–572. doi:10.1016/j.ibusrev.2007.06.003

Bornay-Barrachina, M., De la Rosa-Navarro, D., López-Cabrales, A., & Valle-Cabrera, R. (2012). Employment relationships and firm innovation: The double role of human capital. *British Journal of Management*, *23*(2), 223–240. doi:10.1111/j.1467-8551.2010.00735.x

Braungart, R. G., & Braungart, M. M. (2003). *Research in political sociology*. Greenwich, CT: JAI Press.

Brozova, H., & Subrt, T. (2008). Competency mapping and modelling in system design. *Scientia Agriculturae Bohemica*, *39*(2), 125–131.

Bruno, G. S. F., Crinò, R., & Falzoni, A. M. (2012). Foreign direct investment, trade, and skilled labour demand in Eastern Europe. *Labour*, *26*(4), 492–513. doi:10.1111/labr.12001

Buchholtz, A., Ribbens, B., & Houle, I. (2003). Takeover resistance and executive succession. *Academy of Management Journal*, *46*(4), 506–514. doi:10.2307/30040642

Burke, K. (2006). *From standards to rubrics in 6 steps*. Heatherton, Victoria: Hawker Brownlow Education.

Čadil, J., Petkovová, L., & Blatná, D. (2014). Human capital, economic structure and growth. *Procedia Economics and Finance*, *12*, 85–92. doi:10.1016/S2212-5671(14)00323-2

Caligiuri, P., & Di Santo, V. (2001). Global competence: What is it and can it be developed through global assignments? *Human Resource Planning*, *24*(3), 27–35.

Caligiuri, P., & Tarique, I. (2012). Dynamic cross-cultural competencies and global leadership effectiveness. *Journal of World Business*, *47*(4), 612–622. doi:10.1016/j.jwb.2012.01.014

Calza, F., Aliane, N., & Cannavale, C. (2013). Cross-cultural bridges in European firms' internationalization to Islamic countries: The key role of cultural competence. *EuroMed Journal of Business*, *8*(2), 172–187. doi:10.1108/EMJB-07-2013-0038

Cantwell, J., & Mudambi, R. (2005). MNE competence-creating subsidiary mandates. *Strategic Management Journal*, *26*(12), 1109–1128. doi:10.1002/smj.497

Capelli, P. (1993). Are skill requirements rising? Evidence form production and clerical jobs. *Industrial & Labor Relations Review*, *46*(3), 515–530. doi:10.1177/001979399304600305

Carpenter, M. A., Sanders, W. G., & Gregersen, H. B. (2001). Bundling human capital with organizational context: The impact of international assignment experience on multinational firm performance and CEO pay. *Academy of Management Journal*, *44*(3), 493–512. doi:10.2307/3069366

Caselli, F., & Coleman, J. W. II. (2006). The world technology frontier. *The American Economic Review*, *96*(3), 499–522. doi:10.1257/aer.96.3.499

Cassar, G. (2006). Entrepreneur opportunity costs and intended venture growth. *Journal of Business Venturing*, *21*(5), 610–632. doi:10.1016/j.jbusvent.2005.02.011

Cassiman, B., & Venugelers, R. (2006). In search of complementarity in innovation strategy: Internal R&D and external knowledge acquisition. *Management Science*, *52*(1), 68–82. doi:10.1287/mnsc.1050.0470

Castellacci, F. (2007). Technological regimes and sectoral differences in productivity growth. *Industrial and Corporate Change*, *16*(6), 1105–1145. doi:10.1093/icc/dtm033

Castellani, D., & Zanfei, A. (2003). Technology gaps, inward investments and productivity of European firms. *Economics of Innovation and New Technology*, *12*(6), 555–576. doi:10.1080/714933761

Cerrato, D., & Piva, M. (2012). The internationalization of small and medium-sized enterprises: The effect of family management, human capital and foreign ownership. *Journal of Management & Governance*, *16*(4), 617–644. doi:10.1007/s10997-010-9166-x

Chani, M. I., Jan, S. A., Pervaiz, Z., & Chaudhary, A. R. (2014). Human capital inequality and income inequality: Testing for causality. *Quality & Quantity*, *48*(1), 149–156. doi:10.1007/s11135-012-9755-7

Chen, B. L., Chen, H. J., & Wang, P. (2011). Labor-market frictions, human capital accumulation, and long-run growth: Positive analysis and policy evaluation. *International Economic Review*, *52*(1), 131–160. doi:10.1111/j.1468-2354.2010.00622.x

Chen, C., & Huang, J. (2009). Strategic human resource practices and innovation performance: The mediating role of knowledge management capacity. *Journal of Business Research*, *62*(1), 104–114. doi:10.1016/j.jbusres.2007.11.016

Chen, H. J. (2012). Social status, human capital formation and the long-run effects of money. *Journal of Economics*, *105*(3), 225–246. doi:10.1007/s00712-011-0227-7

Chen, L. F., & Chien, C. F. (2011). Manufacturing intelligence for class prediction and rule generation to support human capital decisions for high-tech industries. *Flexible Services and Manufacturing Journal*, *23*(3), 263–289. doi:10.1007/s10696-010-9068-x

Cheshire, P., & Magrini, S. (2000). Endogenous processes in European regional growth: Convergence and policy. *Growth and Change*, *31*(4), 455–479. doi:10.1111/0017-4815.00140

Chowdhury, S., Schulz, E., Milner, M., & Van de Voort, D. (2014). Core employee based human capital and revenue productivity in small firms: An empirical investigation. *Journal of Business Research*, *67*(11), 2473–2479. doi:10.1016/j.jbusres.2014.03.007

Clement, M. B., Koonce, L., & Lopez, T. J. (2007). The roles of task-specific forecasting experience and innate ability in understanding analyst forecasting performance. *Journal of Accounting and Economics*, *44*(3), 378–398. doi:10.1016/j.jacceco.2007.04.002

Coates, T. T., & McDermott, C. M. (2002). An exploratory analysis of new competencies: A resource based view perspective. *Journal of Operations Management*, *20*(5), 435–450. doi:10.1016/S0272-6963(02)00023-2

Coff, R. W. (2002). Human capital, shared expertise, and the likelihood of impasse in corporate acquisitions. *Journal of Management*, *28*(1), 107–128. doi:10.1177/014920630202800107

Colombo, M. G., & Grilli, L. (2005). Founders' human capital and the growth of new technology-based firms: A competence-based view. *Research Policy*, *34*(6), 795–816. doi:10.1016/j.respol.2005.03.010

Crook, T. R., Todd, S. Y., Combs, J. G., Woehr, D. J., & Ketchen, D. J. (2011). Does human capital matter? A meta-analysis of the relationship between human capital and firm performance. *The Journal of Applied Psychology*, *96*(3), 443–456. doi:10.1037/a0022147 PMID:21244126

Crujeiras, B., & Jiménez-Aleixandre, M. P. (2013). Challenges in the implementation of a competency-based curriculum in Spain. *Thinking Skills and Creativity*, *10*, 208–220. doi:10.1016/j.tsc.2013.07.001

Dainty, A. R. J., Cheng, M. I., & Moore, D. R. (2005). Competency-based model for predicting construction project managers' performance. *Journal of Management Engineering*, *21*(1), 2–9. doi:10.1061/(ASCE)0742-597X(2005)21:1(2)

Davidsson, P., & Honig, B. (2003). The role of social and human capital among nascent entrepreneurs. *Journal of Business Venturing*, *18*(3), 301–331. doi:10.1016/S0883-9026(02)00097-6

Deshpande, A. P. (2014). Application of the competency modelling approach: Determining the ideal profile of the Orthopaedic surgeons. *Procedia: Social and Behavioral Sciences*, *133*, 12–19. doi:10.1016/j.sbspro.2014.04.164

Di Liberto, A. (2008). Education and Italian regional development. *Economics of Education Review*, *27*(1), 94–107. doi:10.1016/j.econedurev.2006.08.004

Díaz-Fernández, M., Lopez-Cabrales, A., & Valle-Cabrera, R. (2014). A contingent approach to the role of human capital and competencies on firm strategy. *BRQ Business Research Quarterly*, *17*(3), 205–222. doi:10.1016/j.brq.2014.01.002

Dickmann, M., & Doherty, N. (2010). Exploring organizational and individual career goals, interactions, and outcomes of developmental international assignments. *Thunderbird International Business Review*, *52*(4), 313–324. doi:10.1002/tie.20353

Dimitratos, P., Liouka, I., & Young, S. (2014). A missing operationalization: Entrepreneurial competencies in multinational enterprise subsidiaries. *Long Range Planning*, *47*(1–2), 64–75. doi:10.1016/j.lrp.2013.10.004

Dimov, D. P., & Shepherd, D. A. (2005). Human capital theory and venture capital firms, exploring home runs and strike outs. *Journal of Business Venturing*, *20*(1), 1–21. doi:10.1016/j.jbusvent.2003.12.007

Draganidis, F., & Mentzas, G. (2006). Competency based management: A review of systems and approaches. *Information Management & Computer Security*, *14*(1), 51–64. doi:10.1108/09685220610648373

Dubois, D. D. (1998). *The competency casebook: Twelve studies in competency-based performance improvement*. Amherst, MA: Human Resource Development Press.

Eiling, E. (2013). Industry-specific human capital, idiosyncratic risk, and the cross-section of expected stock returns. *The Journal of Finance*, *68*(1), 43–84. doi:10.1111/j.1540-6261.2012.01794.x

Evald, M. R., Klyver, K., & Christensen, P. R. (2011). The effect of human capital, social capital, and perceptual values on nascent entrepreneurs' export intentions. *Journal of International Entrepreneurship*, *9*(1), 1–19. doi:10.1007/s10843-010-0069-3

Evans, P., Pucik, V., & Barsoux, J. (2002). *The global challenge: Frameworks for international human resource management*. Boston, MA: McGraw–Hill.

Faggian, A., & McCann, P. (2009). Human capital and regional development. In R. Capello & P. Nijkamp (Eds.), *Handbook of regional growth and development theories* (pp. 133–152). Cheltenham, UK: Edward Elgar. doi:10.4337/9781848445987.00015

Feeny, D. F., & Willcocks, L. P. (1998). Core IS capabilities for exploiting information technology. *MIT Sloan Management Review*, *39*(3), 9–21.

Foss, G. F., Janken, J. K., Langford, D. R., & Patton, M. M. (2004). Using professional specialty competencies to guide course development. *The Journal of Nursing Education*, *43*(8), 368–375. PMID:15344373

Ghere, G., King, J. A., Stevahn, L., & Minnema, J. (2006). A professional development unit for reflecting on program evaluator competencies. *The American Journal of Evaluation*, *27*(1), 108–123. doi:10.1177/1098214005284974

Ghosh, S., & Mastromarco, C. (2013). Cross-border economic activities, human capital and efficiency: A stochastic frontier analysis for OECD countries. *World Economy*, *36*(6), 761–785. doi:10.1111/twec.12010

Giordano, A., & Pagano, A. (2013). Brazil in the transition towards knowledge economy: Between qualification and internationalization of human capital. *Transition Studies Review*, *20*(1), 19–31. doi:10.1007/s11300-013-0267-5

Girma, S., Gong, Y., & Görg, H. (2009). What determines innovation activity in Chinese state-owned enterprises? The role of foreign direct investment. *World Development*, *37*(4), 866–873. doi:10.1016/j.worlddev.2008.07.017

Glaeser, E. L. (1994). Why does schooling generate economic growth? *Economics Letters*, *44*(3), 333–337. doi:10.1016/0165-1765(94)90020-5

Glaeser, E. L., & Resseger, M. G. (2010). The complementarity between cities and skills. *Journal of Regional Science*, *50*(1), 221–244. doi:10.1111/j.1467-9787.2009.00635.x

Glaeser, E. L., Scheinkman, J., & Shleifer, A. (1995). Economic growth in a cross-section of cities. *Journal of Monetary Economics*, *36*(1), 117–143. doi:10.1016/0304-3932(95)01206-2

Goetz, S. J., & Hu, D. (1996). Economic growth and human capital accumulation: Simultaneity and expanded convergence tests. *Economics Letters*, *51*(3), 355–362. doi:10.1016/0165-1765(96)00827-0

Goldin, C. (2001). The human capital century and American leadership: Virtues of the past. *The Journal of Economic History*, *61*(2), 263–292. doi:10.1017/S0022050701028017

Guillen, M. F., & Garcia-Canal, E. (2009). The American model of the multinational firm and the "new" multinationals from emerging economies. *The Academy of Management Perspectives*, *23*(2), 23–35. doi:10.5465/AMP.2009.39985538

Guo, W., Xiao, H., & Yang, X. (2012). An empirical research on the correlation between human capital and career success of knowledge workers in enterprise. *Physics Procedia*, *25*, 715–725. doi:10.1016/j.phpro.2012.03.148

Gupta, A., & Govindarajan, V. (2002). Cultivating a global mindset. *The Academy of Management Executive*, *16*(1), 116–126. doi:10.5465/AME.2002.6640211

Hamel, G. (1994). The concept of core competence. In G. Hamel & A. Henee (Eds.), *Competence based competition* (pp. 11–33). Chichester, UK: John Wiley & Sons.

Harpan, I., & Draghici, A. (2014). Debate on the multilevel model of the human capital measurement. *Procedia: Social and Behavioral Sciences*, *124*, 170–177. doi:10.1016/j.sbspro.2014.02.474

Harris, C. M., Pattie, M. W., & McMahan, G. C. (2015). Advancement along a career path: The influence of human capital and performance. *Human Resource Management Journal*, *25*(1), 102–115. doi:10.1111/1748-8583.12047

Harris, K. J., Kacmar, K. M., & Carlson, D. S. (2006). An examination of temporal variables and relationship quality on promotability ratings. *Group & Organization Management*, *31*(6), 677–699. doi:10.1177/1059601106286889

Harvey, M. G., & Novicevic, M. M. (2005). The challenges associated with the capitalization of managerial skills and competencies. *International Journal of Human Resource Management*, *16*(8), 1374–1398. doi:10.1080/09585190500220424

Hayton, J. C., & McEvoy, G. M. (2006). Guest editors' note. *Human Resource Management*, *45*(3), 291–294. doi:10.1002/hrm.20127

Heitor, M., Horta, H., & Mendonça, J. (2014). Developing human capital and research capacity: Science policies promoting brain gain. *Technological Forecasting and Social Change*, *82*(1), 6–22. doi:10.1016/j.techfore.2013.07.008

Hervas-Oliver, J. L., Sempere-Ripoll, F., & Boronat-Moll, C. (2014). Process innovation strategy in SMEs, organizational innovation and performance: A misleading debate? *Small Business Economics*, *43*(4), 873–886. doi:10.1007/s11187-014-9567-3

Hevey, D. (1997). The UK National (and Scottish) vocational qualification system: State of the art or in a state? *International Journal of Training and Development*, *1*(4), 242–258. doi:10.1111/1468-2419.00024

Higón, D. A., Antolín, M. M., & Manez, J. A. (2011). Multinationals, R&D, and productivity: Evidence for UK manufacturing firms. *Industrial and Corporate Change*, *20*(2), 641–659. doi:10.1093/icc/dtr007

Hitt, M. A., Bierman, L., Shimizu, K., & Kochhar, R. (2001). Direct and moderating effects of human capital on strategy and performance in professional service firms: A resource-based perspective. *Academy of Management Journal*, *44*(1), 13–29. doi:10.2307/3069334

Honjo, Y., Kato, M., & Okamuro, H. (2014). R&D investment of start-up firms: Does founders' human capital matter? *Small Business Economics*, *42*(2), 207–220. doi:10.1007/s11187-013-9476-x

Hsieh, S. I., & Hsu, L. L. (2013). An outcome-based evaluation of nursing competency of baccalaureate senior nursing students in Taiwan. *Nurse Education Today*, *33*(12), 1536–1545. doi:10.1016/j.nedt.2013.01.012 PMID:23428366

Hughes, R. E. (2003). Skill or diploma? The potential influence of skill-based pay systems on sources of skills acquisition and degree programs. *Work Study*, *52*(4), 179–183. doi:10.1108/00438020310479018

Hunter, L. W., Bernhardt, A., Hughes, K. L., & Skuratowicz, E. (2001). It's not just the ATMs: Technology, firm strategies, jobs and earnings in retail banking. *Industrial & Labor Relations Review*, *54*(2), 402–424. doi:10.1177/001979390105400222

Huselid, M. A. (1995). The impact of human resource management practices on turnover, productivity, and corporate financial performance. *Academy of Management Journal*, *38*(3), 635–672. doi:10.2307/256741

Hussinger, K. (2010). On the importance of technological relatedness: SMEs versus large acquisition targets. *Technovation*, *30*(1), 57–64. doi:10.1016/j.technovation.2009.07.006

Intagliata, J., Ulrich, D., & Smallwood, N. (2000). Leveraging leadership competencies to produce leadership brand: Creating distinctiveness by focusing on strategy and results. *Human Resource Planning*, *23*(3), 12–23.

Iranzo, S., & Peri, G. (2009). Schooling externalities, technology, and productivity: Theory and evidence from U.S. states. *The Review of Economics and Statistics*, *91*(2), 420–431. doi:10.1162/rest.91.2.420

Iyer, K. C., & Jha, K. N. (2006). Critical factors affecting schedule performance: Evidence from Indian construction projects. *Journal of Construction Engineering and Management*, *132*(8), 871–881. doi:10.1061/(ASCE)0733-9364(2006)132:8(871)

Jackson, S. E., & Schuler, R. S. (1995). Understanding human resource management in the context of organizations and their environments. *Annual Review of Psychology*, *46*(1), 237–264. doi:10.1146/annurev.ps.46.020195.001321 PMID:19245335

Judge, T., Thoresen, C., Pucik, V., & Welbourne, T. (1999). Managerial coping with organizational change: A dispositional perspective. *The Journal of Applied Psychology*, *92*(1), 107–127. doi:10.1037/0021-9010.84.1.107 PMID:17227155

Kabanoff, B., & Brown, S. (2008). Knowledge structures of prospector, analyzers, and defenders: Content, structure, stability, and performance. *Strategic Management Journal*, *29*(2), 149–171. doi:10.1002/smj.644

Kasemsap, K. (2014a). Strategic innovation management: An integrative framework and causal model of knowledge management, strategic orientation, organizational innovation, and organizational performance. In P. Ordóñez de Pablos & R. Tennyson (Eds.), *Strategic approaches for human capital management and development in a turbulent economy* (pp. 102–116). Hershey, PA, USA: IGI Global. doi:10.4018/978-1-4666-4530-1.ch007

Kasemsap, K. (2014b). The role of knowledge sharing on organisational innovation: An integrated framework. In L. Al-Hakim & C. Jin (Eds.), *Quality innovation: Knowledge, theory, and practices* (pp. 247–271). Hershey, PA, USA: IGI Global. doi:10.4018/978-1-4666-4769-5.ch012

Kasemsap, K. (2015a). Developing a framework of human resource management, organizational learning, knowledge management capability, and organizational performance. In P. Ordoñez de Pablos, L. Turró, R. Tennyson, & J. Zhao (Eds.), *Knowledge management for competitive advantage during economic crisis* (pp. 164–193). Hershey, PA, USA: IGI Global. doi:10.4018/978-1-4666-6457-9.ch010

Kasemsap, K. (2015b). The role of data mining for business intelligence in knowledge management. In A. Azevedo & M. Santos (Eds.), *Integration of data mining in business intelligence systems* (pp. 12–33). Hershey, PA, USA: IGI Global. doi:10.4018/978-1-4666-6477-7.ch002

Kato, M., Okamuro, H., & Honjo, Y. (2015). Does founders' human capital matter for innovation? Evidence from Japanese start-ups. *Journal of Small Business Management*, *53*(1), 114–128. doi:10.1111/jsbm.12094

Kayes, D. C., Kayes, A. B., & Yamazaki, Y. (2005). Essential competencies for cross-cultural knowledge absorption. *Journal of Managerial Psychology*, *20*(7), 578–589. doi:10.1108/02683940510623399

Kim, T. (2015). Impacts of learning interventions on organizational human capital and performance. *Performance Improvement Quarterly*, *27*(4), 7–28. doi:10.1002/piq.21180

Koziol, L., Koziol, W., Wojtowicz, A., & Pyrek, R. (2014). An outline of a compensation system based on human capital theory. *Procedia: Social and Behavioral Sciences*, *148*, 551–558. doi:10.1016/j.sbspro.2014.07.078

Krammer, S. M. S. (2010). International R&D spillovers in emerging markets: The impact of trade and foreign direct investment. *The Journal of International Trade & Economic Development*, *19*(4), 591–623. doi:10.1080/09638190902792464

Kreng, V. B., & Huang, M. (2009). A discussion on international assignments performance and the constructing mechanism of career success development. *International Journal of Human Resource Management*, *20*(7), 1487–1502. doi:10.1080/09585190902983330

Kwon, S., Wadholm, R. R., & Carmody, L. E. (2014). Assessing competencies: An evaluation of ASTD's Certified Professional in Learning and Performance (CPLP) designation. *Evaluation and Program Planning*, *44*, 48–58. doi:10.1016/j.evalprogplan.2014.01.002 PMID:24565949

LaDuke, S. (2002). Ethical issues in pain management. *Critical Care Nursing Clinics of North America*, *14*(2), 165–170. doi:10.1016/S0899-5885(01)00006-5 PMID:12038502

Lan, J., Kakinaka, M., & Huang, X. (2012). Foreign direct investment, human capital and environmental pollution in China. *Environmental and Resource Economics*, *51*(2), 255–275. doi:10.1007/s10640-011-9498-2

Lan, J., & Munro, A. (2013). Environmental compliance and human capital: Evidence from Chinese industrial firms. *Resource and Energy Economics*, *35*(4), 534–557. doi:10.1016/j.reseneeco.2013.05.003

Lawler, E. E. I. (1994). From job-based to competency-based organizations. *Journal of Organizational Behavior*, *15*(1), 3–15. doi:10.1002/job.4030150103

Leonard-Barton, D. A. (1992). Core capabilities and core rigidities: A paradox in managing new product development. *Strategic Management Journal*, *13*(S1), 111–125. doi:10.1002/smj.4250131009

Lepak, D. P., & Snell, S. A. (1999). The human resource architecture: Toward a theory of human allocation and development. *Academy of Management Review*, *24*(1), 31–48. doi: 10.2307/259035

Li, H., Liu, Q., Li, B., Fraumeni, B., & Zhang, X. (2014). Human capital estimates in China: New panel data 1985–2010. *China Economic Review*, *30*(C), 397–418. doi:10.1016/j.chieco.2014.07.006

Libbee, M. (2001). Assessment as a diagnostic tool. *The Journal of Geography*, *100*(4), 175–178. doi:10.1080/00221340108978437

Lin, J. Y. (2014). Effects on diversity of R&D sources and human capital on industrial performance. *Technological Forecasting and Social Change*, *85*(1), 168–184. doi:10.1016/j.techfore.2013.08.010

Lin, S. C., Kim, D. H., & Wu, Y. C. (2013). Foreign direct investment and income inequality: Human capital matters. *Journal of Regional Science*, *53*(5), 874–896. doi:10.1111/jors.12077

Ling, F. Y. Y., & Ma, Y. (2014). Effect of competency and communication on project outcomes in cities in China. *Habitat International*, *44*, 324–331. doi:10.1016/j.habitatint.2014.07.002

Long, C. S. (2013). Success factors of human resource profession in Malaysia: A quantitative study. *New Horizons in Adult Education and Human Resource Development*, *25*(2), 49–61. doi:10.1002/nha.20016

Lucas, R. Jr. (1988). On the mechanics of economic development. *Journal of Monetary Economics*, *22*(1), 3–42. doi:10.1016/0304-3932(88)90168-7

Mah, J. S. (2010). Foreign direct investment inflows and economic growth: The case of Korea. *Review of Development Economics*, *14*(4), 726–735. doi:10.1111/j.1467-9361.2010.00584.x

Mansfield, R. S. (1996). Building competency models: Approaches for HR professionals. *Human Resource Management*, *35*(1), 7–18. doi:10.1002/(SICI)1099-050X(199621)35:1<7::AID-HRM1>3.0.CO;2-2

Marrelli, A. F. (1998). An introduction to competency analysis and modeling. *Performance Improvement*, *37*(5), 8–17. doi:10.1002/pfi.4140370505

Martin, B. C., McNally, J. J., & Kay, M. J. (2013). Examining the formation of human capital in entrepreneurship: A meta-analysis of entrepreneurship education outcomes. *Journal of Business Venturing*, *28*(2), 211–224. doi:10.1016/j.jbusvent.2012.03.002

Masters, J. K., & Miles, G. (2002). Predicting the use of external labor arrangements: A test of the transaction costs perspective. *Academy of Management Journal*, *45*(2), 431–442. doi:10.2307/3069357

Maznevski, M. L., & DiStefano, J. J. (2000). Global leaders are team players: Developing global leaders through membership on global teams. *Human Resource Management*, *39*(2–3), 195–208. doi:10.1002/1099-050X(200022/23)39:2/3<195::AID-HRM9>3.0.CO;2-I

Mendenhall, M. E., & Oddou, G. (1985). The dimensions of expatriate acculturation: A review. *Academy of Management Review*, *10*(1), 39–47. doi: 10.2307/258210

Mendenhall, M. E., & Stahl, G. K. (2000). Expatriate training and development: Where do we go from here? *Human Resource Management*, *39*(2–3), 251–265. doi:10.1002/1099-050X(200022/23)39:2/3<251::AID-HRM13>3.0.CO;2-I

Mengistu, A. A., & Adhikary, B. K. (2011). Does good governance matter for FDI inflows? Evidence from Asian economies. *Asia Pacific Business Review*, *17*(3), 281–299. doi:10.1080/13602381003755765

Mezias, J. M., & Scandura, T. A. (2005). A needs-driven approach to expatriate adjustment and career development: A multiple mentoring perspective. *Journal of International Business Studies*, *36*(5), 519–538. doi:10.1057/palgrave.jibs.8400159

Miles, R., & Snow, C. C. (1978). *Organizational strategy, structure and process*. New York, NY: McGraw–Hill.

Mirabile, R. J. (1997). Everything you wanted to know about competency modeling. *Training & Development*, *51*(8), 73–77.

Moav, O., & Neeman, Z. (2012). Saving rates and poverty: The role of conspicuous consumption and human capital. *The Economic Journal*, *122*(563), 933–956. doi:10.1111/j.1468-0297.2012.02516.x

Möller, K., Gamerschlag, R., & Guenther, F. (2011). Determinants and effects of human capital reporting and controlling. *Journal of Management Control*, *22*(3), 311–333. doi:10.1007/s00187-011-0138-3

Morris, M. H., Webb, J. W., Fu, J., & Singhal, S. (2013). A competency-based perspective on entrepreneurship education: Conceptual and empirical insights. *Journal of Small Business Management*, *51*(3), 352–369. doi:10.1111/jsbm.12023

Nahapiet, J., & Goshal, S. (1998). Social capital, intellectual capital, and the organizational advantage. *Academy of Management Review*, *23*(2), 242–266. doi: 10.2307/259373

Noorbakhsh, F., Paloni, A., & Youssef, A. (2001). Human capital and FDI inflows to developing countries: New empirical evidence. *World Development*, *29*(9), 1593–1610. doi:10.1016/S0305-750X(01)00054-7

O'Connell, J., Gardner, G., & Coyer, F. (2014). Beyond competencies: Using a capability framework in developing practice standards for advanced practice nursing. *Journal of Advanced Nursing*, *70*(12), 2728–2735. doi:10.1111/jan.12475 PMID:25109608

O'Sullivan, L. (1999). The distinction between stable and dynamic cross-cultural competencies: Implications for expatriate trainability. *Journal of International Business Studies*, *30*(4), 709–725. doi:10.1057/palgrave.jibs.8490835

Oddou, G., Mendenhall, M. E., & Ritchie, J. B. (2000). Leveraging travel as a tool for global leadership development. *Human Resource Management*, *39*(2–3), 159–172. doi:10.1002/1099-050X(200022/23)39:2/3<159::AID-HRM6>3.0.CO;2-J

Olfert, M. R., Jelinski, M., Zikos, D., & Campbell, J. (2012). Human capital drift up the urban hierarchy: Veterinarians in Western Canada. *The Annals of Regional Science*, *49*(2), 551–570. doi:10.1007/s00168-011-0448-2

Ordonez, B. (2014). Competency-based education: Changing the traditional college degree power, policy, and practice. *New Horizons in Adult Education and Human Resource Development*, *26*(4), 47–53. doi:10.1002/nha3.20085

Osana, H. P., & Seymour, J. R. (2004). Critical thinking in preservice teachers: A rubric for evaluating argumentation and statistical reasoning. *Educational Research and Evaluation*, *10*(4–6), 473–498. doi: 10.1080/13803610512331383529

Pablo-Romero, M. P., & Gómez-Calero, M. P. (2013). A translog production function for the Spanish provinces: Impact of the human and physical capital in economic growth. *Economic Modelling*, *32*, 77–87. doi:10.1016/j.econmod.2013.01.040

Palacios-Marques, D., Gil-Pechuán, I., & Lim, S. (2011). Improving human capital through knowledge management practices in knowledge-intensive business services. *Service Business*, *5*(2), 99–112. doi:10.1007/s11628-011-0104-z

Pehrsson, A. (2004). Strategy competence: A successful approach to international market entry. *Management Decision*, *42*(6), 758–768. doi:10.1108/00251740410542320

Peng, M. W., Sun, S. L., & Markóczy, L. (2015). Human capital and CEO compensation during institutional transitions. *Journal of Management Studies*, *52*(1), 117–147.

Pennings, J. M., Lee, K., & van Witteloostuijn, A. (1998). Human capital, social capital and firm dissolution. *Academy of Management Journal*, *41*(4), 425–440. doi:10.2307/257082

Ployhart, R. E., & Moliterno, T. P. (2011). Emergence of the human capital resource: A multilevel model. *Academy of Management Review*, *36*(1), 127–150. doi:10.5465/AMR.2011.55662569

Ployhart, R. E., Weekley, J. A., & Baughman, K. (2006). The structure and function of human capital emergence: A multilevel examination of the attraction–selection–attrition model. *Academy of Management Journal*, *49*(4), 661–677. doi:10.5465/AMJ.2006.22083023

Pollak, A. (2013). Growth and convergence when technology and human capital are complements. *Economic Inquiry*, *51*(1), 31–45. doi:10.1111/j.1465-7295.2012.00454.x

Popham, W. J. (1997). What's wrong – and what's right – with rubrics. *Educational Leadership*, *55(2)*, 72–75. doi: 17239567

Porter, M. E. (1980). *Competitive strategy: Techniques for analyzing industries and competitors*. New York, NY: Free Press.

Pozzi, F., Bottino, R. M., & Persico, D. (2014). Enhancing human capital in TEL research: A case study from the STELLAR Network of Excellence. *Computers in Human Behavior*, *31*, 425–431. doi:10.1016/j.chb.2013.10.062

Prahalad, C. K., & Hamel, G. (1990). The core competence of the corporation. *Harvard Business Review*, *68*(3), 79–91.

Qadri, F., & Waheed, A. (2014). Human capital and economic growth: A macroeconomic model for Pakistan. *Economic Modelling*, *42*, 66–76. doi:10.1016/j.econmod.2014.05.021

Racela, O. C. (2014). Customer orientation, innovation competencies, and firm performance: A proposed conceptual model. *Procedia: Social and Behavioral Sciences*, *148*, 16–23. doi:10.1016/j.sbspro.2014.07.010

Ren, Y., Yuan, Y., & Zhang, Y. (2014). Human capital, household capital and asset returns. *Journal of Banking & Finance*, *42*, 11–22. doi:10.1016/j.jbankfin.2014.01.028

Rigby, D., & Zook, C. (2002). Open market innovation. *Harvard Business Review*, *80*(10), 80–89. PMID:12389463

Robinson, K. C., & McDougall, P. P. (2001). Entry barriers and new venture performance: A comparison of universal and contingency approaches. *Strategic Management Journal*, *22*(6–7), 659–685. doi:10.1002/smj.186

Rodriguez, P., Patel, R., Bright, A., Gregory, D., & Gowing, M. (2002). Developing competency models to promote integrated HR practices. *Human Resource Management*, *41*(3), 309–324. doi:10.1002/hrm.10043

Rosell-Martinez, J., & Sanchez-Sellero, P. (2012). Foreign direct investment and technical progress in Spanish manufacturing. *Applied Economics*, *44*(19), 2473–2489. doi:10.1080/00036846.2011.564155

Rugman, A. M., & Verbeke, A. (2001). Subsidiary-specific advantages in multinational enterprises. *Strategic Management Journal*, *22*(3), 237–250. doi:10.1002/smj.153

Rugman, A. M., Verbeke, A., & Nguyen, Q. T. K. (2011). Fifty years of international business theory and beyond. *Management International Review*, *51*(6), 755–786. doi:10.1007/s11575-011-0102-3

Rychen, D. S. (2001). Introduction. In D. S. Rychen & L. H. Salganik (Eds.), *Defining and selecting key competencies* (pp. 1–15). Seattle, WA: Hogrefe and Huber.

Salvato, C., & Rerup, C. (2011). Beyond collective entities: Multilevel research on organizational routines and capabilities. *Journal of Management*, *37*(2), 468–490. doi:10.1177/0149206310371691

Santarelli, E., & Tran, H. T. (2013). The interplay of human and social capital in shaping entrepreneurial performance: The case of Vietnam. *Small Business Economics*, *40*(2), 435–458. doi:10.1007/s11187-012-9427-y

Schildt, H., Maula, M. V. J., & Keil, T. (2005). Explorative and exploitative learning from external corporate ventures. *Entrepreneurship Theory and Practice*, *29*(4), 493–515. doi:10.1111/j.1540-6520.2005.00095.x

Schlitte, F. (2012). Local human capital, segregation by skill, and skill-specific employment growth. *Papers in Regional Science*, *91*(1), 85–106. doi:10.1111/j.1435-5957.2011.00373.x

Schmidt, F. L., & Hunter, J. E. (1998). The validity and utility of selection methods in personnel psychology: Practical and theoretical implications of 85 years of research findings. *Psychological Bulletin*, *124*(2), 262–274. doi:10.1037/0033-2909.124.2.262

Schulz, E., Chowdhury, S., & Van de Voort, D. (2013). Firm productivity moderated link between human capital and compensation: The significance of task-specific human capital. *Human Resource Management*, *52*(3), 423–439. doi:10.1002/hrm.21537

Shaffer, M., Harrison, D., Gregersen, H., Black, J., & Ferzandi, L. (2006). You can take it with you: Individual differences and expatriate effectiveness. *The Journal of Applied Psychology*, *91*(1), 109–125. doi:10.1037/0021-9010.91.1.109 PMID:16435942

Shapiro, J. M. (2006). Smart cities: Quality of life, productivity, and the growth effects of human capital. *The Review of Economics and Statistics*, *88*(2), 324–335. doi:10.1162/rest.88.2.324

Sherer, P. D. (1995). Leveraging human assets in law firms: Human capital structures and organizational capabilities. *Industrial & Labor Relations Review*, *48*(4), 671–691. doi:10.1177/001979399504800405

Shin, H., Sok, S., Hyun, K. S., & Kim, M. J. (2015). Competency and an active learning program in undergraduate nursing education. *Journal of Advanced Nursing*, *71*(3), 591–598. doi:10.1111/jan.12564 PMID:25384709

Simon, C. J. (2004). Industrial reallocation across US cities, 1977–1997. *Journal of Urban Economics*, *56*(1), 119–143. doi:10.1016/j.jue.2004.03.005

Simon, C. J., & Nardinelli, C. (2002). Human capital and the rise of American cities, 1900–1990. *Regional Science and Urban Economics*, *32*(1), 59–96. doi:10.1016/S0166-0462(00)00069-7

Smit, R., & Birri, T. (2014). Assuring the quality of standards-oriented classroom assessment with rubrics for complex competencies. *Studies in Educational Evaluation*, *43*, 5–13. doi:10.1016/j.stueduc.2014.02.002

Snell, C. C., Youndt, M. A., & Wright, P. M. (1996). Establishing a framework for research in strategic human resource management: Merging resource theory and organizational learning. In G. R. Ferris (Ed.), *Research in personnel and human resource management* (pp. 61–90). Greenwich, CT: JAI Press.

Song, M., Nason, R. W., & Di Benedetto, C. A. (2008). Distinctive marketing and information technology capabilities and strategic types: A cross-national investigation. *Journal of International Marketing*, *16*(1), 4–38. doi:10.1509/jimk.16.1.4

Soosay, C. A. (2005). An empirical study of individual competencies in distribution centers to enable continuous innovation. *Creativity and Innovation Management*, *14*(3), 299–310. doi:10.1111/j.1467-8691.2005.00348.x

Spencer, L. M., & Spencer, S. M. (1993). *Competence at work: Models for superior performance*. New York, NY: John Wiley & Sons.

Stark, O., & Dorn, A. (2013). International migration, human capital formation, and saving. *Economics Letters*, *118*(3), 411–414. doi:10.1016/j.econlet.2012.11.032

Stevahn, L., King, J. A., Ghere, G., & Minnema, J. (2005). Establishing essential competencies for program evaluators. *The American Journal of Evaluation*, *26*(1), 43–59. doi:10.1177/1098214004273180

Stevenson, H. H., & Jarillo, J. C. (1990). A paradigm of entrepreneurship: Entrepreneurial management. *Strategic Management Journal*, *11*(4), 17–27.

Subramaniam, M., & Youndt, M. (2005). The influence of intellectual capital on the types of innovative capabilities. *Academy of Management Journal*, *48*(3), 450–463. doi:10.5465/AMJ.2005.17407911

Succar, B., Sher, W., & Williams, A. (2013). An integrated approach to BIM competency assessment, acquisition and application. *Automation in Construction*, *35*, 174–189. doi:10.1016/j.autcon.2013.05.016

Tano, S. (2014). Regional clustering of human capital: School grades and migration of university graduates. *The Annals of Regional Science*, *52*(2), 561–581. doi:10.1007/s00168-014-0599-z

Teece, D. J., Pisano, G., & Shuen, A. (1997). Dynamic capabilities and strategic management. *Strategic Management Journal*, *18*(7), 509–533. doi:10.1002/(SICI)1097-0266(199708)18:7<509::AID-SMJ882>3.0.CO;2-Z

Teixeira, A. A. C., & Fortuna, N. (2010). Human capital, R&D, trade, and long-run productivity. Testing the technological absorption hypothesis for the Portuguese economy, 1960–2001. *Research Policy*, *39*(3), 335–350. doi:10.1016/j.respol.2010.01.009

Teixeira, A. A. C., & Tavares-Lehmann, A. T. (2014). Human capital intensity in technology-based firms located in Portugal: Does foreign ownership matter? *Research Policy*, *43*(4), 737–748. doi:10.1016/j.respol.2014.01.001

Tomohara, A., & Yokota, K. (2011). Foreign direct investment and wage inequality: Is skill upgrading the culprit? *Applied Economics Letters*, *18*(8), 773–781. doi:10.1080/13504851.2010.491448

Trichet, F., & Leclère, M. (2003). A framework for building competency-based systems dedicated to human resource management. In N. Zhong, Z. Ras, S. Tsumoto, & E. Suzuki (Eds.), *Foundations of intelligent systems* (pp. 633–639). Heidelberg, Germany: Springer–Verlag.

Tzeremes, N. G. (2014). The effect of human capital on countries' economic efficiency. *Economics Letters*, *124*(1), 127–131. doi:10.1016/j.econlet.2014.05.006

Ulrich, D., & Lake, D. (1991). Organizational capability: Creating a competitive advantage. *The Academy of Management Executive*, *5*(1), 77–92. doi:10.5465/AME.1991.4274728

Vandeveer, M., & Norton, B. (2005). From teaching to learning: Theoretical foundations. In D. Billings & J. Halstead (Eds.), *Teaching in nursing* (pp. 259–261). Philadelphia, PA: Saunders/Elsevier.

Verdin, P. J., & Williamson, P. J. (1994). Core competencies, competitive advantages and market analysis: Forging the links. In G. Hamel & A. Henee (Eds.), *Competence based competition* (pp. 77–110). Chichester, UK: John Wiley & Sons.

Wang, E. C. (2010). Determinants of R&D investment: The Extreme-Bounds-Analysis approach applied to 26 OECD countries. *Research Policy*, *39*(1), 103–116. doi:10.1016/j.respol.2009.11.010

Wang, K. J., & Lestari, Y. D. (2013). Firm competencies on market entry success: Evidence from a high-tech industry in an emerging market. *Journal of Business Research, 66*(12), 2444–2450. doi:10.1016/j.jbusres.2013.05.033

Wernerfelt, B. (1984). A resource based view of the firm. *Strategic Management Journal, 5*(2), 171–180. doi:10.1002/smj.4250050207

Williamson, O. E. (1975). *Markets and hierarchies: Analysis and antitrust implications*. New York, NY: Free Press.

Winters, J. V. (2013). Human capital externalities and employment differences across metropolitan areas of the USA. *Journal of Economic Geography, 13*(5), 799–822. doi:10.1093/jeg/lbs046

Wright, P. M., & McMahan, G. C. (1992). Theoretical perspectives for strategic human resource management. *Journal of Management, 18*(2), 295–320. doi:10.1177/014920639201800205

Wright, P. M., & McMahan, G. C. (2011). Exploring human capital: Putting 'human' back into strategic human resource management. *Human Resource Management Journal, 21*(2), 93–104. doi:10.1111/j.1748-8583.2010.00165.x

Yan, A., Guorong, Z., & Hall, D. T. (2002). International assignments for career building: A model of agency relationships and psychological contracts. *Academy of Management Review, 27*(3), 373–391. doi: 10.5465/AMR.2002.7389910

Yanagihara, M., & Lu, C. (2013). Cash-in-advance constraint, optimal monetary policy, and human capital accumulation. *Research in Economics, 67*(3), 278–288. doi:10.1016/j.rie.2013.06.001

Youndt, M. A., Subramaniam, M., & Snell, S. A. (2004). Intellectual capital profiles: An examination of investments and returns. *Journal of Management Studies, 41*(2), 335–361. doi:10.1111/j.1467-6486.2004.00435.x

Young, S., & Tavares, A. T. (2004). Multilateral rules on FDI. Do we need them? Will we get them? A developing country perspective. *Transnational Corporations, 13*(1), 1–30.

Zarutskie, R. (2010). The role of top management team human capital in venture capital markets: Evidence from first-time funds. *Journal of Business Venturing, 25*(1), 155–172. doi:10.1016/j.jbusvent.2008.05.008

Zingheim, P. K., & Schuster, J. R. (2003). Competencies and rewards: Substance or just style? *Compensation and Benefits Review, 35*(5), 40–44. doi:10.1177/0886368703256932

## ADDITIONAL READING

Bojica, A. M., & Fuentes-Fuentes, M. M. (2011). Knowledge acquisition and corporate entrepreneurship: Insights from Spanish SMEs in the ICT sector. *Journal of World Business, 47*(3), 397–408. doi:10.1016/j.jwb.2011.05.007

Campbell, B. A., Coff, R., & Kryscynski, D. (2012). Rethinking sustained competitive advantage from human capital. *Academy of Management Review, 37*(3), 376–395. doi:10.5465/amr.2010.0276

Chang, S., Chen, D., & Wu, T. (2012). Developing a competency model for safety professionals: Correlations between competency and safety functions. *Journal of Safety Research*, *43*(5–6), 339–350. doi:10.1016/j.jsr.2012.10.009 PMID:23206506

D'Este, P., Mahdi, S., Neely, A., & Rentocchini, F. (2012). Inventors and entrepreneurs in academia: What types of skills and experience matter? *Technovation*, *32*(5), 293–303. doi:10.1016/j.technovation.2011.12.005

Folloni, G., & Vittadini, G. (2010). Human capital measurement: A survey. *Journal of Economic Surveys*, *24*(2), 248–279. doi:10.1111/j.1467-6419.2009.00614.x

Galliè, E. P., & Legros, D. (2012). Firms' human capital, R&D and innovation: A study on French firms. *Empirical Economics*, *43*(2), 581–596. doi:10.1007/s00181-011-0506-8

Ganotakis, P. (2012). Founders human capital and the performance of UK new technology based firms. *Small Business Economics*, *39*(2), 495–515. doi:10.1007/s11187-010-9309-0

Gao, Q., Zhai, F., Yang, S., & Li, S. (2014). Does welfare enable family expenditures on human capital? Evidence from China. *World Development*, *64*, 219–231. doi:10.1016/j.worlddev.2014.06.003

Giarratana, M. S., & Torrisi, S. (2010). Foreign entry and survival in a knowledge-intensive market: Emerging economy countries' international linkages, technology competences, and firm experience. *Strategic Entrepreneurship Journal*, *4*(1), 85–104. doi:10.1002/sej.84

Grichnik, D., Brinckmann, J., Singh, L., & Manigart, S. (2014). Beyond environmental scarcity: Human and social capital as driving forces of bootstrapping activities. *Journal of Business Venturing*, *29*(2), 310–326. doi:10.1016/j.jbusvent.2013.02.006

Hanushek, E. A. (2013). Economic growth in developing countries: The role of human capital. *Economics of Education Review*, *37*, 204–212. doi:10.1016/j.econedurev.2013.04.005

Hsieh, Y. H., & Chen, H. M. (2011). Strategic fit among business competitive strategy, human resource strategy, and reward system. *Academy of Strategic Management Journal*, *10*(2), 11–32.

Huang, K. F. (2011). Technology competencies in competitive environment. *Journal of Business Research*, *64*(2), 172–179. doi:10.1016/j.jbusres.2010.02.003

Jones, G., & Potrafke, N. (2014). Human capital and national institutional quality: Are TIMSS, PISA, and national average IQ robust predictors? *Intelligence*, *46*, 148–155. doi:10.1016/j.intell.2014.05.011

Kottaridi, C., & Stengos, T. (2010). Foreign direct investment, human capital and nonlinearities in economic growth. *Journal of Macroeconomics*, *32*(3), 858–871. doi:10.1016/j.jmacro.2010.01.004

Lee, Y. F., Altschuld, J. W., & Lee, L. S. (2012). Essential competencies for program evaluators in a diverse cultural context. *Evaluation and Program Planning*, *35*(4), 439–444. doi:10.1016/j.evalprogplan.2012.01.005 PMID:22391617

Lejonqvist, G., Eriksson, K., & Meretoja, R. (2012). Evidence of clinical competence. *Scandinavian Journal of Caring Sciences*, *26*(2), 340–348. doi:10.1111/j.1471-6712.2011.00939.x PMID:22059740

Linton, J., & Walsh, S. (2013). The effect of technology on learning during the acquisition and development of competencies in technology-intensive small firms. *International Journal of Entrepreneurial Behaviour and Research*, *19*(2), 165–186. doi:10.1108/13552551311310365

Marler, J. H. (2012). Strategic human resource management in context: A historical and global perspective. *The Academy of Management Perspectives*, *26*(1), 6–11. doi:10.5465/amp.2012.0063

Maula, M. V. J., Keil, T., & Zahra, S. A. (2013). Top management's attention to discontinuous technological change: Corporate venture capital as an alert mechanism. *Organization Science*, *24*(3), 926–947. doi:10.1287/orsc.1120.0775

Paganini, M. C., & Egry, E. Y. (2011). The ethical component of professional competence in nursing: An analysis. *Nursing Ethics*, *18*(4), 571–582. doi:10.1177/0969733011408041 PMID:21646322

Rauch, A., & Rijsdijk, S. A. (2013). The effects of general and specific human capital on long-term growth and failure of newly founded businesses. *Entrepreneurship Theory and Practice*, *37*(4), 923–941. doi:10.1111/j.1540-6520.2011.00487.x

Semeijn, J. H., Van Der Heijden, B. I. J. M., & Van Der Lee, A. (2014). Multisource ratings of managerial competencies and their predictive value for managerial and organizational effectiveness. *Human Resource Management*, *53*(5), 773–794. doi:10.1002/hrm.21592

Shah, B. K., & Lonie, J. M. (2012). Assessing the cultural competency of practicing community pharmacists: A pilot study. *Currents in Pharmacy Teaching and Learning*, *4*(4), 240–246. doi:10.1016/j.cptl.2012.05.003

Teixeira, A. A. C., & Shu, L. (2012). The level of human capital in innovative firms located in China. Is foreign capital relevant? *Journal of the Asia Pacific Economy*, *17*(2), 343–360. doi:10.1080/13547860.2012.668095

Tomczyk, D., Lee, J., & Winslow, E. (2013). Entrepreneurs' personal values, compensation, and high growth firm performance. *Journal of Small Business Management*, *51*(1), 66–82. doi:10.1111/j.1540-627X.2012.00374.x

Unger, J., Rauch, A., Frese, M., & Rosenbusch, N. (2011). Human capital and entrepreneurial success: A meta-analytical review. *Journal of Business Venturing*, *26*(3), 341–358. doi:10.1016/j.jbusvent.2009.09.004

Uzunboylu, H., & Hursen, C. (2011). Lifelong learning competence scale (LLLCS): The study of validity and reliability. *H.U. Journal of Education*, *41*, 449–460.

Vernon, R., Chiarella, M., & Papps, E. (2011). Confidence in competence: Legislation and nursing in New Zealand. *International Nursing Review*, *58*(1), 103–108. doi:10.1111/j.1466-7657.2010.00853.x PMID:21281301

Winters, J. V. (2014). STEM graduates, human capital externalities, and wages in the U.S. *Regional Science and Urban Economics*, *48*(1), 190–198. doi:10.1016/j.regsciurbeco.2014.07.003

Zamyatina, O. M., Minin, M. G., Denchuk, D. S., & Sadchenko, V. O. (2015). Analysis of engineering invention competencies in standards and programmes of engineering universities. *Procedia: Social and Behavioral Sciences*, *171*, 1088–1096. doi:10.1016/j.sbspro.2015.01.270

Zivin, J. G., & Neidell, M. (2013). Environment, health, and human capital. *Journal of Economic Literature*, *51*(3), 689–730. doi:10.1257/jel.51.3.689

## KEY TERMS AND DEFINITIONS

**Competency:** A cluster of related abilities, commitments, knowledge, and skills that enable employee and organization to effectively act in job and situation.

**Competitive Advantage:** A superiority gained by an organization when it can provide the same value as its competitors but at a lower price, or can charge higher prices by providing greater value through differentiation.

**Globalization:** The process enabling financial and investment markets to operate internationally, largely as a result of deregulation and improved communications.

**Human Capital:** The collective skills, knowledge, or other intangible assets of individuals that can be used to create economic value for the individuals, their employers, or their community.

**Knowledge Creation:** The formation of new ideas through interactions between explicit and tacit knowledge in individual human minds.

**Knowledge Management:** The strategies and processes designed to identify, capture, structure, value, leverage, and share an organization's intellectual assets to enhance its performance and competitiveness.

**Organizational Innovation:** The process of translating an idea or invention into a good or service that creates organizational value.

**Organizational Performance:** An analysis of a company's performance as compared to goals and objectives.

# Chapter 2
# An Empirical Analysis of 7ps' Elements on Tourists Satisfaction: A Case from Bishnupur

**Nilanjan Ray**
*Netaji Mahavidyalaya, India*

**Raj Kumar**
*Benaras Hindu University, India*

**Dillip Kumar Das**
*The University of Burdwan, India*

**Kaushik Chakraborty**
*Kazi Nazrul University, India*

## ABSTRACT

*Marketing plays a vital role to develop the tourism and encourage the tourists to visit the destination and involve the people to enhance their socio economic condition as well. The purpose of this study is to explore three research questions about marketing strategies, about marketing tools and integrated promotional strategies in general and in this particular destination. This study aims to analyze with the help of a questionnaire of 150 respondents. This present study concentrates on impact of 7Ps on Tourists satisfaction. Collected data has analyzed by regression model. There is a great scope of tourism because every village has unique art, culture, folklore, heritage, and lifestyle and so on. Due to lack of proper marketing practices, tourism has facing different problems to pursue parallel with the main stream entrepreneurs. This study is relevant for balancing the demand and supply of tourism motivational requirement indicators which can offer better tourism service excellence in Bishnupur. It will also play a vital role in terms of the policy implication and to analyze the impact for attaining sustainable tourism development in Bishnupur.*

## INTRODUCTION

Tourism is one of the fastest growing industry next to the oil & jewelry industry. Tourism has emerged as a new mantra for alternative economic development. Tourism concept has been tested and already applied for alternative development of a nation and proved to give positive result. As per World Tour-

DOI: 10.4018/978-1-4666-9908-3.ch002

ism Council, tourism is contributing around 10% to the world wide GDP projected to rise nearly 11% by 2014. West Bengal has the wide variety of attractions in terms of tourist destinations from bustling Kolkata with its historical evidence to the beauty of lush green country side. The state is endowed with all the diversities of the nature that is the tourist's attractions or dream. West Bengal Tourism Development Corporation is foreseeing an investment of Rs 150 crore in the next couple of years just for promoting river tourism. The investment would go towards renovating heritage shore along the Ganges as well as developing a Marina with speed boats, para-sailing and cruise boats facilities. Tourisms greatest potential benefit is to earn money and attached with different allied activities. This involvement can translate into numerous positive economic opportunities for society and development communities. Tourism in West Bengal has much to offer to the world. West Bengal has rich tradition, culture, craft and so on which can emerge as a rich potential tourism destination. Tourism development means more income profits for tourist's related business. The lifestyle of the Indian village includes the education and the occupation and lifestyle of the villagers. If there is Industrialization in India still the majority of the people depends on agriculture. The person of India is also engaged in the various arts, culture and handicrafts and the tourism in the country is also the major occupation of the country. As per the report of

West Bengal Human Development, 2004 depicts that economy in the West Bengal province has improved especially in terms of agricultural production largely due to the effective function of the Panchayet system. The most remarkable acceleration of growth occurred in agriculture. West Bengal is a land of stupendous dimension with a rich handicraft, handlooms, folklore, wild life etc. West Bengal is a land of splendid destination with rich cultural heritage, historical heritage, flora & fauna, spectacular beaches & mountains & wildlife. There is a few states in India with the various variety that West Bengal has offered. Tourism has various dimensions in various aspects like economic, social, demographic, technological, geographical, cultural, natural, and so many fields. The attractions of tourists are also has been grownup on the above stated types of dimensions. Tourism now also laid down emphasis on the areas. In the context of socio-economic objectives it is necessary to take vital steps which are constructive and positive. West Bengal has the right specifications to become different tourism segmentation in India like tourism, heritage tourism, pilgrimage tourism particularly. There are varieties of occupational practices in India as well as west Bengal province which reflects different types of socio economic culture. Tourism in West Bengal has recently got some attentive developmental steps. West Bengal is a province in Eastern India which has various tourism dimensions with a rich culture, festivals, handicraft, folklore, river, pilgrimage so on. West Bengal is a land of stupendous dimension with a rich handicraft, handlooms, folklore, wild life etc. Ballavpur Danga in Birbhum District and Mukutmonipur in Bankura District have been undertaken as the tourism potential site in the Endogenous Tourism Project in collaboration with Ministry of Tourism Government of India and UNDP. The heritage of Bengal includes different dimension like at Purulia District specialize of traditional folk music and dance like Chou dance, Baul, Classical Music as well as at Bishnupur District consists major heritage, cultural and varities of handicrafts potentialities. Vishnupur is specialized for Vishnupur Gharana Classical folk lore, cane and bamboo work, cane work, silk textiles clay work and many more.

## Survey of Existing Literature

According to R. N. Kaul (1985) points out that "one of the reasons for travel has been the desire to widen one's knowledge and understanding about other peoples, places and countries, study their culture, customs, ways of life and heritage, and satisfy ones curiosity about them. As per Scheme of Tourism:

"any form of tourism that showcase the life, art, culture, heritage at location there by benefiting the local community economically and socially as well as enabling interaction between tourists and locals." According to Campbell (1999) et al., "development of tourism in Costa Rica found that though the residents there have a positive attitude towards tourism they had limited awareness of employment and investment opportunities. He also highlighted that for the communities to further benefits from tourism it was essential that some amount of formal planning and interventions are done by the Govt". Krippendrof has defined marketing in tourism as follows: "Marketing in tourism is to be understood as the systematic and the coordinated execution of business policy by tourist undertakings whether private or state owned at local, regional, national or international level to achieve to optimal satisfaction of the needs of identifiable consumer groups and in doing so to achieve an appropriate return." According to Philip Kotler et al. (2002), any place that is able to clearly communicate its distinctiveness can compete in tourism, as long as it consistently offers something attractive and remains accessible. Robert & Hall (2004) has defined that "there is a need for tourism to be differentiated from main stream tourism, eco-tourism, and geo-tourism" and is argued that the context of tourism challenges the "Traditional" approach the marketing. According to Beeton & Sue (2004), "Branding has become a central element of tourism destinations, with image being the singular most significant element of brand, which needs to be very seriously considered in the context of tourism. Therefore it is a salient to look at the images presented by the popular, mass media and consider how they relate to tourism in general and more specifically in tourism". In the point of view of advertising Middleton & Clarke (2001) stated "one classic communication tool used by marketing managers as part of marketing campaigns to develop awareness, understanding, interest and motivation amongst a target audience". Tradition marketing concepts is focus on the product, but the concepts have been transit to customers' satisfaction (Kuo, 2003). In the point of view of promotion, Huang (2002) mentioned that the sales for tourism industry is via surveys, analysis and forecast the tourism market, tourism product design, packaging and, pricing; Further promote tourism commodities, trading techniques, documents or transfer service through value-added upgrade to explore, and expand and meet the travel consumer goods or travel to the tourist demand business services. Zeithaml (1988) mentioned that from the consumer's point of view price is a consumer to get a product to be abandoned or the price of sacrifice. "Price" is the most important factor affecting the profitability of companies, which is one of factors considered for the consumer decision-making. A brief retrospective of the literature in marketing reveals for developing marketing programmes (Mc Cleary, 1987; Frechtling, 1987), identifying the tourist or segmenting the market (Crask, 1981; Calatone & Johar, 1984; Woodside & Jacobe, 1985), advertising/communications and conversion studies (Woodside & Motes, 1981). According to Ray et al. (2012) in the context of tourism impact stated that Tourism in India is expected to play a key role in the country's economic growth, human resource, culture, wealth of the country in terms of foreign exchange earnings, etc. Simultaneously, it has a direct bearing on local culture, socio-economic pattern of life, traditions, food habit, language, values & ethics of the local people due to frequent visits of national and international tourists in attractive tourist destinations.

## Objectives of the Study

The main objectives of the study are:

1. To study different pattern of 7Ps elements at Bishnupur.
2. To identify vital factors each elements of 7Ps.

3. To study the tourists satisfaction in the context of 7Ps components.

## Methodology

This study is based on both primary and secondary data. Observation and Survey methods have also been used in conducting this research study. For fulfillment of the objectives of this study, observation method and survey method are the main technical tools. The Sample size was restricted to 150 respondents. Sources of secondary data collected were legal documents, official statistics, reports, articles, publications and other documents, reports of self-government bodies and organizations websites. Collected data has been analyzed by regression analysis by SPSS 20.

# ANALYSIS AND DISCUSSION

## Impact of Marketing Mix Elements on Tourist's Satisfaction (see table 1)

### Research Questions

*Is there Significant Relation between Tourists' Satisfaction and Marketing Mix?*

Hypotheses

*Table 1. 7Ps Classifications of Tourism Elements Available at Bishnupur*

| | |
|---|---|
| Product | Cultural assets, Agricultural products, Scenic value, Handicraft, |
| Price | Revenue oriented, Room price, Price of food and beverages, |
| Promotion | Fairs and trade show, Exhibitions, Broachers, Advertising, PR Cell, television and radio, |
| Place | Availability on demand, parking facilities, |
| Physical evidence | Water Bodies, Rest house, availability of guide, attractive guest house, good room service facilities, pleasant atmosphere, |
| Process | Administration, Easy booking, |
| People | Politeness, responsible skilled personnel, rapid willingness and attentiveness to the customer. |

$\mathbf{H_{01}}$: Product and Tourists' satisfaction are negatively related each other
$\mathbf{H_{02}}$: Price and Tourists' satisfaction are negatively related each other
$\mathbf{H_{03}}$: Place and Tourists' satisfaction are negatively related each other
$\mathbf{H_{04}}$: Promotion and Tourists' satisfaction are negatively related each other
$\mathbf{H_{05}}$: People and Tourists' satisfaction are negatively related each other
$\mathbf{H_{06}}$: Process and Tourists' satisfaction are negatively related each other
$\mathbf{H_{07}}$: Physical Evidence and Tourists' satisfaction are negatively related each other

To understand the strength of the relationship of tourism product and Tourists satisfaction, the simple regression analysis was performed in order to predict the dependent variable from the independent variable (predictor) where satisfaction was considered as the dependent variable and tourism product was considered as the independent variable for this study. The results of simple regression analysis are given below in the following tables:

## Null Hypothesis: 1

**$H_{01}$:** Tourists' satisfaction is independent of product
**$H_{a1}$:** Tourists' satisfaction is dependent of product

To understand the strength of the relationship of Product and Tourists satisfaction, the simple regression analysis was performed in order to predict the dependent variable from the independent variable (predictor) where satisfaction was considered as the dependent variable and Product was considered as the independent variable for this study. The results of simple regression analysis are given in tables 2-5.

*Table 2. Variables Entered/Removed*

| Model | Variables Entered | Variables Removed | Method |
|---|---|---|---|
| 1 | Product | . | Enter |

a. Dependent Variable: TOURISM_SATISFACTION
b. All requested variables entered.

*Table 3. Model Summary[b]*

| Model | R | R Square | Adjusted R Square | Std. Error of the Estimate | Change Statistics | | | | |
|---|---|---|---|---|---|---|---|---|---|
| | | | | | R Square Change | F Change | df1 | df2 | Sig. F Change |
| 1 | .611[a] | .374 | .367 | .934 | .374 | 58.510 | 1 | 98 | .000 |
| a. Predictors: (Constant), PRODUCT b. Dependent Variable: TOURISM_SATISFACTION | | | | | | | | | |

Above table depicts that the model summary. Here R square which represents the proportion of variation in the dependent variable that can be explained by the independent variable. Critical value of R- square should be between 0 and 1. A higher value is better. From the above table R- square is .374.

*Table 4. ANOVA[a]*

| Model | | Sum of Squares | df | Mean Square | F | Sig. |
|---|---|---|---|---|---|---|
| 1 | Regression | 51.082 | 1 | 51.082 | 58.510 | .000[b] |
| | Residual | 85.558 | 98 | .873 | | |
| | Total | 136.640 | 99 | | | |

a. Dependent Variable: TOURISM_SATISFACTION
b. Predictors: (Constant), PRODUCT

From the above table ANOVA result depicts that F = 58.510 and P= .000 established the significance of the relationship between Product and tourists satisfaction.

*Table 5. Coefficients[a]*

| Model | | Unstandardized Coefficients | | Standardized Coefficients | t | Sig. | 95.0% Confidence Interval for B | |
|---|---|---|---|---|---|---|---|---|
| | | B | Std. Error | Beta | | | Lower Bound | Upper Bound |
| 1 | (Constant) | 1.310 | .294 | | 4.458 | .000 | .727 | 1.893 |
| | PRODUCT | .598 | .078 | .611 | 7.649 | .000 | .443 | .754 |

a. Dependent Variable: TOURISM_SATISFACTION

Above table depicts that standardized coefficient Beta and t value of product are Beta .611, t = 7.649, P= .000 which also proved that a strong evidence a relation between Product and tourists Satisfaction. So there is not so good enough evidence to accept null hypothesis and alternative hypothesis has been accepted.

## Null Hypothesis: 2

**$H_{01}$:** Tourists' satisfaction is independent of Price
**$H_{a1}$:** Tourists' satisfaction is dependent of Price

To understand the strength of the relationship of price and Tourists satisfaction, the simple regression analysis was performed in order to predict the dependent variable from the independent variable (predictor) where satisfaction was considered as the dependent variable and price was considered as the independent variable for this study. The results of simple regression analysis are given in tables 6-9.

*Table 6. Variables Entered/Removed[a]*

| Model | Variables Entered | Variables Removed | Method |
|---|---|---|---|
| 1 | PRICE[b] | . | Enter |

a. Dependent Variable: TOURIST_SATISFACTION
b. All requested variables entered.

*Table 7. Model Summary[b]*

| Model | R | R Square | Adjusted R Square | Std. Error of the Estimate | Change Statistics | | | | |
|---|---|---|---|---|---|---|---|---|---|
| | | | | | R Square Change | F Change | df1 | df2 | Sig. F Change |
| 1 | .574[a] | .329 | .322 | .967 | .329 | 48.066 | 1 | 98 | .000 |

a. Predictors: (Constant), PRICE
b. Dependent Variable: TOURIST_SATISFACTION

Above table depicts that the model summary. Here R square which represents the proportion of variation in the dependent variable that can be explained by the independent variable. Critical value of R- square should be between 0 and 1. A higher value is better. From the above table R- square is .329.

*Table 8.* **ANOVA**[a]

| Model | | Sum of Squares | df | Mean Square | F | Sig. |
|---|---|---|---|---|---|---|
| 1 | Regression | 44.964 | 1 | 44.964 | 48.066 | .000[b] |
| | Residual | 91.676 | 98 | .935 | | |
| | Total | 136.640 | 99 | | | |

a. Dependent Variable: TOURIST_SATISFACTION b. Predictors: (Constant), PRICE

From the above table ANOVA result depicts that F = 48.066 and P= .000 established the significance of the relationship between Product and tourists satisfaction.

*Table 9. Coefficients*[a]

| Model | | Unstandardized Coefficients | | Standardized Coefficients | t | Sig. | 95.0% Confidence Interval for B | |
|---|---|---|---|---|---|---|---|---|
| | | B | Std. Error | Beta | | | Lower Bound | Upper Bound |
| 1 | (Constant) | 1.679 | .272 | | 6.174 | .000 | 1.139 | 2.218 |
| | PRICE | .521 | .075 | .574 | 6.933 | .000 | .372 | .670 |

a. Dependent Variable: TOURIST_SATISFACTION

Above table depicts that standardized coefficient Beta and t value of product are Beta .574, t = 6.933, P= .000 which also proved that a strong evidence a relation between Price and tourists Satisfaction. So there is not so good enough evidence to accept null hypothesis and alternative hypothesis has been accepted.

## Null Hypothesis: 3

$H_{01}$: Tourists' satisfaction is independent of Place

$H_{a1}$: Tourists' satisfaction is dependent of Place

To understand the strength of the relationship of place and Tourists satisfaction, the simple regression analysis was performed in order to predict the dependent variable from the independent variable (predictor) where satisfaction was considered as the dependent variable and place was considered as the independent variable for this study. The results of simple regression analysis are given in tables 10-13.

*Table 10. Variables Entered/Removed*[a]

| Model | Variables Entered | Variables Removed | Method |
|---|---|---|---|
| 1 | PLACE[b] | . | Enter |

a. Dependent Variable: TOURIST_SATISFACTION

b. All requested variables entered.

*Table 11. Model Summary[b]*

| Model | R | R Square | Adjusted R Square | Std. Error of the Estimate | Change Statistics | | | | |
|---|---|---|---|---|---|---|---|---|---|
| | | | | | R Square Change | F Change | df1 | df2 | Sig. F Change |
| 1 | .611[a] | .374 | .367 | .934 | .374 | 58.510 | 1 | 98 | .000 |

a. Predictors: (Constant), PLACE

b. Dependent Variable: TOURIST_SATISFACTION

Above table depicts that the model summary. Here R square which represents the proportion of variation in the dependent variable that can be explained by the independent variable. Critical value of R- square should be between 0 and 1. A higher value is better. From the above table R- square is .374.

*Table 12. ANOVA[a]*

| Model | | Sum of Squares | df | Mean Square | F | Sig. |
|---|---|---|---|---|---|---|
| 1 | Regression | 51.082 | 1 | 51.082 | 58.510 | .000[b] |
| | Residual | 85.558 | 98 | .873 | | |
| | Total | 136.640 | 99 | | | |

a. Dependent Variable: TOURIST_SATISFACTION

b. Predictors: (Constant), PLACE

From the above table ANOVA result depicts that F = 58.510 and P= .000 established the significance of the relationship between Place and tourists satisfaction.

*Table 13. Coefficients[a]*

| Model | | Unstandardized Coefficients | | Standardized Coefficients | t | Sig. | 95.0% Confidence Interval for B | |
|---|---|---|---|---|---|---|---|---|
| | | B | Std. Error | Beta | | | Lower Bound | Upper Bound |
| 1 | (Constant) | 1.310 | .294 | | 4.458 | .000 | .727 | 1.893 |
| | PLACE | .598 | .078 | .611 | 7.649 | .000 | .443 | .754 |

a. Dependent Variable: TOURIST_SATISFACTION

Above table depicts that standardized coefficient Beta and t value of product are Beta .574, t = 7.649, P= .000 which also proved that a strong evidence a relation between Place and tourists Satisfaction. So there is not so good enough evidence to accept null hypothesis and alternative hypothesis has been accepted.

## Null Hypothesis: 4

$\mathbf{H_{01}}$: Tourists' satisfaction is independent of Tourism Process

$\mathbf{H_{a1}}$: Tourists' satisfaction is dependent of Tourism Process

To understand the strength of the relationship of Process and Tourists satisfaction, the simple regression analysis was performed in order to predict the dependent variable from the independent variable (predictor) where satisfaction was considered as the dependent variable and Process was considered as the independent variable for this study. The results of simple regression analysis are given in tables 14-17.

*Table 14. Variables Entered/Removed[a]*

| Model | Variables Entered | Variables Removed | Method |
|---|---|---|---|
| 1 | PROCESS[b] | . | Enter |

a. Dependent Variable: TOURIST_SATISFACTION
b. All requested variables entered.

*Table 15. Model Summary[b]*

| Model | R | R Square | Adjusted R Square | Std. Error of the Estimate | Change Statistics | | | | |
|---|---|---|---|---|---|---|---|---|---|
| | | | | | R Square Change | F Change | df1 | df2 | Sig. F Change |
| 1 | .271[a] | .073 | .064 | 1.137 | .073 | 7.759 | 1 | 98 | .006 |

a. Predictors: (Constant), PROCESS
b. Dependent Variable: TOURIST_SATISFACTION

Above table depicts that the model summary. Here R square which represents the proportion of variation in the dependent variable that can be explained by the independent variable. Critical value of R- square should be between 0 and 1. A higher value is better. From the above table R- square is .073 it depicts that the value is good enough.

*Table 16. ANOVAa*

| Model | | Sum of Squares | df | Mean Square | F | Sig. |
|---|---|---|---|---|---|---|
| 1 | Regression | 10.024 | 1 | 10.024 | 7.759 | .006[b] |
| | Residual | 126.616 | 98 | 1.292 | | |
| | Total | 136.640 | 99 | | | |

a. Dependent Variable: TOURIST_SATISFACTION
b. Predictors: (Constant), PROCESS

From the above table ANOVA result depicts that F = 7.759 and P= .000 established the significance of the relationship between Process and tourists satisfaction.

*Table 17. Coefficients[a]*

| Model | | Unstandardized Coefficients | | Standardized Coefficients | t | Sig. | 95.0% Confidence Interval for B | |
|---|---|---|---|---|---|---|---|---|
| | | B | Std. Error | Beta | | | Lower Bound | Upper Bound |
| 1 | (Constant) | 2.634 | .311 | | 8.469 | .000 | 2.017 | 3.251 |
| | PROCESS | .236 | .085 | .271 | 2.785 | .006 | .068 | .404 |

a. Dependent Variable: TOURIST_SATISFACTION

Above table depicts that standardized coefficient Beta and t value of product are Beta .271, t = 2.785, P= .006 which also proved that a strong evidence a relation between Process and tourists Satisfaction. So there is not so good enough evidence to accept null hypothesis and alternative hypothesis has been accepted.

## Null Hypothesis: 5

**$H_{01}$:** Tourists' satisfaction is independent of Physical Evidence
**$H_{a1}$:** Tourists' satisfaction is dependent of Physical Evidence

To understand the strength of the relationship of Physical Evidence and Tourists satisfaction, the simple regression analysis was performed in order to predict the dependent variable from the independent variable (predictor) where satisfaction was considered as the dependent variable and Physical Evidence was considered as the independent variable for this study. The results of simple regression analysis are given in tables (18-21).

*Table 18. Variables Entered/Removed[a]*

| Model | Variables Entered | Variables Removed | Method |
|---|---|---|---|
| 1 | PHYSICAL_EVIDENCE[b] | . | Enter |

a. Dependent Variable: TOURIST_SATISFACTION
b. All requested variables entered.

*Table 19. Model Summary[b]*

| Model | R | R Square | Adjusted R Square | Std. Error of the Estimate | Change Statistics | | | | |
|---|---|---|---|---|---|---|---|---|---|
| | | | | | R Square Change | F Change | df1 | df2 | Sig. F Change |
| 1 | .611[a] | .374 | .367 | .934 | .374 | 58.510 | 1 | 98 | .000 |

a. Predictors: (Constant), PHYSICAL_EVIDENCE
b. Dependent Variable: TOURIST_SATISFACTION
Above table depicts that the model summary. Here R square which represents the proportion of variation in the dependent variable that can be explained by the independent variable. Critical value of R- square should be between 0 and 1. A higher value is better. From the above table R- square is .374.

*Table 20. ANOVA[a]*

| Model | | Sum of Squares | Df | Mean Square | F | Sig. |
|---|---|---|---|---|---|---|
| 1 | Regression | 51.082 | 1 | 51.082 | 58.510 | .000[b] |
| | Residual | 85.558 | 98 | .873 | | |
| | Total | 136.640 | 99 | | | |

a. Dependent Variable: TOURIST_SATISFACTION
b. Predictors: (Constant), PHYSICAL_EVIDENCE
From the above table ANOVA result depicts that F = 58.510 and P= .000 established the significance of the relationship between Physical evidence and tourists satisfaction.

*Table 21. Coefficients[a]*

| Model | | Unstandardized Coefficients | | Standardized Coefficients | t | Sig. | 95.0% Confidence Interval for B | |
|---|---|---|---|---|---|---|---|---|
| | | B | Std. Error | Beta | | | Lower Bound | Upper Bound |
| 1 | (Constant) | 1.310 | .294 | | 4.458 | .000 | .727 | 1.893 |
| | PHYSICAL_EVIDENCE | .598 | .078 | .611 | 7.649 | .000 | .443 | .754 |

a. Dependent Variable: TOURIST_SATISFACTION

Above table depicts that standardized coefficient Beta and t value of product are Beta .611, t = 7.649, P= .000 which also proved that a strong evidence a relation between Physical evidence and tourists Satisfaction. So there is not so good enough evidence to accept null hypothesis and alternative hypothesis has been accepted.

## Null Hypothesis: 6

**$H_{01}$:** Tourists' satisfaction is independent of Promotion
**$H_{a1}$:** Tourists' satisfaction is dependent of Promotion

To understand the strength of the relationship of Promotion and Tourists satisfaction, the simple regression analysis was performed in order to predict the dependent variable from the independent variable (predictor) where satisfaction was considered as the dependent variable and Promotion was considered as the independent variable for this study. The results of simple regression analysis are given in tables 22-26.

*Table 22. Variables Entered/Removed[a]*

| Model | Variables Entered | Variables Removed | Method |
|---|---|---|---|
| 1 | PROMOTION[b] | . | Enter |

a. Dependent Variable: TOURIST_SATISFACTION
b. All requested variables entered.

*Table 23. Model Summary[b]*

| Model | R | R Square | Adjusted R Square | Std. Error of the Estimate | Change Statistics | | | | |
|---|---|---|---|---|---|---|---|---|---|
| | | | | | R Square Change | F Change | df1 | df2 | Sig. F Change |
| 1 | .666[a] | .444 | .438 | .881 | .444 | 78.117 | 1 | 98 | .000 |

a. Predictors: (Constant), PROMOTION
b. Dependent Variable: TOURIST_SATISFACTION

Above table depicts that the model summary. Here R square which represents the proportion of variation in the dependent variable that can be explained by the independent variable. Critical value of R- square should be between 0 and 1. A higher value is better. From the above table R- square is .444.

*Table 24. ANOVA[a]*

| Model | | Sum of Squares | df | Mean Square | F | Sig. |
|---|---|---|---|---|---|---|
| 1 | Regression | 60.607 | 1 | 60.607 | 78.117 | .000[b] |
| | Residual | 76.033 | 98 | .776 | | |
| | Total | 136.640 | 99 | | | |

a. Dependent Variable: TOURIST_SATISFACTION

b. Predictors: (Constant), PROMOTION

From the above table ANOVA result depicts that F = 78.117 and P= .000 established the significance of the relationship between Product and tourists satisfaction.

*Table 25. Coefficients[a]*

| Model | | Unstandardized Coefficients | | Standardized Coefficients | t | Sig. | 95.0% Confidence Interval for B | |
|---|---|---|---|---|---|---|---|---|
| | | B | Std. Error | Beta | | | Lower Bound | Upper Bound |
| 1 | (Constant) | 1.195 | .269 | | 4.444 | .000 | .661 | 1.728 |
| | PROMOTION | .620 | .070 | .666 | 8.838 | .000 | .481 | .759 |

a. Dependent Variable: TOURIST_SATISFACTION

Above table depicts that standardized coefficient Beta and t value of product are Beta .666, t = 8.838, P= .000 which also proved that a strong evidence a relation between Promotion and tourists Satisfaction. So there is not so good enough evidence to accept null hypothesis and alternative hypothesis has been accepted.

*Table 26. 7Ps Framework at Bishnupur*

| | |
|---|---|
| Product | Cultural assets, Agricultural products, Scenic value, Handicraft, |
| Price | Revenue oriented, Room price, Price of food and beverages, |
| Promotion | Fairs and trade show, Exhibitions, Broachers, Advertising, PR Cell, television and radio, |
| Place | Availability on demand, parking facilities, |
| Physical evidence | Water Bodies, Rest house, availability of guide, attractive guest house, good room service facilities, pleasant atmosphere, |
| Process | Administration, Easy booking, |
| People | Politeness, responsible skilled personnel, rapid willingness and attentiveness to the customer. |

From the above study prove that tourists' satisfaction is related with product, price, place, promotion, physical Evidence, process, people. The findings also prove that Product package has the significant role for satisfaction. Price also moderate which can lead the strong relationship with tourists satisfaction. Bishnupur has good scenic beauty and good environment also lead the strong relationship with satisfaction. Promotion itself has significant relationship with tourist satisfaction. West Bengal Tourism Department plays a vital role for promotional activities. Physical Evidence also play a vital role for tourist satisfaction. Reservation process and Admission process both are very easy which can lead to increase tourist satisfaction. People are very eager to help tourists which also increase tourist's satisfaction. Good quality of Brochures on the villages of Bishnupur as a spiritual and rural destination may be produced containing detailed tourism information regarding accommodation, prices travel, schedules, attractions, for tourists in the villages and the pattern of different activities available including auxiliary and ancillary services through illustrations, roadmap, and graphic design of the cover and the layout of the Brochures and other promotional tools.

## Major Challenges in Promoting Tourism in Bishnupur

- To increase advertisement expenditure.
- To create a strong and positive image about areas of Bengal in general and Bishnupur in particular.
- Effectively positioning the destination in front of both domestic as well as foreign tourist.
- To increase the duration of stay of the tourists at various destination.
- Training of youth and NGOs, VCCs, SHGs operating in these areas
- To preserve of the villages the preservation and development of local.
- To maintain the drainage system, garbage disposal system, sanitation and hygiene system
- To promote the states culture and tradition in the NRI market.
- How effective documentation can be prepare in form of brochures, cards, websites etc. for depicting the site attractions, which leads to marketing the sites among both domestic as well as foreign tourists.
- A vital aspect of the Tourism Scheme was to check the migration of the artisans from the village. To tackle the problem of migration, the artisans in different categories like stone Carvers, pot makers, wood carvers, painters, weavers etc. have been given trainings and exposure sits. Their product has been effectively promoted via different means and they have been taught about product diversification and demand of market, which has ultimately enhanced their income and stopped the migration

## Findings

In the point of view in product five parameters were selected to analysis this dimension of marketing mix. The score of Handicraft value is high due to it is a vital tourism product as per respondents and the lowest score belongs to other tourism elements available at Bishnupur. Few respondents complained about sometimes they were deprived from various allied or auxiliary tourism elements from host communities.

In the context of price four parameters were selected. Among these parameters room price is very nominal or low according to the respondents. There are private hotels and restaurants at Bishnupur who take care of large number of tourists. Transportation Cost is comparatively high as per respondents. Most of the respondents shared their view in the context of handicraft that the price of handiwork at Bishnupur and outside Bishnupur quite same. Low prices would easily and quickly attract clients, but this is an inefficient way to seek for sustained success in the market (Vitkienë, 2002; Kotler, 2003).

In the point of view of place in 7Ps context, five parameters were selected. Among these parameters car parking facilities were given highest score and communication facilities were given the lowest score. Bishnupur gets overcrowded at the time of celebration or on festive occasion tourists who came with their cars, found it easy to park. On the other hand communication facilities and availability on demand services are not so satisfactory due to lack of up dated technological application and easy accessibility of different forms of tourism services also low scores too. Some respondents depict that when they want to move from one destination to another tourist destination sometimes monopoly attitude exist in the service providers like rickshaw puller, taxi/cab etc.

In the context of promotion of marketing mix dimension, four elements were selected. Among four parameters PR Cell has the highest score and publications has the lowest score. According to respondents Public relation plays a very vital role in the promotional activity of any tourist destination. At Bishnupur, well executed PR Cell may be established with the support of the Department of Tourism West Bengal as per respondents. Respondents have agreed that Fairs & Trade shows or quality Brochures carry more weightage than publications. According to them Fairs & Trade shows / Brochures have stronger impact in their minds compared to any publication. Good quality of Brochures on the villages of Bishnupur as a spiritual and destination may be produced containing detailed tourism information regarding accommodation, prices travel, schedules, attractions, for tourists in the villages and the pattern of different activities available including auxiliary and ancillary services through illustrations, roadmap, and graphic design of the cover and the layout of the Brochures.

Physical Evidence is one of the vital elements. Attractive environment of meditation belongs to highest score and lowest score belongs to availability of guide. Recreation and room service facilities were satisfactory. According to respondents at Bishnupur guide is necessary for provides assistance, information and cultural, historical and contemporary heritage interpretation to people on organized tours, individual clients, educational establishments at religious and historical sites, and other significant interest.

In the process dimension has three parameters. Among them highest score belongs to easy booking and lowest score belongs to Government sanctions. Most of the Government officials agreed to offer their full support to the safety and security of the community development subject to government sanction of the requisite fund.

## CONCLUSION

Its boom time for travel and tourism sector in India .Eastern India has emerged as the front runner in its growth chart. West Bengal is replete with business and tourism potential. The travel and tourism sector has entered a take off stage and it is going to scale a great height in near future. It is growing every day, every month and every year with a steady pace. Both the growth promise must not lead to mind less complacency. At a time when expansion looks assured in the travel and tourism sector, it calls for some hard thinking. Has west Bengal realized its optimum potential in the sector? Has the state government done enough in promoting travel and tourism, particularly tourism in the state? What are its priorities? Has the private sector made Adequate Contribution to the travel and tourism in the east? Has the centre extended a helping hand in this regard?

It does not need any serious analysis to say that despite their immense potential west Bengal don't figure prominently in the tourism map of India. Internationally the eastern India is yet to make a true mark. The number of domestic and foreign tourist visiting west Bengal and the neighboring states has been on the rise in the last few years. The rising trend may yield some satisfaction. But a comparison with other states and regions in India shows that the east region particularly West Bengal have failed to measure up to their potential. The reason is simple. While other states are doing all around publicity to attract tourists, West Bengal is lagging behind in its visibility campaign.

## REFERENCES

Ashley, C. (2000), The Impacts of Tourism on Livelihoods: Namibia's Experience. Overseas Development Institute. London: Portland House, Stag Place.

Ashley, C., & Jones, B. (1999). Joint ventures between communities and tourism investors: Experience in Southern Africa. *Presentation to Fair Trade and Tourism Conference*, London.

Beerli, A., & Martin, J. D. (2004). Factors influencing destination image. *Annals of Tourism Research, 31*(3), 657–681. doi:10.1016/j.annals.2004.01.010

Calantone, R. J., & Johar, J. S.Calatone & Johar. (1984). Seasonal segmentation of the tourism market using a benefit segmentation framework. *Journal of Travel Research, 23*(2), 14–24. doi:10.1177/004728758402300203

Colley, R. H. (1961). *Defining advertising goals for measured advertising results*. New York: Association of National Advertisers.

Coltman, M. M. (1989). *Tourism Marketing*. New York: Van Nostrand Reinhold.

Crask, M. R. (1981). Segmenting the vacationer market: Identifying the vacation preferences, demographics and magazine readership of each group. *Journal of Travel Research, 20*(2), 29–34. doi:10.1177/004728758102000205

Crompton, J. L. (1979). Motivations for pleasure vacations. *Annals of Tourism Research, 6*(4), 408–424. doi:10.1016/0160-7383(79)90004-5

Czinkto, M. R., & Ronkainen, I. A. (2001). *International Marketing* (6th ed.). Orlando: Harcourt College Publishers.

Dspace. (n. d.). Retrieved from www.dspace.iimk.ac.in

Etzel, M. J., & Wahlers, R. G. (1985). The use of request promotional material by pleasure travelers. *Journal of Travel Research, 23*(4), 2–6.

Freachtling, D. C. (1987). Five issues in tourism marketing in the 1990s. *Tourism Management, 8*(2), 177–178. doi:10.1016/0261-5177(87)90030-6

Huang, L., & Hsien-T, T. (2002). *The effects of electronic commerce on business management of travel agencies* [PhD Thesis]. Nation Chung San University.

Incredible India. (n. d.). Retrieved from www.incredibleindia.org

India Tourism. (n. d.). Retrieved from www.tourism.nic.in

Kaul, R. N. (1985). *Dynamics of Tourism*. New Delhi: Starling Publishers.

Kotler, P. H., Armstrong, G., Saunders, J., & Wong, V. (2003). *Rinkodaros Principai*. Kaunas.

McCleary, K. W. (1987). A framework for national tourism marketing. *International of Hospitality Management, 6*(3), 169–175. doi:10.1016/0278-4319(87)90051-X

Middleton, V., & Clarke, J. (2001). *Marketing in Travel and Tourism* (3rd ed.). Roshester, Kent: MPG Books Ltd., Bodmin.

Nigel, M. (2003). *Advertising in Tourism and Leisure: British Library Cataloguing in of National Advertiser*. New York Publication.

Page, S. J. (2009). *Tourism Management and Managing Change* (3rd ed.). Elsevier Ltd.

Ray, N., & Das, D. K. (2011). 3Hs Tourism, an Alternative Approach of Developing Tourism at Bishnupur: An Empirical Study. *South Asian Journal of Tourism and Heritage*, *4*(2).

Ray, N., Das, D. K., Sengupta, P., & Ghosh, S. (2012). Tourism and its Impact on Socio- Economic Condition: Evidence from West Bengal, India *Global. Journal of Business Research*, *6*(2).

Roberts, L., & Derek, H. (2004). Consuming the country side: Marketing for tourism. *Journal of Vacation Marketing*, *10*(3), 253–263. doi:10.1177/135676670401000305

Rowley, J. (1998). Promotion and marketing communication in the information market place. *Journal of Library Review*, *47*(8), 383–387. doi:10.1108/00242539810239543

Sharma (2000), *Tourism Education Principle, Theories, Practices*. New Delhi: Kanishka Publisher.

Sue, B. (2004). Tourism in Australia–Has the gaze altered? Tracking images through film and tourism promotion. *International Journal of Tourism Research*, *6*(3), 125–135. doi:10.1002/jtr.479

Vitkienë, E. (1998). Paslaugø rinkodaros organizacinë sistema ir jos valdymas. In *Ekonomika ir vadyba-98* (pp. 454–458). Kaunas: Technologija.

Walker Orville, C., Boyd, H. W., Jmullins, J., & Larreche, C. (2001). *Marketing Strategy, translated by A. Rabi and Izadi*. Teheran: Cultural Research Bureau.

Woodside, A. G. & Jacobe. (1985). Steps two in benefit segmentation: Learning the benefits realized by major travel market. *Journal of Travel Research*, *26*(1), 2–7.

Woodside, A. G., & Motes, W. H. (1981). Sensitivity of market segments to separate advertising strategies. *Journal of Marketing*, *45*(1), 63–73. doi:10.2307/1251721

Zeithaml, V. A. (1988). Consumer perceptions of price, quality, and value: Ameans-end model and synthesis of evidence. *Journal of Marketing*, *52*(3), 2–22. doi:10.2307/1251446

## ADDITIONAL READING

Fisher, R.J., & Price, L.L. (1991). International Pleasure Motivation and Post Vacation Culture Attitude Change. *Journal of Leisure Research,* 23(3), 193-208.

Fodness, D. (1994). Measuring Tourist Motivation. *Annals of Tourism Research*, *21*(3), 555–581. doi:10.1016/0160-7383(94)90120-1

Hirschman, E. C. (1984). Experience seeking: A Subjectivist Perspective of Consumption. *Journal of Business Research, 12*(1), 115–136. doi:10.1016/0148-2963(84)90042-0

Lane, B. (1994). What is rural tourism. *Journal of Sustainable Tourism, 2*(7), 23–30.

Parrincello, G. R. (1993). Motivation & Anticipation in Post Industrial Tourism. *Annals of Tourism Research, 20*(2), 233–249. doi:10.1016/0160-7383(93)90052-5

Pearce, P., Morrison, A. M., & Rutledge, J. L. (1998). *Tourism: Bridges across Continents*. Sydney: McGraw-Hill.

## KEY TERMS AND DEFINITIONS

**Cultural Adaptability:** The socio-political, infrastructural as well as financial ability of an individual or a society to accept and acknowledge the cultural constituents.

**Tourism:** Tourism is a social, cultural and economic phenomenon related to the movement of people to places outside their usual place of residence. Tourism comprises the activities of persons travelling to and staying in places outside their usual environment for not more than one consecutive year for leisure, business and other purposes not related to the exercise of an activity remunerated from within the place visited.

**Tourist:** Someone who travels for pleasure and recreation and exchange of culture.

# Chapter 3
# Assets Management of the Indian Pharma Sector in the Changing Socio-Cultural and Business Environment of Post-Liberalization Era:
## A Comparative Study on Select Multinational and Domestic Companies

**Kaushik Chakraborty**
*Kazi Nazrul University, India*

## ABSTRACT

*Efficiency of assets management is an absolutely unavoidable issue in accomplishing the wealth maximization objective of business. In India, the changing scenario in the front of demographic, social and cultural made a prominent impact on the growth of pharmaceutical industry. In fact, during the last two decades the changing socio-cultural and business environment of India witnessed a rapid change in various managerial as well as financial applications of the Indian pharma sector. Assets management is no doubt a vital part of the overall strategy for achieving financial objectives of any industry. In this backdrop, the present study empirically investigates the relationship between the efficiency of assets management and profitability of the Indian pharmaceutical industry during the period 1998-99 to 2012-13 and also examines whether its findings conform to the theoretical arguments. Besides this, the paper also tries to make a comparison, in respect of the efficiency of assets management, between multinational and domestic companies in the Indian pharmaceutical industry during the same period to know whether changing socio-cultural and business environment gives an age to domestic companies in respect of assets management or not. The sample size of the study consists of ten pharmaceutical companies by taking five multinational and five domestic companies from the Indian pharmaceutical industry. The issues analyzed in this study have been tackled using relevant statistical tools and techniques.*

DOI: 10.4018/978-1-4666-9908-3.ch003

## 1. INTRODUCTION

Assets management is essential for the day-to-day and long-term operations of a company. With the opening up of Indian economy since the year 1991, noticeable changes occurred in the practice of assets management. In fact, as a result of the socio-cultural and business environment in Indian corporate sector has failed to maintain its conventional practices of assets management during the post-liberalization era. So, it is high time to analyze the efficiency of assets management of the Indian corporate sector in the post-liberalization period. In this backdrop, the present study seeks to analyze the efficiency of assets management in the Indian pharmaceutical industry during the period 1998-99 to 2012-13 and also to examine whether its findings conform to the theoretical arguments. Besides this, the paper has also made a modest effort to compare the aspect of the efficiency of assets management practices of multinational companies with that of the domestic companies of the Indian pharmaceutical industry during the same period to know whether the changing socio-cultural and business environment gives any advantage to domestic companies in respect of assets management or not.

The remainder of this paper is organized as follows. Section 2 deals with the review of the existing literature relating to the assessment of efficiency of assets management. Section 3 narrates the objectives of the study. In Section 4 the methodology adopted in the study is explained. Section 5 presents the findings of the study. In Section 6 concluding remarks are given.

## 2. REVIEW OF EXISTING LITERATURE

Before entering into the empirical work, a quick look through the existing literature on the analysis of efficiency of assets management seems desirable. A considerable number of empirical studies on assets management have been carried out by different researchers in India during the last four decades. But a very few studies relating to the assessment of efficiency of assets management have been conducted in India during the post-liberalisation era. The following paragraphs provide very brief explanation of some significant studies so far carried out in India on the issue.

Khatick and Singh (2003) in their work on Eircher Ltd. during the period 1994-95 to 1998-99 showed that there was a positive impact of inventory management of the company towards improving the efficiency of its liquidity management.

Ghosh and Maji (2004) conducted a study on the evaluation of the efficiency of the working capital management of Indian cement industry during the period 1992-93 to 2001-02. This study identified no consistency regarding betterment of efficiency in working capital management of the selected cement companies during the study period.

Sur et al. (2007), made a comparative study of the efficiency of asset management of Colgate-Palmolive (India) Ltd. in the pre-liberalisation period (1980-81 to 1991-92) and in the post-liberalisation era (1992-93 to 2003-04). The study observed a significant negative influence of the company's inventory management on its profitability during the post-liberalisation period.

The study conducted by Azhagaiah and Gejalakshmi (2007) for examining the efficiency of working capital management of thirty selected companies in Indian textile industry during the period 1995-96 to 2005-06 concluded that the efficiency of managing current assets of the companies under study was one of the contributory factors towards improving their profitability.

Sur and Chakraborty (2010) studied the efficiency of working capital management of fifty companies (from ten industries which have been selected from manufacturing sector) during the period 1997-98 to 2008-09. The study made an analysis of relative efficiency-profitability status of the selected ten industries during the study period and observed that the food producing industry maintained a nice blend of efficiency of investment in working capital management and overall profitability during the period under study.

From the above discussion it is clear that in recent past many studies have made an analysis of the relationship between efficiency of assets management and profitability, but not a single study have made a comparative study on the issue between multinational and domestic companies' from the same industry of a country. Moreover, in many cases the findings of the studies have failed to provide any definite conclusion. Furthermore, there are many intricacies in measuring the efficiency of assets management of a Company. In order to bridge the gap the present study has been undertaken by taking into account ten companies from the Indian pharmaceutical industry consisting of five multinational and five domestic companies using necessary tools in connection with financial analysis as well as relevant statistical techniques. The pharmaceutical industry which is the lifeline industry in any country, has been chosen here because its contribution towards the growth, development and welfare of the economy as well as forming a strong human capital and intellectual property rights in a country cannot be ignored.

## 3. OBJECTIVES OF THE STUDY

This study has the following objectives:

- To measure the extent of relationship between efficiency of fixed assets management and profitability of the selected companies and to compare the said matter of the multinational companies with that of the domestic companies in Indian pharmaceutical sector.
- To evaluate the degree of correlation between efficiency of inventory management and profitability of the enterprises under study as well as to compare the said aspect of multinational companies with that of the domestic companies during the period under study.
- To analyze the closeness of association between efficiency of debtors management and profitability of the companies under study and to compare the said matter of selected multinational companies with that of the selected domestic pharmaceutical companies during the study period.
- To analyze the closeness of association between efficiency of total assets management and profitability of the companies under study and to compare the said matter of selected multinational companies with that of the selected domestic pharmaceutical companies during the study period.
- To assess the joint effect of fixed assets management, inventory management, debtors management and total assets management of the selected multinational and domestic companies on their earnings performance as well as to compare the said matter of multinational companies with that of domestic companies under study.
- To examine whether the findings of the study conform to the theoretical arguments.

## 4. METHODOLOGY OF THE STUDY

The study is based on ten (consisting of five multinational and five domestic companies) pharmaceutical companies which have been selected from Indian pharmaceutical sector following purposive sampling procedure. The selected five multinational and five domestic companies have been listed in Appendix 1. The data of the selected companies for the period 1998-99 to 2012-13 used in this study have been taken from secondary sources i.e. Capitaline Corporate Database of Capital Market Publishers (I) Ltd. Mumbai. The data used in this paper pertains to the yearend figures of each financial year under study. In fact, in order to capture the impact of the changing socio-cultural and business environment on assets management of Indian pharmaceutical sector, the post-liberalization period has been considered in this study. Although liberalization process started in India from July 1991, it is obvious that its effect could not be reflected clearly during the initial years of liberalization. Thus, for accounting for the effects of liberalization, financial year 1998-99 has been treated as the initial year of the period under study. For analysis of the data, ratio analysis as well as various statistical tools and techniques have been used. The ratios relating to the measurement of efficiency of assets management which have been used in this study are: (a) fixed assets turnover ratio (FATR), (b) inventory turnover ratio (ITR) (c) debtors turnover ratio (DTR) and total assets turnover ratio (TATR). FATR, ITR, DTR and TATR measure efficiency of fixed assets turnover ratio, efficiency of inventory management, efficiency of credit management and efficiency of total assets management respectively. So, these four ratios have been used in this study as the independent variables indicating the efficiency of assets management. The profitability measures which have been selected for this study are return on capital employed (ROCE) and return on net worth (RONW). ROCE and RONW have been used as dependent variable in this study. The degree of relationship between efficiency of assets management and profitability has been assessed through correlation coefficients between the selected measures of assets management and profitability taking into account their magnitudes (i.e. by Pearson's simple correlation coefficient), ranking of their magnitudes (i.e. by Spearman's rank correlation coefficient) and the nature of their associated changes (i.e. by Kendall's correlation coefficients). For studying the joint influence of the selected measures relating to the efficiency of assets management on the profitability, multiple correlation and multiple regression techniques have been applied. In order to examine whether the computed values of correlation coefficients and partial regression coefficients are statistically significant or not, t test has been used. The multiple correlation coefficients have been tested by F test.

## 5. FINDINGS OF THE STUDY

**A.** In Table 1, Table 2, Table 3 and Table 4 (appendix I), the effect of efficiency of assets management on profitability in the Indian pharmaceutical industry has been evaluated. This has been done by computing Karl Pearson's simple correlation coefficient, Kendall's correlation coefficient and Spearman's rank correlation coefficient between selected profitability measures (ROCE and RONW) and the selected ratios relating to the efficiency of assets management for each of the ten companies (five multinational and five domestic) under study.

(i) Table 1 shows that out of thirty correlation coefficients between FATR and ROCE in the selected companies, twenty-two coefficients were positive, out of which eleven coefficients were found to be sta-

*Table 1. Analysis of Correlation Between Fixed Assets Management and Profitability of the Selected Companies in the Indian Pharmaceutical Industry*

| | Company | Correlation coefficient between FATR and ROCE | | | Correlation coefficient between FATR and RONW | | |
|---|---|---|---|---|---|---|---|
| | | **Pearson** | **Kendall** | **Spearman** | **Pearson** | **Kendall** | **Spearman** |
| Multinational Company | Abbott | -0.330 | -0.333 | -0.400 | -0.549* | -0.543** | -0.779** |
| | Astrazeneca | -0.007 | 0.276 | 0.329 | 0.025 | 0.314 | 0.329 |
| | Fulford | -0.072 | 0.172 | 0.259 | 0.044 | 0.230 | 0.295 |
| | Glaxosmithkline | 0.685** | 0.352 | 0.586* | 0.773** | 0.467* | 0.675** |
| | Merck | -0.322 | -0.249 | -0.352 | -0.402 | -0.287 | -0.433 |
| Domestic Company | Aurobindo | 0.929** | 0.771** | 0.886** | 0.796** | 0.581** | 0.729** |
| | Cadila | 0.164 | 0.038 | 0.038 | 0.207 | -0.038 | -0.048 |
| | Cipla | 0.844** | 0.657** | 0.839** | 0.697** | 0.524** | 0.711** |
| | Dr Reddy's | 0.868** | 0.689** | 0.836** | 0.839** | 0.574** | 0.836** |
| | Ipca | 0.139 | 0.039 | 0.127 | 0.166 | 0.019 | 0.095 |

Note: * Significant at 5 per cent level

** Significant at 1 per cent level

Source: Compiled and computed from 'Capitaline Corporate Database' of Capital Market Publishers (I) Ltd., Mumbai.

*Table 2. Analysis of Correlation Between Inventory Management and Profitability of the Selected Companies in the Indian Pharmaceutical Industry*

| | Company | Correlation coefficient between ITR and ROCE | | | Correlation coefficient between ITR and RONW | | |
|---|---|---|---|---|---|---|---|
| | | **Pearson** | **Kendall** | **Spearman** | **Pearson** | **Kendall** | **Spearman** |
| Multinational Company | Abbott | 0.212 | 0.162 | 0.179 | 0.093 | -0.086 | -0.068 |
| | Astrazeneca | 0.424 | 0.402* | 0.563* | 0.391 | 0.402* | 0.563* |
| | Fulford | 0.769** | 0.670** | 0.845** | 0.707** | 0.651** | 0.820** |
| | Glaxosmithkline | 0.607* | 0.200 | 0.504 | 0.698** | 0.390* | 0.650** |
| | Merck | 0.107 | -0.029 | -0.018 | -0.035 | -0.105 | -0.146 |
| Domestic Company | Aurobindo | 0.863** | 0.555** | 0.681** | 0.696** | 0.383* | 0.499 |
| | Cadila | -0.158 | -0.019 | -0.043 | -0.220 | 0.038 | -0.038 |
| | Cipla | 0.231 | 0.162 | 0.382 | 0.047 | 0.105 | 0.236 |
| | Dr Reddy's | 0.864** | 0.486* | 0.614* | 0.874** | 0.448* | 0.514* |
| | Ipca | 0.281 | 0.211 | 0.268 | 0.378 | 0.191 | 0.277 |

Note: * Significant at 5 per cent level

** Significant at 1 per cent level

Source: Compiled and computed from 'Capitaline Corporate Database' of Capital Market Publishers (I) Ltd., Mumbai.

*Table 3. Analysis of Correlation Between Debtors Management and Profitability of the Selected Companies in the Indian Pharmaceutical Industry*

| | Company | Correlation coefficient between DTR and ROCE | | | Correlation coefficient between DTR and RONW | | |
|---|---|---|---|---|---|---|---|
| | | Pearson | Kendall | Spearman | Pearson | Kendall | Spearman |
| Multinational Company | Abbott | 0.208 | 0.143 | 0.318 | 0.066 | 0.048 | 0.039 |
| | Astrazeneca | -0.399 | -0.143 | -0.193 | -0.427 | -0.219 | -0.261 |
| | Fulford | 0.109 | 0.191 | 0.236 | 0.023 | 0.134 | 0.189 |
| | Glaxosmithkline | 0.731** | 0.429* | 0.618* | 0.750** | 0.429* | 0.625* |
| | Merck | -0.840** | -0.581** | -0.786** | -0.855** | -0.505** | -0.718** |
| Domestic Company | Aurobindo | 0.914** | 0.657** | 0.789** | 0.820** | 0.695** | 0.775** |
| | Cadila | -0.758** | -0.562** | -0.729** | -0.684** | -0.467* | -0.650** |
| | Cipla | 0.744** | 0.581** | 0.729** | 0.525* | 0.448* | 0.564* |
| | Dr Reddy's | 0.530* | 0.029 | 0.143 | 0.574* | 0.163 | 0.283 |
| | Ipca | 0.061 | -0.057 | -0.130 | -0.054 | -0.115 | -0.206 |

Note: * Significant at 5 per cent level
** Significant at 1 per cent level
Source: Compiled and computed from 'Capitaline Corporate Database' of Capital Market Publishers (I) Ltd., Mumbai.

*Table 4. Analysis of Correlation Between Total Assets Management and Profitability of the Selected Companies in the Indian Pharmaceutical Industry*

| | Company | Correlation coefficient between TATR and ROCE | | | Correlation coefficient between TATR and RONW | | |
|---|---|---|---|---|---|---|---|
| | | Pearson | Kendall | Spearman | Pearson | Kendall | Spearman |
| Multinational Company | Abbott | 0.255 | 0.200 | 0.339 | 0.248 | 0.181 | 0.239 |
| | Astrazeneca | 0.159 | 0.038 | 0.046 | -0.173 | 0.077 | 0.082 |
| | Fulford | 0.395 | 0.306 | 0.416 | 0.534* | 0.364 | 0.466 |
| | Glaxosmithkline | -0.748** | -0.364 | -0.593* | -0.788** | -0.402* | -0.613* |
| | Merck | 0.739** | 0.517** | 0.726** | 0.757** | 0.517** | 0.708** |
| Domestic Company | **Aurobindo** | **0.934**** | **0.771**** | **0.911**** | **0.795**** | **0.581**** | **0.729**** |
| | Cadila | 0.473 | 0.406* | 0.495 | 0.482 | 0.387* | 0.516* |
| | Cipla | 0.897** | 0.676** | 0.839** | 0.854** | 0.619** | 0.786** |
| | Dr Reddy's | 0.825** | 0.651** | 0.811** | 0.812** | 0.534** | 0.676** |
| | Ipca | 0.624* | 0.444* | 0.564* | 0.664** | 0.483* | 0.620* |

Note: * Significant at 5 per cent level
** Significant at 1 per cent level
Source: Compiled and computed from 'Capitaline Corporate Database' of Capital Market Publishers (I) Ltd., Mumbai.

tistically significant, whereas the remaining eight correlation coefficients were negative, and statistically insignificant. Thus, in the majority of the companies under study a positive relationship between firm's efficiency of fixed assets management and profitability was observed. Infact, no negative relationship between firm's efficiency of fixed assets management and profitability was statistically significant. Theoretically, higher the FATR, the greater is the efficiency of fixed assets management and the larger is the scope of profitability. Taking all the selected companies separately, the computed values of correlation coefficient between FATR and ROCE in a substantial portion of the sample companies conform to the accepted principle. Besides this, a comparative analysis between multinational and domestic companies under study with reference to the impact of their efficiency of fixed assets management on profitability has been conducted here. Table 1 exhibits that, in case of multinational companies, out of total fifteen correlation coefficients between FATR and ROCE seven coefficients were positive, out of which two coefficients were statistically significant. Remaining eight coefficients were negative, and statistically insignificant. Whereas, in case of domestic companies, out of fifteen correlation coefficients between FATR and ROCE, all the fifteen coefficients were positive out of which nine coefficients were found to be statistically significant. Thus, in the majority of the domestic companies under study (compared to the multinational companies under study) a positive relationship between companies' efficiency of fixed assets management and profitability was noticed.

Table 1 also depicts that out of thirty correlation coefficients between FATR and RONW in the selected companies, twenty-two coefficients were positive, out of which twelve coefficients were found to be statistically significant whereas the remaining eight correlation coefficients were negative, out of which three negative coefficients were found to be statistically significant. Theoretically, higher the FATR, the greater is the efficiency of asset management and larger is the scope of profitability. Taking all the selected companies separately, the computed values of correlation coefficient between FATR and RONW in a substantial portion of the sample companies conform to the accepted principle. Besides this, a comparative analysis between multinational and domestic companies under study with reference to the impact of their efficiency of fixed assets management on profitability has been conducted here. Table 1. exhibits that, in case of multinational companies, out of total fifteen correlation coefficients between FATR and RONW nine coefficients were positive, out of which three coefficients were statistically significant. Remaining six coefficients were negative, out of which three coefficients were found to be statistically significant. Whereas, in case of domestic companies, out of fifteen correlation coefficients between FATR and RONW thirteen coefficients were positive out of which nine coefficients were found to be statistically significant. Thus, in the majority of the domestic companies under study (compared to the multinational companies under study) a positive relationship between companies' efficiency of fixed assets management and profitability was noticed.

(ii) Table 2 exhibits that out of thirty correlation coefficients between ITR and ROCE in the selected companies, twenty-five coefficients were positive, out of which twelve coefficients were statistically significant while the remaining five correlation coefficients were negative, and statistically insignificant. It is an accepted principle that the higher the ITR, the greater is the efficiency of inventory management and the larger is the scope of profitability. Taking all the selected companies separately, the computed values of correlation coefficient between ITR and ROCE in a substantial portion of the sample companies conform to the accepted principle. Besides this, an attempt has also been made to compare the effect of multinational companies' efficiency of inventory management on overall profitability with that of the domestic companies under study. Table 2 also discloses that in case of multinational companies out of total fifteen correlation coefficients between ITR and ROCE, thirteen coefficients were positive, out of which six coefficients were statistically significant. Remaining two coefficients between ITR and ROCE were negative and statistically insignificant. In case of domestic companies out of total fifteen correlation coefficients between ITR and ROCE twelve coefficients were positive, out of which six coefficients were statistically significant whereas the rest three correlation coefficients between ITR and ROCE were negative and statistically insignificant. Thus in case of both multinational and domestic companies under study majority of the companies recorded a positive relationship between companies' efficiency of inventory management and profitability was noticed during the period under study.

Table 2 also exhibits that out of thirty correlation coefficients between ITR and RONW in the selected companies, twenty-three coefficients were positive, out of which thirteen coefficients were statistically significant while the remaining six correlation coefficients were negative, and statistically insignificant. It is an accepted principle that the higher the ITR, the greater is the efficiency of inventory management and the larger is the scope of profitability. Taking all the selected companies separately, the computed values of correlation coefficient between ITR and RONW in a substantial portion of the sample companies conform to the accepted principle. Besides this an attempt has also been made to compare the effect of multinational companies' efficiency of inventory management on profitability with that of the domestic companies under study. Table 2. also discloses that in case of multinational companies out of total fifteen correlation coefficients between ITR and RONW, ten coefficients were positive, out of which eight coefficients were statistically significant. Remaining five coefficients between ITR and RONW were negative and statistically insignificant. In case of domestic companies out of total fifteen correlation coefficients between ITR and RONW thirteen coefficients were positive, out of which five coefficients were statistically significant whereas the rest two correlation coefficients between ITR and RONW were negative and statistically insignificant. Thus in case of both multinational and domestic companies under study majority of the companies recorded a positive relationship between companies' efficiency of inventory management and profitability was noticed during the period under study.

(iii) Table 3 reveals that out of thirty correlation coefficients between DTR and ROCE, nineteen coefficients were positive, out of which ten coefficients were found to be statistically significant. Remaining eleven coefficients between DTR and ROCE were negative, of which only six coefficients were found to be statistically significant. Generally speaking, the faster the DTR the lower is the relative investment in receivables and the higher is the efficiency as well as profitability. The computed values of correlation coefficient between DTR and ROCE in the majority companies under study conform to the principle. A comparative study on the effect of multinational companies' efficiency of debtors' management on profitability with that of the domestic companies under study has also been made in Table 3. Table 3 depicts that while considering only multinational companies, out of total fifteen correlation coefficients between DTR and ROCE, nine coefficients were positive, of which three correlation coefficients were statistically significant whereas remaining six coefficients were negative, out of which three correlation coefficients were statistically significant. In case of only domestic companies under study, out of fifteen correlation coefficients between DTR and ROCE, ten coefficients were positive, out of which seven coefficients were statistically significant. Remaining five correlation coefficients between DTR and ROCE were negative, of which three coefficients were statistically significant. Thus in case of domestic companies under study majority of the relationships between companies' efficiency of debtors' management and overall profitability were positive and noticeable.

Table 3 also reveals that out of thirty correlation coefficients between DTR and RONW, eighteen coefficients were positive, out of which ten coefficients were found to be statistically significant. Remaining twelve coefficients between DTR and RONW were negative, of which only six coefficients were found to be statistically significant. Generally speaking, the faster the DTR the lower is the relative investment in receivables and the higher is the efficiency as well as profitability. The computed values of correlation coefficient between DTR and ROCE in the majority companies under study conform to the principle. A comparative study on the effect of multinational companies' efficiency of debtors' management on profitability with that of the domestic companies under study has also been made in Table 3. Table 3. depicts that while considering only multinational companies, out of total fifteen correlation coefficients between DTR and RONW, nine coefficients were positive, of which three correlation coefficients were statistically significant whereas remaining six coefficients were negative, out of which three correlation coefficients were statistically significant. In case of only domestic companies under study, out of fifteen correlation coefficients between DTR and RONW, nine coefficients were positive, out of which seven coefficients were statistically significant. Remaining six correlation coefficients between DTR and RONW were negative, of which three coefficients were statistically significant. Thus in case of domestic companies under study majority of the relationships between companies' efficiency of debtors' management and overall profitability were positive and noticeable.

(iv) Table 4 reveals that out of thirty correlation coefficients between TATR and ROCE, twenty-seven coefficients were positive, out of which sixteen coefficients were found to be statistically significant. Remaining only three coefficients between TATR and ROCE were negative and statistically significant. Generally speaking, the faster the TATR the lower is the relative investment in total assets and the higher is the efficiency as well as profitability. The computed values of correlation coefficient between TATR and ROCE in the majority companies under study conform to the principle. A comparative study on the effect of multinational companies' efficiency of total assets management on profitability with that of the domestic companies under study has also been made in Table 4. Table 4 exibits that while considering only multinational companies, out of total fifteen correlation coefficients between TATR and ROCE, twelve coefficients were positive, of which three correlation coefficients were statistically significant whereas remaining three coefficients were negative, out of which one correlation coefficient was statistically significant. In case of only domestic companies under study, out of fifteen correlation coefficients between TATR and ROCE, fifteen coefficients were positive, out of which thirteen coefficients were statistically significant. Thus in case of domestic companies under study majority of the relationships between companies' efficiency of total assets management and overall profitability were positive and noticeable.

Table 4 also reveals that out of thirty correlation coefficients between TATR and RONW, twenty-six coefficients were positive, out of which eighteen coefficients were found to be statistically significant. Remaining four coefficients between TATR and RONW were negative, of which only three coefficients were found to be statistically significant. Generally speaking, the faster the TATR the lower is the relative investment in total assets and the higher is the efficiency as well as profitability. The computed values of correlation coefficient between TATR and ROCE in the majority companies under study conform to the principle. A comparative study on the effect of multinational companies' efficiency of debtors' management on profitability with that of the domestic companies under study has also been made in Table 4. Table 4. depicts that while considering only multinational companies, out of total fifteen correlation coefficients between TATR and RONW, eleven coefficients were positive, of which four correlation coefficients were statistically significant whereas remaining four coefficients were negative, out of which three correlation coefficients were statistically significant. In case of only domestic companies under study, out of fifteen correlation coefficients between TATR and RONW, all coefficients were positive, out of which fourteen coefficients were statistically significant. Thus in case of domestic companies under study majority of the relationships between companies' total assets management and profitability were positive and noticeable.

**B.** The joint influence of the selected ratios indicating efficiency of assets management on the profitability of each of the companies under study has been studied in Table 5 (appendix I). The multiple regression equation which has been fitted in this study for each company is: ROCE= $B_0 + B_1$.FATR + $B_2$.ITR +$B_3$.DTR+$B_4$.TATR where $B_0$ is the constant, $B_1$, $B_2$,$B_3$ and $B_4$ are the partial regression coefficients.

Table 5 exhibits that when FATR increased by one unit, the ROCE went up in four out of the selected ten companies but the increase in ROCE was found to be statistically significant in only Dr Reddy's whereas for one unit increase in FATR, the ROCE came down in remaining six companies, out of which in case of three companies (Abbott, Fulford and Cadila) the partial regression coefficient was found to be statistically significant. In case of multinational companies under study when FATR increased by one unit, the ROCE improved (statistically insignificant) in two out of five multinational companies, whereas for one unit improvement of FATR, the ROCE came down in three out of total five multinational companies and the decrease in ROCE was found to be statistically significant in case of two companies (Abbott and Fulford) under study. On the other hand, in case of domestic companies under study when FATR increased by one unit, the ROCE improved in two out of five multinational companies and the

*Table 5. Analysis of Multiple Regression of ROCE on FATR, ITR, DTR and TATR of the Selected Companies in the Indian Pharmaceutical Industry*

| Company | | Partial regression coefficients | | | | Constant $B_0$ |
|---|---|---|---|---|---|---|
| | | $B_1$ (FATR) | $B_2$ (ITR) | $B_3$ (DTR) | $B_4$(TATR) | |
| Multinational Company | Abbott | -2.980 (-2.130)* | 1.767 (1.535) | 0.297 (0.433) | 12.950 (2.153)* | 6.289 (0.268) |
| | Astrazeneca | 3.442 (0.777) | 3.172 (2.372)** | -0.401 (-0.260) | -20.088 (-1.647) | 52.100 (4.800) |
| | Fulford | -2.839 (-2.031)* | 10.013 (4.002)*** | -0.075 (-0.062) | 8.552 (2.775)** | -4.064 (-0.111) |
| | Glaxosmithkline | 5.394 (1.488) | -11.353 (-1.539) | 0.744 (1.131) | -1.304 (-0.071) | 75.255 (1.298) |
| | Merck | -1.131 (-0.393) | 3.006 (3.238)*** | -2.078 (-1.355) | 14.932 (4.282)*** | 8.999 (0.339) |
| Domestic Company | Aurobindo | 2.038 (0.376) | 0.312 (0.141) | 2.474 (0.517) | 3.861 (0.216) | -4.251 (-0.383) |
| | Cadila | -2.575 (-2.113)* | 2.686 (2.272)** | -2.599 (-5.091)*** | 6.940 (2.589)** | 19.751 (3.525) |
| | Cipla | -4.571 (-1.584) | 1.878 (0.578) | 1.046 (2.761)** | 34.072 (3.869)*** | -15.583 (-1.055) |
| | Dr Reddy's | 11.010 (1.968)* | 1.815 (0.551) | 0.245 (0.063) | 13.919 (1.172) | -32.889 (-3.057) |
| | Ipca | -7.527 (-1.381) | -3.696 (-0.562) | -1.195 (-0.449) | 44.134 (2.668)** | -0.333 (-0.011) |

Note: Figures in the parentheses indicate t values,

* Significant at 10 per cent level, ** Significant at 5 per cent level, *** Significant at 1 per centevel,

Source: Compiled and computed from 'Capitaline Corporate Database' of Capital Market Publishers (I) Ltd., Mumbai.

Regression Equation of ROCE on FATR, ITR, DTR and FATR: ROCE = $B_0$+$B_1$.FATR+$B_2$.ITR+$B_3$.DTR+$B_4$.TATR increase in ROCE was found to be statistically significant in one company (Dr Reddy's), whereas for one unit improvement of FATR, the ROCE came down in rest three domestic companies under study and the decrease in ROCE was found to be statistically significant in case of one company (Cadila) under study. Thus, the study of the partial regression coefficients shown in the regression equation of ROCE on FATR, ITR, DTR and TATR which was fitted in this study reveals that in case of two domestic companies (Aurobindo and Dr. Reddy's) and two multinational companies (Astrazeneca and Glaxosmitkline) the effect of efficiency of fixed assets management on profitability was positive during the study period.

For one unit increase in ITR, the ROCE increased in eight companies whereas it reduced in the remaining two companies under study. The increase in ROCE were found to be statistically significant in four companies (Astrazeneca, Fulford, Merck and Cadila). Table 5 also discloses that in case of multinational companies, when ITR improved by one unit, the ROCE stepped up in four out of the five companies under study and the increase in ROCE was found to be statistically significant in three companies (Astrazeneca, Fulford and Merck), whereas for one unit increase in ITR, the ROCE decreased (statistically insignificant) in one company. In case of domestic companies when ITR increased by one unit, the ROCE went up in four companies, out of which in one case (Cadila) the increase in ROCE was statistically significant whereas for one unit increase in ITR, the ROCE detoriated (statistically insignificant) in one domestic company (Ipca). Thus, the study of the partial regression coefficients shown in the regression equation of ROCE on FATR, ITR, DTR and TATR which was fitted in this study reveals that majority of both multinational and domestic companies under study recorded the positive effect of efficiency of inventory management on profitability during the study period.

When DTR increased by one unit, the ROCE stepped up in five companies, but this change was found to be statistically significant in case of only one company (Cadila) whereas the decrease in ROCE due to one unit increase in DTR was found in the remaining five companies, out of which in one company (Cadila), the partial regression coefficient was found to be statistically significant. In case of multinational companies under study, when DTR increased by one unit, the ROCE improved (statistically insignificant) in two out of five multinational companies, whereas for one unit improvement of DTR, the ROCE came down (statistically insignificant) in three companies. On the other hand, in case of domestic companies under study when DTR increased by one unit, the ROCE improved in three companies and the increase in ROCE was found to be statistically significant in one company (Cipla), whereas for one unit improvement of DTR, the ROCE came down in rest two domestic companies under study and the decrease in ROCE was found to be statistically significant in case of one company (Cadila) under study.

For one unit increase in TATR, the ROCE increased in eight companies whereas it reduced in the remaining two companies under study. The increase in ROCE were found to be statistically significant in five companies (Abbott, Fulford, Merck, Cadila and Cipla). Table 5 also discloses that in case of multinational companies, when TATR improved by one unit, the ROCE stepped up in three out of the five companies under study and the increase in ROCE was found to be statistically significant in three companies (Abbott, Fulford and Merck), whereas for one unit increase in TATR, the ROCE decreased (statistically insignificant) in two multinational companies (Astrazeneca and Glaxosmithkline). In case of domestic companies when TATR increased by one unit, the ROCE went up in case of all the five companies under study, out of which in three cases (Cadila, Cipla and Ipca) the increase in ROCE was statistically significant. Thus, the study of the partial regression coefficients shown in the regression equation of ROCE on FATR, ITR, DTR and TATR which was fitted in this study reveals that majority of both multinational and domestic companies under study recorded the positive effect of efficiency of inventory management on profitability during the study period. Thus, the study of the partial regression coefficients shown in the regression equation of ROCE on FATR, ITR, DTR and TATR which was fitted in this study reveals that the effect of efficiency of debtors' management on profitability was positive in case of majority of domestic companies during the study period.

For one unit increase in TATR, the ROCE increased in eight companies whereas it reduced in the remaining two companies under study. The increase in ROCE was found to be statistically significant in four companies (Abbott, Fulford, Merck, Cadila, Cipla and Ipca). Table 5 also discloses that in case of multinational companies, when TATR improved by one unit, the ROCE stepped up in three out of the five companies under study and the increase in ROCE was found to be statistically significant in three companies (Abbott, Fulford and Merck), whereas for one unit increase in TATR, the ROCE decreased (statistically insignificant) in two companies. In case of domestic companies when TATR increased by one unit, the ROCE went up in case of all the five companies, out of which in three cases (Cadila, Cipla and Ipca) the increase in ROCE was statistically significant. Thus, the study of the partial regression coefficients shown in the regression equation of ROCE on FATR, ITR, DTR and TATR which was fitted in this study reveals that majority of domestic companies (compared to multinational companies) recorded the positive effect of efficiency of total asserts management on profitability during the study period.

The joint influence of the selected ratios indicating efficiency of assets management on the profitability (RONW) of each of the companies under study has been studied in Table 6 (appendix I). The multiple regression equation which has been fitted in this study for each company is: $RONW= b_0 + b_1.FATR + b_2.ITR + b_3.DTR + b_4.TATR$ where $b_0$ is the constant, $b_1$, $b_2$, $b_3$ and $b_4$ are the partial regression coefficients.

Table 6 exhibits that when FATR increased by one unit, the RONW went up (statistically insignificant) in four out of the selected ten companies. whereas for one unit increase in FATR, the RONW came down in remaining six companies, out of which in case of three companies (Abbott, Fulford and Cadila) the partial regression coefficient was found to be statistically significant. In case of multinational companies under study when FATR increased by one unit, the RONW improved (statistically insignificant) in two out of five multinational companies, whereas for one unit improvement of FATR, the RONW came down in three out of total five multinational companies and the decrease in ROCE was found to be statistically significant in case of two companies (Abbott and Fulford) under study. On the other hand, in case of domestic companies under study when FATR increased by one unit, the RONW improved in two out of five companies whereas for one unit improvement of FATR, the RONW came down in rest three domestic companies (Cadila, Cipla and Ipca) under study and the decrease in RONW was found to be statistically significant in case of one company (Cadila) under study.

For one unit increase in ITR, the RONW increased in seven companies whereas it reduced in the remaining three companies under study. The increase in RONW was found to be statistically significant in three companies (Abbott, Astrazeneca and Fulford). Table 5 also discloses that in case of multinational companies, when ITR improved by one unit, the RONW stepped up in four out of the five companies under study and the increase in RONW was found to be statistically significant in three companies (Abbott, Astrazeneca and Fulford), whereas for one unit increase in ITR, the RONW decreased (statistically insignificant) in one company (Glaxosmithkline). In case of domestic companies when ITR increased by one unit, the RONW went up in three companies (Cadila, Cipla and Dr Reddy's) whereas for one unit increase in ITR, the RONW detoriated (statistically insignificant) in two domestic companies (Aurobindo and Ipca). Thus, the study of the partial regression coefficients shown in the regression equation of ROCE on FATR, ITR, DTR and TATR which was fitted in this study reveals that majority of both multinational and domestic companies under study recorded the positive effect of efficiency of inventory management on profitability during the study period.

*Table 6. Analysis of Multiple Regression of ROCE on FATR, ITR, DTR and TATR of the Selected Companies in the Indian Pharmaceutical Industry*

| | Company | Partial regression coefficients | | | | Constant $B_0$ |
|---|---|---|---|---|---|---|
| | | $B_1$ (FATR) | $B_2$ (ITR) | $B_3$ (DTR) | $B_4$(TATR) | |
| Multinational Company | Abbott | -3.842<br>(-3.873)*** | 1.511<br>(1.850)* | 0.068<br>(0.141) | 11.144<br>(2.612)** | 12.375<br>(0.745) |
| | Astrazeneca | 4.366<br>(1.295) | 2.085<br>(2.049)* | -0.689<br>(-0.586) | -16.266<br>(-1.752) | 37.774<br>(4.571) |
| | Fulford | -2.066<br>(-1.996)* | 6.739<br>(3.638)*** | 0.285<br>(0.320) | 8.580<br>(3.760)*** | -11.677<br>(-0.431) |
| | Glaxosmithkline | 3.349<br>(1.583) | -4.986<br>(-1.158) | 0.320<br>(0.834) | -1.263<br>(-0.117) | 38.415<br>(1.136) |
| | Merck | -1.689<br>(-0.696) | 0.718<br>(0.919) | -2.959<br>(-2.292)** | 6.144<br>(2.094) | 41.367<br>(1.850) |
| Domestic Company | Aurobindo | 10.848<br>(1.025) | -1.065<br>(-0.248) | 11.870<br>(1.271) | -29.584<br>(-0.848) | -12.251<br>(-0.566) |
| | Cadila | -3.430<br>(-1.070) | 2.167<br>(0.697) | -3.639<br>(-2.711)** | 12.723<br>(1.805) | 29.572<br>(2.007) |
| | Cipla | -7.299<br>(-2.402)** | 2.193<br>(0.640) | 0.481<br>(1.206) | 38.660<br>(4.169)*** | -16.404<br>(-1.055) |
| | Dr Reddy's | 9.036<br>(1.422) | 2.963<br>(0.792) | 1.117<br>(0.252) | 12.271<br>(0.910) | -38.993<br>(-3.190) |
| | Ipca | -9.484<br>(-1.491) | -4.100<br>(-0.533) | -2.673<br>(-0.860) | 57.540<br>(2.979)** | -3.699<br>(-0.101) |

Note: Figures in the parentheses indicate t values,
* Significant at 10 per cent level, ** Significant at 5 per cent level, *** Significant at 2 per cent level, **** Significant at 1 per cent level
Source: Compiled and computed from 'Capitaline Corporate Database' of Capital Market Publishers (I) Ltd., Mumbai.
Regression Equation of RONW on FATR, ITR, DTR and FATR: RONW = $b_0+b_1.FATR+b_2.ITR+b_3.DTR+b_4.TATR$

When DTR increased by one unit, the RONW stepped up in six companies, whereas the decrease in RONW due to one unit increase in DTR was found in the remaining four companies, out of which in two companies (Merck and Cadila), the partial regression coefficient was found to be statistically significant. When DTR increased by one unit, the RONW improved (statistically insignificant) in three out of five multinational companies, whereas for one unit improvement of DTR, the RONW came down in two companies, out of which in case of Merck the negative impact was statistically significant. On the other hand, in case of domestic companies under study when DTR increased by one unit, the RONW improved in three companies, whereas for one unit improvement of DTR, the RONW came down in rest two domestic companies under study and the decrease in RONW was found to be statistically significant in case of one company (Cadila) under study.

For one unit increase in TATR, the RONW increased in seven companies whereas it reduced in the remaining three companies under study. The increase in RONW were found to be statistically significant in four companies (Abbott, Fulford, Cipla and Ipca). Table 6 also discloses that in case of multinational companies, when TATR improved by one unit, the RONW stepped up in three out of the five companies under study and the increase in RONW was found to be statistically significant in two companies (Abbott and Fulford), whereas for one unit increase in TATR, the RONW decreased (statistically insignificant) in two companies. In case of domestic companies when TATR increased by one unit, the RONW went up in four companies, out of which in one case (Cipla and Ipca) the increase in RONW was statistically significant whereas for one unit increase in TATR, the RONW detoriated (statistically insignificant) in one domestic company (Aurobindo). Thus, the study of the partial regression coefficients shown in the regression equation of RONW on FATR, ITR, DTR and TATR which was fitted in this study reveals that majority of both multinational and domestic companies under study recorded the positive effect of efficiency of total assets management on profitability during the study period.

Table 7 (appendix I) reveals that the multiple correlation coefficient of ROCE on FATR, ITR, DTR and TATR in the selected companies ranged between 0.676 (Abbott) and 0.955 (Cipla) under study. This coefficient was found to be statistically significant in seven companies. It implies that the joint influence of firm's efficiency in managing its fixed assets, inventory, debtors and total assets on profitability was notable in these seven companies (Fulford, Glaxosmitkline, Merck, Aurobindo, Cadila, Cipla and Dr Reddy's). The contribution made by the selected variables towards improving ROCE in the companies under study varied between 45.70 percent and 91.20 per cent. Table 7 also exhibits that the multiple correlation coefficient of ROCE on FATR, ITR, DTR and TATR in the selected multinational companies ranged between 0.676 (Abbott) and 0.948 (Merck) whereas the multiple correlation coefficient of ROCE on FATR, ITR, DTR and TATR in selected domestic companies ranged between 0.702 (Ipca) and 0.955 (Cipla). So the range of multiple correlation coefficient of ROCE on FATR, ITR, DTR and TATR in the domestic companies was more than the multinational companies under study. This coefficient was found to be statistically significant in three multinational companies and four domestic companies under study. It denotes that the joint influence of firm's efficiency in managing its fixed assets, inventory, debtors and total assets on profitability was notable in case of three multinational companies (Fulford, Glaxosmithkline, Merck) and four domestic companies (Aurobindo, Cadila, Cipla and Dr Reddy's) during the study period. Besides this, the coefficients of multiple determination in the selected multinational companies reflected that the percentage of the total variation in FATR, ITR, DTR and TATR ranged

*Table 7. Analysis of Multiple Correlation of ROCE on FATR, ITR, DTR and TATR of the Selected Companies in the Indian Pharmaceutical Industry*

| | Company | R | $R^2$ | F |
|---|---|---|---|---|
| | **Abbott** | **0.676** | **0.457** | **2.104** |
| Multinational Company | Astrazeneca | 0.733 | 0.537 | 2.904 |
| | Fulford | 0.894 | 0.799 | 9.916** |
| | Glaxosmithkline | 0.809 | 0.655 | 4.745* |
| | Merck | 0.948 | 0.900 | 22.398** |
| Domestic Company | Aurobindo | 0.936 | 0.877 | 17.809** |
| | Cadila | 0.909 | 0.826 | 11.888** |
| | Cipla | 0.955 | 0.912 | 25.986** |
| | Dr Reddy's | 0.917 | 0.841 | 13.202** |
| | Ipca | 0.702 | 0.493 | 2.435 |

Note: * Significant at 5 per cent level,
** Significant at 1 per cent level
Source: Compiled and computed from 'Capitaline Corporate Database' of Capital Market Publishers (I) Ltd., Mumbai.

between 45.70 per cent and 90.00 per cent, whereas the percentage of the total variation in the ROCE of the selected five domestic companies due to the variation in FATR, ITR, DTR and TATR ranged between 49.30 per cent and 91.20 per cent.

Table 8 reveals that the multiple correlation coefficient of RONW on FATR, ITR, DTR and TATR in the selected companies ranged between 0.743 (Astrazeneca) and 0.919 (Merck) under study. This coefficient was found to be statistically significant in eight companies. It implies that the joint influence of firm's efficiency in managing its fixed assets, inventory, debtors and total assets on profitability was notable in these eight companies (Abbott, Fulford, Glaxosmitkline, Merck, Aurobindo, Cadila, Cipla and Dr Reddy's). The contribution made by the selected variables towards improving RONW in the companies under study varied between 55.30 percent and 84.50 per cent. Table 8. (appendix I) also exhibits that the multiple correlation coefficient of RONW on FATR, ITR, DTR and TATR in the selected multinational companies ranged between 0.743 (Astrazeneca) and 0.919 (Merck) whereas the multiple correlation coefficient of ROCE on FATR, ITR, DTR and TATR in selected domestic companies ranged between 0.748 (Ipca) and 0.912 (Cipla). This coefficient was found to be statistically significant in four multinational companies and four domestic companies under study. It denotes that the joint influence of firm's efficiency in managing its fixed assets, inventory, debtors and total assets on profitability was notable in case of four multinational companies (Abbott, Fulford, Glaxosmithkline, Merck) and four domestic companies (Aurobindo, Cadila, Cipla and Dr Reddy's) during the study period. Besides this, the coefficients of multiple determination in the selected multinational companies reflected that the percentage of the total variation in FATR, ITR, DTR and TATR ranged between 55.30 per cent and 84.50 per cent, whereas the percentage of the total variation in the ROCE of the selected five domestic companies due to the variation in FATR, ITR, DTR and TATR ranged between 55.90 per cent and 83.10 per cent.

*Table 8. Analysis of Multiple Correlation of RONW on FATR, ITR, DTR and TATR of the Selected Companies in the Indian Pharmaceutical Industry*

| | Company | R | $R^2$ | F |
|---|---|---|---|---|
| | **Abbott** | **0.804** | **0.646** | **4.570*** |
| Multinational Company | Astrazeneca | 0.743 | 0.553 | 3.087 |
| | Fulford | 0.907 | 0.822 | 11.566** |
| | Glaxosmithkline | 0.835 | 0.697 | 5.746* |
| | Merck | 0.919 | 0.845 | 13.663** |
| Domestic Company | Aurobindo | 0.839 | 0.704 | 5.948* |
| | Cadila | 0.803 | 0.645 | 4.552* |
| | Cipla | 0.912 | 0.831 | 12.302** |
| | Dr Reddy's | 0.905 | 0.819 | 11.278** |
| | Ipca | 0.748 | 0.559 | 3.172 |

Note: * Significant at 5 per cent level,
** Significant at 1 per cent level
Source: Compiled and computed from 'Capitaline Corporate Database' of Capital Market Publishers (I) Ltd., Mumbai.

## 5. CONCLUDING REMARKS

1. In forty-four out of sixty cases the efficiency of management of fixed assets was positively associated with the profitability and in twenty-three cases the positive association was significant. In the remaining sixteen cases the relationship between FATR and profitability was negative, out of which in three cases the negative association was statistically significant. Thus, the analysis of correlation between FATR and the selected profitability measure reveals that in 73.33 per cent cases a positive association was observed and in 52.27 per cent of these cases the positive association was significant. Therefore, when taken all the companies separately, the study established a strong evidence of positive relationship between efficiency of managing fixed assets and profitability. Besides this, in majority of the domestic companies under study (compared to the multinational companies under study) a positive relationship between companies' efficiency of fixed assets management and profitability prevailed during the study period. In fact, positive relationship between companies' efficiency of fixed assets management and profitability was observed in 53.33 per cent and 93.33 per cent cases of the multinational and domestic companies respectively.
2. A positive correlation between ITR and profitability was found in forty-eight out of sixty cases and the positive correlation was significant in twenty-five cases. The association between ITR and profitability was negative in the remaining twelve cases (statistically insignificant). Thus, the study of correlation between ITR and profitability exhibits that there was a positive relationship between efficiency of inventory management and profitability in 80 per cent cases and in 52.08 per cent of these cases the relationship was found to be statistically significant. Hence, these results provide strong evidence of positive contribution of inventory management towards improving profitability in a substantial portion of the sample companies during the study period. It is also noticeable that in 76.67 per cent cases there was positive relationship between multinational companies' efficiency of inventory management and profitability whereas the positive relationship between domestic companies' efficiency of inventory management and profitability was 83.33 per cent during the study period. Thus in case of both multinational and domestic companies under study majority of the companies recorded a positive relationship between companies' efficiency of inventory management and profitability was noticed.
3. The relationship between DTR and the selected profitability indicators was positive in thirty-seven out of sixty cases and in twenty cases the positive association was significant. In the remaining twenty-three cases DTR was negatively associated with profitability and in twelve cases out of these twenty-three, the negative association was statistically significant. Thus, the analysis of correlation between DTR and ROCE discloses that in 61.67 per cent cases a positive association was found and 54.05 per cent of these positive correlations were statistically significant. While 38.33 per cent of the same was negative. The outcome of the study conforms to the hypothesis in the majority cases that the higher the efficiency of credit management, the higher the profitability. The relationship between companies' efficiency of credit management and profitability were positive in 60 per cent and 63.33 per cent in case of multinational companies and domestic companies respectively. Thus in case of both multinational and domestic companies under study majority of the relationship between companies' efficiency of debtors' management and overall profitability were positive.
4. In fifty-three out of sixty cases the efficiency of total assets management was positively associated with the profitability and in thirty-four cases the positive association was significant. In the remaining seven cases the relationship between TATR and profitability was negative, out of which

in six cases the negative association was statistically significant. Thus, the analysis of correlation between TATR and the selected profitability measures reveals that in 88.33 per cent cases a positive association was observed and in 64.15 per cent of these cases the positive association was significant. Therefore, when taken all the companies separately, the study established a strong evidence of positive relationship between efficiency of managing total assets and profitability. Besides this, in majority of the domestic companies under study (compared to the multinational companies under study) a positive relationship between companies' efficiency of total assets management and profitability prevailed during the study period. In fact, positive relationship between companies' efficiency of total assets management and profitability was observed in 76.67 per cent and 100 per cent cases of the multinational and domestic companies respectively.

5. The study of the partial regression coefficients shown in the regression equation of ROCE on FATR, ITR, DTR and TATR which was fitted in this study reveals that in case of only Dr Reddy's (domestic company) the effect of efficiency of fixed assets management on profitability was positive as well as significant. In four cases including three multinational (Astrazeneca, Fulford and Merck) and one domestic company (Cadila) the impact of inventory management on profitability was positive and significant. The study also shows that the efficiency of credit management in case of Cipla (domestic companies) was positive and significant. In six cases including three multinational (Abbott, Fulford and Merck) and three domestic companies (Cadila, Cipla and Ipca) the impact of total assets management on profitability was positive and significant. While making a comparison between multinational and domestic companies under study, the partial regression coefficients shown in the regression equation of ROCE on FATR, ITR, DTR and TATR which was fitted in this study reveals that in case of two multinational companies (Astrazeneca and Glaxosmithkline) and two domestic companies (Aurobindo and Dr Reddy's) the effect of efficiency of fixed assets management on profitability was positive whereas majority of both multinational (Abbott, Astrazeneca, Fulford and Merck) and domestic companies (Cadila, Cipla and Dr. Reddy's) recorded the positive effect of efficiency of inventory management on overall profitability during the study period. Besides this, the study exhibits that the effect of efficiency of debtors' management on profitability was also positive in case of majority of the multinational (Abbott, Fulford and Glaxosmithkline) and domestic companies (Aurobindo, Cipla and Dr Reddy's) during the period under study. In case of three multinational companies (Abbott, Fulford and Merck) and four domestic companies (Cadila, Cipla, Dr Reddy's and Ipca) the effect of efficiency of total assets management on profitability was positive.
6. The study of the partial regression coefficients shown in the regression equation of RONW on FATR, ITR, DTR and TATR which was fitted in this study reveals that in case of Astrazeneca and Glaxosmithkline (multinational company) the effect of efficiency of fixed assets management on profitability was positive but statistically insignificant. In two cases of domestic (Aurobindo and Dr Reddy's) company the effect of fixed assets management on profitability was positive and statistically insignificant. The impact of inventory management on profitability was positive and significant in three cases of multinational companies (Abbott, Astrazeneca and Fulford). But in case of domestic companies under study the impact of inventory management on profitability was positive but insignificant in three cases (Cadila, Cipla and Dr Reddy's). The study also shows that the efficiency of credit management in case of Aurobindo, Cipla and Dr Reddy's (domestic companies) was positive and insignificant. In three cases of multinational (Abbott, Fulford and Glaxosmithkline) companies the impact of creditors' management on profitability was positive

and insignificant. In case of two multinational companies (Abbott and Fulford) and two domestic companies (Cipla and Ipca) the effect of efficiency of total assets management on profitability was positive and statistically significant.

7. The multiple correlation coefficient of ROCE on FATR, ITR, DTR and TATR denotes that the joint influence of firm's efficiency in managing its fixed assets, inventory, debtors and total assets on profitability was notable in case of three multinational companies (Fulford, Glaxosmithkline, Merck) and four domestic companies (Aurobindo, Cadila, Cipla and Dr Reddy's) during the study period. The multiple correlation coefficient of RONW on FATR, ITR, DTR and TATR denotes that the joint influence of firm's efficiency in managing its fixed assets, inventory, debtors and total assets on profitability was notable in case of four multinational companies (Abbott, Fulford, Glaxosmithkline, Merck) and four domestic companies (Aurobindo, Cadila, Cipla and Dr Reddy's) during the study period.

## REFERENCES

Azagaiah, R., & Gejalakshmi, S. (2007). Working Capital Management – Efficiency Analysis. *Udyog Pragathi*, *31*(3), 15–90.

Chakraborty, K. (2008). Working Capital and Profitability: An Empirical Analysis of their Relationship with Reference to Selected Companies in the Indian Pharmaceutical Industry. *The Icfaian Journal of Management Research*, *VII*(12), 41–59.

Ghosh, S.K., & Maji, S.G. (2004). Utilization of Current Assets and Operating Profitability: An Empirical Study on Cement and Tea Industries in India. *Indian Journal of Accounting*, December, 52-55.

Khatick, S. K., & Singh, P. K. (2003). Liquidity Management in Eicher Ltd. – A Case Study. *The Management Accountant*, *38*(3), 217–220.

Mallik, A. K., & Sur, D. (1998). Working Capital and Profitability: A Case Study in Interrelation. The Management Accountant, November, 805-809.

Sarkar, J. B., & Saha, S. N. (1987). Profitability Crisis & Working Capital Management in the Public Sector in India: A Case Study. The Management Accountant, May, 328-333.

Sur, D., & Chakraborty, K. (2010). Efficiency of Working Capital Management in Indian Corporate Sector: An Empirical Analysis in the Post-liberalisation Era. *GITAM Journal of Management*, *8*(3), 119–138.

Sur, D., & Chakraborty, K. (2011). Evaluating Relationship of Working Capital and Profitability: A Study of Select Multinational Companies in the Indian Pharmaceutical Sector. *The IUP Journal of Management Research*, *X*(2), 7–22.

Sur, D., Chakraborty, K., & Das, S. (2007). Measuring Efficiency of Asset Management of Private Sector Enterprises in India during the Pre- and Post- liberalization Periods: A Study on Colgate-Palmolive (India) Ltd. *The Icfaian Journal of Management Research*, *6*(7), 25–36.

Vijayakumar, A., & Venkatachalam, A. (1995). Working Capital and Profitability- An Empirical Analysis. The Management Accountant, June, 748-750.

# APPENDIX

## List of the Companies Under Study

### Multinational Companies

Abbott
Astrazeneca
Fulford
Glaxosmithkline
Merck

### Domestic Companies

Aurobindo
Cadila
Cipla
Dr Reddy's
Ipca

# Chapter 4

# Can Codes of Conduct Work? Evaluating the Effectiveness of Privatised Corporate Governance

**Shefali Virkar**
*University of Oxford, UK*

## ABSTRACT

*Over the last couple of decades, the world has witnessed a spectacular increase in the size and number of Transnational Corporations (TNCs). This explosion has resulted in the overseas practices of such companies coming under intense scrutiny, and has highlighted that in most cases, governments lack the resources necessary to ensure TNC compliance to international standards in key areas such as labour rights, environmental pollution, and social justice. As a direct result of the failure of national and international attempts to regulate corporate behaviour, recent years have seen the mushrooming of a number of codes aimed at regulating corporate behaviour, and an increased focus on corporate social responsibility. This chapter will attempt to evaluate the effectiveness of such codes of ethical corporate conduct in the light of available evidence, focusing on the conceptualisation of such regulatory mechanisms, and their relationship to the larger corpus of corporate social, commercial, and ethical interactions. The work will then seek to evaluate the effectiveness of such codes as instruments of privatised governance, particularly through the examination of corporate stakeholder behaviour and recent examples of global best practice.*

## INTRODUCTION

The 1980s were marked by a dramatic shift in political ideology that involved a move away from the Keynesian interventionism that had dominated post-World War 2 economics in the North, and towards a growing disillusionment with import substitution in some Southern nations. This move saw the state beginning to withdraw from the over-regulation of the economy, and marked the beginning of an era of rapid economic integration (cf. Carroll & Shabana, 2010; Held, 2013; Jenkins, 2013). The closing years of the 1980s witnessed a tremendous outpouring of foreign direct investment from developed to

DOI: 10.4018/978-1-4666-9908-3.ch004

developing countries, and a simultaneous increase in the size and number of transnational corporations (TNCs) worldwide. The past three decades in particular have seen a progressive removal of restrictions on international flows of capital and goods, policies that have speeded up the expansion of TNCs in the developing world. Historically, national governments have only been able to regulate the activities of foreign-owned firms within their borders; all attempts at international regulation having been largely unsuccessful. To add to this, the policy shifts of the '80s left states even more ill-equipped and unable to regulate the sheer speed and volume of TNC expansion.

In recent years, the growing recognition that the current form of globalisation has provided Transnational Corporations with a distinct advantage in extracting greater gains from productivity and efficiency from international trade has prompted the spotlight to be turned onto the overall impact of transnational corporate activity in the Third World (Bondy et. al., 2008). Increasingly integrated supply chains have left transnationals more vulnerable to potentially adverse publicity, particularly with regard to the behaviour of their subcontractors and suppliers (Carroll & Buchholtz, 2014). This coupled with the advent of greater pressure from Non-Governmental Organisations and consumers has brought into sharp focus the need for Transnational Corporations to adopt some kind of privatised voluntary or semi-formalised self-regulation in order to minimise the extent of their vulnerability to legal wrangles and to adverse publicity (Grace & Cohen, 2013).

Over the last couple of decades, the world has witnessed a spectacular increase in the size and number of Transnational Corporations (TNCs), an explosion that has resulted in the overseas practices of such companies coming under intense scrutiny, and that has highlighted the propensity for some national governments, mainly those of the developing world, to find it difficult to muster the resources necessary to ensure TNC compliance to international standards in key areas such as labour rights, societal health, environmental pollution, and social justice. In some cases, governments have been found to deliberately lower standards in order to entice foreign investment into the country. This has left Transnational Corporations with a virtual *carte blanche* from which to operate, and has resulted in them coming under intense scrutiny and becoming targets of intense criticism from communities and advocacy groups concerned with the negative impacts of corporate activity on the global community.

As a direct result of the failure of local, national, and international level attempts to regulate corporate and other private forms of behaviour, recent years have witnessed an increased focus on idea of *corporate social responsibility* (CSR) as a panacea to the ills of society, and a mushrooming in terms of the breadth and depth of the conceptualisation and the development of both voluntary and formalised codes of corporate ethical conduct (Rodriguez-Dominguez et. al., 2009). In this context, the basic structure of such codified regulatory frameworks has been drawn from the base CSR concept that local, national, and international communities may be dealt with in a fair, ethical, and socially responsible manner for both profit and for human development by commercial entities. This book chapter will attempt to evaluate the effectiveness of codes of ethical corporate conduct as instruments of privatised regulation and corporate governance in the light of available evidence. Through a discussion of the evolution of the ideal, the potential benefits and limitations of codes of ethical corporate conduct will be examined, together with the modes of proliferation and implementation available to transnational entities, and other related controversies.

There is little doubt that corporate codes of ethical conduct represent an important new development in the regulation of the transnational corporation. The chapter seeks to study the effectiveness of such structures of informal regulation as an innovative attempt at privatised governance in a globalising age, through an evaluation of their benefits and limitations, and the presentation of suggestions to improve the efficacy of voluntary corporate codes, together with a brief discussion regarding their role for the future. In illustrating its main thesis through the presentation of international instances and examples of best practice, the chapter will argue that codes of ethical corporate conduct, despite their significant limitations, have the potential to be highly effective tools of grassroots governance that complement the more formalised, established government regulation of international business activity.

## CODES OF ETHICAL CORPORATE CONDUCT: A DISCUSSION OF KEY DEFINITIONS AND CONCEPTS

Of the current literature existing on topics related to the ways in which organizations may codify and consequently influence the behaviour and the interactions of their employees and subsidiary enterprises, a majority of the work written under the broad umbrella of *corporate social responsibility* may be found to deal exclusively with the issue of *corporate codes of conduct* or of *corporate codes of ethics* or of *codes of corporate ethical conduct*, and their impact on industry and on society. Further, most discussions surrounding codes of ethical corporate conduct evaluate the contents of such structures of privatized corporate regulation on the basis of opinions offered regarding their wording, their content, and/or their overtly intrinsic value (Ashkanasy et. al, 2000). Unfortunately, however, very little research to date has been devoted towards discovering whether this form of codified regulatory governance is effective in not only engendering and promoting ethical decision-making behaviour, and identifying forms and examples of international best practice, but also in setting out the scope and forging the direction of the definitional canon with the scholarly field.

Of all the definitional jargon used to describe the conception, development, and effectuation of codes of corporate ethical conduct, the term *corporate social responsibility* remains paramount in popular usage and in business scholarship today, despite other competing, complementary, and overlapping concepts such as *corporate citizenship* (Matten & Crane, 2005), *business ethics* (Svensson et. al., 2010), *stakeholder management* (Carroll & Buchholtz, 2014), and *corporate sustainability* (Kolk, 2006) vying to become the most accepted and widespread descriptor of the given field. The popularisation of the concept of *corporate responsibility to the stakeholder* (anyone affected by international or large-scale business activity), as against the narrower concept of *stockholder/shareholder responsibility* (shown towards an organisation by its backers, funders, and investors), further heightened this need (Carroll & Shabana, 2010).

It is against this backdrop that the past ten years have seen the emergence of a plethora of codes of ethical corporate conduct. Companies, religious groups, activists, consumer bodies, policy makers, bureaucrats and a wide range of civil society institutions have all tried their hand at defining, publicising, and implementing guidelines for a broad array of business practices (Rodriguez-Dominguez et. al, 2009). As a beginning, it is universally accepted that the deeper meaning of corporate social responsibility centres around two base concepts: that of *responsibility*, which is associated with integrity and honesty in commercial transactions and interactions; and that of *society*, or the environment within which a company or an organization operates, in order to guarantee the optimum conditions necessary for the sustainable development and expansion of its activities (Béthoux et. al., 2007).

In relation to this fact and their subject matter, Davis (1988) claimed that all codes of ethics shared at least three characteristics. Firstly, codes asked more of their addressees than would otherwise be expected; second, codes generally governed activities that could not be supervised closely enough to ensure compliance; and third, codes served the long-term interests of companies only if the addressees concurred and complied with the codes without close supervision. Davis (1988) considered a code to be a mere statement of corporate aspirations. Based on this observation, Frankel (1989) identified the existence of three types of codes: described as *inspirational codes*, or codes of ethical conduct that contained statements of ideals to which addressees ought to strive; *regulatory codes*, or coda that comprised a set of detailed rules to govern conduct and that served as a basis for adjudicating grievances; and *educational codes*, or that buttressed the understanding of the prescriptive provisions contained therein through the usage of extensive commentary and/or in-depth interpretation.

This classification, together with other related categorisations of codes of ethical corporate conduct have been used by other scholars in the discipline to further the comprehension of the way in which big business actors' impact global scenarios. For example, Vinten (1990) used the base categorisation proposed by Frankle to develop a similar classification that comprised of three key concepts somewhat redefined: *regulatory codes*, which required one-to-one correspondence between the actual content of the code or guideline and the behaviour it engendered; *aspirational codes*, that provided a standard to be aspired to, whilst recognising that full compliance might rarely be possible; and *educational codes*, whose chief aim was to furnish an enlightened discussion of the issues presented at hand, facilitating informed, individual decisions on the part of the addressee from the stage-cycle at which the matter would left to rest.

Since these preliminary advances in scholarship, the distinction between *inspirational codes* and *prescriptive codes* has further been commonly utilised as yet another axis against which the impact and the efficacy of codes of corporate ethical conduct on transnational business practices has been examined. Sweeny and Siers (1990) criticised prescriptive codes on the grounds that, in practical terms, for codes of corporate conduct embodied only in skeletal guidelines and mission statements, it would be impossible for scholars and business practitioners alike to identify, consider, and resolve all likely moral hazards that addressees might encounter in the face of such implied rigidity minus enforcement. In concurrence with Robin et. al. (1989), they concluded that both categorisations of codes examined were extreme forms of dictates or rules that either prohibited specific actor behaviours, or required them, and suggested that if written and prescriptive, codes need to be both voluminous in depth and in detail and inclusive of enforceable disciplinary measures grounded in natural justice.

This view was further nuanced and enhanced by Dienhart (1995), who warned that codes of ethical corporate conduct were all together inherent defective instruments designed to encourage the most basic rote, non-rational, and machine-like behaviour in participating individuals and groups, and were thereby, on their own, unable to nurture and promote the rational responses and informed, policy-based decisions needed to create and maintain long-term, sustainable ethical transnational commercial behaviour and standard best practice. Dienhart concluded that, consequently, codes of ethical corporate conduct were in themselves not effective in changing behaviour and in altering judgement, as they fell short of reconciling the principled, non-authoritarian nature of ethics as a discipline with the codified system of concrete rules necessary to impose values on individual and collective behaviour and the overall rule of law.

Based on these observations, the classification of codes of conduct has been developed further in recent years, moving away from a mere surface-level take on the commonly applied axes of inspirational and prescriptive, towards a more nuanced distinction based on the linguistic structures employed, rather than on a clear and precise diversity in the nature of either the outcomes of such codes or of who makes the final ethical decision – code author or principal addressee - when a codified system of corporate behaviour is put in place. A final more useful distinction, therefore, is proposed by Farrell et. al (2002), and highlights which codes of ethical corporate conduct are amenable to the measurement of their behavioural outcomes by classifying them as either *allodial* or *decretal*. The former, allodial codes of corporate conduct, do not contain many key operational definitions alongst which they function whilst the latter does, either in detail of the coda itself or in other documentation or by way of shared oral or informally-imparted knowledge. Further, under this schema, only decretal codes engender the behavioural outcomes that can be measured and thus be tested for effectiveness.

It is vital to pause at this point and distinguish between codes of conduct for multinational corporations and corporate codes of ethical conduct. Typically, codes of conduct for multinational and transnational organisations are generalised sets of rules that are externally generated and are to some degree imposed on companies from outside in, whereas corporate codes of ethical conduct are usually voluntary codes adopted by a company to deal with the broader issues usually covered by the mission and vision statements by Tier 1 corporate boards of directors such as human rights, the treatment of clients and consumers, environmental protection, and the resolution of internal labour issues and standardisation differentials (Stohl et. al, 2009).

Today, many people perceive corporate activities to be highly unethical, and to be of having exceedingly low credibility (Brooks, 1989). If an organization wants to promote ethical behaviour, both *in-house* amongst its employees and between its various subsidiary holdings, and *externally* in its dealings with other actors, companies, and government agencies, the full focus of policy and enforcement must fall on those factors that the organization in question can control. Therefore, in trying to understand the academic disciplines of both ethics and business studies, and their relationship to individuals, communities, and organizations, scholarly research has identified five key factors that impact ethical corporate behaviour and transnational decision-making amongst the various actors, groups, and organisations involved (Lewis, 1989): (1) corporate politics, (2) corporate codes of ethics, (3) the morality of various management processes, (4) the significance of teaching business ethics, and (5) studies on the importance of social responsibility, conflict of interest, payoffs, safety, whistle-blowing, training and development, and reward systems. This so-called *Interactionist* model of ethical corporate behaviour may be further nuanced through the assessment of the efficacy and the effectiveness of codes of corporate conduct along a combination of axes including *individual factors*, *ethical philosophy*, *ethical decision ideologies*, *external forces*, and *miscellaneous organizational factors* (Cleek & Leonard, 1998).

Codes can be framed and adopted unilaterally by a company or may be (as a growing trend suggests) drafted by a number of stakeholders including TNCs, Northern and Southern non-governmental organisations, trade unions, shareholders and consumer groups. They may range from a vague declaration of business principles to a more serious, codified, and formalised attempt at corporate self-regulation. Invariably, corporate codes do take cognisance of other available codes of ethical conduct and resolutions drawn up by key international organisations such as the International Labour Organisation (ILO); and in general such codes provide a relatively comprehensive, non-confrontational way for companies to deal with the external pressures resulting from globalisation (Grace & Cohen, 2013).

## THE PSYCHOLOGY BEHIND CODES OF ETHICAL CORPORATE CONDUCT AND THEIR EFFECTIVENESS: FROM HUMAN FACTORS TO HUMAN ACTORS

As research on the topic of codes of ethical conduct in organizations has progressed, a growing interest in the behavioural and contextual issues associated with their conception, development, and implementation has become evident in recent academic scholarship and practitioner literature (O'Donohue & Nelson, 2009). This development may be considered to be the first step in the natural progression of a research stream that began with an initial scholarly interest in the empirical investigations into the implications of formalized and semi-structured modes of private and public governance; both for individual actors and for organizations (McCabe et. al., 1996). Similarly, the practical need to engender and to enforce ethical behaviour within and by transnational organizations, and amongst their constituent actors has, in recent years, increased in its importance to both business owners and to government agencies alike; largely due to developments taking place between the late 1960s and the early 1980s related to the rapidly changing expectations of both academic scholarship and of practitioner circles with regard to the expansion and the performance of these organisations, and the impact of their realization on society (Farrell et. al., 2002). There has also been increasing public interest in attempts made from different ends of the spectrum to understand the nature of corporate ethics and the place of corporate governance mechanisms with the larger framework of national governance, owing to the knowledge that unethical decisions and activities frequently undermine the performance and abilities of not just transnational organizations and their employees but also of society at large (Cleek & Leonard, 1998). During the recession of the early 1980s, for instance, the media and popular attention focused on the many management failures of that period, and the plant closures, layoffs, and numerous bankruptcies that manifested during that decade. A noteworthy example is that of the emergence of Singapore, and of its employment of key trade and commercial exit strategies between the mid-1980s and early 1990s, as an economic powerhouse highly attractive to Foreign Direct Investment and to Transnational Corporations (Hobson & Ramesh, 2002).

The study of actor interactions is fundamental to any evaluation of codes of ethical corporate conduct, as it is important determine the impact that actor interpretations, motivations, and subsequent behaviour have on the conceptualisation, development, and execution of this form of privatised governance and subsequently on policy outcomes. The central issue that needs to be understood, therefore, whilst studying the implications of this form of grassroots governance and regulation, and the impact it has on public sector organisations and on private transnational enterprise through an analysis of actor interactions is thus: *Why do people do what they do?* One approach to understanding behaviour is to look at the composition and at the rationality of individual actors, rather than at a collection of human factors or at the aggregative movement of variables within the transnational economy or within the financial system as a whole (Virkar, 2011). This is largely because political, economic, and societal actors are all driven by a combination of both organisational and institutional roles and duties and by calculated self-interest, with all three sets of interactions being organised around the construction and interpretation of meaning as well as the making of choices (Salvendy, 2012). The main actors in deliberative and policy processes resulting in the creation, evolution, and application of codes of ethical corporate conduct may thus be placed into two groups:

*Internal actors:* who comprise chiefly of those institutional actors responsible for the maintenance, upkeep, and running of a project, including (a) officers of the assembly who are responsible for the operation and day-to-day running of a system such as senior corporate employees and stakeholders, and (b) elected representatives (and their support staff) who monitor and respond to corporate, economic, and financial indicators and stimuli individually and collectively.

*External actors:* who comprise of two distinct categories including (a) those participants, employees, or individuals, or groups who commit to adopt and/or who benefit directly from a code of ethical corporate conduct, and (b) citizens or society at large: those individuals, communities, and groups who may or may not be entitled to participate directly in the governance of the transnational organisation but who nonetheless will invariably impact the outcome of a policy process through their ability to shape and to follow public opinion.

Central to the understanding of the psychology behind the development of codes of ethical corporate conduct is the definition and the in-depth examination of the motives and goals that prompt actors to interact and participate in decision- and policy making processes, given that all behaviour is motivated in some way and that individuals will engage in a particular behaviour in order to achieve a desired end (Atkinson & Birch, 1970). Political and socio-economic actors, in particular, have a complex set of goals including *power*, *income*, *prestige*, *security*, *convenience*, *loyalty* (to an idea, an institution, or the nation), *pride in work well done*, and *a desire to serve the public interest* (as the individual actor perceives it). Added to this, individuals and private citizens tend to participate in politics and economic lobbying for reasons ranging from altruistic to conformist, in order to boost their self-esteem, to self-enhance, and to achieve self-efficacy (Cruickshank et. al., 2010). On the one hand, political and economic actors range from being purely self-interested 'climbers' or 'conservers', motivated entirely by goals which benefit themselves and their *status quo* rather than their organizations or the society at large, to having mixed motives as 'zealots', 'advocates' and 'statesmen', motivated by goals which combine self-interest and altruistic loyalty with larger values (Downs, 1964).

Through an in-depth analysis of the literature concerned with the numerous ways in which organizations may influence the behaviour and decision-making of employees and enterprises, and might participate to raise global standards of living, five actor groups involved in games and interactions related to the design and implementation of codes of ethical corporate conduct might be identified (cf. Ashkanasay et. al, 2000; Virkar, 2011):

1. **Politicians:** The first group identified comprises of elected representatives of various hues, guided and influenced chiefly by electoral imperatives and a need to maintain their public image, and are therefore concerned with directing both key economic policy issues as well as issues of public service delivery.
2. **Administrators / Civil Servants:** This group of actors is guided by their perceptions of existing institutional 'culture' and practices and by their positive (or negative) attitudes towards internal bureaucratic reforms and sectoral functioning such as concerns about the down-sizing of administrative and commercial services to promote 'efficiency' and to negate the sense of being policed by elected government inherent in any form of institutionalised or semi-institutionalised governance.
3. **Individuals, Groups, Organisations, and Agencies Concerned with the Defining of the Standards of Ethical Conduct and the Design of Formalised, Regulatory Code:** This group of actors is responsible primarily for much of the initial groundwork built into the final interpretation and application of codes of ethical corporate conduct and other international standards. In this context, the attitude adopted by individual actors working from privately-funded think-tanks and universities towards ethical behaviour and transnational corporations, and the final approach adopted therein towards the formulation and the application of privatised, grassroots forms of corporate governance, might deviate considerably from the strategies, attitudes, expectations, and outcomes pertaining to those individuals and actor groups co-existing within a more applicative setting.
4. **Citizens:** This is another, particularly interesting group of actors as one is never quite sure what the reaction of the general public would be to the implementation of an innovation or to the formalisation or codification or greater regulation of commercial activity. Whilst in theory citizens should

welcome the introduction of a codified system that simplifies administrative processes towards the common good, in practice it is equally possible that some citizens might not be very happy if a more efficient system involving increased regulation of market and financial activity was put into place.

5. **International Donors:** This final actor group controls the purse-strings within the international arena, and oftentimes comes to the table with 'higher' ideals coloured by the politics and ideas prevalent, oftentimes trending, in international diplomacy (such as the desire to push a particular industry, to the detriment of others, or to see in a particular brand of 'good governance' in the developing world favourable to more developed nations).

For transnational corporation employees and for the public at large, the motivation to adopt and to adhere to a formalized or voluntary code of conduct may be either *intrinsic* or *extrinsic* (Cruickshank et. al., 2010). Intrinsic motives include the desire to feel competent and self-determining, to show altruism, or to seek to increase the welfare of others. Extrinsic motives, in contrast, are usually associated with some sort of external reward in the social, economic, or political sphere. Both these manifest themselves in conditional co-operation, social pressure, thresholds, and the bandwagon effect (Margetts et. al., 2012). In conclusion, therefore, different motives and goals may underlie the same surface behavior, with the social and psychological consequences of participation being perhaps different for different users (i.e. some participate to gain information or support, others to communicate), and the end result being a set of nested, interrelated interactions within the framework of a large meta-game or playing field (cf. Dutton, 1992; Virkar, 2011). Consequently, the motivations and goals for complying with a code of corporate conduct will determine how they will they be perceived and the benefit accrued, by whom, and when.

## ENTER, THE TRANSNATIONAL CORPORATION

In August 1999, at the height of the dotcom boom, while the prices of I.T. stocks were peaking and the 'euphoria of the new millennium' had taken hold of the global economy, a mustachioed sheep-farmer called José Bové won national fame in France (and a jail sentence) for tearing the roof off a local Mc-Donald's with his tractor (Morena, 2013). Bové's message was simple: he just didn't like the taste of the modern global corporation. Anti-globalisation protests since then also took on new venom, particularly when the World Trade Organisation Ministerial Conference met in Seattle later that year chiefly to again target multinational corporate power (Gill, 2000).

*Multinational Corporations* (MNCs) otherwise known as *Transnational Corporations* (TNCs) are generally defined as those companies headquartered in a developed country, having operations around the world (Bondy et. al., 2008). The past few decades have witnessed a spectacular increase in the spread of TNCs worldwide, a trend that has its roots in the late 1980s which saw a tremendous outpouring of foreign direct investment (FDI) from the developed world to less developed countries across the globe. There are approximately 63,000 TNCs and their affiliates operating in the world today, accounting for almost 66% of global trade and 80% of the world's investment, a figure up from early 1990, where the number of companies doing business transnationally exceeded only 35,000 (Pilger, 2014).

It is this virtual explosion, particularly a result of a frenzy of high-profile mergers and acquisitions, which has resulted in the transnational corporation becoming the most visible and highly contested manifestation of economic globalisation (The Economist, 2012). It is small wonder then that TNC practices, especially those implemented in developing countries, have come under increasing scrutiny by an ever-growing body of individuals, public bodies, and Non-Governmental Organisations (NGOs).

Recent controversies have seen TNCs on the one hand as being painted out to be monopolistic monsters that wield tremendous financial and political clout, and who, in their search for profits, are violating labour rights, are surreptitiously propping up corrupt, repressive regimes, are damaging the environment, are bullying governments into adopting lower regulatory tax and environmental standards, and are responsible for ruining global cultural diversity.

Advocates of globalisation on the other hand, both scholars and practitioners, stress the critical role that multinationals play in the creation of relatively better paying jobs, in the transfer of technology from developed to developing countries, in the improvement and the setting of the standards of corporate governance, in the transmittance of Foreign Direct Investment to augment the relatively low quantum of savings in less developed countries, in the enhancement of the overall global standard of living in developing countries particularly through the augmentation of available consumer choices, and in the provision of a higher quality of produce, goods, and services (Asiedu & Lien, 2011).

## THE POTENTIAL BENEFITS OF CODES OF ETHICAL CORPORATE CONDUCT: FIVE STARS, BIG BUCKS

In 1994, Starbucks Coffee was the target of a campaign staged against the sourcing of its coffee beans from export houses that paid Guatemalan coffee growers less than a living wage. The following year it became the first company in the agricultural commodities sector to announce a framework for a comprehensive code of conduct that included the purchase of coffee beans only from suppliers who paid growers a fair wage (Entine & Nichols, 1996). Ten years on, and many "Corporate Conscience" awards later, Starbucks is an oft-quoted example of a company that has not only been successful in implementing its code of conduct, but has also become a trendsetter in the forging of partnerships with farmers' fair-trade co-operatives in poorer countries, and has drafted a wider code in cooperation with both Non Governmental Organisations such as Oxfam (UK) and privately funded think-tanks as the Ford Foundation (USA). Consequently, as a direct result of these initiatives, Starbucks has seen a huge increase in earnings (Fellner, 2008).

The example set by Starbucks goes to show the significant impact that a code of conduct may have on corporate behaviour, and demonstrate the positive benefits that might accrue to the various stakeholders involved. However, despite the recent proliferation of such codes, their implementation remains relatively limited (Mullerat, 2010). Key structural limitations include the initial infrastructure and drivers responsible for their development and dissemination, the number of issues that they address, and the parties to whom such codes of conduct apply (Locke et. al., 2007).

To begin with, a wide range of stakeholders are involved in the drawing up of voluntary codes of corporate conduct, and can be significantly impacted by their adoption (Florini, 2003). Since all parties involved have specific vested interests and agendas that predispose them toward corporate codes, and influence the kinds of behaviour that they would like to ultimately see implemented, limited codes of conduct with very narrow vision give stakeholders adequate room to criticise and reject their scope and coverage (Clean Clothes Campaign, 2001). Model codes drawn up by NGOs and other organisations help in this respect by establishing a benchmark against which company behaviour across an industry may be measured (Mullerat, 2007). A prime example of such a model ethical code is the International Conference of Free Trade Union's *Basic Code of Conduct Covering Labour Practices*, a standard against which the labour policies and practices of TNCs are regularly compared (Mares, 2004).

A second potential benefit is that companies that have established codes of conduct can be held accountable by various civil society bodies and are powerless against criticism should they be caught breaking them (Jenkins, 2001). Although in the absence of independent monitoring, it is difficult sometimes to know whether a company is abiding by the terms of its own code, instant international communications and contact between different stakeholders, particularly NGOs and trade unions, can help reveal cases of violation (Aguilera & Cuervo-Cazzura, 2004). In the mid-1990s, for example, public outrage followed news reports that big sports goods companies like Nike and Reebok were using child labour in Pakistan to stitch footballs after explicitly taking a stand against it in their codes of conduct (Boje & Khan, 2009). In the end, the companies agreed to enter into a joint initiative with local suppliers, the International Labour Organisation, and with NGOs and other quasi-entrepreneurial entities to formulate a comprehensive code whereby they would eliminate child labour from their production lines, whilst at the same time looking after the well being of the families concerned. To date, the implementation of this code has met with considerable success (Schrage, 2004).

Thirdly, the idea of a code of conduct establishes a clear relationship between the economic variables and non-economic factors implicit in business structuring and in rapid globalisation, and the impact one set of indicators has on the other (Somers, 2001). In particular, the emphasis found in codes of conduct is placed on the growing awareness that consumption is not divorced from production, and is not only an activity of exchange based in the marketplace. Codes of conduct, therefore, whilst covering the political, social, and environmental aspects of commercial activity, go beyond dealing what is produced in the open economy and instead seek to shape behaviour related to entire business processes (Gordon & Miyake, 1999). There is, consequently, recognition of a clear link between issues such as the environment and human rights and economic development; and an acknowledgement that in the long run, the state of the former has a significant impact on the latter.

Codes of conduct also force TNCs to publicly take responsibility for the actions of not only themselves, but also those of their suppliers and their subcontractors (Bondy et. al, 2008). Codes of corporate governance, therefore, ensure that companies accept this extended responsibility (and in some cases extended legal liability), and make it tough for them to externalise costs, whether social or environmental, as they are unable to project themselves as remaining squeaky clean in the First World whilst their affiliates behave irresponsibly in the developing world (Jeffcott & Yanz, 2004). To quote a classic example, Nike cannot project itself as being socially responsible if its Korean subcontractors indulge in human and labour rights abuses in Vietnam or Indonesia (Lim & Phillips, 2008).

Finally, the most important consequence of various initiatives to promote codes of conduct, particularly those supported by bilateral and multilateral agencies, is that there has been a definitive change in policy discussions concerning poverty alleviation and globalisation at all levels of government worldwide (Jenkins, 2005). Including the concepts of ethical labour and business standards as routine agenda provisions allows for more inclusive global trade and investment negotiations that ensure that the interests of both local society and the global community at large are protected during the framing of initial political discourse, and are then taken into account whilst formulating policy.

## THE LIMITATIONS: STILL WAITING FOR NIKE TO JUST DO IT

Despite the benefits, there are several limitations to codes of conduct as a means of regulating TNC activity and promoting better conditions in the developing world. Part of the problem lies is the practicality of such codes; the way they are implemented (or in some cases not implemented), and how this implementation is monitored. Other problems relate to the inherent weaknesses within codes of conduct themselves: their definitions, their basic parameters, and their implications; and the failure of such codes to make a significant impact goes beyond merely their application (Jeffcott & Yanz, 2004).

The biggest drawback of voluntary codes of ethical corporate conduct is their limited adoption by TNCs. Many companies use codes of conduct as public relations exercises, issuing expansive statements and participating in joint discussion groups with other non-state actors with little or no real implementation of the policies produced (Talaulicar, 2009). Many codes drawn up by Non-Governmental Organisations and other quasi-private entities are only signed up to by a handful of private sector enterprises, indeed a large number still only exist in draft form (Grace & Cohen, 2013). Significant examples of such codes include the Code of Labour Practices for the Apparel Industry Including Sportswear, and the Ethical Initiative Trading (EIT) Base Code. High profile companies with global operations and large investments in more controversial industries, particularly those involved in the production, sourcing, and distribution of Fast Moving Consumer Goods, of food and food-related comestibles, of apparel and footwear, of pharmaceuticals, and of plastics and other chemical-based articles, tend to sign up faster to global ethical contracts owing to their greater visibility and to their pronounced vulnerability and openness to attack, whilst the majority of smaller players are found to be yet wanting to adopt even the most basic codes developed by themselves internally (Bondy et. al., 2008).

Another weakness relates to the scope and extent of the issues addressed. This is particularly the case with codes dealing with labour issues, which often fail to include aspects of labour rights such as work security, benefits, maternity leave and the like, that are not core to either international labour standards or to ILO priorities (Fisher & Lovell, 2009). In some cases, even basic ILO rights are not included in the final versions of these documents, and codes of conduct may not cover large (often marginalised) groups of workers. For instance, Barrientos (1999) points to the failure of many codes of conduct to cover casualised "flexible" female workers in export processing zones as an example of poor regulatory coverage.

A key limitation of voluntary codes is concerned with issues of monitoring and accountability (Jenkins, 2001). Many complications arise due to the multiplicity of codes and actors, and often it is difficult to determine the main provisions of each code, which enterprises are covered and most importantly which organisation is responsible for monitoring the TNC's compliance to the code and reporting back to the stakeholders. Even relatively 'clean' companies like Unilever have had problems with local partners over compliance issues (Pearson & Seyfang, 2001).

A key structural problem inherent in the conceptualisation, development, and propagation of codes of ethical corporate conduct relates to the sectors of industry and the nature of the adopting organisation covered by outreach of such codes in terms of the ethical and business principles and influences embodied therein (Canary & Jennings, 2008). Studies have shown that codes are common in sectors such as the toys, cosmetics, and footwear and apparel industries, where brand names and public image are relatively important and where production costs comprise a small fraction of the final price. Furthermore, most codes tend not to cover local producers in the South (cf. Sethi, 2003; Jenkins, 2013).

There is a danger that increased reliance on voluntary codes would take away from the state's role in legislation and regulation (Talaulicar, 2009). It is feared that an increased importance of voluntary codes would either be used as a convenient way for companies to override local legislation and institutions, or would result in a steady withdrawal of the state from its responsibilities. The tendency of academic scholarship and of practitioner communities to focus primarily (read: almost solely) on high-profile issues that can potentially damage a company's image both and home and on the world stage is a final key shortcoming that has strong echoes in the drawing up and in the enforcement of voluntary codes of ethical corporate behaviour.

Key domains of private, public, and transnational concern include the continued prevalence of child labour in certain parts of the world and its continued exploitation for profit, together with the environment and the associated travails of disguised environmental degradation, and the exploitation of vulnerable suppliers of bas raw materials and of cheap, low-skilled labour. The corporate budgeting for and the resolution of issues such as these may not concur in full with the priorities of a majority of organisation shareholders, stockholders, and stakeholders, particularly those with interests in the economic South despite many of them being provided for in key national developmental goals and agendas, and may in fact work to the disadvantage of those they intend to help as soon as they are tabled by private sector actors and individuals.

## TNCs AND SOCIAL RESPONSIBILITY: OF PEOPLE AND PROFITS

The global multinational has always painted as an ogre whose chief desire has been to make a profit at any cost, irrespective of who it crushed in its wake, and to be responsible to and for its shareholders only (Grace & Cohen, 2013). As a result, the TNC is still seen to be an evil institution earning its profits at the expense of the economy, the polity and society, particularly the poorest at the bottom of the pyramid. That view, however, is changing rapidly. As the debate in policymaking circles rages over possible solutions to eliminate global poverty, some large companies are trying to spearhead a silent revolution in their host countries (Virkar, 2014). The result is an approach that attempts to combine market forces with a smarter use of existing local infrastructure, particularly through the development and enforcement of corporate codes of conduct (Jenkins, 2013).

Whilst their motives are not altogether altruistic, TNCs act often out of a combination of self-interest and external pressure, global corporations are gradually devoting a growing portion of their resources to the development of societies in which they operate. These activities, issues, and actions that Transnational Corporations need to look into, broadly labelled 'corporate social responsibility' as defined and discussed in previous sections of this chapter, range from the covering of corporate philanthropic obligations to the innovation in and the development of affordable, high quality goods for the poor and to the design of small- and large-scale 'living lab' experiments (Fisher & Lovell, 2009).

A growing new breed of businessmen-turned-philanthropists has emerged to spearhead the movement, including big names such as Microsoft Corp. Chairman William H. Gates III and financier George Soros, who all began by trying to bring a more business-like approach to the development projects that they personally fund (Wang et. al., 2008). In particular, this class of corporate do-gooders stresses on a combination of strong financial incentives coupled with aggressive monitoring together with greater coordination of government and non-government bodies in project execution.

The same approach holds true for development and business projects funded by corporations as well, where key stakeholders need to develop written codes and manifestos, some formal, most of which are informal, in that existing examples of best practice guide, but do not set in stone, the direction that a project takes. The advantages of such codes of corporate conduct are therefore manifold: a substantial amount of money is made available to fund projects, there is altogether greater accountability during the execution of a project, and improved monitoring by TNCs ensures that the money and resources available reach the people they are intended for (Locke et. al., 2007). Furthermore, greater coordination and less duplication between the various agencies on the ground enhances the probability of success.

There is also a growing recognition amongst corporations that it is in their self-interest to enter into and invest in the world's poorest markets; whose individual constituents make up a potential market of trillions of dollars worth of disposable income as a consequence of their sheer number, in spite of their deplorably small *per capita* earnings. Influential management gurus such as C.K. Prahalad, are of the view that businesses, through stimulating commerce and development at the bottom of the economic pyramid (i.e. amongst the world's poorest) could radically improve the lives of billions of people, but *profitably* so, ensuring a win-win situation for both transnational corporations and society. Prahalad and Hammond (2002: P.49) assert, therefore, that "...prosperity can come to the poorest regions only through a direct and sustained involvement of multinational companies". The secret lies in realising that the poor are not averse to spending on goods and services that improve the quality of their lives (Prahalad, 2009). Recent studies have shown, for instance, that although the *per capita* income of rural Bangladesh is less than $200, both the local population and the national government are extremely keen on developing and maintaining sophisticated telecommunications services throughout the country as also lucrative village telephone networks that can generate from between $90 to $1000 *per* month (cf. Ahmed & Chowdhury, 2009; Islam et. al., 2011; Yusuf & Alam, 2011). In that vein, transnational corporations have the technological know-how and innovative capacity to produce low cost, high quality goods suited to meet the needs of the poor. A company, for example, in South Africa made a fortune through selling local villagers an innovation it called the Hippo Roller, essentially a low-cost large rolling water barrel that enables village women and children to fetch water from far away without tiring much (The Hippo Roller Project, 2013).

Further, a growing trend amongst TNCs is that of 'partnering', the formation of partnerships with governments, other public organisations, NGOs, religious groups, and a wide range of civil society institutions towards the creation and long-term sustenance of viable development projects (Prahalad, 2009). A now famous example of such a project is that of Hewlett-Packard's 'living lab' in the Indian village of Kuppam where, through the application of business principles to project execution, the TNC was able to successfully develop a partnership that created viable solutions to help Kuppam's citizens meet their basic survival needs through small-scale digital photography (Dunn & Yamashita, 2006). Partnerships, and the codes of conduct that support them, thus provide the resources that the poor require to help sustain themselves. In essence, they are about achieving long-term development with and sustainably improving standards of living within the regions where multinationals do business, whilst in the process allowing those businesses to prosper as well (Prahalad, 2009).

Today, profits are still the chief focus of any multinational and TNCs are still primarily responsible to their shareholders and stakeholders, circumscribed by draconian rules and regulations. Despite this, there has been a fundamental paradigm shift in thinking, a growing recognition that multinationals can play and will play a major role in helping to alleviate some of society's chief ills and scourges. There is also a growing body of academic literature which suggests that multinationals play a central role in building social capital within the communities they operate in (cf. Jones et. al, 2002; Jenkins, 2005; Carroll & Shabana, 2010). Codes of ethical corporate conduct are, therefore, concerned chiefly with the following areas: Business Conduct and Best Practice, Transnational Political Behaviour, Labour and Organisational Practices, Environmental Policies (Rodriguez-Dominguez, 2009).

## TNC Business Conduct: The Rule of Best Practice?

The economic impact of multinational activity has also come under intense scrutiny and has been the subject of much debate over the past decade. Particular attention has been paid to the role that Transnational Corporations play in the transfer of technology from the developed to the developing world. In this respect, the central question being asked is whether, in the long run, developing countries will benefit from multinational activity within their borders to an equal, if not greater, extent than economies in the developed world. This question gains importance in the light of the fact that the flow of Foreign Direct Investment into a developing economy is generally a one-way process. In other words, given the low amount of surplus capital available for productive investment, developing country partners are generally wholesale recipients of rich-country investment and not themselves frequent investors abroad (Carroll & Shabana, 2010).

A large number of critics, arguing from a variety of standpoints, assert, therefore, that TNCs are of dubious benefit to developing countries on two major counts (Jenkins, 2013): the first reason given is that the economic costs that result from TNC activity may outweigh the overall benefits to the country concerned. For example, multinationals have been accused of destroying indigenous industries by forcing local competition out of business. Sklair (2002) for instance, points out that Triad-based electronics TNCs have stymied the development of electronics companies in all but a few developing countries. Workers in local industries that go out of business are laid off, and are either left unemployed or are then forced into cut-throat competition for scarce lower paying jobs. The second argument put forward is one where the technology and work-flow processes brought into a country by a multinational may be wholly inappropriate to the current economic circumstances; especially when measured according to a number of non-economic, particularly welfare, criteria (Jenkins, 2013). A car manufacturer may, for instance, bring in technology that adds capital value to the industry, but which is, otherwise, wholly useless to a population whose majority can barely eke out a living on bicycles. In some cases, therefore, technology may not be transferred to local entrepreneurs at all, and instead be selfishly guarded by the big company.

In contrast, however, there remain circumstances where TNCs can be beneficial to nascent, even non-existent, local industry. In most cases they are dependent on local enterprises, either for raw materials or as potential customers of their products and services. Similarly, extensive TNC activity boosts local ancillary units and factories that rely on the multinational either for custom or the basic inputs and services provided. These backward and forward linkages result in a win-win situation for both the TNC and for local enterprises, and provide a boost to the national economy as a whole (Andersen & Skjoett-Larsen, 2009). A landmark study done by Holger Görg and Eric Strobl (2003) demonstrated the presence of such *technology spillovers* in the developing world, and their impact on indigenous industry. The study showed that the greatest effects of Multinational Corporation activity were felt by local industry in the high-tech, technology-heavy sectors, and that these impacts were highly positive; in that they levelled the playing field and resulted in fairer competition between local and multinational producers.

Building on these observations, further studies have shown that a combination of technological spillovers into domestic industry and high productivity amongst foreign-owned firms has contributed to an overall rise in the productivity of developing economies (cf. Sener, 2006; Gancia & Bonfiglioli,

2007; Glass & Wu, 2007; Lipsey, 2008). This is because multinationals still remain possibly the most important means for technology transfer from developed to developing nations, more particularly in the global transmission of cutting edge technology as well as the know-how to use it (Glass & Saggi, 1999) Companies based in First World countries possess the resources and the wherewithal to develop new, innovative technologies, and to these get passed on to their foreign affiliates, demonstrated by the simple fact that 70% of payments on international technology royalties are made between parent firms headquartered in the developed world and their foreign affiliates situated elsewhere (Dinopoulos & Segerstrom, 2010).

Yet another related, largely unrecognised role of transnational corporations is that of mobilising the science and technology available to them to address key developmental crises in Third World countries, such as those concerning public health, agricultural productivity, and environmental degradation (Doremus et. al, 1998). Biotechnology, for example, offers an opportunity to produce hardier, pest resistant crops, and an alternative way to eventually feed the world's growing population, provided that biotechnology firms can gear their products towards crops and practices suited to the developing world. Similarly, multinationals can harness science to benefit poorer countries through the innovation and development of effective low cost vaccines (Mudambi et. al., 2007).

More recently, in another example of best practice for development, multinational companies have been opening Research & Development facilities in the developing world in order to be able to adapt themselves to the peculiarities of each individual market. This in turn has resulted in the introduction of much usable technology into the Third World, and as Worasinchai et. al. (2010) points out, is likely to have beneficial effects on industry and employment. In this respect, much of the technological know-how is also transferred through the formation of joint ventures between local companies and Transnational Enterprises (Doremus et.al., 1998). Already joint ventures between multinationals and local partners yield direct benefits to developing economies, a happenstance that can only improve with the continuous lowering of barriers to international trade and regular increases in Third World membership to the World Trade Organisation (Payne, 2010).

## TNC Behaviour in the Political Arena: Footloose and Fancy-Free?

Much reviled and feared is the perceived behaviour of multinational corporations in the political arena. TNCs, possibly due to their sheer size and economic clout, are seen to be gradually putting national governments into what Thomas Friedman (2001: P.101) referred to as "The Golden Straightjacket" that "narrows the political and economic choices of those in power to relatively tight parameters…" Strong corporate lobbying is accused of forcing states to lower taxes and relax regulations, inducing national governments into a "race to the bottom" in an effort to win and keep "footloose" capital within their borders. More serious is the charge that TNCs are in part responsible for propping up repressive, corrupt regimes simply because they are granted favourable business terms (Prahalad, 2009).

Despite the claims of falling tax revenue, studies have proven otherwise (c.f. Commendatore, 2008; Bucovetsky, 2009; Hong & Smart, 2010; The Economist, 2011). For example, a survey conducted by The Economist in 2011 showed that governments around the world are on an average collecting slightly more tax than in 1990 (The Economist, 2011). The same survey revealed that most TNC activity is located in developed countries, the very countries that set and enforce stringent regulations. Furthermore, the very fact that big business has to *lobby* government to do their bidding belies the notion of an omnipotent TNC. In fact, several studies, cited in Tarzi (2002) have shown that despite the enormous clout of TNCs, there has been a trend of increasing ascendancy of several Third World host states with respect to their relationships with Transnational Corporations.

There has been a debate over the past few years regarding the role multinationals play (or do not play) in encouraging the spread of democratic values in the Third World. There are three main strands of thinking that have emerged from this discussion. The more conventional theories of modernisation and globalisation take the view that TNCs have had a benevolent influence on world politics. They are seen as vectors of democratic values and more equitable practices to the Third World, and that the system of global capitalism they work under is fairer than any existing alternative (Asiedu & Lien, 2011).

This view, however, has been challenged from many quarters. For example, the theory of *Bureaucratic Authoritarianism,* first set down by O'Donnell (1979) to describe and to define a type of nation state characterized by a high degree of nepotism, disenfranchisement, and exclusion – both political and economic, uses the example of Latin America to demonstrate the tendency of high levels of modernisation to be strongly correlated with non-democratic forms of government. In this regard, authoritarian regimes may push through policies attractive to TNCs and can guarantee low cost labour to foreign investors with little or any opposition. In short, countries that have both *bureaucratic* and *authoritarian* regimes are most likely to attract high levels of FDI (Avelino et. al., 2005).

A third strand of thinking suggests that, contrary to both *Liberal Free Market Economics* and theories of *Bureaucratic Authoritarianism,* Transnational Corporations are neither hostile nor favourable to democracy (Grace & Cohen, 2013). Indeed, they are willing to operate under *any* form of government that is able to give them a stable business climate and preferential business terms and conditions. It is an interesting fact that, until the 1980s, most developing countries were under authoritarian rule and attracted little or no Foreign Direct Investment. The waves of FDI into Africa, Asia, and Latin America from the mid-1980s onward appear to have coincided with waves of democratisation in a vast majority of these countries (Sklair, 2002). However, it remains unclear as to whether or not TNCs actually play a direct role in the democratisation process within a country. Recently conducted studies have concluded that on the whole, as figures suggest, democratically governed countries are seen as low risk investment locations, and that staunchly democratic regimes attract 70% more FDI than do authoritarian ones (Jenkins, 2013). So much for the claim that transnational corporations support dictatorial regimes.

Another area of the debate focuses on the role played by TNCs operating in zones of conflict, and in particular their conduct in civil war zones. Multinationals have often been accused of creating "war economies," of funding government armies, of arming rebellions and rebel groups, and of protecting dissidents and other criminal elements by buying valuable natural resources from these entities sold to finance their guerrilla operations (Carroll & Shabana, 2010). An oft-quoted example is that of Angola's 'blood diamonds' or 'conflict diamonds' trade, where precious and semi-precious stones of questionable origin were sold to foreign companies clandestinely by rebel groups and sometimes by the government itself to finance the armed conflict in Angola during the 1990s (Grant, 2012). There is little doubt that certain multinational corporations have behaved improperly in host nation states over the past few decades. Indeed there is evidence that goes to show that transnational companies have actively interfered in and taken advantage of the domestic politics of several unstable host countries. There is little doubt too that using bribery to achieve economic goals has not been limited to exceptional cases (Boddewyn, 1988).

A classic example often used to illustrate this point is that of ITT Industries in the 1970s, which allegedly sought to prevent the election of Salvador Allende to the Chilean presidency by pumping large amounts of money into the oppositions' campaign and, after eventual his victory, attempting to engineer his immediate downfall both via legal means and through the unabashed financing of guerrilla warfare

(Sigmund, 1974; Winston, 1999; Legrain, 2002). That said, the political influence that multinational organisations wield may also be put to positive use, albeit when exercised to buttress existing policy when put under pressure from consumers and political lobby groups. Several TNCs have, for instance, disinvested and moved away from countries whose governments and leaders have flouted democratic norms and openly violated human rights (Carroll & Shabana, 2010). Sklair (2002) gives us the example of South Africa during the apartheid era, and of how sustained exclusion from the global economy and the continuous absence of FDI withheld through global economic sanctions by the rest of the world in protest against the abysmal treatment of the local black population, began to hurt the very people for whom apartheid was designed to benefit.

## Transnational Corporations and Labour Practices: No Sweat

The most concrete effect of multinationals in developing countries is in terms of the jobs they create and destroy. It has become a fashion among detractors of globalisation to condemn TNC operations in the developing world as exploitative of workers – when jobs both skilled and unskilled are shifted abroad, the wages paid are much lower than those commanded by the same jobs in the developed world; and at the bottom end of the scale defenceless, unorganised workers have no choice but to labour in "sweatshop" conditions for a pittance (Klein, 1999). To quote a prominent trade unionist (Mazur, 2000: 82): "...Millions of workers are losing out in a global economy that disrupts traditional economies and weakens the ability of governments to assist them. They are left to fend for themselves within failed states against destitution, famine and plague. They are forced to migrate, to offer their labour at wages below subsistence, sacrifice their children, and cash in on their natural environments and often their personal health – all in a desperate struggle to survive." Women, some argue, are particularly at risk as they are preferred employees in Export Processing Zones (EPZs) where employers feel they can get away by paying them lower wages, subjecting them to harsh working conditions (Barrientos, 2002).

Despite this view of the global business corporation, a growing body of empirical evidence concludes that foreign ownership in fact raises the average wage in a country by improving labour productivity and by expanding the scale of production, both of which lead to better working conditions. Workers in multinationals consistently earn higher wages than the average wage paid by local firms, far in excess of the minimum wage set by the government. A seminal study conducted by Edward M. Graham of the Institute for International Economics, results showed that the wages paid by Transnational Corporations and their affiliates to poor-country workers are about double the local manufacturing wage, and those paid to workers from middle-income countries was about 1.8 times as great (Graham, 1994).

A similar series of studies centering around Nike subcontract factories in Vietnam and Indonesia, conducted by students from the Amos Tuck School at Dartmouth College in the 1990s, showed further that not only did workers earn a wage that was far above the government-mandated minimum wage, but also that employment in a Nike factory was economically more attractive to entry-level workers than any other available job opportunity in the local area (Mihaly, 1999). Moreover, the presence of the factory itself had greatly benefited the population of the surrounding area. These studies also revealed that the conditions of work in these factories were much better than those of local factories (Calzini et. al., 1997). Similar studies conducted by the International Labour Organisation (ILO) and the US Department for Labour, as well as econometric analysis done by prominent economists, reinforce the notion of the wage premium that comes to employees working for a multinational corporation relative to their counterparts in small-scale industry (cf.Bartley, 2007; Eckle & Egger, 2009). Women in EPZs, far from being exploited, are able to take home a much higher wage than they would normally be able to earn (Avelino et. al. 2005). Lower wages in comparison to Western standards merely reflect the difference in productivity of developing country workers, the lower cost of living and the market value of labour as compared to those from the industrialised countries.

Global corporations are also accused of being attracted to markets where labour is poorly protected. It is alleged that lack of organisation helps multinationals keep labour costs down. However, there is no convincing evidence (statistical or otherwise) to support this claim. Far from discouraging unionisation, scholarly and practitioner studies appear to show that TNCs make use of the inherent organisation of workers prevalent in a country to increase the efficiency of their organisations (Grace & Cohen, 2013). However, the media image of this type of transnational activity is poor; the globalised media also plays a key role in the process of deterring companies from abusing worker rights (Diller, 1999), through both the emergence of global conglomerates with operations in both mainstream and grassroots media (Zadek, 2004), and as a consequence of the newsworthiness and subsequent close scrutiny of Transnational Corporation activity surrounding the abuse of labour rights in the developing world (Virkar, 2014).

In conclusion, it would be fair to say that while there have been a number of controversies surrounding the behaviour of TNCs, their affiliates and subcontractors, for example the treatment of East-Asian workers in the footwear industry, they are more exceptions than the general rule (Farrell et. al., 2002). Multinationals offer Third-World workers the chance of a relatively higher paid job in better working conditions than what are offered by local alternatives (Jenkins, 2013). They also contribute to the economic prosperity of the surrounding neighbourhood, buying raw materials and sourcing labour locally, and through the setting-up ancillary industries. By and large, they do not coerce governments to lower their standards as regards labour rights, but instead work within existing frameworks, often using labour organisation to their advantage. As regards women, while TNCs are not generally actively committed to promoting feminism they do introduce more egalitarian employment practices, and even amongst the bottom rungs of the workforce provide relatively good job opportunities for women (Sklair, 2002).

## Transnational Corporations and the Environment: Breathe Easy!

Perhaps no aspect of globalisation worries people more than the impact of TNC activity on the environment. This concern is only natural – we all live on the same planet. In recent times, environmental problems are increasingly being acknowledged as having global implications and are seen to be the result of the steep cumulative increase in the production and the consumption of environmentally-sensitive goods and services (Kolk & Pinkse, 2008). Global warming, overfishing, greenhouse gas emissions, and the depletion of the ozone layer are all buzzwords in environmental circles, and at the heart of all these issues appears to lie the omnipotent, ever-present, big, bad Transnational Corporation.

Multinationals are extensively involved in environmentally significant activities. For instance they are major producers and consumers of ozone-depleting chlorofluorocarbons. Critics see multinationals as marauding giants, recklessly destroying the environment in their pursuit for profits. Environmentalists' biggest fear is that multinationals flock to developing countries to exploit their rich natural resources and take advantage of their lax environmental regulations. For example, when the North American Free Trade Agreement (NAFTA) was signed in 1992, one of the main objections to the agreement stemmed from the fear that polluting industries from America and Canada would shift to Mexico to take advantage of its lax environmental standards (Eskeland & Harrison, 1997). This is known as the 'pollution haven hypothesis' – the enforcement of strict environmental regulations in developed nations will relocate polluting industries to poorer countries with relatively lax environmental norms (Levinson & Taylor, 2008).

By fleeing from countries that impose higher environmental standards, multinationals encourage countries, particularly in the developing world, to engage in a 'race to the bottom' in environmental standards. Governments give many Transnational Corporations the environmental equivalent of tax breaks, that ultimately have detrimental effects on not only the national, but the global environment. *Maquiladora* activity on the Mexican border as a consequence of the NAFTA is an oft-quoted example (Cañas & Gilmer, 2009). A large amount of foreign direct investment also flows into developing countries for natural resource extraction, and this too can take a heavy toll on the environment (French, 1998). Worse still multinationals are often accused of using environmentally hazardous techniques to exploit the natural resource wealth of developing countries. In addition, over-exploitation poses a serious threat to both the sustainability of resources and the surrounding ecosystem. This is particularly true in industries such as logging and mining (Kinoshita & Campos, 2003). A related argument is that TNCs promote a consumption culture, which, in turn, fuels the consumption of already scarce resources.

On the face of it, the logic behind such a hypothesis seems easy to understand. It costs time and money to conform to environmental standards and greater expenditure leads to lower profit margins, sacrilege to profit-maximising firms (Antweiler et. al, 1998). However, despite widespread belief, little empirical evidence exists to support the theory. In fact, econometric studies have shown that freer trade is good for the environment (Stern, 2004; Frankel & Rose, 2005) and that host country standards have very little impact on FDI inflows, either qualitatively or quantitatively (Smarzynska & Wei, 2001). In recent times, as a consequence of greater scrutiny by the media and concerned civil society bodies, examples like those of the Mexican maquiladora area are becoming less widespread, particularly in the light of them being potential public relations disasters. Studies conducted by Wagner & Timmins (2009) in the mid-2000s that have shown a positive correlation between high standards and low levels of 'pollution-intensive' FDI have proved limited in terms of the scope of industries and countries surveyed.

Furthermore, other factors such as political stability, developed financial institutions and legal systems, availability of land, market size, and labour force participation, play a greater role in influencing an TNC's choice of location than do environmental standards. This is partly due to fact that pollution abatement costs constitute only a tiny fraction of total costs, even in highly polluting industries such paper (5% of value added) and organic chemicals (8%), and consequently the impact of abatement costs on location is small (Eskeland & Harrison, 1997). Most companies welcome higher environmental standards, as they result in a better quality of life for the surrounding people and, by implication, a healthier more able work force. Still others find environmental clean-up services highly lucrative, and are vying to enter developing markets (Forstater, 2006).

Lastly, foreign firms are by and large less polluting than their domestic counterparts, largely due to their visibility, resources and access to 'clean' technology (Manderson & Kneller, 2012). All this evidence does not mean that pollution havens do not exist, or that pollution is not an issue for developing countries. It does, however, have broad implications for policymaking, and implies that a shift from specific investors to a more general focus on pollution abatement is in order (Kearsley & Riddel, 2010).

The significance of TNC practices and their impact on the environment cannot be understated. The relationship between environmental standards and levels of pollution, and its implications is also extremely important in the context of development. Whilst general trend of findings from studies related to the environmental impact of TNC activity contradict theories such as the pollution-haven hypothesis, it must not be inferred that the presence of multinationals is indisputably good for recipient countries (Lundan, 2004). Hazardous industries are still found in countries that have rudimentary environmental standards and monitoring systems, and they do fuel demand that can lead to wanton over-consumption and destruction of the environment. However such findings do refute the claim that transnational corporations are indisputably bad, and show that under the right circumstances companies are willing to put their technology and finances to the good of the environment (Jenkins, 2013).

Given that most efforts made by TNCs are done out of a certain degree of self interest – the prospect of good publicity from the undertaking of such projects or the maintenance of a richer, healthier developing world willing to spend on goods and services – it is important that the codes of conduct developed to lend support to these projects allow entire communities to benefit from substantial funds and resources, skills and technology, and to in the long-run enable people to lift themselves out of grinding poverty permanently (Prahalad, 2009). This because, as discussed earlier, the informality of corporate governance allows for many a fancy corporate social responsibility scheme to become mere eyewash, mere gimmickry, with very little being done beyond the elaborate corporate statements.

## CONCLUSION: TOWARDS A MIRAGE OR MECCA?

The idea that transnational corporations have a major role to play in development and social policy reflects the growing global reach of international business and the increasing complexity of the private sector and of the global financial system in the world today. This book chapter is one of the first to analyse the effectiveness of codes of corporate ethical conduct as an attempt at privatised governance, considering their implications for and impact on the behaviour and interactions of individual actors, groups, and organisations through a presentation of global examples of best practice. The discussion presented herein evaluates the usefulness, necessity, and potential of such formalized and semi-formal modes of governance as a preliminary attempt in bridging the conspicuous dearth of studies available in scholarly and practitioner literature that surround the actual conception, development, and implementation of codes of conduct in transnational corporations. As evidenced by the examples presented throughout this work, the limitations of these codes are real, and if they are to go beyond mere rhetoric to become effective regulatory tools, their shortcomings will have to be addressed.

It has been suggested that multi-stakeholder codes are more effective than unilaterally developed ones, as they are more inclusive and take into account views from a broad spectrum of stakeholders. This in turn can help ensure that their content is not limited to include only the basic standards recommended by international conventions, but also covers other issues that may affect the various stakeholders involved. For any code to succeed, the Transnational Corporation concerned must be genuinely committed to its implementation. It must ensure that it follows a uniform, non-discriminatory policy in all the countries of the world wherein it operates in, and that its policies take into account the requirements of all the players involved in the supply chain. The organisation must also be willing to put its money where its mouth is, and finally, to ensure this degree of commitment, the code put forward must provide for an efficient, unbiased monitoring, reporting, and enforcement system.

*Codes of conduct can work.* However, they are not automatic solutions to the negative effects of globalisation – they require the investment of a large amount of time, money, and resources from all the stakeholders involved if they are to be truly useful. Consequently, this researcher argues that whilst codes of ethical corporate behaviour may initially be adopted by transnational organisations for compulsory legal reasons, related especially to corporate social responsibility standards, they clearly lose character and function once incorporated into regular practice unless built upon concrete foundations and maintained. This in itself is a significant contribution to the canon, as it cautions against much of the optimism prevalent in those other scholarly and practitioner works which consider the adoption of both voluntary and authoritarian codes by TNCs to be indicative of their being successful in addressing corporate ethical and regulatory deficiencies.

Finally, the chapter contributes to the literature on the global spread of management practices, arguing that corporate social responsibility, and codes of ethical corporate conduct in particular, may be considered as recent examples of management concepts and tools that have consistently proliferated globally, and that have led to the convergence of management best practice worldwide. Voluntary codes of corporate conduct, no matter how effective, are no substitute for national legislation. It is important to always remember, in conclusion, the primacy of the state in ensuring basic freedoms and the rule of law, whilst at the same time using corporate codes of ethical conduct and other similar forms of semi-formal, privatised governance as a means of complementing basic state law-enforcement functions. Coupled with civil society pressure, voluntary codes of conduct could help to reinforce, in particular, the statutory regulations that deliver sustained improvements in corporate standards, and that society would be able to move towards Zadek's 'Mecca' by benefiting from sustained improvements in labour, health, and other standards. However, only time will tell if the corporate world is serious enough about pursing the practical strategies necessary to undertake this pilgrimage.

## REFERENCES


Ahmed, K., & Chowdhury, T. A. (2009). Performance Evaluation of SMEs. *International Journal of Business and Management*, *4*(7), 126–133. doi:10.5539/ijbm.v4n7p126

Andersen, M., & Skjoett-Larsen, T. (2009). Corporate Social Responsibility in Global Supply Chains. *Supply Chain Management: An International Journal*, *14*(2), 75–86. doi:10.1108/13598540910941948

Ashkanasy, N. M., Falkus, S., & Callan, V. J. (2000). Predictors of Ethical Code Use and Ethical Tolerance in the Public Sector. *Journal of Business Ethics*, *25*(3), 237–253. doi:10.1023/A:1006001722137

Asiedu, E., & Lien, D. (2011). Democracy, Foreign Direct Investment and Natural Resources. *Journal of International Economics*, *84*(1), 99–111. doi:10.1016/j.jinteco.2010.12.001

Barrientos, S. W. (2002). Flexible Female Employment and Ethical Trade in the Global Economy. In P. Newell, S. Rai, & A. Scott (Eds.), *Development and the Challenge of Globalisation* (pp. 143–158). London: ITDG Publishing. doi:10.3362/9781780441108.010

Bartley, T. (2007). Institutional Emergence in an Era of Globalization: The Rise of Transnational Private Regulation of Labor and Environmental Conditions. *American Journal of Sociology*, *113*(2), 297–351. doi:10.1086/518871

Bondy, K., Matten, D., & Moon, J. (2008). Multinational Corporation Codes of Conduct: Governance Tools for Corporate Social Responsibility? *Corporate Governance: An International Review*, *16*(4), 294–311. doi:10.1111/j.1467-8683.2008.00694.x

Bucovetsky, S. (2009). An Index of Capital Tax Competition. *International Tax and Public Finance, 16*(6), 727–752. doi:10.1007/s10797-008-9093-9

Canary, H. E., & Jennings, M. M. (2008). Principles and Influences in Codes of Ethics: A Centering Resonance Analysis Comparing Pre- and Post-Sarbanes-Oxley Codes of Ethics. *Journal of Business Ethics, 80*(2), 263–278. doi:10.1007/s10551-007-9417-1

Cañas, J., & Gilmer, R. W. (2009). The Maquiladora's Changing Geography. *The Federal Reserve Bank of Dallas: Second Quarter, 2009*, 10–14.

Carroll, A., & Buchholtz, A. (2014). *Business and Society: Ethics, Sustainability, and Stakeholder Management*. Stamford, CT: Cengage Learning.

Carroll, A. B., & Shabana, K. M. (2010). The Business Case for Corporate Social Responsibility: A Review of Concepts, Research and Practice. *International Journal of Management Reviews, 12*(1), 85–105. doi:10.1111/j.1468-2370.2009.00275.x

Chonko, L. B., Wotruba, T. R., & Loe, T. W. (2003). Ethics Code Familiarity and Usefulness: Views on Idealist and Relativist Managers Under Varying Conditions of Turbulence. *Journal of Business Ethics, 42*(3), 237–252. doi:10.1023/A:1022261006692

Clean Clothes Campaign. (2001, March) Controlling Corporate Wrongs: The Liability of Multinational Corporations, *Report of the IRENE Seminar*. Retrieved from http://www.cleanclothes.org/publications/corp-8.htm

Cleek, M. A., & Leonard, S. L. (1998). Can Corporate Codes of Ethics Influence Behavior? *Journal of Business Ethics, 17*(6), 619–630.

Commendatore, P., Currie, M., & Kubin, I. (2008). Footloose Entrepreneurs, Taxes and Subsidies. *Spatial Economic Analysis, 3*(1), 115–141. doi:10.1080/17421770701774914

Cruickshank, P., Edelmann, N., & Smith, C. (2010). Signing an e-Petition as a Transition from Lurking to Participation. In H. J. Scholl & M. Janssen (Eds.), *Electronic Government and Electronic Participation: Joint Proceedings of Ongoing Research and Projects of IFIP EGOV and IFIP ePart 2010* (pp. 275–282). Linz, Austria: Trauner Verlag.

Davidson, K. (2009). Ethical Concerns at the Bottom of the Pyramid: Where CSR Meets BOP. *Journal of International Business Ethics, 2*(1), 22–32.

Diller, J. (1999). A Social Conscience in the Global Marketplace? Labour Dimensions of Codes of Conduct, Social Labelling and Investor Initiatives. *International Labour Review, 138*(2), 99–129. doi:10.1111/j.1564-913X.1999.tb00062.x

Dinopoulos, E., & Segerstrom, P. (2010). Intellectual Property Rights, Multinational Firms, and Economic Growth. *Journal of Development Economics, 92*(1), 13–27. doi:10.1016/j.jdeveco.2009.01.007

Diving Into the Rich Pool. (2011, September 24). *The Economist*.

Doremus, P., Keller, W. W., Pauly, L. W., & Reich, S. (1998). *The Myth of the Global Corporation*. Princeton, N.J.: Princeton University Press.

Downs, A. (1964). *Inside Bureaucracy*. Boston: Little Brown.

Eckel, C., & Egger, H. (2009). Wage bargaining and Multinational Firms. *Journal of International Economics*, *77*(2), 206–214. doi:10.1016/j.jinteco.2009.01.004

Farrell, B. J., Cobbin, D. M., & Farrell, H. M. (2002). Codes of Ethics: Their Evolution, Development and Other Controversies. *Journal of Management Development*, *21*(2), 152–163. doi:10.1108/02621710210417448

Fellner, K. (2008). *Wrestling With Starbucks: Conscience, Capital, Cappuccino*. New Brunswick, N.J.: Rutgers University Press.

Fisher, C., & Lovell, A. (2009). *Business Ethics and Values: Individual, Corporate, and International Perspectives* (3rd ed.). Harlow: Pearson Education.

Forstater, M. (2006). Green Jobs: Public Service Employment and Environmental Sustainability. *Challenge*, *49*(4), 58–72. doi:10.2753/CHA0577-5132490405

Frankel, J. A., & Rose, A. K. (2005). Is Trade Good or Bad for the Environment? Sorting out the Causality. *The Review of Economics and Statistics*, *87*(1), 85–91. doi:10.1162/0034653053327577

Gancia, G., & Bonfiglioli, A. (2008). North–South Trade and Directed Technical Change. *Journal of International Economics*, *76*(2), 276–295. doi:10.1016/j.jinteco.2008.03.010

Gill, S. (2000). Toward a Postmodern Prince? The Battle in Seattle as a Moment in the New Politics of Globalisation. *Millennium*, *29*(1), 131–140. doi:10.1177/03058298000290010101

Glass, A. J., & Wu, X. (2007). Intellectual Property Rights and Quality Improvement. *Journal of Development Economics*, *82*(2), 393–415. doi:10.1016/j.jdeveco.2005.08.002

Gordon, K., & Miyake, M. (2001). Business Approaches to Combating Bribery: A Study of Codes of Conduct. *Journal of Business Ethics*, *34*(3/4), 161–173. doi:10.1023/A:1012517622479

Grace, D., & Cohen, S. (2013). *Business Ethics* (5th ed.). Oxford: Oxford University Press.

Graham, E. M., & Wilkie, C. (1994). Multinationals and the Investment Provisions of the NAFTA. *The International Trade Journal*, *8*(1), 9–38. doi:10.1080/08853909408523791

Grant, J. (2012). The Kimberly Process at Ten: Reflections on a Decade of Efforts to End the Trade in Conflict Diamonds. In P. Lujala & S. A. Rustad (Eds.), *High-Value Natural Resources and Peacebuilding* (pp. 151–179). London: Earthscan Press.

Held, D. (2013). *Global Covenant: The Social Democratic Alternative to the Washington Consensus*. Cambridge: Polity Press.

Henderson, H. (2000). Life Beyond Global Economic Warfare. In J. N. Pieterse (Ed.), *Global Futures: Shaping Globalisation* (pp. 63–82). London: Zed.

Hobson, J. M., & Ramesh, M. (2002). Globalisation Makes of States What States Make of It: Between Agency and Structure in the State/Globalisation Debate. *New Political Economy*, *7*(1), 5–22. doi:10.1080/13563460120115499

Hong, Q., & Smart, M. (2010). In Praise of Tax Havens: International Tax Planning and Foreign Direct Investment. *European Economic Review*, *54*(1), 82–95. doi:10.1016/j.euroecorev.2009.06.006

Hopkins, M. (2003). *The Planetary Bargain – CSR Matters*. London: Earthscan.

International Labour Organisation. (2013) *Codes of Conduct for Multinationals*. Retrieved from http://www.itcilo.it/english/actrav/telearn/global/ilo/guide/main.htm

International Labour Organisation. (2013). *Statistical Information and Monitoring Programme on Child Labour (2013)*. Retrieved from http://www.ilo.org/public/english/standards/ipec/simpoc/index.htm

Islam, M. A., Khan, M. A., Obaidullah, A. Z. M., & Alam, M. S. (2011). Effect of Entrepreneur and Firm Characteristics on the Business: Success of Small and Medium Enterprises (SMEs) in Bangladesh. *International Journal of Business and Management*, *6*(3), 289–299.

Jeffcott, B., & Yanz, L. (2013). Voluntary Codes of Conduct: Do They Strengthen or Undermine Government Regulation and Worker Organising? *Maquila Solidarity Network*. Retrieved from http://www.maquilasolidarity.org/resources/codes/volcodes99.htm

Jenkins, R. (2001). Corporate Codes of Conduct: Self Regulation in a Global Economy. *Technology, Business and Programme Paper # 2*, UNRISD. Retrieved from http://www.natural-resources.org/minerals/CD/docs/other/jenkins.pdf

Jenkins, R. (2013). *Transnational Corporations and Uneven Development: The Internalization of Capital and the Third World*. London: Routledge Press.

Kearsley, A., & Riddel, M. (2010). A Further Inquiry into the Pollution Haven Hypothesis and the Environmental Kuznets Curve. *Ecological Economics*, *69*(4), 905–919. doi:10.1016/j.ecolecon.2009.11.014

Kinoshita, Y., & Campos, N. F. (2003). Why Does FDI Go Where it Goes? New Evidence from the Transitional Economies (Working Paper). International Monetary Fund Press, Washington, D.C..

Legrain, P. (2002). *Open World: The Truth About Globalisation*. London: Abacus Press.

Levinson, A., & Taylor, M. S. (2008). Unmasking the Pollution Haven Effect. *International Economic Review*, *49*(1), 223–254. doi:10.1111/j.1468-2354.2008.00478.x

Lipsey, R. E. (2010). Measuring The Location Of Production In A World Of Intangible Productive Assets, FDI, And Intrafirm Trade. *Review of Income and Wealth. International Association for Research in Income and Wealth*, *56*(s1), S99–S110. doi:10.1111/j.1475-4991.2010.00385.x

Lundan, S. M. (2004). Multinationals, NGOs and Regulation: Greenpeace and the Global Phase-Out of Chlorine Bleaching. In S. M. Lundan (Ed.), Multinationals, Environment and Global Competition (pp.147– 170). Oxford: JAI (Elsevier) Press.

Maassen, G. F. (1999). *An International Comparison of Corporate Governance Models: A Study on the Formal independence and Convergence of One-Tier and Two-Tier Corporate Boards of Directors in the United States of America, the United Kingdom and the Netherlands. Ph.D. Series in General Management, Nr. 31*. N.L.: Rotterdam School of Management.

Manderson, E., & Kneller, R. (2012). Environmental Regulations, Outward FDI and Heterogeneous Firms: Are Countries Used as Pollution Havens? *Environmental and Resource Economics*, *51*(3), 317–352. doi:10.1007/s10640-011-9500-z

Mareş, R. (2004). *Business and Human Rights: a Compilation of Documents (Vol. 13)*. Leiden: Martinus Nijhoff Publishers.

Margetts, H. Z., John, P., Escher, T., & Reissfelder, S. (2011). Social Information and Political Participation on the Internet: An Experiment. *European Political Science Review*, *3*(3), 321–344. doi:10.1017/S1755773911000129

Matten, D., & Crane, A. (2005). Corporate Citizenship: Toward an Extended Theoretical Conceptualization. *Academy of Management Review*, *30*(1), 166–179. doi:10.5465/AMR.2005.15281448

McClintock, B. (1999). The Multinational Corporation and Social Justice: Experiments in Supranational Governance. *Review of Social Economy*, *57*(4), 507–522. doi:10.1080/00346769900000019

Mihaly, E. B. (1999). Multinational Companies and Wages in Low-Income Countries. *Journal of Small & Emerging Business Law*, *3*(1), 1–26.

Morena, E. (2013). The French *Confédération Paysanne* (CP) as Anti-Capitalist 'Peasant' Movement. In C. F. Fominaya & L. Cox (Eds.), *Understanding European Movements: New Social Movements, Global Justice Struggles, Anti-Austerity Protest* (pp. 94–108). London: Routledge Press.

Mudambi, R., Mudambi, S., & Navarra, P. (2007). Global Innovation in MNCs: The Effect of Subsidiary Innovation and Teamwork. *Journal of Product Innovation Management*, *24*(5), 442–455. doi:10.1111/j.1540-5885.2007.00262.x

O'Donnell, G. (1978). Reflections on the Patterns of Change in the Bureaucratic Authoritarian State. *Latin American Research Review*, *13*(1), 3–38.

O'Donohue, W., & Nelson, L. (2009). The Role of Ethical Values in an Expanded Psychological Contract. *Journal of Business Ethics*, *90*(2), 251–263. doi:10.1007/s10551-009-0040-1

Payne, A. (2010). How many Gs are there in 'Global Governance' After the Crisis? The Perspectives of the 'Marginal Majority' of the World's States. *International Affairs*, *86*(3), 729–740. doi:10.1111/j.1468-2346.2010.00908.x

Pearson, R., & Seyfang, G. (2001). New Hope or False Dawn: Voluntary Codes of Conduct, Labour Regulation and Social Policy in a Globalising World. *Global Social Policy*, *1*(1), 48–78. doi:10.1177/146801810100100104

Prahalad, C. K. (2009). *The Fortune at the Bottom of the Pyramid, Revised and Updated 5th Anniversary Edition: Eradicating Poverty Through Profits*. New Jersey: Wharton School Publishing.

Rodriguez-Dominguez, L., Gallego-Alvarez, I., & Garcia-Sanchez, I. M. (2009). Corporate Governance and Codes of Ethics. *Journal of Business Ethics*, *90*(2), 187–202. doi:10.1007/s10551-009-0035-y

Salvendy, G. (2012). *Handbook of Human Factors and Ergonomics* (4th ed.). New Jersey: John Wiley and Sons. doi:10.1002/9781118131350

Schrage, E. J. (2004, January). *Promoting Worker Rights through Private Voluntary Initiatives: Public Relations or Public Policy? A Report to the US Department of State*. Retrieved from http://www.uichr.org/content/act/sponsored/gwri/report.pdf

Şener, F. (2006). *Intellectual Property Rights and Rent Protection in a North-South Product-Cycle Model. Manuscript*. Schenectady: Union College Press.

Sethi, S. P. (2003). *Setting Global Standards: Guidelines for Creating Codes of Conduct in Multinational Corporations*. Hoboken, N.J.: John Wiley & Sons.

Sigmund, P. E. (1974). The "Invisible Blockade" and the Overthrow of Allende. *Foreign Affairs*, *52*(2), 322–340. doi:10.2307/20038052

Somers, M. J. (2001). Ethical Codes of Conduct and Organizational Context: A Study of the Relationship between Codes of Conduct, Employee Behaviour and Organizational Value. *Journal of Business Ethics*, *30*(2), 185–195. doi:10.1023/A:1006457810654

Spar, D. L. (1998). The Spotlight and the Bottom Line: How Multinationals Export Human Rights. *Foreign Affairs*, *77*(2), 7–12. doi:10.2307/20048784

Official Website: Corporate Social Responsibility Initiatives. (2013). Starbucks Coffee Company. Retrieved from http://www.starbucks.com/aboutus/csr.asp

Stern, D. I. (2004). The Rise and Fall of the Environmental Kuznets Curve. *World Development*, *32*(8), 1419–1439. doi:10.1016/j.worlddev.2004.03.004

Stohl, C., Stohl, M., & Popova, L. (2009). A New Generation of Corporate Codes of Ethics. *Journal of Business Ethics*, *90*(4), 607–622. doi:10.1007/s10551-009-0064-6

Svensson, G., Wood, G., & Callaghan, M. (2010). A Comparison of Business Ethics Commitment in Private and Public Sector Organizations in Sweden. *Business Ethics (Oxford, England)*, *19*(2), 213–232. doi:10.1111/j.1467-8608.2010.01585.x

Talaulicar, T. (2009). Barriers Against Globalizing Corporate Ethics: An Analysis of Legal Disputes on Implementing U.S. Codes of Ethics in Germany. *Journal of Business Ethics*, *84*(3), 349–360. doi:10.1007/s10551-009-0199-5

Tarzi, S. M. (2002). International Norms, Trade, and Human Rights: A Perspective on Norm Conformity. *The Journal of Social, Political, and Economic Studies*, *27*(2), 187–202.

Thai Labour Campaign. (2013). *Can Corporations Promote Labour Standards? Evidence from the Thai Footwear and Apparel Industry*. Retrieved from http://www.thailabour.org/docs/CodesReport

Virkar, S. (forthcoming). The Globalisation of the Media: Towards Cultural Homogeneity? In J. M. Alcántara-Pilar, S. del Barrio-García, E. Crespo-Almedros, & L. Porcu (Eds.), Analyzing the Cultural Diversity of Consumers in the Global Marketplace. Hershey, PA, USA: IGI Global.

Wagner, U., & Timmins, C. D. (2009). Agglomeration Effects in Foreign Direct Investment and the Pollution Haven Hypothesis. *Environmental and Resource Economics*, *43*(2), 231–256. doi:10.1007/s10640-008-9236-6

Wang, H., Choi, J., & Li, J. (2008). Too Little or Too Much? Untangling the Relationship Between Corporate Philanthropy and Firm Financial Performance. *Organization Science*, *19*(1), 143–159. doi:10.1287/orsc.1070.0271

Winston, M. E. (1999). Human rights and International Political Economy in Third World Nations: Multinational Corporations, Foreign Aid, and Repression. *Human Rights Quarterly*, *21*(3), 824–830. doi:10.1353/hrq.1999.0036

Worasinchai, L., & Bechina, A. A. A. (2010). The Role of Multinational Corporations (MNCs) in Developing R & D in Thailand: The Knowledge Flow Between MNCs and University. *Electronic Journal of Knowledge Management*, *8*(1), 171–180.

Yusuf, M. A., & Alam, Q. (2011). Empowering Role of the Village Phone Program in Bangladesh: In Retrospect, in Prospect. *Journal of Information Technology Impact*, *11*(1), 35–50.

Zadek, S. (2004). The Path to Corporate Responsibility. *Harvard Business Review*, *82*(12), 125–132. PMID:15605571

## ADDITIONAL READING

Compa, L. (2001). Trade Unions, NGOs and Corporate Codes of Conduct. *International Union Rights*, *3*. Retrieved from http://www.citinv.it/associazioni/CNMS/archivio/strategie/tradeU_NGO.html

Cutler, A. C., Haufler, V., & Porter, T. (1999). *Private Authority and International Affairs*. Albany: State University of New York Press.

Eden, L., & Potter, E. H. (1993). *Multinationals in the Global Political Economy*. New York, N.Y.: St. Martin's Press. doi:10.1007/978-1-349-22973-4

Entine, J., & Nichols, M. (1996). Corporate Codes of Conduct. *Better World Zine*, 5. Retrieved from http://www.betterworld.com/BWZ/9608/editor.htm

Fridd, P., & Sainsbury, J. (1999). The Role of Voluntary Codes of Conduct and Regulation – A Retailer's View. In S. Picciotto & R. Mayne (Eds.), *Regulating International Business: Beyond Liberalisation* (pp. 221–234). London: Macmillan Press. doi:10.1007/978-1-349-27738-4_12

Kearney, N. (1999). Corporate Codes of Conduct: the Privatised Application of Labour Standards. In S. Picciotto & R. Mayne (Eds.), *Regulating International Business: Beyond Liberalisation* (pp. 205–220). London: Macmillan Press. doi:10.1007/978-1-349-27738-4_11

Knight, D. (2001, June 13). Environment-Finance: Corporate Codes of Conduct Deemed Insufficient. *InterPress Service*. Retrieved from http://www.globalpolicy.org/reform/2001/corpcode0613.htm

Mayne, R. (1999). Regulating TNCs: The Role of Voluntary and Governmental Approaches. In S. Picciotto & R. Mayne (Eds.), *Regulating International Business: Beyond Liberalisation* (pp. 235–254). London: Macmillan Press. doi:10.1007/978-1-349-27738-4_13

Michael, B. (2013) Codes of Corporate Conduct: Moving from Order to Progress. Available at: http://users.ox.ac.uk/~scat1663/Publications/Papers/Codes%20in%India.PDF

Ronit, K., & Schneider, V. (1999). *Private Organisations in Global Politics*. London: Routledge Press.

Sethi, S. P. (2002). Corporate Codes of Conduct and the Success of Globalisation. *Ethics & International Affairs*, *16*(1), 89–106. doi:10.1111/j.1747-7093.2002.tb00377.x

Svensson, G., Wood, G., & Callaghan, M. (2004). A Comparison Between Corporate and Public Sector Business Ethics in Sweden. *Business Ethics (Oxford, England)*, *13*(2-3), 166–184. doi:10.1111/j.1467-8608.2004.00361.x

United States Centre for International Business. (2013). *Codes of Conduct: A Review of Recent Initiatives*. Retrieved from http://www.uscib.org/index.asp?documentID=1357

## KEY TERMS AND DEFINITIONS

**Business Ethics:** Defined as the practical application of a guiding set of values or high moral code within an organisational, usually commercial or financial setting; governed by a general focus on what is right or good for the organisation and its stakeholders.

**Corporate Social Responsibility:** Is a concept embodied in the fair, ethical, and socially responsible treatment for profit of transnational corporation employees, local communities, and other stakeholders; particularly to increase human development and the standards of living of stakeholders both internal and external to a commercial enterprise.

**Codes of Corporate Ethical Conduct:** Or *Corporate Codes of Ethics* or *Corporate Codes of Conduct*, defined as formalized public statements of corporate principles, precepts, guidelines, and rules of conduct that govern international, intra-organisational, and interpersonal practices and relations.

**Transnational Corporation (TNC):** Or *Multinational Corporation (MNC)* or *Transnational Enterprise (TNE)* or *Multinational Enterprise (MNE)*, defined as a large and increasingly complex company or commercial conglomerate that operates and holds investments in more than one country.

# Chapter 5
# Financial Inclusion in India:
## An Assessment

**Rohit Bhattacharya**
*Dhirendra Mahila Post Graduate College, India*

## ABSTRACT

*The concept of Financial Inclusion is not a new one. It has become a catchphrase now and has attracted the global attention in the recent past. Lack of accessible, affordable and appropriate financial services has always been a global problem. It is estimated that about 2.9 billion people around the world do not have access to formal sources of banking and financial services. India is said to live in its villages, a convincing statement, considering that nearly 72% of our population lives there. However, a significant proportion of our 650,000 odd villages does not have a single bank branch to boast of, leaving swathes of the rural population in financial exclusion. RBI has reported that the financial exclusion in India leads to the loss of GDP to the extent of one per cent (RBI, Working Paper Series (DEPR): 8/2011). Financially excluded people, consistently, depend on money lenders even for their day to day needs, borrowing at excessive rates to finally get caught in a debt trap. In addition, people in far-off villages are completely unaware of financial products like insurance, which could protect them in adverse situation. Therefore, financial inclusion is a big necessity for our country as a large chunk of the world's poor resides here. Access to finance by the poor and vulnerable groups is a prerequisite for poverty reduction and social cohesion. Present paper is an attempt to highlight the present efforts of financial inclusion in India its future road map, its challenges etc.*

## OBJECTIVES OF THE STUDY

- To review the present status of the financial inclusion in India in particular and the world general.
- To highlight the measures taken by the Government of India and RBI for promoting financial Inclusion.

DOI: 10.4018/978-1-4666-9908-3.ch005

## METHODOLOGY OF THE STUDY

Secondary research was conducted to review the present status of financial inclusion in India. Research methodology explains and chooses the best (in terms of quality and economy) way of doing it. The information and data for the research can be collected through primary as well as secondary sources i.e. published articles, journals, newspapers, reports, books and websites." Various graphs and tables have been used. Data has been collected from the websites of the Reserve Bank of India and also taken from various committee reports submitted to Government of India on Financial Inclusion.

## INTRODUCTION

With the progress of the Indian economy, especially when the focus is on the achievement of sustainable development, there must be an attempt to include maximum number of participation from all the sections of the society. But the lack of awareness and financial literacy among the rural population of the country is hindering the growth of the economy as majority of the population does not have access to formal credit. This is a serious issue for the economic progress of the country. In order to overcome such barriers, the banking sector emerged with some technological innovations such as automated teller machines (ATM), credit and debit cards, internet banking, etc. Though introduction of such banking technologies brought a change in the urban society, a majority of the rural population is still unaware of these changes and is excluded from formal banking (Srikanth, 2013).

Financial inclusion enables improved and better sustainable economic and social development of the country. It helps in the empowerment of the underprivileged, poor and women of the society with the mission of making them self-sufficient and well informed to take better financial decisions. Financial inclusion takes into account the participation of vulnerable groups such as weaker sections of the society and low income groups, based on the extent of their access to financial services such as savings and payment account, credit insurance, pensions etc. Also the objective of financial inclusion exercise is easy availability of financial services which allows maximum investment in business opportunities, education, save for retirement, insurance against risks, etc. by the rural individuals and firms (Agarwal, 2014).

The penetration of financial services in the rural areas of India is still very low. The factors responsible for this condition can be looked at from both supply side and demand side and the major reason for low penetration of financial services is, probably, lack of supply. The reasons for low demand for financial services could be low income level, lack of financial literacy, other bank accounts in the family, etc. On the other hand, the supply side factors include no bank branch in the vicinity, lack of suitable products meeting the needs of the poor people, complex processes and language barriers (Chakrabarty, 2012),

## DEFINITION OF FINANCIAL INCLUSION

- *Financial inclusion refers to universal access to a wider range of financial services at a reasonable cost. These include not only banking products but also other financial services such as insurance and equity products.* The household access to financial services includes access to contingency planning, credit and wealth creation. Access to contingency planning would help for future savings such as retirement savings, buffer savings and insurable contingencies and access to credit includes emergency loans, housing loans and consumption loans. On the other hand, access to wealth creation includes savings and investment based on household's level of financial literacy and risk perception (Planning Commission, 2009).

- Financial inclusion as *the process of ensuring access to financial services and timely and adequate credit where needed by vulnerable groups such as weaker sections and low income groups at an affordable cost.* The meaning of financial inclusion is delivery of financial services to the low income groups especially the excluded sections of the population with the provision of equal opportunities. The main target is the access of financial services for better standard of living and income (Rangarajan, 2008).
- *Financial inclusion is the process of ensuring access to appropriate financial products and services needed by all sections of society including vulnerable groups such as weaker sections and low income groups at an affordable cost in a fair and transparent manner by mainstream institutional players.* This issue started gaining importance recently in the news media (Chakrabarty, 2011).
- Rangarajan's committee on financial inclusion defines it as: Financial inclusion may be defined as the process of access to financial services and timely and adequate credit where needed by vulnerable groups such as weaker sections and low income groups at an affordable cost (Rangarajan, 2008).
- The financial services include the entire gamut - savings, loans, insurance, credit, payments etc. The financial system has to provide its function of transferring resources from surplus to deficit units but both deficit and surplus units are those with low incomes, poor background etc. By providing these services, the aim is to help them come out of poverty. So far, the focus has only been on delivering credit (it is called as microfinance but is microcredit) and has been quite successful (Rangarajan, 2008).

*Figure 1. An overview of Financial Inclusion Services*

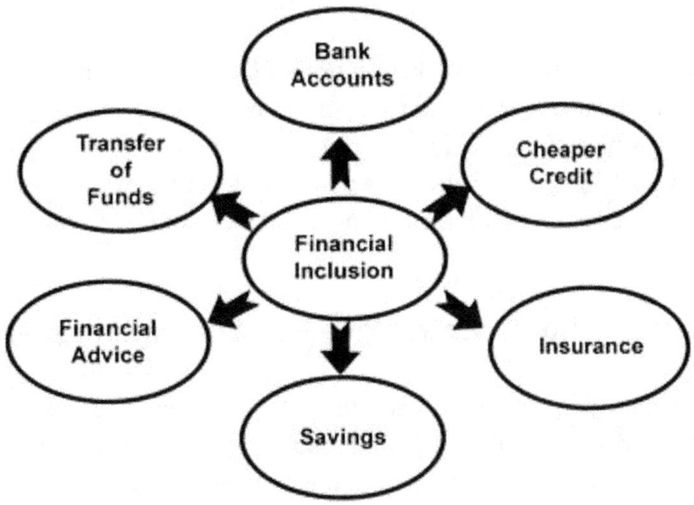

## NEED OF FINANCIAL INCLUSION

According to the United Nations the main goals of inclusive finance are as follows:

1. Access at a reasonable cost of all households and enterprises to the range of financial services for which they are "bankable," including savings, short and long-term credit, leasing and factoring, mortgages, insurance, pensions, payments, local money transfers and international remittances.
2. Sound institutions, guided by appropriate internal management systems, industry performance standards, and performance monitoring by the market, as well as by sound prudential regulation where required
3. Financial and institutional sustainability as a means of providing access to financial services over time
4. Multiple providers of financial services, wherever feasible, so as to bring cost-effective and a wide variety of alternatives to customers (which could include any number of combinations of sound private, non-profit and public providers) (Arunaachalam, 2008).

There has been a many objectives related to the need for financial Inclusion such as:

- **Economic Objectives:** For the equitable growth in all the sections of the society leading to a reduction of disparities in terms of income and savings the financial inclusion can serve as a boom for the underdeveloped and developing nations.
- **Mobilization of Savings:** If the weaker sections are provided with the facility of banking services the savings can be mobilized which is normally piled up at their households can be effectively utilized for the capital formation and growth of the economy.
- **Larger Market for the financial system:** To serve the requirements and need of the large section of society there is a surging need for the larger market for the financial system which opens up the avenue for the new players in the financial sector and can lead to growth of banking sector also.
- **Social Objectives:** Poverty Eradication is considered to be the main sole objective of the financial inclusion scheme since they bridge up the gap between the weaker section of society and the sources of livelihood and the means of income which can be generated for them if they get loans and advances.
- **Sustainable Livelihood:** Once the weaker section of society got some money in loan form they can start up their own business or they can support their education through which they can sustain their livelihood. Thus financial inclusion is turn out to be boom for the low income households.
- **Political Objectives:** There are certain other political objectives which can be achieved with the wider inclusion of lower strata in the society and an effective direction can be given to the government programmes.

### Outreach of Banking Sector Country Wise Position: India vis-à-vis the World

Geographic and demographic penetration indicates the outreach of banking sector. Geographic penetration can be measured in terms of number of bank branches per 1000 Square Kilometers (sq km) and number of ATMs per 1000 sq km. larger number of branches and ATMs per sq km. The following table represents the comparison of Geographic and Demographic penetration of Banking Services of various countries (Table 1).

*Table 1.*

| Country | Geographic Penetration | | Demographic Penetration | |
|---|---|---|---|---|
| | No of bank branches per 1000 sq km | No of ATMs per 1000 sq km | No of branches per 100,000 People | No of ATMs per 100,000 People |
| Korea | 65.02 | 436.88 | 13.40 | 40.03 |
| U.K | 45.16 | 104.46 | 18.35 | 42.45 |
| India | 22.57 | - | 6.30 | - |
| Indonesia | 10.00 | 5.73 | 8.44 | 4.84 |
| USA | 9.81 | 38.43 | 30.86 | 120.94 |
| Mexico | 4.09 | 8.91 | 7.63 | 16.63 |
| Brazil | 3.05 | 3.72 | 14.59 | 17.82 |
| China | 1.83 | 5.25 | 1.33 | 3.80 |
| Russia | 0.19 | 0.53 | 2.24 | 6.28 |

Source: Beck, Demirguc-Kunt and Soledad Martinez Peria (2005)

As per Trends and Progress of Banking in India, RBI, 2006-07 (Appendix Table III.35), end March 2007 there were 27,088 ATMs of Scheduled Commercial Banks in India. As can be seen from the above table India being the developing nation and having a large number of rural sector still it lags behind in providing the basic facility of opening of number of bank branches in the rural areas.

## Survey Reports on Financial Inclusion

A financial inclusion survey was conducted by World Bank team in India between April-June, 2011, which included face to face interviews of 3,518 respondents. The sample excluded the north eastern states and remote islands representing approximately 10 per cent of the total adult population. The survey suggest in developing countries India lags behind in opening bank accounts, but is much closer to the global average when it comes to borrowing from formal institutions. In India, 35 per cent of people had formal accounts versus the global average of 50 per cent and the average of 41 per cent in developing economies as can be seen from the Table 1 (Demirguc–Kunt and Leora, 2012). The survey also points to the slow growth of mobile money in India, where only 4 per cent of adults in the Global Findex sample report having used a mobile phone in the past 12 months to pay bills or sends or receive money. Keeping in view the goal of bringing banking services to identified 74,414 villages with population above 2,000 by March 2012, and thereafter progressively to all villages over a period of time, the Reserve Bank advised commercial banks that while preparing their Annual Branch Expansion Plan (ABEP), they should allocate at least 25 per cent of the total number of branches proposed to be opened during the year in unbanked rural centers.

## Key Statistics on Financial Inclusion in India: A Survey

Thus a lot has to be done to bridge the gap between the formal financial institutions and the rural people needs. To make them aware of the fact about the facilities available for their benefit and which can help

India to turn out to a developed nation from a developing nation. As can be seen from the below table-2 that the financial inclusion plan has shown a tremendous growth in the past two years. Banks are gaining momentum in areas like opening up of new banking outlets in rural areas, deploying new business correspondents (BCs), opening of new frills accounts, granting more credit through KCC(Kisan Credit Card) AND GCC"s(General Purpose Credit Card).

## INITIATION AND PROGRESS OF FINANCIAL INCLUSION CONCEPT IN INDIA

In India, financial inclusion first featured in 2005, when it was introduced by K C Chakraborty, the chairman of Indian Bank. Mangalam Village became the first village in India where all households were provided banking facilities. Norms were relaxed for people intending to open accounts with annual deposits of less than Rs. 50,000. General credit cards (GCCs) were issued to the poor and the disadvantaged with a view to help them access easy credit. In January 2006, the Reserve Bank permitted commercial banks to make use of the services of non-governmental organizations (NGOs/SHGs), micro-finance institutions, and other civil society organizations as intermediaries for providing financial and banking services. These intermediaries could be used as business facilitators or business correspondents by commercial banks. The bank asked the commercial banks in different regions to start a 100% financial inclusion campaign on a pilot basis. As a result of the campaign states or U.T.s like Pondicherry, Himachal Pradesh and Kerala announced 100% financial inclusion in all their districts. Reserve Bank of India's vision for 2020 is to open nearly 600 million new customers' accounts and service them through a variety of channels by leveraging on IT. However, illiteracy and the low income savings and lack of bank branches in rural areas continue to be a roadblock to financial inclusion in many states and there is inadequate legal and financial structure.

## MAJOR MILESTONES IN FINANCIAL INCLUSION IN INDIA (tables 3-4)

1969 Nationalization of Banks
1971 Establishment of priority Sector Lending Banks
1975 Establishment of Regional Rural Banks
1982 Establishment of NABARD
1992 Launching of the Self Help Groups bank Linkage Programme
1998 NABARD sets a goal for linkage one million SHGs by 2008
2000 Establishment of SIDBI foundation for Micro Credit
2005 One million SHF linkage target achieved three years ahead of date 2006 Committee on Financial Inclusion 2007 Proposed Bill on Micro Finance Regulation introduced in parliament
2008 Committee submitted its final report on Financial Inclusion to Union Finance Minister in January

### New Initiatives Taken by GOI

- **PradhanMantri Jan DhanYojna:-** PM NarendraModi's ambitious initiative financial inclusion scheme PrradhanMantri Jan DhanYojna has made its way into the Guinness World Record for opening the highest number of bank accounts in the least time. Launched by PM Modi in Aug-28,

*Table 3. Financial Inclusion Progress: Banks and RRBS*

| | Year ended March 2010 | Year ended March 2014 |
|---|---|---|
| Banking Outlets in Villages- Branches | 33,378 | 46,126 |
| Banking Outlets in Villages- Branchless Mode | 34,316 | 3,37,678 |
| Banking Outlets in Villages- Total | 67,694 | 3,83,804 |
| Urban Locations covered through BCs | 447 | 60,730 |
| Basic Savings Bank Deposit A/c through branches (No. in million) | 60.2 | 126.0 |
| Basic Savings Bank Deposit A/c through branches (Amt. in billion) | 44.3 | 273.3 |
| Basic Savings Bank Deposit A/c through BCs (No. in million) | 13.3 | 116.9 |
| Basic Savings Bank Deposit A/c through BCs (Amt. in billion) | 10.7 | 39.0 |
| Basic Savings Bank Deposit Accounts Total (No. in million) | 73.5 | 243.0 |
| Basic Savings Bank Deposit Accounts Total (Amt. in billion) | 55.0 | 312.3 |
| Overdraft facility availed in Basic Savings Bank Deposit Accounts (No. in million) | 0.2 | 5.9 |
| Overdraft facility availed in Basic Savings Bank Deposit Accounts (Amt. in billion) | 0.1 | 16.0 |
| KCCs – (No. in million) | 24.3 | 39.9 |
| KCCs – (Amt. in billion) | 1,240.1 | 3,684.5 |
| GCC - (No. in million) | 1.4 | 7.4 |
| GCC - (Amt. in billion) | 35.1 | 1,096.9 |
| Information and Communication Technology A/Cs-BC- Transaction - (No. in million) (During the year) | 26.5 | 328.6 |
| Information and Communication Technology A/Cs-BC- Transactions - (Amt. in billion) (During the year) | 6.9 | 524.4 |

Source: Reserve Bank of India, Survey Report of the Committee on Medium-term Path on Financial Inclusion (2013-2014)

*Table 4. Measures Taken by GOI, RBI and NABARD*

| | | |
|---|---|---|
| Customer Service Centres | Role of NGOs, SHGs and MFIs | Financial Inclusion Technology Fund |
| Credit Counselling Centres | BF and BC models Micro Pension Model | Separate Plan for Urban Financial Inclusion and |
| Adhaar Scheme | Nationwide Electronic Financial Inclusion System | Electronic Benefit Transfer Scheme |
| The National Agricultural Insurance Scheme | Project Financial Literacy | Financial Literacy through Audio Visual medium –Doordarshan |
| No-frill Account | National Rural Financial Inclusion Plan | Banks and RRBs for setting up of Financial Literacy Centres |
| General Credit Card Project on Processor Cards | Financial Inclusion Fund | Farmers' Club Program |
| Micro Finance Development Fund | Project on "e-Grama" SHG-Post Office Linkage | Rural Volunteers as Book Writers |

Source: Reserve Bank of India, Survey Report of the Committee on Medium-term Path on Financial Inclusion (2013-2014).

2014, the govt. had given banks the deadline of Jan-26, 2015 to open 10 crore accounts. However banks had achieved the target set by the govt. a month before of the deadline. 99.74 percent household in the country have been covered by Jan DhanYojna. The Finance secretary has said according to reports 11.43 crore accounts were opened by banks across the country as of Jan 16, of this 8.24 crore accounts had zero balance. Public sector banks alone opened 9.60 crore accounts followed by RRB's which opened about 2 crore accounts. 13 private sector banks together open just 36 lakhs accounts.

The main purpose of this scheme was to enrolling over 7.5 crore households and to open their accounts. The scheme has been started with a target to provide "Universal access to banking facilities" starting with "Basic Banking Accounts" with overdraft facility of Rs. 5000 after six months and Rupay debit card with inbuilt accident insurance cover of Rs. 1 lakh, life insurance cover of Rs. 30,000 and RupayKishan Card. In next phase, micro insurance & pension scheme will also be added. This scheme also provide the facility of mobile banking through normal phones which were earlier only available with smart phones. So we can say that this scheme is a giant effort towards financial inclusion and provide the poor and vulnerable people of India all financial services under one umbrella.

- **PradhanMantriJeevanJyoti, PradhanMantriSurakshaYojna & Atal Pension Yojna:** "A large proportion of India's population is without insurance of any kind, health accidental or life. Worrying, as our young population ages, it is also going to be pension-less. Encourage by success of JhanDhanYojna, we propose to work towards creating a universal social security system for all Indians that will ensure that no Indian citizen will have to worry about illness, accidents or penury in old age." These words delivered by finance minister Sri Arun Jately clearly focus the main purpose of these three schemes.

Main highlights of these schemes are that Pradhan Mantri Jeevan Jyotiyojna provides 2 Lakhs Rs Life Insurance cover for an Individual for just Rs 330 p.a., PradhanMantriSurakshaYojna provide 2 Lakhs Rs Accidental Insurance for an Individual for just Rs. 12 p.a. and Atal Pension Yojna provides up to 5,000 Rs per month pension at very low per month contribution made by an individual depended on his age of entering in this scheme. So we can say that it is a gambit of social security plans offered to the poor, vulnerable and unorganized working sector that can make the way to a giant step towards financial inclusion.

## PROBLEMS AND CHALLENGES

1. Since independence, the Government had been dependent on its machinery first and then, after nationalization, on banks to reach the poor. But government machinery suffered all the demerits of bureaucracy and corruption and hence, failed miserably.
2. Banks also could not succeed in reaching the poor society because of many reasons.
    a. First, most of the Indians Banks were in government hands till the late nineties their employees were looking for a "salary", not for achieving the 'national target'.
    b. Second, banks have to follow certain rules which sometimes create bottlenecks in their targets of reaching the poor. For example, no bank will give a cheque book of ATM facility to a poor

man unless he has a minimum of Rs. 1000 in his account; which means if a poor man opens a bank account, he stills remains in the "stone age".(Subbiah, 2014)

3. Financial literacy is very low in India. Forget about BPL people, even the educated urban population is financially illiterate. Many college going students still cannot write cheques and a major part of white collar working class people need consultants to fill simple income tax returns.
4. Due to financial illiteracy, most of the people do not maintain proper records or books of accounts. This leads proper records or books of accounts. This leads to removing of these people from the financial services of the banks (Agarwal, 2010).

To sum up, banks need to redesign their business strategies to incorporate specific plans to promote financial inclusion of low income groups treating it both a business opportunity as well as a corporate social responsibility.

## CONCLUSION

For standing out on a global platform India has to look upon the inclusive growth and financial inclusion is the key for inclusive growth. There is a long way to go for the financial inclusion to reach to the core poor (Bhaskarans, 2006). According to K.C. Chakrabarty (2011) RBI Deputy Governor, "Even today the fact remains that nearly half of the Indian population doesn't have access to formal financial services and are largely dependent on money lenders". Mere opening of no-frill bank accounts is not the purpose or the end of financial inclusion while formal financial institutions must gain the trust and goodwill of the poor through developing strong linkages with community-based financial ventures and cooperative. New fresh initiatives taken by GOI towards opening of massive bank a/c through the scheme of PMJDY providing financial and social security through DBTL scheme, PMJJY, PMSY and APY schemes to reach out to poor and vulnerable section of the society are way forward to financial inclusion. Financial Inclusion has not yielded the desired results and there is long road ahead but no doubt it is playing a significant role and is working on the positive side.

## REFERENCES

Agarwal, A. (2010). Financial Inclusion: Challenges and Opportunities. *Proceedings of the 23rd Skoch Summit*.

Agarwal, P. (2014). Financial Inclusion in India: a Review and Initiatives and Achievements. *IOSR Journal of Business and Management*, 16(6).

Arunachalam, R.S. (2008, January). Scoping paper on Financial Inclusion: Considerations and recommendations for UNDP. The UNDP lasting solutions to development challenges.

Beck, T., Demirguc-Kunt, A., & Peria, M.S.M. (2005). *Reaching Out: Access to and use of banking services across countries*. World Bank Policy Research (WPS 3754).

Bhaskarans, R. (2006). *Financial Inclusion: What needs to be done?* New Delhi: Reading on Financial Inclusion, IIBF & Taxman.

Chakrabarty, K.C. (2011, September). Financial Inclusion (Keynote address), Mumbai.

Chakrabarty, K.C. (2012, November).Financial Inclusion: Issues in Measurement and Analysis (Keynote address). *Proceedings of the BIS-BNM Workshop on Financial Inclusion Indicators*, Kuala Lumpur.

Demirguc–Kunt, A., & Klapper, L. (2012, April). Measuring Financial Inclusion (Policy Research Working Paper 6025). *World Bank*.

Rangarajan, C. (2008, January). Report of the committee on financial inclusion. *GOI*.

Srikanth, R. (2013, September). A Study on - Financial Inclusion - Role of Indian Banks in Reaching Out to Unbanked and Backward Areas. *International Journal of Applied Research and Studies*, 2(9).

Subbiah, N. (2014). Role of banks in financial inclusion. *Research Journal of Commerce and Behavioural Science*, 1(4).

Survey Report of the Committee on Medium-term Path on Financial Inclusion (Year 2013-2014). (2014). Reserve Bank of India.

# Chapter 6
# Perception of Residents on Ecotourism in Uttarakhand

**Shalini Singh**
*Sunbeam College for Women, India*

## ABSTRACT

*Uttarakhand has immense tourism potential for growth of tourist traffic. With the adverse effect of mass tourism and a growing environmental awareness, ecotourism now represents the fastest growing sub sector of the tourism industry, generating billions of dollars annually. Ecotourism plays an important role in economic, socio- cultural and environmental development of the society. Therefore the present research answers the question as to how does ecotourism affect the local community, economy, culture and the environment. According to the collected data the results of the study indicated that when residents in the community were asked to reveal ecotourism impacts, they assessed the perception of impacts in both negative and positive ways.*

## INTRODUCTION

Tourism in Uttarakhand has increased by 168 per cent (213 per cent according to the Uttarakhand tourism department) over the past twelve years. Unregulated and unplanned growth in tourism has led to environmental degradation. The state is a site of high biodiversity value, but is facing growing threats from a variety of sources including commercial logging, farming practices and tourism. The consequences of unchecked tourism in the state were seen on 16th June, when cloudbursts and extreme rains caused massive flooding and devastation in the state. As concern grows over the loss of both natural and cultural heritage in the region, attention is turning to strategies, which seek to link conservation with tourism development and generate incentives to conserve the resources.

Ecotourism is a tool for sustainable development in the region. It is defined by Ceballos-Lascuraintghjm (1996), of the World Conservation Union (IUCN), as an environmentally responsible trave0l and visitation to relatively undisturbed natural areas, in order to enjoy and appreciate nature (and any accompanying cultural features-both past and present) that promotes conservation, has low visitor negative impact and provides for beneficially active socio-economic involvement of local populations. Ecotourism means conservation of environment and to provide economic benefits to the local communities

DOI: 10.4018/978-1-4666-9908-3.ch006

## NEED AND SIGNIFICANCE OF THE STUDY

Uttarakhand has immense ecotourism potential for growth of tourist traffic and to provide lively hood to local communities. It is undoubtedly India's most beautiful canvas studded with green strokes, wild splash and quaint highlights. Ecotourism holds a very bright future and has acquired a great significance in the recent times but this potential has not been tapped effectively. The importance of environmental education is an important component of ecotourism. It has both positive and negative impacts. As concern grows over the loss of natural heritage in the area, it appears that this is the ideal time to facilitate ecologically and socially responsible to support the local community. Therefore the present study evaluates the perceptions of environmental, economical and socio-cultural impact of ecotourism in Uttarakhand.

### Study Area

In the present research, Uttarakhand has been selected as it has immense ecotourism potential for growth of tourist traffic. It is divided into two broad regions Garhwal and Kumaon. So, Hardwar, (Rishikesh) and Dehradun, (Mussoorie) districts from Garhwal region and Nanital, (Corbet National Park) and Almora from Kumaon region were selected deliberately by the researcher.

### Data Collection Techniques

The present study makes use of both primary as well as secondary data. For the selection of sample, Convenience sampling method was applied in this survey. Wide range of data was collected through secondary sources mainly from Directorate of Tourism Dehradun. References from research papers, books, articles, internets and newspapers were taken appropriately for interpretation of data.

### Survey Instrument

The questionnaire that was used for the local people perception regarding the environmental and socio-cultural impact of ecotourism consisted of two sections. The first part of the questionnaire gathered demographic information. The second part consisted of item that utilizes a 5- point Liker scale. The anchors include strongly agree, agree, undecided, disagree, strongly disagree

### Sample Size

Respondents younger than age 18 were automatically excluded. A total sample size of 110 local people participated in the study.

### Research Question

How Does Ecotourism Affect the Quality of Life of Local Community?

### Data Processing

In this study the method of collecting and gathering data from a part of population was used by the structured questionnaire. The software approach for the data analysis in this research was SPSS 12.version.

*Table 1. Age Distribution*

| Age | Frequency | %age |
|---|---|---|
| 18-25 | 42 | 42.0 |
| 26-32 | 25 | 25.0 |
| 33-40 | 21 | 21.0 |
| 41 and above | 12 | 12.0 |
| Total | 100 | 100.0 |

## Data Collection Analysis

### Age of Respondents

As indicated earlier, the current study targets those individuals aged 18 years or over within the areas investigated. This research identifies four different categories of respondent ages. Results of the current study indicate that out of the 100 respondents, majority of the respondents (67%) were of young age, (18-32), 21% were of middle age (33-42) and only 12% were of old age (41 and above). Hence it can be said that opinion stated here in this study is of younger generations. The age distribution of the respondents is shown below in table 1

### Gender of Respondents

Gender is the second demographical attribute outlined in this part of the research. Results of the data analysis indicated that 62% of the total respondents were males and that over 38% of the respondents were female. The result indicated in figure 1 shows an almost unequal distribution of males and females.

*Figure 1. Gender Distribution of respondents*

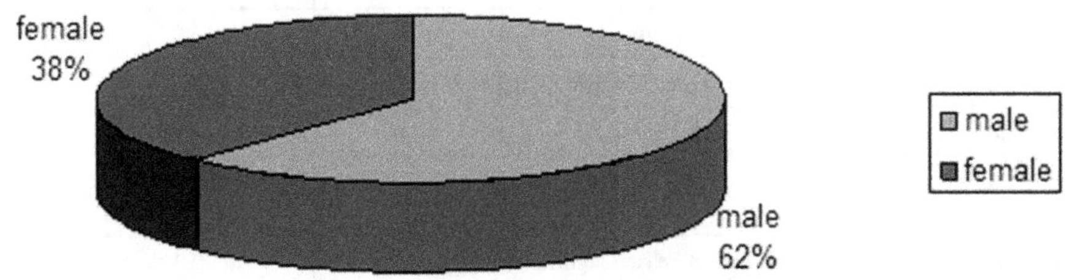

## Educational Level of respondents

Education is an issue critical to societal development. The current research identifies five different categories in respect of educational level, ranging from no education to university degree. Overall, the results indicate that 47% of the total respondents were holders of a university degree against 25% with secondary education certificates. 22% of the respondents were holder of high school degree and 3% had primary education and only 3% of the respondents had no education. What is really interesting in the data analysis results is that, almost 47% of the people who responded were holder of University degree.

## Descriptive analysis Of Respondents (Tables 2-4)

The first questionnaire that was designed to investigate the perception of local people towards environmental, economic and socio-cultural impacts of ecotourism consisted of 29 questions.

Table illustrates the responses of the study population (measured by Mean and Standard Deviation) on questions (1-10) of the research questionnaire.

## Results of Hypotheses Testing

To answer the research question following hypotheses were made and the results of the study indicated that when residents in the community were asked to reveal ecotourism impacts, they assessed the perception of ecotourism impact in both negative and positive ways.

*Table 2. Perceptions of respondents towards the Economic impacts of ecotourism*

| *Q #* | | *RESULT* | |
|---|---|---|---|
| | | *MEAN* | *S.D* |
| 1 | Ecotourism brings important economic benefits to the residents of the community | 4.10 | 1.049 |
| 2 | One of the most important aspects of ecotourism is that it has created investment and variety of jobs for the residents in the community | 4.13 | 1.169 |
| 3 | Due to ecotourism infrastructure at Uttaranchal has been enhanced such as roads, schools, hospitals, restaurants etc. | 4.02 | 1.205 |
| 4 | Ecotourism generates tax revenue for the local government | 3.75 | 1.343 |
| 5 | Working in ecotourism makes me feel insecure about my future employment | 3.97 | 1.242 |
| 6 | Our standard of living has increased due to tourist spending in the community | 3.99 | 1.226 |
| 7 | Ecotourism generates foreign exchange earnings for the National government | 4.09 | 1.045 |
| 8 | Local people are participating in ecotourism related activities, like guide and home stays. | 3.98 | 1.286 |
| 9 | The price of many goods and services has increased significantly because of ecotourism | 2.12 | 1.241 |
| 10 | Real estate prices have increased because of ecotourism | 2.62 | 1.523 |

*Table 3.* ***Perceptions of respondents towards the Socio-cultural impacts of ecotourism***

| Q # | Statement | Mean | S.D |
|---|---|---|---|
| 11 | Ecotourism encourages a variety of cultural activities for local residents | 3.22 | 1.586 |
| 12 | Ecotourism helps local culture alive and maintain cultural identity | 4.04 | 1.109 |
| 13 | Ecotourism has increased the image of Uttaranchal and its local culture pride | 4.02 | 1.044 |
| 14 | The cultural exchange between residents and tourist is valuable and pleasant for the residents | 3.96 | 1.196 |
| 15 | Increased ecotourism causes more recreational facilities for local residents | 3.55 | 1.328 |
| 16 | Results in unpleasantly overcrowded in parks and the surroundings. | 3.30 | 1.520 |
| 17 | The commercial demand of tourist causes change in style and traditional arts and craft | 2.48 | 1.521 |
| 18 | Alcoholism and Prostitution has increased due to tourist arrival in the region | 3.14 | 1.456 |
| 19 | Earnings from ecotourism, has attracted children in the community to drop out school at an early age. | 3.15 | 1.465 |
| 20 | Ecotourism has increased crime in the region | 3.08 | 1.440 |

*Table 4. Perceptions of respondents towards the Environmental impacts of ecotourism*

| Q # | Statement | Mean | S. D. |
|---|---|---|---|
| 21 | Ecotourism brings environmental pollution | 2.81 | 1.489 |
| 22 | Ecotourism activities like rafting and camping causes water pollution in the lakes and basin | 3.26 | 1.468 |
| 23 | Tourists littering destroys the beauty of the landscape | 3.46 | 1.480 |
| 24 | Ecotourism produces noise, littering and congestion | 2.80 | 1.470 |
| 25 | Ecotourism has contributed to preservation of the natural environment and protection of the wildlife in the community | 3.84 | 1.228 |
| 26 | Ecotourism imposes less negative impact on the state natural resources | 3.79 | 1.297 |
| 27 | Hotels, Airlines and other related tourism business throw away tons of garbage a year | 3.80 | 1.287 |
| 28 | Ecotourism has improved the ecological environment in the community in many ways | 3.19 | 1.488 |
| 29 | Ecotourism does not contribute to the negative effect of vegetation and loss of meadows and green space | 2.96 | 1.377 |

*$H_1$: There will be a significant relationship between environmental impacts of ecotourism and demographic variables such as age, level of education and income.*

In the study the correlation coefficient was used to measures the strength of linear between the environmental impact of ecotourism and the demographic variables. The results revealed that there is no significant relationship between the demographic variables and the environmental impact, explicitly the result confirmed that the sig. value of correlation for the whole set of variables is not statistically significant. As a result, the null hypothesis is rejected (table 5).

*Table 5. (see annexture 1) Correlation between environmental impact and age and income*

| | Environment | Income of respondents | Age of respondents |
|---|---|---|---|
| Income | -.098 | | |
| Age | -.092 | .088 | |
| Education | .130 | -.100 | .115 |

(P>0.5)

***$H_2$*:There will be a significant relationship between the perceptions of the economic impacts of ecotourism and the demographic variables such as age, level of education and income.**

This result revealed that there was no significant relationship between the perceptions of economic impacts of ecotourism and the demographic variables such as education and level of education, explicitly that the sig. value of correlation for the whole set of variables is not statistically significant. In addition the result of the study revealed that there was significant negative relationship between economic impact of ecotourism and age (-.270**) where the correlation was significant at 0.01 level. Undoubtedly, the later result confirms that the perception of economic impact of ecotourism has influenced the young people. As a result, the hypothesis can be accepted only for age (table 6).

***$H_3$*: There will be a significant relationship between the perceptions of sociocultural impacts of ecotourism and demographic variables such as age, level of education and income.**

The result of the hypothesis shows that there is no significant relationship between age and sociocultural impact as that the sig. value of correlation for the whole set of variables is not statistically significant. In addition the result of the study revealed that there was significant positive relationship between sociocultural impact of ecotourism and income (.275*) where the correlation was significant at 0.05 level.

Undoubtedly, the later result confirms that the level of income influences the perceptions of the local people towards the sociocultural impacts of ecotourism. As a result the hypotheses can be accepted with respect to income. See table 7

## Findings and Discussions

Ecotourism activities have affected the environment both in the positive and the negative ways. In addition the result of the study revealed that there was no significant relationship between the perceptions of environmental impacts of ecotourism and the demographic variables such as age, income and level of

*Table 6. Correlation between economic impact and age, level of education and income*

| | Economic | Income of respondent | Age of respondent | Education of respondent |
|---|---|---|---|---|
| Income | .075 | | | |
| Age | -.270** | -.077 | | |
| Education | -.102 | .055 | .258 | |

** P<-0.01

*Table 7. Correlation between sociocultural impact and demographic variables*

| | Sociocultural | Age of respondents | Education of respondents | Income of respondents |
|---|---|---|---|---|
| **Age** | .174 | | | |
| **Education** | .009 | .115 | | |
| **income** | **.257*** | .088 | -.100 | |

** (P< 0.05)

education. The residents strongly reported that ecotourism brings environmental pollution. They agreed that though its ecotourism activities but tourists littering destroys the beauty of the landscape. Activities like rafting produces water pollution in the lakes and rivers. The Mountaineers uses unguided Himalayan treks and trails, which causes severe damage to sensitive flora and fauna. The Ecotourism activities like camping in remote areas are responsible for the destruction of vegetation, soil, river sand and pollution of the river Ganga. The camp sites are also responsible for disturbing the wildlife of the region. On the other side it has also affected the environment of the people in positive ways. It has contributed to preservation of the natural environment and protection of the wildlife in the community. Due to ecotourism many parks (Nanda Devi Park was closed in 1982 and in 1988 it was converted into Biosphere reserves) have been protected from environmental degradation and a regular care is taken to preserve the important wildlife and national parks. It imposes less negative impact on the state natural resources It has improved the ecological environment in the community in many ways. For example Night treks for tourists have been voluntarily discontinued in Camp Kyari as the villagers realized that they disturbed wild animals.

Regarding the economic impact of ecotourism result of the hypotheses stated that the economic impact of ecotourism was found more on the young people and thus we can that more and more youth are being involved in ecotourism activities. The residents believed that ecotourism has brought important economic benefits to them and has improved their economic situations.

Ecotourism affects the socio-culture of the residents in both positive and negative ways however the positive effects were found more on the local people. The result of the study revealed that the perception of the positive socio-cultural impact was more on higher income group people compare to lower income group people. The vast majority of the respondents believe that ecotourism has increased the image of Uttaranchal and its local culture pride, that it creates more recreational facilities for local residents. In contrast the ecotourism development has also negatively affected the socio-cultural environment of the people. Respondents reported that crime, alcoholism and prostitution have increased in the region, especially due to foreign tourists coming to the region. Tourists leave behind their life style and spending pattern and the youths of the region are more affected by the life style of the tourists and they copy their behaviour and living style.

## REFERENCES

Alambath, M. (2008). Forest faces the evils of ecotourism. *Iftrac Tourism World*, *1*, 42–45.

Alhasant, S. (2008). *Socio-cultural Impacts of Tourism on the local community at Jordan*. Coventry University.

Anil, K. (2007). Tourism: Impact of Negative Factors On The Host Community-Case Of Kerala. *The Journal of Business Studies*, *4*(8), 39–43.

Bansal, S. P. (2002). Socio-cultural impact of tourism in Himachal Pradesh according to Bansal and Garg. In Tourism in New Millennium (pp. 370-390). Chandigarh: Abhishek Publications.

Bansal, S. P. (2002). Ecotourism vis a vis Holistic Regional Development according to D.Singhai & Gautam. In Tourism in New Millennium (pp. 331-348). Chandigarh: Abhishek Publications.

Beeler, B. G. (2000). *Opportunities and threat to local sustainable development: Introducing ecotourism to Venado Island, Costa Rica* [Thesis]. Lund University, Sweden.

Lindberg, K., Wood, M.E., & Engeldrum, D. (1999). *Ecotourism a Guide for Planner and Managers* (Vol. 2). Dehradun: Natraj Publishers.

Lindberg, K. (1993). *Hawkins, D.E. Ecotourism: A Guide for Planners and Managers* (Vol. 1). North Bennington, VT: The Ecotourism Society.

Malviya, S. (2005). Tourism, Environment and the Society (pp. 62-72). Delhi: Isha Books.

Nigam, D. (2002). Tourism Environment and development of Garhwal Himalaya (pp. 43-48). New Delhi: Mittal Publications.

Nigam, S. C. (2002). Ecotourism and Sustainable Development (pp. 1-2). New Delhi: Rajat Publications.

Vogelsong, H. (2001). *Assessing the Economic Impact of Ecotourism Developments on the Albermarle/ Pamlico Region*. Retrieved from www.cabi.org

Ward, N.K. (1997). *Ecotourism: Reality or Rhetoric*. Retrieved from www.planeta.com

# Chapter 7
# Women's Empowerment and Socio-Economic Development in MENA Region:
## Adaptation to Trade Policies and Access to Market for Promoting Entrepreneurship

**Malek Jihene**
*University El Manar, Tunisia*

## ABSTRACT

*Women plays a vital role in business and they are a major resource potential in entrepreneurship. Unfortunately, women entrepreneurs tend to face greater obstacles in access to credit, market knowledge, business needs and by the limits of trade agreements and the constraints of trade policies. Thus, there is a need for more efficient policies for the development of female entrepreneurship. The chapter offer analysis of state of the empowerment of women in the globalization. Then, the analysis of the theoretical foundations is for justifying the role of women as entrepreneur and promoter of gender equality and constraints that they are facing. Then, it is an opportunity to offer a brief overview about women in the socio-economic development in MENA region. Finally, the question is how to create policies for the business sector to promote their empowerment. A SWOT analysis is done to explore challenges and limits and offer some recommendations .This chapter is an opportunity to explore new area about the degree of adaptation of women's entrepreneur to the trade policies rules.*

## INTRODUCTION

Global interest in the development of female entrepreneurship and exploring policies to support recently increased due to the gender gap in entrepreneurial activity. On the other hand, the under-development of female entrepreneurship represents an untapped potential for prosperity growth. Through entrepreneurial activities, women create jobs, generate income to reduce poverty, achieve economic independence and contribute to sustainable development. Although there is a great, need of creating more favorable condi-

DOI: 10.4018/978-1-4666-9908-3.ch007

tions for the development and strengthening of women's entrepreneurship. Therefore, policies better designed and funded strong and targeted measures at increasing women's empowerment. Thus, empowering women economically need it is to improve the following goals: increase the rate of entrepreneurship of women who go through improved policies, strengthen the institutional support and establish a public-private dialogue, improve women's access to credit and financial services, improve services business development and reduce gender inequality in access to information and markets.

Unfortunately, in developing world women entrepreneurs tend to face greater obstacles in access to credit due to systemic failures and market knowledge and business needs. In addition, financial institutions and providers of business development do not serve them, and they often lack access to consumer and market opportunities for business networks. Then, the access to market for women entrepreneur and the building of networking relation is constraint by the limits of trade agreements and the constraints of trade policies. In addition, women entrepreneur are facing everywhere the rule and mechanisms of Trade policy at the national level for cross-border trade activities, which is intertwined with domestic fiscal, monetary and labor market policies, and linked to other policies such as foreign aid and investment, structural adjustment, debt and development. Indeed, Trade liberalization entails the deregulation of foreign investment through the reduction of barriers to international trade, such as tariffs. Liberalization also means instituting macroeconomic reforms such as export promotion. Indeed, with trade liberalization, countries are encouraged to specialize in particular goods and services according to their own comparative advantage. Women entrepreneurs are facing trade rules and can participate to the building of comparative advantage and adapt the WTO rules in different sectors.

This chapter is an opportunity to explore the empowerment of women on socio-economic development. Firstly, the Analysis of the theoretical foundations is justifying the role of women as entrepreneur and gender equality in growth and to analysis the limits and constraints of women's entrepreneurs. Then, it is an opportunity to offer a brief overview about role and importance of women in the socio-economic development in MENA region. Then, is the analysis of actual state of the empowerment of women from the actual state of women in the Universal Millennium Goals and Sustainable Development Goals post-2015. And a comparative analysis is done to explain disparities between determinants of women's economic empowerment and also between countries. Finally, the question is how to create policies for the business sector to promote the empowerment of women and how they are adopted and implemented for developing countries. Finally, some recommendations are offered to expand economic opportunities for women.

## BACKGROUND: LITERATURE REVIEW

### Analysis of the Theoretical Foundations Justifying the Role of Women as Entrepreneur and Gender Equality in Growth

Women's empowerment is a critical aspect of achieving gender equality. Women's empowerment is achieved when women and girls acquire the power to act freely and fulfill their potential. While empowerment comes from within individuals themselves, cultures, societies, and institutions creating conditions that facilitate the possibilities for empowerment. The process of empowerment involves changes to multiple aspects of a woman's life. The World Bank (2007) defined women's economic empowerment principally on markets, which is, "…making markets work for women and empowering women to compete in markets". Access to markets is important because inequality prevents women from having equal access to productive resources and economic opportunities. Indeed, economic empowerment is the capacity of women to participate, contribute and benefit from growth processes as said Eyben (2008). Economic empowerment increases women's access to economic resources and opportunities including jobs, financial services, property and other productive assets, skills development and market information. In fact, women's economic participation and empowerment are fundamental to strengthening women's rights and enabling women to have control and influence in society. Unfortunately, women are facing failures limiting their empowerment especially in facing trade liberalization and trade rules.

## What about the Impact of Trade Policy on Gender Equality and the empowerment of Women in Theoretical Foundations and Empirical Studies?

In analyzing the relation between gender inequality, globalization and economic growth, there is an effect of trade policy on economic and social activities. Indeed, due to socio-cultural, political and economic factors, women tend to be more affected by the negative effects of trade liberalization than man. In addition, they are facing challenges when it comes to taking advantage of the opportunities trade offers due to gender biases in education and training. Gender inequalities in the distribution of income and command of resources is existing, as well as unequal access to productive inputs such as credit, land, and technology, etc. Some studies on gender and globalization have found that higher trade openness may not necessarily lead to higher gender equality. Indeed, Forsythe, Korzeniewicz, Majid, Weathers and Durrant (2003) examined the effect of economic reforms and economic growth on gender inequality. Their results suggest that besides policies, socio-economic characteristics play a role in gender equality. They found that macroeconomic policies including changes in trade policy do not explain only gender inequality. And Morrison, Raju and Sinha (2007) argued that gender equality occurs through greater access of women to land and credit market and their enhanced decision making power within households. While a large number of studies have found that gender equality and economic growth are positively related, the increased trade opportunities through increased employment and output that are expected to benefit all population groups including women. Baliamoune-Lutz (2006) found that increased trade openness leads to an increase in gender inequality in Africa. Indeed, the increased trade openness leads to increase in the supply of unskilled labour and causes gender inequality to increase. Then, Shultz (2005) examined the relationship between trade liberalization and economic status of women and showed that trade restrictions in the form of tariffs, quotas or other restrictions such as, on foreign exchange lead to low trade and affect women's education and health. The study indicated that trade liberalization and globalization through spillover effects and increased demand for female labour could lead to increased education and health facilities for women. In addition, Seguino (2006) examined the impact of globalization on gender equality and suggest that economic growth has not been beneficial for gender equality in the Latin American and Caribbean countries and it has actually had negative effect on some indicators due to out-migration of women in low paid insecure jobs and men's increased financial insecurity because of their reduced earnings leading to domestic violence. The study also measured the impact of four variables on gender equity in well-being-female as: bargaining power, structure of production, macroeconomic condition, and government spending. Her results showed that production structure or shift to manufacturing impacts gender equity positively. In addition, Pande (2007) urged argued that women in the informal sector with poor access to land, credit, education and health facilities remain marginalized despite globalization. Because, they are often exploited by working long hours and paid low wages and in the same time safer from lack voice and participation. He pointed out that the emergence of self-help groups, which provide finance to women to start entrepreneurial ventures is a beneficial initiative. Some other studies as Fontana et al. (1998), Fontana and Wood (2000), Cağatay (2001) also found that in the agricultural based economies trade actually leads to increase in gender inequality. And Stotsky (2006) argued also that inequalities in women's opportunities limit their ability to take advantage of beneficial macroeconomic and structural policies especially on sub-Saharan Africa.

Market access and enterprise development have been considered as fundamental policies through which developing countries can be engaged in international trade. However, liberalization under the WTO rules has not significantly increased women's access to credit, nor has it provided more opportunities to use domestic savings for entrepreneurial activities due to some limits as structural gender inequalities in property rights and ownership. Rather than introducing policies to support women's access to credit, liberalisation policies have perpetuated the discrimination against poor women in the mainstream financial market by focusing on urban areas and more profitable economic sectors and the exclusion of poor women in the informal sector and operate mostly in SMEs that have to reply on the informal financial sector as said Randriamaro (2001).

In addition, changes in investment regimes mean that foreign investors are not held to particular performance requirements by the governments of the countries in which they operate. Because, they will be able to produce goods in country at competitive prices, which can lead to the displacement of weaker economic actors as women from their segments of the domestic markets. This is likely to have adverse impacts on women-owned and other SMEs. For this reasons, some case studies suggest that regional trading arrangements are likely to offer opportunities that are the best suited to women, who are mostly small-scale producers and traders. Because they do not need large export markets and may find neighbouring markets more familiar and easier to deal with. Especially, in informal cross-border trade. In addition, the Bridge Report (2006) offered also some recommendations for businesswomen, facing trade policies and rules limiting their level of economic empowerment, as: increase understanding of laws, regulations, standards and policy processes related to trade, develop members' management, financial and negotiating skills, focus on the production and commercialisation of high value-added products in the sectors and segments where there are some comparative advantage, including through the upgrading of production, the creation of cooperatives and other forms of clustering and networking at the national, regional and international levels to increase economies of scale and bargaining power, and to address global competition, make full use of ICTs for market contacts, information, and business opportunities opened up by them and to promote women members' understanding of the potentials of fair and ethical trade schemes to promote gender equality .

Otherwise, in analyzing the role of technological learning in competitive environment, the UNCTAD Report (2009) offer some remarks that trade policies have a significant impact on the viability of micro and small enterprises and thus affect the large number of women who own or work in these businesses. Trade integration may offer opportunities for enterprises to grow; it also exposes them to international competition. In fact, SME generally operate in protected markets and a swift increase in foreign competition forces them to grow and upgrade technologically. In fact, technological learning and upgrading is one of the processes that firms must go through in order to become more competitive, which requires adaptation.

Unfortunately, women entrepreneurs in developing countries often have less access to marketing networks, capital, credit and technical knowledge, all of which are essential to improving production competitiveness. In this regard, policies aimed specifically at facilitating access to credit for small enterprises, organizing exporter associations and providing technical training on the compliance requirements of the export markets are likely to smooth the transition of small and micro enterprises to an open market environment. In addition, there are a need to some support that should also be provided to women entrepreneurs to improve their business management skills. Thus, the priority is to remove barriers to female entrepreneurship and promote inclusive financial services and to be adapted to trade policies. Indeed, private sector development should support female entrepreneurs by removing the barriers to the development of women-owned enterprises. However, most women in low-income and developing countries have micro or small enterprises operating mainly in the informal economy and are almost invisible in large and medium enterprises due to multiple obstacles as: limited access to education and training, few are members of business associations, have less freedom to select their business sector, and are subject to discriminatory attitudes in property, marital and inheritance laws. Indeed, those can be relied to personal savings or on contributions from relatives to fund their enterprises, and without property ownership, they lack collateral to access credit from financial institutions. They also face administrative barriers as well as lack of information, which limit business development and hinder graduation from the informal to the formal economy.

Thus, enabling women to become successful in business development requires addressing underlying new policy and regulatory constraints. Thereby women's access to economic resources and business support to start, formalize and expand their businesses can be ensured. In order to be successful, sector policies need to continue supporting business training, start-up services and mentorship for women linked to micro-finance while promoting measures that set the basic for a more business-enabling environment and inclusive financial systems. In fact, many programmes exist in the developing world that offer small-scale entrepreneurship training for women, provide market information, promote market access through, for example, trade fairs, and improve business management and financial skills. In addition, services through business incubators are offered to young people, men and women, and a few are offered exclusively to women and girls. Training programmes designed to suit the needs of women do exist as well as programmes that set criteria ensuring that at least a certain percentage of participants are women. These are examples of initiatives, which can be developed. In addition, access to non-collateralized credit is important for starting or growing businesses but the size and duration of loans women may need is also important to be fixed in the valuable limit. Even when loans are accessible, they are often too small to provide sufficient capital to start or grow an enterprise. There are a need of measures to address these issues include investing in product development that responds to the need for larger loans and longer terms in micro-credit programmes and setting up equity lines as incentives for commercial banks to lend to women. In another case, start-up investments in micro-finance can be also an effective solution.

There are various factors, which can justify the divergence orientation of women to become entrepreneur and empower their self. Acquiring resources, as funds essential for their new venture, constitutes one of the key hindrances for women as said Orser et al., (2006) and Fuller-Love, (2008). In fact, women face many difficulties in raising finance and only a small percentage of women manage to raise venture capital as notified in Brush (2002). Indeed, the possibility to obtain venture capital is dependent on the industry in which an entrepreneur operates. The fact that fewer women engage in entrepreneurship based on technological innovations results, due to education. Because, women are under-represented in science and technology related fields as advanced in OECD Report (2004). Some evidence supporting the idea that women, making financial decisions, are more risk averse than men and they have lower turnover expectations in Harding, (2007). Other studies prove that men are more willing to grow their new venture in order to achieve financial success, whereas women recognize financial success as only one of many reasons to achieve growth in Brush, Cooper, (2012). According to Minniti (2005), fewer women know other entrepreneurs and deem their skills as adequate to run a business. Apart from education and industry choice, issues and that man are more confident in their success and abilities than women. So developing confidence in female entrepreneurs is one of important aspect that should be considered. In addition, Ascher (2012), basing on research recognises individual motivation, demography, economic and social environments, education, family networks and unemployment as the factors affecting female entrepreneurship, including the manner of perception. Among motivational factors, the author enumerates: the need for autonomy and flexibility, the need to generate income, the need for achievement, self-determination and personal growth, the need for change, frustration, boredom and dissatisfaction with the present job, previous unfriendly work environment, etc. In addition, In the Report of World Bank-IFC (2012), equal opportunities for women in business and the workplace depend on the interplay of various economic, social and cultural factors. This report recognized many issues that affect women's economic opportunities, but focused on one particular area, which are: aspects of the formal legal and regulatory environment that enable women to manage their own businesses find and maintain jobs. Although many women in developing economies work or start businesses in the informal economy that when women move from the informal to the formal economy, they obtain greater opportunities in higher-paying industries, greater social protection and formal mechanisms for recourse should their rights be denied.

## MAIN FOCUS OF THE CHAPTER

There is a need for women to participate actively in the achievement of global goals during many years and to pursue gender empowerment. Moving from the Universal Millennium Goals to sustainable development goals offer new areas for women's economic empowerment.

### Women from Universal Millennium Goals to Sustainable Development Goals

The UN and the international community have made significant progress in advancing gender equality and empowerment of women and girls. Since the adoption of the Beijing Declaration and Platform for Action, there has been steady progress towards areas that include eliminating gender disparity in primary school attendance; access to sexual and reproductive health-care services; an increase in the number of women in national parliaments in some regions and an increase in women's labour market participation. In many countries, gender inequality persists and women continue to face discrimination in access to education, work and economic assets, and be active in government's participation. For example, in every developing region, women tend to hold less secure jobs than men, with fewer social benefits as advanced in the Millennium Development Goals Report (2014).

Actually, the on-going intergovernmental discussions on Sustainable Development Goals provide an important opportunity to build on the lessons learnt from the Millennium Development Goals. Otherwise, the role of women is essential in sustainable development in a number of international norms and agreements with the goal 5 which is focused on empowerment of women, by: ensuring women's full and effective participation and equal opportunities for leadership at all levels of decision-making in political, economic, and public life; undertaking reforms to give women equal rights to economic resources, as well as access to ownership and control over land and other forms of property, financial services, inheritance, and natural resources in accordance with national laws; enhancing the use of enabling technologies, to promote women's empowerment and adopt and strengthen sound policies and enforceable legislation for the promotion of gender equality and the empowerment of all women and girls at all levels .

In the same time, the role of women is existing in the others sustainable development goals related to the area of: poverty food security, sustainable agriculture; education, sustainable management of water and sanitation, productive employment and decent work, resilient and sustainable cities and to combat climate change. There are some recommendations in this area notified in the Report of UN Women (2014) that accelerate the realization of gender equality as: assess investments in services and infrastructure in terms of the gender-specific costs, benefits and risks they present for the realization of women's and girls' rights and capabilities, with particular focus on the poorest groups; prioritize investments to ensure universal access to water, with specific attention to distance, quality, affordability and the ways in which women use water, with a view to reducing unpaid care work; ensure access to clean, private and safe sanitation for all women and girls that is responsive to gender-specific needs and addressing the risk of violence in accessing sanitation facilities; invest at scale in efficient solid-fuel stoves or cooking technologies that use cleaner fuels, especially in rural and peri-urban areas, and encourage stove uptake by involving women in stove design, testing and social marketing; invest at scale in initiatives to provide basic and affordable electricity access to unserved and underserved populations, particularly rural populations, with a view to enabling health-care facilities to function; supporting income generation and educational attainment; and reducing women's unpaid care work, enabling them to enjoy leisure time; ensure women's full and equal participation and leadership in decision-making processes at all levels to determine investment in and usage of water, sanitation and energy technologies at the household, local, national, regional and global levels and finally develop public-private-civil sector alliances that enable investments at scale to guarantee universal access to essential services and infrastructure, while ensuring compliance with human rights standards. Globally, all this goals are including in the new area of sustainable development goals post-2015 and can be part of new strategies that will be implemented to empower women and promote gender equality. Thus, the transition from universal millennium goals to sustainable development goals require to take on account that empowering women need to include the goals and initiatives that are not achieved by the last goals and to add new areas as: access to water, sanitation, clean cook stoves and electricity are the backbone of a decent quality of life and there is significant underinvestment in these areas, relative to the global need and this domains are directly connected to environmental sustainability.

One of the most constraints needed to be included in the sustainable development goals is the transition of women entrepreneur from the informal to formal sector. For Example, MENA's having one of the largest informal sectors in the world and women entrepreneurs are facing significant difficulties. There is a need for some policies, those have the effect of encouraging the transfer of activities from the informal economy to the formal economy in my opinion. Indeed, political and legal context for promoting entrepreneurship by lowering the costs of starting and operating a business, including through simplified procedures for reporting and licensing, regulation appropriate and reasonable and fair taxation need to be implemented. It also reinforces the benefits of legalization: easy access to business customers, credit conditions advantageous legal protection, contract enforcement, access to technology, subsidies, and foreign exchange markets as local and international markets. After become part in the formal sector, the question is how the competitiveness of entrepreneurship's in global value chains can be improved by increasing women's access to technical assistance contracts, scientific and technical cooperation, creation joint activities, training programs and information, industrial franchise, patent license or expertise, partnership network for research of opportunities.

## Women Empowerment Indexes in the MENA Countries

In front of the new globalization process and multilateral rules, women's entrepreneurship and empowerment need new policies, laws, formal agencies and institutions that can be implemented to make easier the entrepreneurship process.

Since independence, Arab and North African countries have struggled with multiple challenges. In the World Economic Forum Report (2014), the Middle East and North Africa region closed 60% of its overall gender gap in 2014. Despite experiencing the biggest absolute improvement compared to 2013, the region remains in the sixth position. It continues to rank last on the economic participation and opportunity sub-index, with only 42% of the economic gender gap closed. Compared to 2006, the region saw the third-largest improvement on the overall Index score. The region has also shown the third largest relative change compared to its own 2006 overall Index score. In the area of Economic Participation and Opportunity, three countries from the region are above average, as Tunisia and Algeria. However, most countries from the region have had varying degrees of success at integrating women into the economy and in decision-making in order to reap the benefits of this investment: Tunisia (123) and Algeria (126). Egypt holds the 129th position. Next are Morocco (133) and Jordan (134). Jordan is followed by Lebanon (135). In addition, Turkey is ranking 125nd due to the high performing on the economic participation and opportunity sub-index. As showed in Table 1, there are some few disparities between countries and from one year to another.

In addition, in the GEM Report (2012) offered also an outlook about the state Women's participation in entrepreneurship that varies markedly in the MENA countries. Lower female total entrepreneurial activity levels are evident at either end of the economic development scale. Overall participation in entrepreneurship, females, is typically higher in factor-driven economies, most likely due to such factors as an undersupply of jobs and the ability or tendency toward operating in the informal sector. The MENA region, however, reports the lowest total entrepreneurial activity levels among women need more development economically and which need more target policies. In general, female TEA rates in economies and regions track similarly to that of males, albeit at lower levels (see Table 2).

While the MENA region has a high proportion of early development-stage, factor driven economies, participation rates in entrepreneurship run almost opposite to this region's southern neighbors. In addition, the lowest levels of female TEA can be seen in this region. Women also rarely run established businesses with a problem of high discontinuance rates which is not accompanied by a lot of startup efforts. In addition, with regard to attitudes, women show moderate levels on most of the indicators. The issue, however, is more around gender gaps. Additionally, women also appear to have trouble converting their intentions into actual starts. For every woman entrepreneur in the MENA region, there are the highest average proportion of necessity motives. Women entrepreneurs in this region have large families. They

*Table 1. North Africa and Middle East GCI and sub-index empowerment of women:*

| | Algeria | Egypt | Jordan | Lebanon | Morocco | Tunisia | Turkey |
|---|---|---|---|---|---|---|---|
| **GCI index** | 0.618 | 0.606 | 0.597 | 0.592 | 0.599 | 0.627 | 0.618 |
| **Sub-index economic participation and opportunity** | 0.393 | 0.461 | 0.358 | 0.432 | 0.4 | 0.436 | 0.453 |

Source: The Global Gender Gap (2014)

*Table 2. Total Entrepreneurial Activity (TEA) for Female Adults (18 – 64 years) in 67 Economies:*

| Country | Development Stage | TEA Rate (% Adult Population Female) | Established Business Ownership Rate (% Adult Population) | Discontinuing a Business in the Rate Past Year (% Adult Population) | At Least a Post-Secondary Degree | Business Have One Founder (%TEA) |
|---|---|---|---|---|---|---|
| Algeria | Factor-efficiency | 5 | 1 | 33 | 45 | 50 |
| Egypt | Factor-efficiency | 2 | 1 | 2 | 24 | 51 |
| Tunisia | Factor-efficiency | 3 | 7 | 11 | 33 | 95 |
| Turkey | Factor-innovation | 7 | 3 | 8 | 51 | 43 |

Source: Global Entrepreneurship Monitor, 2012

operate primarily one-woman businesses with no employees. What is distinct about the MENA region, though, is that despite some positive attitudes and intentions among women, as well as necessity drivers, there is a need for more women to start businesses. The high discontinuance rates may be a signal of the difficulties faced by women in this region when they do start. In addition, although showing better gender parity than other developed regions, entrepreneurship seems to attract young and middle class women. Among women entrepreneurs, youth rates are 63% higher than those in the 35 to 65-age range and nearly 90% of female entrepreneurs in this economy that operate their businesses on their own, without other founders: the highest of all the regions. At the same time, they are highly likely to employ others.

In analyzing the entrepreneurship perceptions of women in the MENA regions, there are some recommendations:

- There is a strong link between women's perceptions about entrepreneurship and their entering this activity (see Table 3). Where women believed there were good opportunities for starting businesses, and where they had confidence, ability and spirit for this activity, there were more female entrepreneurs.
- Women are facing difficulties moving from one phase to another in the entrepreneurship process. At the front end, intent is not always accompanied by actual starts. Women may want to start businesses in many cases, but the problematic idea is this intent is translating into action. At the later stages of the process, there are many cases that are discontinuing or not sustaining their business into maturity.

*Table 3. Entrepreneurial Perceptions for Women in some MENA Economies by Economic Development Level*

| Countries | Sees Good Opportunities | Has Capabilities to Start | Fear to Failure for those Seeing Opportunities | Intend to Start in the Next Three Years (Non-Entrepreneurs) | Personally Know as Entrepreneurs |
|---|---|---|---|---|---|
| Algeria | 43 | 49 | 37 | 20 | 55 |
| Egypt | 53 | 45 | 38 | 35 | 23 |
| Tunisia | 23 | 50 | 24 | 16 | 28 |
| Turkey | 35 | 37 | 36 | 12 | 24 |

Source: Global entrepreneurship Monitor (2013) women's Report

*Table 4. Percentage of Women New and Established Business Owners with No Employees in some MENA Economies, and Economic Development Level*

| Countries | Percent New Business Owners with No Employees | Percent Established Business Owners with No Employees |
|---|---|---|
| Algeria | 5 | 12 |
| Egypt | 2 | 0 |
| Tunisia | 42 | 30 |
| Turkey | 10 | 5 |

Source: Global entrepreneurship Monitor (2013) women's Report

- Women more often operate businesses as single founders and without employees (see Table 4). However, they cannot leverage the ideas, abilities, resources and connections of co-founders. Thus, these is limiting the contribution to the ability to grow a business, which can due to cultural value and how this is perceived in male versus female businesses.
- Industry participation in women's entrepreneurship shows a dominance of consumer-oriented business activity, and accompanying that, less industry sector diversity. In some cases, well educated women may be running lower potential businesses. This may indicate either a mismatch between their education levels and confidence, or a lack of more relevant training for entrepreneurship. Because they are not engaged in sectors that typically rely on capital and knowledge.
- Women often start businesses out of necessity because they have large households and low education levels, perhaps leading to shorter term concerns and low entry-barrier businesses, yet fewer longer term prospects.
- Low rates of international business activities among women are evident. While the size of the internal market and competitive characteristics may explain these results, an overly local focus may represent missed opportunities for women.
- Young women entrepreneurs is may benefit from venturing out at an age when they have fewer family-related financial obligations and, being at the start of their careers, when they have fewer opportunity costs associated with higher level positions and salaries as employees. Early entrepreneurial endeavors may benefit young women even as they seek other career pursuits later on (as entrepreneurial employees, repeat entrepreneurs or as investors, managers or value chain participants with other entrepreneurs).
- Finance accounts for twice the proportion of business discontinuance among women, the visibly associated with sophisticated financial systems for entrepreneurship is needed.
- Women have lower aspirations for growing their businesses. This finding raises questions about education and policy. While most of these policies may be considered gender neutral at first time, inside of each are issues to be addressed, such as entrepreneurship training programs for women that emphasize economic core types of business rather than growth, and policies that increase social welfare benefits for corporate women.
- Addressing women's entrepreneurship in many societies will require a combination of broader efforts and more targeted ones as those providing better access to education, and these efforts will enhance entrepreneurial activity. However, some wide-ranging initiatives, like promoting societal role models, may be less effective when women are facing many constraints.

- Broader initiatives are needed to take into account the overall conditions in the environment. It may be worthwhile to assess the evolution of attitudes, both in how women see the environment around them and how they perceive themselves relative to this activity.
- Opportunities to encourage and support women entrepreneurs should not wait for conditions to improve in an economy or region. Targeted efforts may therefore be warranted; for example, role models might be more effective for women in early stage educational programs In addition, education and training programs may focus on growth and sustainability of the business as well as the start-up and nascent phases.

Globally, this analysis provide a wealth of information to stimulate conversations and improve understanding about the women that start businesses and the ecosystem in which they operate. The ultimate goal is to enable women of all kinds and in all places to have the opportunities and resources to successfully exercise their entrepreneurial ambitions.

## THE COMPARATIVE ANALYSIS

### SWOT Analysis and Success Stories of Women's Entrepreneurship in Tunisia

The female population in Tunisian in 2013 is 5,431,418 and the percentage of Women in the Workforce is 28%. In fact, the gender gap index in 2014 is reflecting the high level of women economic empowerment in the country especially the economic participation as 0.627% in 2014. The SWOT analysis demonstrate the strength and weakness of women's economic empowerment activities in Tunisia and what about opportunities and threats for Tunisian women. As analyzed in the SWOT analysis bellow, women are operating largely in as leader, researcher, entrepreneur and change maker in the Tunisian society (see Table 5). They have a high level in enterprise due to the socio-cultural behavior. They are mostly graduated due to the good quality of education's policies in the country. The mainstreaming of women in science, technology and innovation is efficient because a high level of women as R&D personal due to the high number of women working on research laboratory and center. In addition, the situation of women's entrepreneur in Tunisia need more target actions, new rules and more appropriate strategies. Indeed, the need of more access to credit, property and other land for creating women's SME and the implementation of network to facilitate the transfer of knowledge and franchise. In the same time, the majority of women have large access to information provided by microfinance institution due to training and capacity building of their employees. In the same time, rural women are needing more program of financial and economic literacy. Unfortunately, the majority of women entrepreneur are one founder due to the presence of familiar SME and also due to the economic autonomy of women.

In another hand, there are some weakness as a high level of unemployment female in the non-agricultural sector which is due to the less development of women's entrepreneurship in this sector. In addition, there is a need for more economic and financial literacy and also education for women by capacity building in banking service. In addition, a more tertiary-level student education for female in university need to be increased to give the chance to women as engineer, researcher to build some innovative projects. Unfortunately, a few access by women to lands and credit due to the few target financial tools and accessibility to money and also the lack of regional financial institution in rural area explain the limited number of women entrepreneur in the regional level. This situation call for the creation of new agency,

*Table 5. SWOT analysis of women's entrepreneurship and economic empowerment for Tunisia case*

| Strength | Index | Weakness | Index |
|---|---|---|---|
| **Employment and Leadership** | | **Employment and leadership** | |
| Ability of women to rise to positions of enterprise leadership | 4.5 | Female, male adult unemployment rate (as % of female, male labour force) | 27.4, 15.0 |
| **Science, technology and research** | | Share of women employed in the non-agricultural sector (% of total non-agricultural employment) | 25 |
| Percentage of PhD graduates (female, male) | 53,47 | Percentage of women, men with an account at a formal financial institution | .25, 39 |
| Percentage of total R&D personnel (FTE) (female, male) | 50,51 | **Science, technology and research** | |
| **Rights and norms** | | Percentage of tertiary-level STEM students (female, male). | 48, 52 |
| Women's access to credit | 0.0 | Percentage of tertiary-level STEM graduates (female, male) | 43, 57 |
| Women's access to property other than land | 0.0 | **Rights and norms** | |
| | | Women's access to land ownership | 0.5 |
| **Women, business and law** | | **Women, business and law** | |
| Can an unmarried and married woman register a business in the same way as a man? | yes | Are there specific tax deductions or credits that are applicable only to women? | no |
| Can an unmarried and married woman open a bank account in the same way as a man? | yes | What is the minimum loan amount covered in the private credit bureau or public credit registry (as a percentage of income per capita)? | 0% |
| Do microfinance institutions provide information to private credit bureaus or public credit registries? | yes | Do retailers provide information to private credit bureaus or public credit registries? | No |
| **Rates and Profile of Women Entrepreneurs** | | **Rates and Profile of Women Entrepreneurs** | |
| At Least a Post-Secondary Degree (% TEA)-female | 33 | Do utility companies provide information to private credit bureaus or public credit registries? | No |
| Businesses Have One Founder (% TEA)-female | 95 | Total Entrepreneurial Activity (TEA) Rate (% Adult Population)-female | 3 |
| | | Established Business Ownership Rate (% Adult Population)-female | 2 |
| | | Discontinuing a Business in the Past Year (% Adult Population)-female | 11 |
| **Entrepreneurial perception for women** | | **Entrepreneurial perception for women** | |
| Has Capabilities to Start | 50 | Sees Good Opportunities-female | 23 |
| | | Fear of Failure for those Seeing Opportunities-female | 24 |
| | | Intend to Start in the Next Three Years (Non-Entrepreneurs)-female | 16 |
| | | Personally Knows an Entrepreneur | 28 |
| **Necessity and Opportunity Motives for Women Entrepreneurs (TEA)** | | **Necessity and Opportunity Motives for Women Entrepreneurs (TEA)** | |
| Opportunity-Motives (% TEA)-Female | 69 | Necessity-Motives (% TEA)-female | 28% |
| **Percentage of Women New and Established Business Owners with No Employees** | | **Percentage of Women New and Established Business Owners with No Employees** | |
| Percent New Business Owners With No Employees-female | 49 | Percent Established Business Owners With No Employees-female | 30 |
| Opportunities | | Threats | |
| High level of women's leader in enterprise due to the socio-cultural behavior of Tunisian women. | | High level of unemployment female as labor force and especially in the non-agricultural sector due to the less development of women's entrepreneurship in non-agriculture sector | |

*continued on following page*

*Table 5. Continued*

| Strength | Index | Weakness | Index |
|---|---|---|---|
| High percentage of women with PhD due to the target policies of higher education | | Luck of economic and financial literacy especially in banking service. | |
| High level of women as R&D personal due to the high number of women working on research laboratory and center | | The need of more tertiary-level student education for female in university oriented in STEM | |
| The need of more access to credit, property and other land for creating women's SME and the implementation of network to facilitate the transfer of knowledge and franchise | | Little access by women to lands, loan and credit due to the few target financial tools and accessibility to money and a lack of regional financial institution especially in rural area. | |
| The facility to register a business by women which need more electronic system to promote doing business in rural area | | Lack of reforms to offer new legislative incitation as tax deductions or credit applicable for women's | |
| The accessibility to information provided by microfinance institutions due to the training and capacity building of their employees | | The majority of women entrepreneur are one founder due to the presence of familiar SME. | |
| Women entrepreneur are motivated and has capabilities to start their own firms and by more access to opportunities | | High women's firm with only one employees due to the economic autonomy of women | |

Source: WEF report (2014), GEM report (2012). Survey data, responses on a 1-to-7 scale (1 = worst score, 7 = best score) and Data on a 0-to-1 scale (1 = worst score, 0 = best score); Women, business and law Report (2014): "creating economic opportunity for women", Global Entrepreneurship Monitor (2012) Women's Report; WDI-World Bank (2014).

adaptation of public institution to new challenges and the implementation of new financial association and structure in rural area. Globally, new reforms can offer new legislative incitation as tax or credit for women's entrepreneur limiting the level of investment by women.

## RECOMMENDATIONS

In summary, there some recommendations offered and needed to be integrated in the policies of women's empowerment in developing countries especially MENA countries.

- A gender-responsive trade policy is needed. Because, there is a need to incorporate gender perspectives into trade policy design and implementation to better understanding the specific challenges and opportunities that women face from trade policy and to maximize opportunities; facilitating the successful integration of women into more technologically advanced and dynamic sectors of the economy; avoiding the increase of gender disparities and mitigating the existing; and facilitating women's empowerment.
- Trade integration may offer opportunities for such enterprises to grow; it also exposes them to international competition and constraints. Different policy measures in trade provide specific entry points to mainstream gender issues in international trade as: trade liberalization agreements; unilateral liberalization as unilateral reduction of tariffs on intermediate inputs in productive sectors with high female employment; tax incentives to encourage exports from women-owned enterprises, etc. Thus, several coordinated and gender-sensitive policies are needed in areas such as fiscal policies, education, labor, training, innovation, financing, to mention a few. For this reason, trade policies and measures can be adapted to foster women's empowerment as part of the strategy to strengthen integration into the international trading system and make globalisation more inclusive. Thus, a gender-sensitive approach to trade must involve a vision of trade as an integral component of wider development efforts to promote sustainable development. Explicit and specific

attention to gender issues in trade and development policies, strategies and operational actions is crucial to maximising the gains for gender equality and minimising the costs that can arise.

- Making visible formal the contribution of women in economic growth. Indeed, women power have exceptional multi-tasking skills in balancing responsibilities of home towards their families and relatives, unpaid, and workplace in the organized labour market, or in self-employed small business or in subsistence farming, fishing, forestry and mining. Paradoxically, this force of women power is underutilized and underexploited. Women, especially poor women, work in the most physically exacting, poorly paid, labor-intensive tasks, often in inclement, unhygienic and stressful conditions. Women's contribution to productive activities is largely undervalued and unrecognized. These constrain is reducing their bargaining power in the market. There a need of new policies, rules, strategies those have the effect of encouraging the transfer of activities from the informal economy to the formal economy. Indeed, political and legal context for promoting entrepreneurship by offering a more competitive business environment for women's entrepreneurs by lowering the costs of starting and operating a business, including through simplified procedures for reporting and licensing, regulation appropriate and reasonable and better taxation need to be implemented. It also improving the benefits of legalization: easy access to business customers, credit conditions advantageous legal protection, contract enforcement, access to technology, subsidies, and foreign exchange markets as local and international markets.
- Harnessing the power of women for trade, growth and development in the globalization is both a top-down and bottom-up process. It is the responsibility of women; at all levels as Government and private sector as women entrepreneurs, civil society, and academia; among women's groups, and in different economic sectors to engender development. From the top down, there is the introduction of gender-sensitive aspects into the foreign trade policy by the policymakers at the top. From the bottom-up process, some innovations include: new business models such as cluster development for small enterprises or incubation services that provide full support for the development of new small industries; supporting the creation of association of women entrepreneurs and their activities; introducing changes to representation in business associations, such as cooperatives or producer networks, to allow women's or participation of women.
- There is a need for women to proactively pursue gender empowerment. They need to persevere in gender sensitization at all levels, create networks to promote common interests, be bold in initiating new activities and adapting to changing technologies. For women entrepreneurs to be successful they need: good ideas to create business; steadfast in achieving the goal; take calculated risks; and the support of the family. In addition, the transition to formal sector through deliberate measures and actions that purposely target and empower women to participate at international and national levels of public policymaking as well as among stakeholders within countries to maximize potential gains.
- Integrated approach to gender mainstreaming is also important. Indeed, trade policy and women's empowerment must be situated within wider national development strategies. Such supportive policies are needed in both central and state Governments. Support to women entrepreneurs should be strengthened, as they are mostly self-motivated and can be effective agents of change for many women. Financial opportunities for women, such as credit facilities, need to be created to enable women, especially entrepreneurs, to engage in trading activities. Information on market opportunities need to be made more easily available to women to enable them to get a better deal for their production. Small and medium-sized enterprises with women workers or entrepreneurs must

be provided more support to be competitive in national and international markets. Investment and industrial policies, including entrepreneurial development, should emphasize women's empowerment. Special tax incentives should be extended to women-owned enterprises for encouraging exports. Building of trade-related infrastructure, including rural areas and rural markets, to encourage more women participation in trade is needed.

## FUTURES RESEARCH DIRECTIONS

Women's economic empowerment through more flexible access to trade and market is one of the main goals to increase women's entrepreneurship in MENA countries. How new rules of trade can be more appropriate with women's empowerment and more access to the international market and in another hand? A combined strategies between fiscal instruments and trade instruments can offer solutions for women entrepreneurs actually? How the entrepreneurship in sustainable development can offer new area to explore new kind of projects offering to women more large freedom to face trade rules.

## CONCLUSION

Due to the gender gap in entrepreneurial activities, there is a need for more efficient policies for the development of female entrepreneurship. Policies better designed and funded strong and targeted measures at increasing women's empowerment. In addition, improved policies, institutional support and establish a public-private dialogue are important to improve women's access to credit and financial services, improve services business development and access to information and markets. More access to consumer and market opportunities for business networks are needed also. In the same time, the access to market for women entrepreneur and the building of networking need to be adapted to trade agreements and constraints of trade policies. The franchise contract can also be a solution a solution to facilitating the technology transfer and knowledge. In addition, a new area of adaptation is need in women's policies to be more efficient and to offer new positive result in the economic empowerment of women.

## REFERENCES

Arora, R.U. (2012). Gender inequality, economic development, and globalization: a state level analysis of India. *Journal of Developing Areas*, 41(1).

Baliamoune-Lutz, M. (2006). Globalization and Gender: Is Africa Different? *Journal of African Economies*, *16*(2), 301–348. doi:10.1093/jae/ejl037

Cağatay, N. (2001). *Trade, Gender and Poverty», Background Paper for UNDP"s Report on Trade and Sustainable Human Development*. UNDP.

Concept Note. (2015, March 6). Advancing Gender Equality and Empowerment of Women and Girls for a Transformative Post-2015 Development Agenda.

Eyben, R., et al. (2008). *Conceptualizing empowerment and the implications for pro-poor growth.* Brighton, Institute of Development Studies, University of Sussex.

Fontana, M., Joekes, S., & Masika, R. (1998). Global Trade Expansion and Liberalization: Gender Issue and Impact (Bridge Report no. 42). Brighton, UK, IDS.

Fontana, M., & Wood, A. (2000). Modeling the Effects of Trade on Women, at Work and at Home. *World Development, 28*(7), 1173–1190. doi:10.1016/S0305-750X(00)00033-4

Forsythe, N., Korzeniewicz, R. P., Majid, N., Weathers, G., & Durrant, V. (2003). *Gender inequalities, economic growth and economic reform: A preliminary longitudinal evaluation, No. 2003/45.* Geneva: International Labour Office.

Global Monitor entrepreneurship Report. (2012).Women's Report.

Millennium development goals. (2014). UN.

Morrison, A., Raju, D., & Sinha, N. (2007). Gender Equality, Poverty and Economic Growth (Policy Research Working Paper No. WPS4349). Washington DC, World Bank.

Okali, C. (2011). *Integrating Social Difference, Gender and Social Analysis into Agricultural Development.* Brighton, UK: Future Agricultures.

Pande, R. (2007). Gender, Poverty and Globalization in India. *Development, 50*(2), 134–140. doi:10.1057/palgrave.development.1100367

Randriamano, Z. (2006). *Gender and trade: overview report, Bridge Report, Institute of development Studies. OCDE (2011). Women economic empowerment », Issues Paper, June 2011; OCDE and DAC Network on Gender Equality.* GENDERNET.

Seguino, S. (2006). The great equalizer: Globalization effects on gender equality in Latin America and the Caribbean (MPRA Paper No. 6509). Retrieved from http://mpra.ub.uni-muenchen.de/6509

Shultz, T. P. (2005). *Does the Liberalization of Trade Advance Gender Equality in Schooling and Health?* (Working Papers). Economic Growth Center, Yale University.

Stotsky, J. G. (2006). *Gender and its Relevance to Macroeconomic Policy: A Survey (No. WP/06/233).* Washington: Fiscal Affairs Department, International Monetary Fund.

UNCTAD. (2009). Mainstreaming gender in trade policy. Note by the UNCTAD secretariat TD/B/C.I/EM.2/2/Rev.1. Retrieved from http://www.unctad.org/en/docs/ciem2d2_en.pd

Women survey on the role of women in development 2014: gender equality and sustainable development. (2014). UNWomen, New York.

World Bank. (2007). *Gender working towards greater equality, Gender equality as smart economics: A World Bank group action plan.* Washington, DC: World Bank.

# Chapter 8
# A Measurement-Based E-Government Portals' Maturity Model

**Abdoullah Fath-Allah**
*ENSIAS, Mohammed V University, Morocco*

**Rafa E. Al-Qutaish**
*ETS, University of Québec, Canada*

**Laila Cheikhi**
*ENSIAS, Mohammed V University, Morocco*

**Ali Idri**
*ENSIAS, Mohammed V University, Morocco*

## ABSTRACT

*E-government portals are playing an important role in facilitating the citizens' life. The e-government services can be executed by citizens without any time and location constraints, which results in great benefits for them. Therefore, governments should pay a special attention when designing, developing and maintaining their e-government portals. In order to achieve this, they need to follow worldwide e-government portals' best practices that would contribute in the enhancement of the portals' quality. Moreover, such best practices can be used to benchmark or rank the portals by measuring the presence of those best practices. This issue is addressed in this chapter by proposing a measurement based e-government portals' maturity model to help governments identify their portals' maturity stage and also provide guidelines and recommendations to move to an upper stage of maturity.*

## INTRODUCTION

E-government is the use of information technologies by e-government agencies to change the way governments are dealing with citizens, businesses and other arms of governments (World Bank, 2011). E-government has many advantages for its stakeholders. In fact, it transforms the way the stakeholders are dealing with governments, since transactions can be completed without having the need to visit the governmental offices (Fath-ALLAH, Cheikhi, Al-Qutaish, & Idri, 2014c). There are many types of e-governments such as: Government-to-Citizen (G2C), Citizen-to-Government (C2G), Government-to-Business (G2B), Business-to-Government (B2G), Government-to-Government (G2G), Government-to-Nonprofit (G2N), Nonprofit-to-Government (N2G), and Government-to-Employee (G2E) (Fang,

DOI: 10.4018/978-1-4666-9908-3.ch008

2002). Furthermore, there are many delivery channels of e-government, such as: wide area networks, the internet and mobile computing (World Bank, 2011). In this chapter, we are concerned about G2C e-government portals.

E-government portals are changing the way citizens are interacting with their governments; the citizens can execute services anytime and anywhere. For this purpose, governments should pay a special attention when developing those e-governments portals. However, e-government is considered an emerging field in which practical recommendations or best practices are considered very important (Assar, 2011). This means that governments should benefit from the worldwide best practices and recommendations when building those e-government portals. E-government maturity models can be used for this purpose. They can also be used to help governments improve their portals' maturity by providing guidelines and best practices to be implemented in order to move to an upper stage of maturity.

In this chapter we provide a background and summary on the literature review which has been conducted to build the e-government portals' best practice model (eGPBPM), and the initial maturity stages of the measurement based e-government portals' maturity model (MBeGPMM) in section 1. Then, section 2 provides a detailed overview of the MBeGPMM with its corresponding best practice subcategories. Section 3 presents the architectural view of the MBeGPMM and describes its components, whereas, section 4 explains the procedural view of the MBeGPMM and clarifies its lifecycle and calculation methodology. Finally, we give directions for future work in section 5 and conclude the chapter in section 6.

## BACKGROUND

As mentioned earlier, e-government portals are becoming a daily necessity for the citizens. They are considered a crucial aspect of good governance. However, e-government is a field where practical recommendations are considered important features for its prosperity (Assar, Boughzala, & Isckia, 2011). Hence, agencies should benefit from the worldwide experience and best practices when building e-government portals. E-government maturity models can be used for this purpose, that is; they can help agencies identify their portals' maturity and provide best practices and recommendations to implement to move to higher stages of maturity.

In order to build the new maturity model, we have conducted previous research studies as the following: 1) build a best practice model for e-government portals, 2) analyze the existing maturity models in the literature. An overview of these two studies in presented below.

### Best Practice Model

Many e-government portals' best practices have been raised in the literature. Such best practices are from research papers, case studies, industry practices and international standards. But, unfortunately those best practices are not logically grouped. Moreover, some authors may raise the same best practice with the same meaning, but with different wordings (Fath-ALLAH, Cheikhi, Al-Qutaish, & Idri, 2014b). For instance, customer centricity could be named as: user focus, customer-centric, user-centric or customer intention (Berntzen & Olsen, 2009; Forfás, 2008; The European Centre for Total Quality Management, 2002; World Bank, 2005). However, all these wordings mean the same thing; which is to design the e-government portal from a customer perspective. This un-structuration may cause ambiguities for the designers of the e-government portals. Hence, it becomes a necessity to unify all the e-government portals' best practices into a best practice model that will help the designers build e-government portals in an easy way; the eGPBPM model was proposed in (Fath-ALLAH et al., 2014b).

This model is composed of five best practice categories. Each category contains its corresponding subcategories and each subcategory contains its corresponding best practices, as the following:

1. Back-end category includes best practices that run in background and usually the users do not see them, such as: system, data processing and business logic best practices. This includes the following best practice subcategories: interoperability, use of standards, modularity, security, privacy, single sign on, delegation and reusability.
2. Front-end Web design category includes best practices that the user usually interacts with and sees and is related to the design of the portal. This includes the following best practice subcategories: one stop shop, ease of navigation, personalization, industrialization and structuration.
3. Front-end Web content category includes best practices that the user usually interacts with and sees and is related to the information and content of the portal. This includes the following best practice subcategories: relevancy, accessibility, search engines, periodical change, rich content, interactive games, mobile applications, statements, translations, understandability, help and responsiveness.
4. External category includes best practices that are loosely coupled with the technical aspects of the portal. This category is mostly related to the integration of the citizen in the e-government process and to the marketing of the portal. This includes the following best practice subcategories: e-participation, sociability, advertising, referencing, incentives, contests, emailing, data analytics, contact information and performance ratings.
5. Service category includes best practices that are related to the services present in the portal that can be executed by citizens. This includes the following best practice subcategories: service customer centricity, service interoperability, service help, payments, workflows, service performance ratings, user forms and service responsiveness.

## Maturity Models

E-government maturity models are a set of stages (from basic to advanced ones) that can be used to determine the maturity stage of an e-government portal. In software engineering, there are many e-government maturity models. We have conducted a study which investigates in details a set of 25 maturity models provided in the literature and compared them according to different criteria, such as: stages' names, number of stages, year, country, focus and features (Fath-ALLAH, Cheikhi, Al-Qutaish, & Idri, 2014a). We have noticed in this comparison that the maturity models suffer from some limitations (Fath-ALLAH et al., 2014a, 2014c, 2015). First of all, the models are not built based on a unified best practice model; this explains the difference in terms of best practices' coverage by each maturity model. Second, some maturity models were built without any input from the other models; as a result, there are different wordings of the best practices, and some maturity models are missing many best practices already raised by other authors. Last but not least, the maturity models provide only a way to rank the portals without providing directions and guidelines for agencies to move to higher stages of maturity. These inconsistencies can cause ambiguities and misunderstandings for the designers of the e-government portals. Therefore, the design of a new maturity model that should tackle these limitations represents a research challenge in software engineering. This maturity model should be based on a best practice model and use the output of the existing maturity models in the literature. Moreover, the model will allow agencies to measure their portals' maturity and identify the missing best practices at any maturity stage. On top of that, the model will also provide guidelines for agencies to move to higher stages of maturity.

The first step to build the MBeGPMM is to identify the most important stages of maturity by analyzing the 25 maturity models. In fact, we noticed that the models present large similarities between them in terms of stages' focus. Hence, we have grouped the maturity models' stages into 4 categories that represent the stages of the MBeGPMM. These categories are as the following (Fath-ALLAH et al., 2014a):

1. The presence stage: the purpose of this stage is to present information to the citizens. The portal at this stage serves as a way to post static information or pages to the citizens.
2. The interaction stage: the purpose of this stage is to allow citizens to interact with the government. An example is the use of emails as a way to interact with citizens.
3. The transaction stage: the purpose of this stage is to allow citizens to complete transactions or execute online services over the web. This stage features great care over security and privacy of the transactions.
4. The integration stage: the purpose of this stage is information sharing between various agencies and the inclusion of the citizen in the e-government process. This stage focuses also on advanced features such as: transformation, one stop shop and e-participation.

The second step is to identify the corresponding stage of maturity (among those four stages) for each best practice subcategory with respect to the 25 studied maturity models in (Fath-ALLAH et al., 2015). This information is important, since it allows us to build the MBeGPMM by figuring out the corresponding stage of maturity for each best practice subcategory of our eGPBPM model (see Table 1). For instance, the best practice subcategory 'search engines' (first column) was mentioned by three maturity models (second column) in their stage that focuses on interaction (third column). This includes Siau & Long (Siau & Long, 2005), Kim & Grant (Kim & Grant, 2010) and Almazan & Gil-Garcia (Almazan & Gil-Garcia, 2008) maturity models. However, the other 22 maturity models do not cover this best practice subcategory.

## MBeGPMM: Maturity Stages' Best Practices

As mentioned earlier, the MBeGPMM is composed of four maturity stages (presence, interaction, transaction and integration). In this section, we present the results of the mapping performed between the best practice subcategories of the eGPBPM model and these four maturity stages. This mapping is conducted based on the purpose of both: the best practices subcategories and the four maturity stages. Table 1 was also taken into consideration to perform this mapping, since it gives us the same information from a literature point of view. As a result, each maturity stage will have its corresponding best practice subcategories. Figure 1 presents the result of this mapping which will be discussed in a detailed view in the next subsections.

*Table 1. Mapping between the eGPBPM subcategories, MMs and our 4 stages of maturity*

| eGPBPM Subcategory | Maturity Models (MMs) | MMs' Corresponding Stage |
|---|---|---|
| Relevancy | UN, Windley, Deloitte & Touche | Integration |
| Accessibility | West | Integration |
| Search engines | Siau & Long, Kim & Grant, Almazan & Gil-Garcia | Interaction |
| Periodical change | Almazan & Gil-Garcia, Hiller & Belanger, Siau & Long | Presence |
| Rich content | UN, West, World Bank | Presence |
| | Wescott | Transaction |
| Translation | UN | Presence |
| | West | Integration |
| Statements | Windley | Presence |
| | West | Integration |
| Contact Information | Windley | Presence |
| | World Bank | Interaction |
| Emailing | Windley, Chandler & Emanuel, Siau & Long, Moon, Gartner, Alhomod | Interaction |
| | Wescott | Transaction |
| | West | Integration |
| Security | UN, World Bank, Shahkooh, Almazan & Gil-Garcia, UK National Audit Office, Deloitte & Touche | Transaction |
| | Cisco, Windley | Integration |
| Privacy | Chandler & Emanuel, Deloitte & Touche | Transaction |
| | Hiller & Belanger | Integration |
| Personalization | Cisco | Presence |
| | Almazan & Gil-Garcia | Interaction |
| | Siau & Long, Almazan & Gil-Garcia, UK National Audit Office | Transaction |
| | Cisco, West, Deloitte & Touche | Integration |
| Help | Windley | Interaction |
| | Wescott | Integration |
| Customer Centricity | Almazan & Gil-Garcia | Transaction |
| | Deloitte & Touche, Andersen & Henriksen, UN, Windley | Integration |
| Payments | Windley | Interaction |
| | Cisco, Reddick, UN, Alhomod, Hiller & Belanger, Moon, Howard, Shahkooh, Siau & Long, Kim & Grant, Almazan & Gil-Garcia, UK National Audit Office, Netchaeva, Deloitte & Touche | Transaction |
| | Deloitte & Touche, Windley, Wescott | Integration |
| Workflows | UK National Audit Office | Transaction |
| | Windley | Integration |

*continued on following page*

*Table 1. Continued*

| eGPBPM Subcategory | Maturity Models (MMs) | MMs' Corresponding Stage |
|---|---|---|
| User forms | Cisco | Presence |
| | Windley | Interaction |
| | Layne & Lee, Chen, UN, Alhomod, Hiller & Belanger, Moon, World Bank, Shahkooh, Siau & Long | Transaction |
| | Windley | Integration |
| Interoperability | Layne & Lee, Cisco, Chen, UN, Alhomod, Hiller & Belanger, Moon, Shahkooh, Siau & Long, Chandler & Emanuel, Kim & Grant, Windley, Almazan & Gil-Garcia, Deloitte & Touche, UK National Audit Office, Wescott | Integration |
| One stop shop | Reddick | Transaction |
| | West, Deloitte & Touche, Layne & Lee, Hiller & Belanger, Shahkooh, Siau & Long, Almazan & Gil-Garcia, Wescott, UK National Audit Office, Netchaeva | Integration |
| E-participation | Hiller & Belanger, Moon, World Bank, Howard, Windley, Almazan & Gil-Garcia | Interaction |
| | Layne & Lee, UN, Wescott | Transaction |
| | Cisco, UN, West, Hiller & Belanger, Moon, Shahkooh, Siau & Long, Wescott, Kim & Grant, Netchaeva, Almazan & Gil-Garcia | Integration |
| Sociability | UN | Integration |

## Presence Stage

The purpose of the presence stage is to present information on the Web; this means that the website serves as way to present information and content to the citizens such as: news, laws, publications, databases and interactive maps. Therefore, the best practices of this stage should focus on information and content of the portal. This includes the following best practice subcategories:

1. **Ease of Navigation:** It allows citizens to navigate in the portal and find information easily, especially when this information is broad and large; it does not make sense to present information to the citizens that is hardly found.
2. **Structuration:** It helps the users and search engines find pages easily. Structuration helps also the citizens to stay oriented in the Website and know exactly where they are in the portal, and what other options are available to them. For instance, a portal that contains a large amount of unstructured information will bring a feeling to the citizens that they are lost and disoriented in the portal.
3. **Industrialization:** It is related to compliance with industrial standards. An example is the published recommendations by the World Wide Web Consortium (W3C) under Web Content Accessibility Guidelines 2.0 (WCAG 2.0) which was accepted under ISO/IEC 40500. This standard provides guidelines to build accessible portals for citizens with or without disabilities.
4. **Relevancy:** It helps making information presented in the portal relevant to the citizens' interests. For instance, information should not be organized from an organizational perspective; however the citizen needs to find information grouped by his group of interest, such as themes and target groups and not by organizations and departments.

*Figure 1. MBeGPMM maturity stages' best practice subcategories*

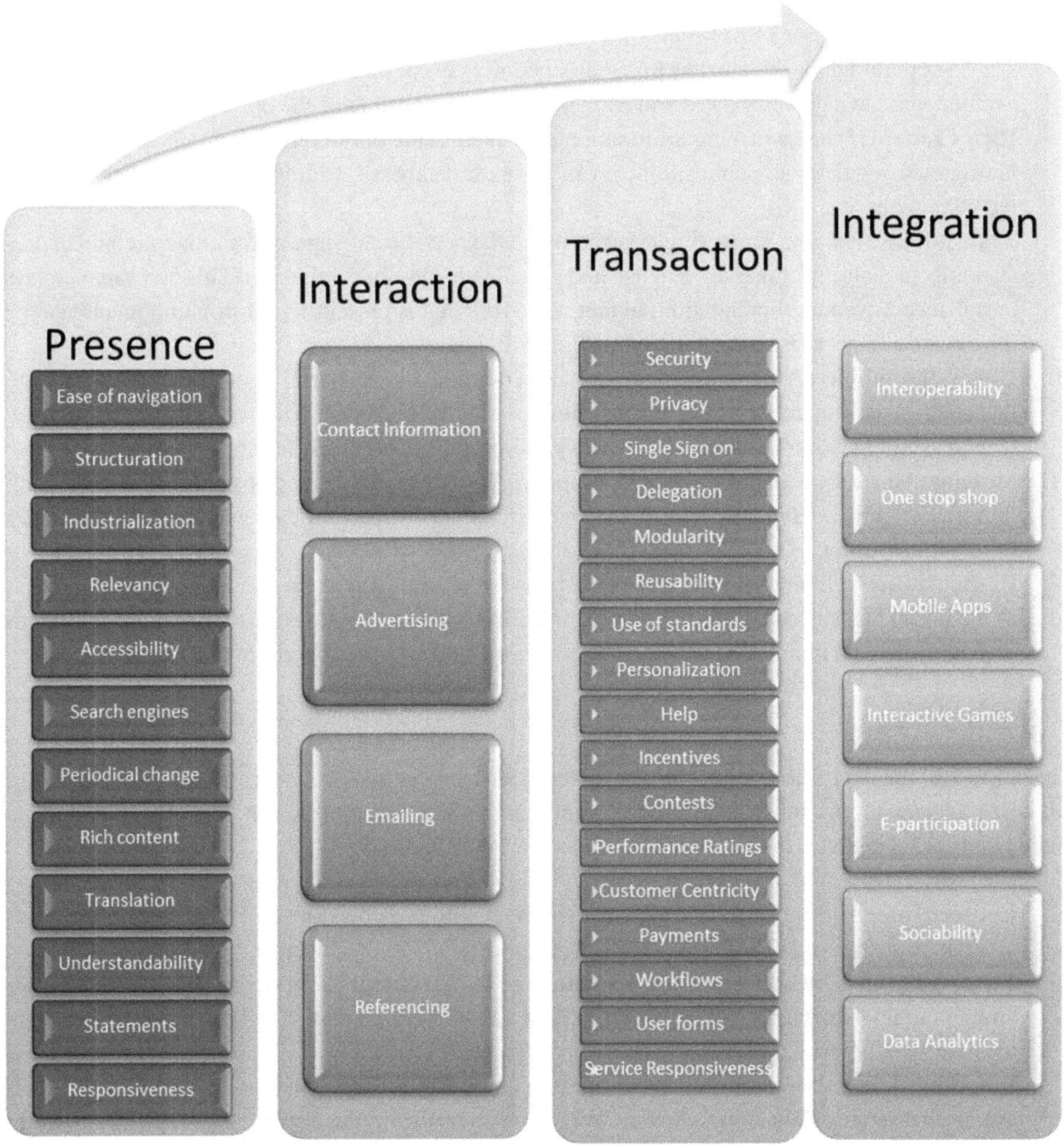


5. **Accessibility:** It helps making information presented in the portal accessible for all visitors. This encourages the use of the portal since it allows a wide range of citizens to access the portals including those with disabilities such as people with vision or hearing deficiencies.
6. **Search Engines:** It helps citizens find information presented in the portal easily. For instance, if the portal contains large amount of information such as: codes, laws, images, videos, or news, it will be difficult for the citizens to browse all this data to look for specific information. Therefore,

an enhanced search engine that allows the possibility to narrow and make various filters on the search will make this information easier to find.

7. **Periodical Change:** It helps keeping information presented in the portal up-to-date. For instance, it is disappointing for the citizens to see an upcoming event that occurred in the past. This can be avoided via: having expiry dates and team of editors responsible of the portal's timeliness.
8. **Rich Content:** It helps making information presented in the portal broad and rich, such as codes, laws, news, regulations, publications, press releases, databases, audio/video clips, Webcasts, interactive maps, etc.
9. **Translations:** It allows presenting information in the portal in a language the citizens could understand (local dialects for natives, English and other languages for foreigners). This helps making the portal accessible for all population. In fact, a website that is presenting information in a language the citizens do not master creates a huge digital divide.
10. **Understandability:** It helps making information presented in the portal written in a plain language that can be easily understood by citizens. Besides that, writing information in a difficult language is increasing the digital divide and is making the portals inaccessible for some population.
11. **Statements:** An example of statements is copyrights and disclaimers. Copyrights help protecting information presented in the portal. Moreover, disclaimers help avoiding penalties for the accuracy of this information.
12. **Responsiveness:** It helps having a short response time when navigating and viewing information in the portal. This is considered important since information that takes a large amount of time to load, may give an impression to the citizens that the portal is improperly functioning.

## Interaction Stage

The purpose of the interaction stage is to allow interaction between governments and citizens. Therefore, the best practices of this stage should focus on interaction and communication between governments and citizens. This includes the following best practice subcategories:

1. **Contact Information:** It allows citizens to interact with the government. Examples are: 'contact us' link or posting email addresses and phones of officials in the portal.
2. **Advertising:** It allows the government to promote the portal and its services. This allows the government to interact with citizens as it provides a way of communication with them. An example is to advertise the portal and its services in the internet.
3. **Emailing:** It provides governments a way to interact with citizens via emails. An example is the use of newsletters. This allows citizens to receive emails from the agency after registering in the newsletter.
4. **Referencing:** It allows agencies to interact with citizens by making the portal accessible and easily findable in search engines. An example is Search Engine Optimization (SEO), which consists of making the portal more visible in search engines such as: Google and Yahoo.

## Transaction Stage

The purpose of the transaction stage is to allow citizens to make transactions by executing online services. An example of service is a 'birth registry' that allows citizens to register a new born, and the transaction is the process of completing the service. Therefore, the best practices that focus on allowing citizens to execute transactions and complete services (making a request and having a response) are related to this stage. These are as the following:

1. **Security:** It helps protecting the personal data exchanged between citizens and governments during transactions, this helps making the transactions secure and protects the citizens' data. An example is the use of digital signatures for authentication and encryption.
2. **Privacy:** It protects private data exchanged between citizens and governments during completion of transactions from any disclosure. An example is compliance with Platform for Privacy Preferences (P3P).
3. **Single Sign On:** It is related to authentication or signing in into the portal only one time. This should give citizens access to all services and systems with a single login. For instance, some transactions require the citizen to log in to the portal to verify his identity. Moreover, signing in into the portal is mandatory in order to show to the citizens the list of executed services that are in progress.
4. **Delegation:** It allows citizens to execute e-government services or complete transactions on behalf of other persons or entities. This can be done by allowing citizens to create delegations for delegates. The delegates can then execute services on behalf of them.
5. **Modularity:** It helps building and maintaining e-government services. An example of modularity is the use of Service Oriented Architecture (SOA), which consists of breaking down the application into small modules called services.
6. **Reusability:** It helps building and maintaining e-government services. An example of reusability is the reuse of open source modules (such as Google Calendar and WordPress) or services that are already available before starting any new development.
7. **Use of Standards**: It helps maintaining e-government services by enabling flexibility and ease of change in requirements. Examples of standards are: Extensible Markup Language (XML), JavaScript Object Notation (JSON) and Dublin core metadata.
8. **Personalization:** It offers the possibility for citizens to personalize the portal and its functionalities according to their needs. For instance, citizens need to sign in into the portal to access a personalized section, such as a 'MyPage' section.
9. **Help:** It assists the citizens during the execution of e-government services by providing live support such as: click to chat, Frequently Asked Questions (FAQs) and videos explaining the navigation process.
10. **Incentives:** It encourages the citizens to opt for the online services. In fact, incentives, promotes and increases service usage, since it concerns privileging online users over the traditional ones (those visiting public offices).
11. **Contests:** It encourages citizens to become producers of e-government services. In fact, contests or organizing competitions help exploit the problem solving skills of the users and hence, achieve great service usage.
12. **Performance Ratings:** It allows the citizens to rate the e-government services upon using them. An example is the use of feedback icons and emoticons to score the portal and its services. This is more related to e-government services.
13. **Service Customer Centricity:** It helps building citizen centric services and ensuring that the services are designed for the citizen and not for the organization. This is achieved by observing users trying e-government services using observatory methods and eye tracking techniques.

14. **Payments:** It offers a way for citizens to pay for the e-government services via credit/debit cards or electronic banking. An example is the possibility for citizens for pay for taxes, fines and fees.
15. **Workflows:** It allows citizens to track the status of the executed services. This can be achieved using dashboards, where the citizens can see the status of their executed services.
16. **User Forms:** It is considered a part of the e-government services. In fact the user forms are submitted and filled by the citizen during the execution of services. It is important to check that these forms are suitable and easy to use. For instance, having drop down menus when necessary and using mandatory fields.
17. **Service Responsiveness:** It focuses on having short response time when executing e-government services. In fact, services that take a large amount of time to execute or fail frequently, may prevent the citizens from reusing the portal.

### Integration Stage

The purpose of the integration or transformation stage is integration between governments, that is; joining governments together to exchange information between agencies from the same or different jurisdictions. This stage includes best practice subcategories that are either related to integration between governments or to the involvement of the citizen in the e-government process. The stage also covers subcategories that are considered advanced features. This includes the following best practice subcategories:

1. **Interoperability:** It is related to integration between governments to work together and exchange information. An example is to share information between agencies from the same or different jurisdictions.
2. **One Stop Shop:** It is considered an example of integration between agencies into one portal giving a 'one agency feel'. The citizen could access all the e-government services in a single point of entry.
3. **Mobile Applications:** This is related to mobile applications that can be installed on mobile devices. This is considered an advanced feature.
4. **Interactive Games:** An example is decision games to increase citizen awareness. This is considered an advanced feature.
5. **E-Participation:** It is related to the involvement of the citizen in the e-government process. An example is to allow citizens to interact with each other or with governmental officers. This can be achieved using tools such as: chat rooms and comment forms.
6. **Sociability:** It is related to the involvement of the citizen in the e-government process using social networks and tools, such as: Facebook and Twitter.
7. **Data Analytics:** It relates to analyzing the data for insights and decision making. This is considered an advanced feature. An example is the use of sentiment analysis in social networks to analyze conversations and discussions.

## MBeGPMM: Architectural View

The MBeGPMM is a hierarchical framework composed of four levels. The first level contains the four maturity stages. Each maturity stage contains its corresponding best practice categories and subcategories in the second level. Moreover, each best practice subcategory is associated with its corresponding

*Figure 2. Components of the MBeGPMM*

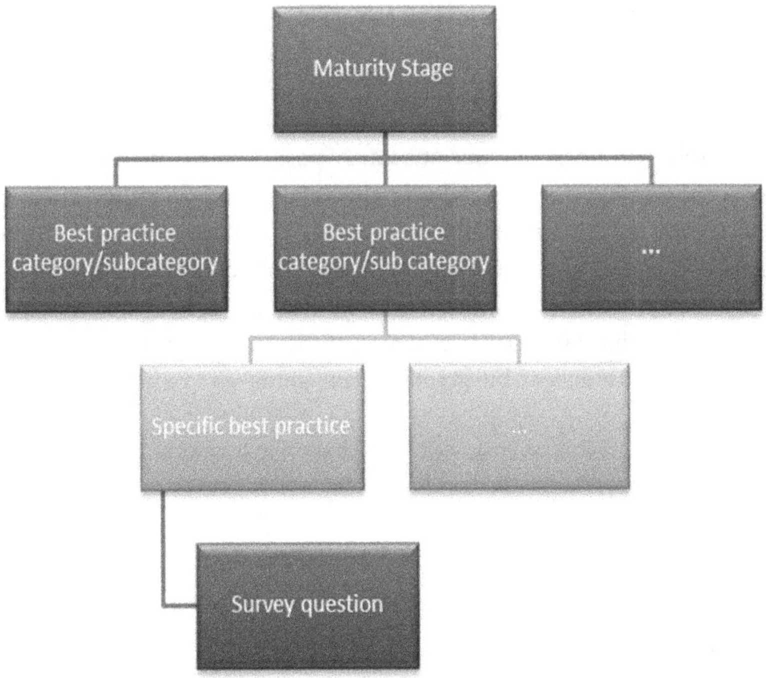


specific best practices in the third level. The fourth level contains the survey questions that measure the presence/absence of those best practices. Figure 2 shows the components of the MBeGPMM.

## First Level: Maturity Stages

The MBeGPMM is composed of four maturity stages as described previously. The first maturity stage is presence, which focuses mainly on presenting information to the citizens. The second stage is interaction, which focuses on interaction between citizens and governments. The third stage is transaction, which focuses on allowing citizens to make transaction and execute online services. Finally, the fourth stage is integration, which focuses on integration between agencies from the same or different jurisdictions.

## Second Level: Best Practice Categories/ Subcategories

The best practices categories/subcategories for each maturity stage were described in details in the previous sections. This subsection summarizes the best practice categories/subcategories for each maturity stage.

- The first maturity stage covers best practices that are related to presence on the Web from the Web content and Web design best practice categories. This includes the following best practice subcategories: ease of navigation, structuration, industrialization, relevancy, accessibility, search engines, periodical change, rich content, translations, understandability, statements, and responsiveness.

- The second maturity stage covers best practices that are related to interaction between citizens and governments from the external best practice category. This includes the following best practice subcategories: contact information, advertising, emailing, and referencing.
- The third maturity stage covers best practices related to back-end, web design, web content, external and service categories that are related to allowing citizens to make transactions over the Web. This includes the following best practice subcategories: security, privacy, single sign on, delegation, modularity, reusability, use of standards, personalization, help, incentives, contests, performance ratings, service customer centricity, payments, workflows, user forms, and responsiveness.
- The fourth maturity stage covers best practices that are related to integration and e-participation from the back-end, web design, web content, external and service best practice categories. This includes the following best practice subcategories: accessibility, interoperability, one stop shops, mobile applications, accessibility, interactive games, e-participation, sociability, and data analytics.

## Third Level: Specific Best Practices

As explained earlier, each best practice subcategory contains its corresponding specific best practices. This subsection gives an overview on the specific best practices for each maturity stage (presence, interaction, transaction and integration).

## Presence Stage

The portal at this stage is easy to navigate, intuitive and visually pleasing. The users can perform their activities in a user friendly way (Sørum, 2011).The portal provides a list of frequently searched items and most used services (Georgescu & Georgescu, 2008; Peters, Janssen, & van Engers, 2004; Seifert & McLoughlin, 2007; UNDESA, 2012; West, 2007). Besides that, the portal features clear menu structure and its main menu is maintained in all the pages of the portal (Rodríguez, Welicki, Giulianelli, & Vera, 2008; The European Centre for Total Quality Management, 2002). Moreover, the portal is similar in appearance with other governmental Websites (Kumar, Mukerji, Butt, & Persaud, 2007; West, Adam Deitch, Miguel A. Porrúa Vigón, & Federico Sobisch, 2004). The portal has a clear structure (The European Centre for Total Quality Management, 2002) and contains sitemaps for the users and XML sitemaps for search engines. Moreover, industry guidelines, such as compliance with Web Content Accessibility Guidelines WCAG 2.0 (W3C, 2012) are followed. Besides that, information is relevant and grouped by themes and target groups (European Commission, 2009, 2010; West, 2007). Moreover, the information is at the right level of detail (Sørum, 2011). The portal is accessible to people with vision and hearing deficiencies (UNDESA, 2012). Moreover, HTLM broken links are monitored (The European Centre for Total Quality Management, 2002; West, 2007). Besides that, the portal features enhanced search engines with many search options (Berntzen & Olsen, 2009; European Commission, 2010; The European Centre for Total Quality Management, 2002; UNDESA, 2012). These search engines are used in conjunction with metadata (Peters et al., 2004). The portal's content is changed periodically and features expiry or review dates (Choudrie, Ghinea, & Weerakkody, 2004; The European Centre for Total Quality Management, 2002; United Nations, 2012). Moreover, the portal's content is rich and the portal offers a broad range of information (Georgescu & Georgescu, 2008; UNDESA, 2012; United Nations, 2012). Furthermore, the portal's content is translated to local dialects (UNDESA, 2012), official languages (European Commission, 2010), other languages for foreigners (European Commission, 2009; Georgescu & Georgescu, 2008; United Nations, 2008; West, 2007) and especially English (Berntzen & Olsen, 2009). Moreover, the portal's content is clear to understand and is written in a plain language (Delone, 2003; DeLone & McLean, 1992; Plain Language Action and Information Network (PLAIN), 2014; Sørum, 2011; West et al., 2004). Furthermore, the portal features disclaimers, copyrights, privacy and security statements (European Commission, 2009, 2010; Georgescu & Georgescu, 2008; Kumar et al., 2007; Makolm, 2002; The European Centre for Total Quality Management, 2002). Finally, the portal's pages are responsive and can be quickly downloaded, and the pictures are not overdone as they slow down browsers (The European Centre for Total Quality Management, 2002).

## Interaction Stage

The portal at this stage features contact information such as: emails, phones, address, key persons to contact (Rohleder & Jupp, 2004; West, 2004, 2007; Windley, 2002). A 'contact us' link that allows citizens to interact with the agency is made available (United Nations, 2008). Moreover, there is a timely response to emails, and turnaround time mechanisms to respond to submitted requests are put in place (United Nations, 2008). Information regarding the users' possibility to complain is also present in the portal (European Commission, 2013). The portal is advertised in printed brochures, television, radio and internet (West et al., 2004). Moreover, there is a use of email systems and push technology (such as: email subscriptions and newsletters) (N.A.O., 2002; West, 2004). Eventually, the portal can be easily accessed via search engines and the SEO best practices are assessed and enhanced (Alsmadi, Al-Kabi, & Wahbeh, 2012; Papadomichelaki & Mentzas, 2012).

## Transaction Stage

At this stage, there is a great care over security. There is a use of digital signatures for both: encryption and authentication (Posch, Posch, Tauber, Zefferer, & Zwattendorfer, 2011). The portal is secured against hacking attacks such as: SQL injections and denial of service attacks. Moreover, real-time backups and recovery mechanisms are put in place. Besides that, privacy is an important concern at this stage. P3P privacy guidelines are followed and HTML get forms and cookies are avoided (Choudrie et al., 2004). On top of that, personal information is not shared with third parties and there is a role-based authorization access for officials (Makolm, 2002; Papadomichelaki & Mentzas, 2012). Besides that, single sign on and delegation mechanisms are made available at this stage (Posch et al., 2011). Moreover, the application is broken down into small modules called services such as the use of SOA (Klischewski & Askar, 2010). Next to that, Web 2.0 modules (such as WordPress) and standards (such as: XML, SOAP and Dublin core metadata) are used at this stage (Alasem, 2009; Assar et al., 2011; Forfás, 2008). Moreover, the stage also features personalization options such as: personal accounts (European Commission, 2010; United Nations, 2008), storage space for the citizens (European Commission, 2009) and possibility to tailor the content and services of interest. Help is provided in the form of FAQs (European Commission, 2009, 2010; UNDESA, 2012), live support (European Commission, 2010) and guided tours (Bhattacharya, Gulla, & Gupta, 2012). Incentives are made available to motivate the users to use the Web channel (UNDESA, 2012). Besides that, public data is made available (Assar et al., 2011) and contests are organized to motivate citizens to create services. Furthermore, feedback icons and surveys are used to allow citizens to rate the portal and its services (European Commission, 2009, 2010). The services are customer centric and designed for the citizens in mind. For this purpose, observatory and eye tracking techniques are used to observe users trying e-government services (European Commission, 2009). Ethnographic work is also used, which consists of grouping users according to some socio-cultural criteria like age and educational level (European Commission, 2009). Citizens can complete online payments using credit cards or online banking (Berntzen & Olsen, 2009; Makolm, 2002). Besides that, the users can track the status of their executed services via dashboard or emails (United Nations, 2012). Next to that, user forms which are filled by the citizens during the execution of online services are enhanced and user friendly (Makolm, 2002). Eventually, the services are fast and do not take a large amount of time to be executed.

## Integration Stage

At this stage, the portal is vertically and horizontally integrated. This means that departments from the same or different jurisdictions are able to exchange information with each other. Moreover, the e-government services are also integrated. This means that a service can trigger other services or notify agencies with higher and lower levels (national, regional, federal, provincial or municipal) within the same or different jurisdictions. Moreover, a Chief Information Officer (CIO) is responsible of managing cross-agency coordination (Rohleder & Jupp, 2004; United Nations, 2008). Besides, other features that help achieve interoperability are also used, such as: the use of standards (Al-Khouri, 2011; Forfás, 2008; Posch et al., 2011), and SOA or Web services (Klischewski & Askar, 2010). The portal provides a large number of services and covers almost all federal ministries, federal provinces, local authorities, and municipalities (United Nations, 2012). This is a real one stop shop portal. The portal also features mobile applications and interactive games (United Nations, 2012). E-participation tools such as: chat rooms, comment forms (ask questions and receive answers), blogs, surveys and polls are also present at this stage (Berntzen & Olsen, 2009; European Commission, 2009; The European Centre for Total Quality Management, 2002; UNDESA, 2012; United Nations, 2008, 2012). Besides that, feedback is gathered from users and nonusers (European Commission, 2009; United Nations, 2008). This feedback is integrated into the portal in a regular manner (Georgescu & Georgescu, 2008; Iribarren et al., 2008; Kumar et al., 2007). On top of that, the portal is present in social media Websites such as: Facebook, Twitter, WordPress, YouTube, and Flickr (UNDESA, 2012). Moreover, data is analyzed for insights and decision making. This helps governments take reliable decisions (Lee & Kwak, 2012). Website performance is also measured (Kim & Grant, 2010; Layne & Lee, 2001; Lee & Kwak, 2012) using tools such as Google Analytics. Eventually, sentiment analysis tools which allow the analysis of online conversations on social websites (such as: Facebook, LinkedIn, Twitter, blogging sites and wikis) are also used (Andreasson, Millard, & Snaprud, 2012).

## Fourth Level: Survey Questions

The last level of the MBeGPMM is composed of the survey questions. Each survey question allows measuring its corresponding specific best practice. Let's take for example the structuration best practice subcategory. It contains two specific best practices as the following: 1) use of sitemaps, 2) use of XML sitemaps for search engines. This means that this subcategory will have two survey questions. Each question will measure the presence/absence (i.e. yes/no binary scoring) of the specific best practice. Figure 3 shows the survey questions for the structuration best practice subcategory.

*Figure 3. Survey questions of the structuration best practice subcategory*

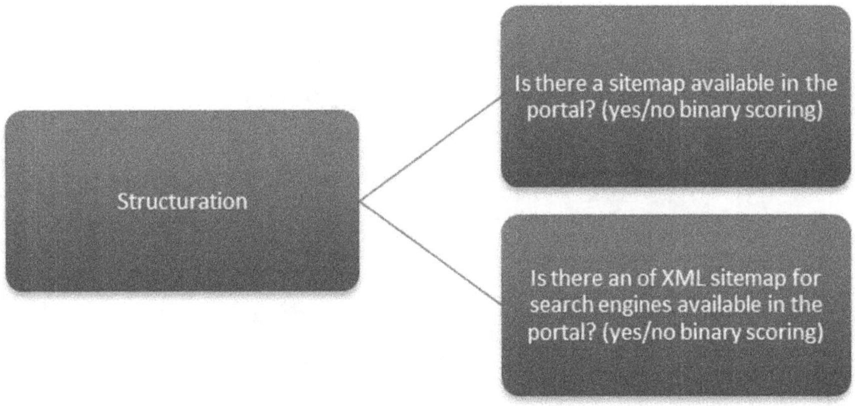


## MBeGPMM: Procedural View

In this section, we explain the MBeGPMM life cycle and how it can allow agencies to identify their portals' maturity stage and provide guidelines to move to an upper stage of maturity. Afterwards, the section explains how the maturity stage's compliance with best practices is calculated.

### MBeGPMM Life Cycle

The MBeGPMM life cycle is composed of five steps. The first step is to define the maturity stage to be measured (first time the stage is presence). The survey questions corresponding to the maturity stage being measured can be executed in the second step. Afterwards, the SCwBP (Subcategory's Compliance with Best Practices) for each best practice subcategory can be calculated using the output of the survey in the third step. The MSCwBP (Maturity Stage's Compliance with Best Practices) can be calculated by equally weighting all its corresponding SCwBPs in the fourth step.

The output of the survey will provide agencies with guidelines and missing best practices to be implemented in order to move to a higher stage of maturity. Once the agency has completed all the missing best practices, it can move to the next stage of maturity and execute its corresponding survey. This process is cyclic and can be repeated until the e-government portal reaches a good MSCwBP in the integration stage. This process is summarized in Figure 4.

### Calculation Methodology

As presented earlier, the MBeGPMM is an e-government portal maturity model based on measurement of best practices. Each best practice subcategory contains a set of survey questions that measure the presence/absence of the specific best practices within this subcategory. The scoring of the survey questions can be one of these forms:

- Binary scoring (1|0) that measures the presence/absence of the best practice.
- Percentage scoring such as ratios or the scores obtained in automatic Web tools.
- Equally weighted scoring for survey questions with multiple responses.

*Figure 4. MBeGPMM process*

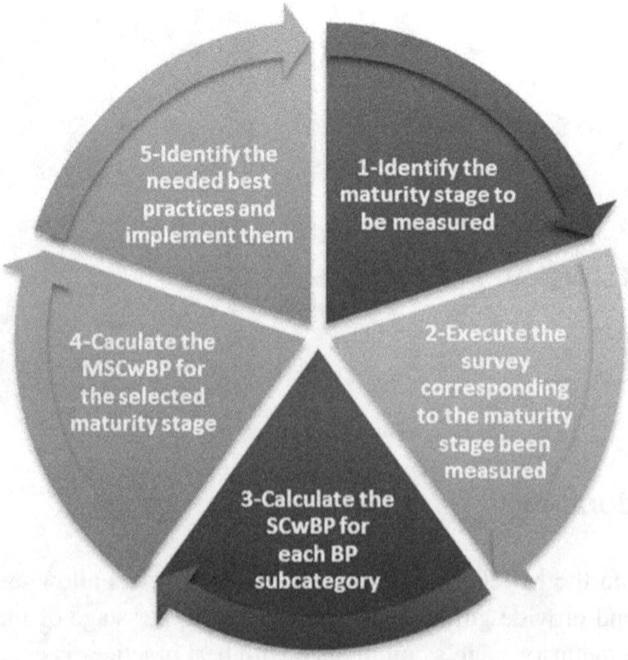


In our calculation, we assume that the survey questions and the best practice subcategories are equally weighted.

The first step is to calculate the SCwBP for all the best practice subcategories belonging to the measured maturity stage. This can be done by equally weighing the survey questions' output for each best practice subcategory. Equation 1 can be used for this purpose:

$$SCwBP = \left( \sum_{i=1}^{n} SQ(i) \right) / n \qquad (1)$$

where:

*SCwBP = Subcategory's compliance with Best Practices*
*n = Number of survey questions in the corresponding best practice subcategory*
*SQ = Survey question output*

In the second step, the MSCwBP can be calculated by equally weighing the corresponding best practice subcategories' SCwBP. Equation 2 can be used for this purpose (Al-Qutaish & Abran, 2011):

$$MSCwBP = \left( \sum_{i=1}^{m} SCwBP(i) \right) / m \qquad (2)$$

where:

*MSCwBP = Maturity Stage's Compliance with Best Practices*
*m = Number of subcategories in the corresponding maturity stage*
*SCwBP = Subcategory's compliance with Best Practices*

## FUTURE RESEARCH DIRECTIONS

The MBeGPMM can be used to help agencies identify their portals' maturity stage and figure out the missing practices the portal should satisfy in order to reach a higher stage of maturity. This model is also based on a list of structured best practices that allows the designers to build portals that satisfy the worldwide e-government portals' best practices. Thus, this model moves beyond the benefits of the actual maturity models and provides the process and the calculation methodology. The process of the MBeGPMM can be done manually or using a web based application. A future research is needed in order to finalize this framework by completing the list of survey questions for each best practice subcategory for the four maturity stages.

## CONCLUSION

In this chapter, we have built a measurement based e-government portals' maturity model. This model is based on a set e-government portals' best practices that we have identified in the literature. This has allowed us to build an e-government portals' best practice model in (Fath-ALLAH et al., 2014b). Second, based on the review of the 25 maturity models that exist in the literature, we have identified the most important stages of maturity (Fath-ALLAH et al., 2014a, 2014c). Then, we have provided a detailed view of the four maturity stages of our maturity model and their corresponding best practice subcategories.

Afterwards, we have explained the architectural view of the MBeGPMM, which is composed of four stages (presence, interaction, transaction and integration). Each stage has its corresponding best practice categories and subcategories, and each best practice subcategory has its corresponding specific best practices. These specific best practices can be measured using the survey questions.

At last, we have explained the cyclic process of the MBeGPMM that allows both: calculating the maturity stage of the e-government portal, and determining the missing best practices at any stage of maturity using the output of the survey. The formulas used to calculate the maturity stage's compliance with best practices were also provided.

## REFERENCES

W3C. (2012). Web Content Accessibility Guidelines. Retrieved from http://www.w3.org/WAI/intro/wcag

Al-Khouri, A. M. (2011). An Innovative Approach for E-Government Transformation. arXiv Preprint arXiv:1105.6358. Retrieved from http://arxiv.org/abs/1105.6358

Al-Qutaish, R. E., & Abran, A. (2011). A Maturity Model of Software Product Quality. *Journal of Research & Practice in Information Technology*, 43(4), 307-327. Retrieved from http://search.ebscohost.com/login.aspx?direct=true&profile=ehost&scope=site&authtype=crawler&jrnl=1443458X&AN=87525733&h=HZhdR3x4ibqL7aU3c%2B9zIsOv37eI%2Bbn5kDNyjOgdGWxtuF5WNSkG9PbkjezkKex8OnAfORK%2F4jx%2FA8ZsKNrW0w%3D%3D&crl=c

Alasem, A. (2009). An overview of e-government metadata standards and initiatives based on Dublin Core. *Electronic Journal of E-Government*, *7*(1), 1–10.

Almazan, R. S., & Gil-Garcia, J. R. (2008). E-Government Portals in Mexico. Retrieved from http://www.igi-global.com/chapter/electronic-government-concepts-methodologies-tools/9818

Alsmadi, I., Al-Kabi, M., & Wahbeh, A. (2012). A Conceptual Organization for Websites Metrics and E-Government Websites: A Case Study. *International Journal of Information Communication Technologies and Human Development*, *4*(1), 93–117. doi:10.4018/jicthd.2012010107

Andreasson, K., Millard, J., & Snaprud, M. (2012). Evolving e-government benchmarking to better cover technology development and emerging societal needs. *Proceedings of the 6th International Conference on Theory and Practice of Electronic Governance* (pp. 430–439). Retrieved from http://dl.acm.org/citation.cfm?id=2463811

Assar, S. (2011). *Practical studies in e-Government.* Springer. Retrieved from http://books.google.be/books?hl=fr&lr=&id=DzZk-Riel_MC&oi=fnd&pg=PR9&dq=Practical+Studies+in+E-Government&ots=twg6CbeZ3T&sig=J31HDADy1ndhCjGpZH3ycgcGmXY

Assar, S., Boughzala, I., & Isckia, T. (2011). eGovernment trends in the Web 2.0 era and the open innovation perspective: an exploratory field study. In *Electronic Government* (pp. 210–222). Springer. Retrieved from http://link.springer.com/chapter/10.1007/978-3-642-22878-0_18

Berntzen, L., & Olsen, M. G. (2009). Benchmarking e-government-a comparative review of three international benchmarking studies. *Proceedings of the Third International Conference on Digital Society ICDS '09* (pp. 77–82). Retrieved from http://ieeexplore.ieee.org/xpls/abs_all.jsp?arnumber=4782854

Bhattacharya, D., Gulla, U., & Gupta, M. P. (2012). E-service quality model for Indian government portals: Citizens' perspective. *Journal of Enterprise Information Management*, *25*(3), 246–271. doi:10.1108/17410391211224408

Choudrie, J., Ghinea, G., & Weerakkody, V. (2004). Evaluating global e-government sites: A view using Web diagnostics tools. *Electronic Journal of E-Government*, *2*(2), 105–114.

Delone, W. H. (2003). The DeLone and McLean model of information systems success: A ten-year update. *Journal of Management Information Systems*, *19*(4), 9–30.

DeLone, W. H., & McLean, E. R. (1992). Information systems success: The quest for the dependent variable. *Information Systems Research*, *3*(1), 60–95. doi:10.1287/isre.3.1.60

European Commission. (2009). Benchmark Measurement of European eGovernment services, 8th Benchmark Measurement. Retrieved from http://www.capgemini.com/sites/default/files/resource/pdf/Benchmark_Measurement_of_European_eGovernment_services.pdf

European Commission. (2010). *Digitizing Public Services in Europe: Putting ambition into action, 9th Benchmark Measurement. Report Prepared by Capgemini* , IDC, Sogeti, IS-Practice and Indigov, RAND Europe and the Danish Technological Institute for the Directorate General for Communications Networks, Content and Technology.

European Commission. (2013). *Public Services Online 'Digital by Default or by Detour? Assessing User Centric eGovernment performance in Europe – eGovernment Benchmark 2012. Report Prepared by Capgemini* , IDC, Sogeti, IS-Practice and Indigov, RAND Europe and the Danish Technological Institute for the Directorate General for Communications Networks, Content and Technology.

Fang, Z. (2002). E-government in digital era: concept, practice, and development. International Journal of the Computer, the Internet and Management, 10(2), 1–22.

Fath-Allah, A., Cheikhi, L., Al-Qutaish, R. E., & Idri, A. (2014a). *E-Government Maturity Models: A Comparative Study*.

Fath-Allah, A., Cheikhi, L., Al-Qutaish, R. E., & Idri, A. (2014b). E-Government Portals Best Practices: A Comprehensive Survey.

Fath-Allah, A., Cheikhi, L., Al-Qutaish, R. E., & Idri, A. (2014c). *Towards a Measurement-Based E-Government Portals Maturity Model*.

Fath-Allah, A., Cheikhi, L., Al-Qutaish, R. E., & Idri, A. (2015). E-Government Portals' Maturity Models: A Best Practices' Coverage Perspective. *Journal of Software*. Retrieved from http://www.jsoftware.us

Forfás. (2008). *eGovernment: International Best Practices*. Retrieved from http://www.forfas.com/media/forfas080916_eGovernment.pdf

Georgescu, M., & Georgescu, I. (2008). Do We Need a Powerful E-Government. *Communications of the IBIMA*, 5.

Iribarren, M., Concha, G., Valdes, G., Solar, M., Villarroel, M. T., Gutiérrez, P., & Vásquez, Á. (2008). Capability maturity framework for eGovernment: A multi-dimensional model and assessing tool. In *Electronic Government* (pp. 136–147). Springer. Retrieved from http://link.springer.com/chapter/10.1007/978-3-540-85204-9_12

Kim, D.-Y., & Grant, G. (2010). E-government maturity model using the capability maturity model integration. *Journal of Systems and Information Technology*, *12*(3), 230–244. doi:10.1108/13287261011070858

Klischewski, R., & Askar, E. (2010). Success factors of developing G2G services: the case of Egypt. *Proceedings of the 4th International Conference on Theory and Practice of Electronic Governance* (pp. 152–160). Retrieved from http://dl.acm.org/citation.cfm?id=1930354

Kumar, V., Mukerji, B., Butt, I., & Persaud, A. (2007). Factors for successful e-government adoption: A conceptual framework. *Electronic Journal of E-Government*, *5*(1), 63–76.

Layne, K., & Lee, J. (2001). Developing fully functional E-government: A four stage model. *Government Information Quarterly*, *18*(2), 122–136. doi:10.1016/S0740-624X(01)00066-1

Lee, G., & Kwak, Y. H. (2012). *An Open Government Maturity Model for social media-based public engagement*. Government Information Quarterly. Retrieved from http://www.sciencedirect.com/science/article/pii/S0740624X1200086X

Makolm, J. (2002). Best practice in e-government. In *Electronic Government* (pp. 370–374). Springer. Retrieved from http://link.springer.com/chapter/10.1007/978-3-540-46138-8_60

N.A.O. (2002). Government on the Web II. Retrieved from http://www.nao.org.uk/publications/0102/government_on_the_web_ii.aspx

Papadomichelaki, X., & Mentzas, G. (2012). e-GovQual: A multiple-item scale for assessing e-government service quality. *Government Information Quarterly*, *29*(1), 98–109. doi:10.1016/j.giq.2011.08.011

Peters, R. M., Janssen, M., & van Engers, T. M. (2004). Measuring e-government impact: existing practices and shortcomings. *Proceedings of the 6th international conference on Electronic commerce* (pp. 480–489). Retrieved from http://dl.acm.org/citation.cfm?id=1052281

Plain Language Action and Information Network (PLAIN). (2014). What is Plain Language? Retrieved from http://www.plainlanguage.gov/whatisPL/

Posch, K. C., Posch, R., Tauber, A., Zefferer, T., & Zwattendorfer, B. (2011). Secure and Privacy-Preserving eGovernment—Best Practice Austria. In Rainbow of computer science (pp. 259–269). Springer; Retrieved from http://link.springer.com/chapter/10.1007/978-3-642-19391-0_19 doi:10.1007/978-3-642-19391-0_19

Rodríguez, R. A., Welicki, L., Giulianelli, D. A., & Vera, P. M. (2008). Measurement framework for evaluating e-governance on municipalities' websites. Proceedings of the 2nd international conference on Theory and practice of electronic governance (pp. 381–387). Retrieved from http://dl.acm.org/citation.cfm?id=1509176

Rohleder, S. J., & Jupp, V. (2004). eGovernment leadership: High performance, maximum value. Accenture.

Seifert, J. W., & McLoughlin, G. J. (2007). State e-government strategies: Identifying best practices and applications. Retrieved from http://oai.dtic.mil/oai/oai?verb=getRecord&metadataPrefix=html&identifier=ADA471212

Siau, K., & Long, Y. (2005). Synthesizing e-government stage models–a meta-synthesis based on meta-ethnography approach. *Industrial Management & Data Systems*, *105*(4), 443–458. doi:10.1108/02635570510592352

Sørum, H. (2011). An empirical investigation of user involvement, website quality and perceived user satisfaction in eGovernment environments. In Electronic Government and the Information Systems Perspective (pp. 122–134). Springer. Retrieved from http://link.springer.com/chapter/10.1007/978-3-642-22961-9_10 doi:10.1007/978-3-642-22961-9_10

The European Centre for Total Quality Management. (2002, July). E-Government A Best Practice Perspective.

UNDESA. (2012). UN E-Government Survey 2012: E-Government for the People (United Nations). New York, United States. Retrieved from http://unpan1.un.org/intradoc/groups/public/documents/un/unpan048065.pdf

United Nations. (2008). Main Features Reviewed by the United Nations e-Government Survey. Retrieved from http://unpan1.un.org/intradoc/groups/public/documents/un/unpan029361.pdf

United Nations. (2012). Compendium of Innovative E-government Practices (Vol. IV). UN. Retrieved from http://books.google.com/books?hl=en&lr=&id=tX83tuHyv7AC&oi=fnd&pg=PA3&dq=Compendium+of+Innovative+E-government+Practices&ots=9nBmYhcl8r&sig=vxiObuDH_rwak-FkYYLxVZ1FS3g

West, D. M. (2004). E-Government and the Transformation of Service Delivery and Citizen Attitudes. *Public Administration Review*, *64*(1), 15–27. doi:10.1111/j.1540-6210.2004.00343.x

West, D.M., & Deitch, A. (2004). Development of e-government strategies in Chile, Canada and Brazil. Retrieved from http://portal.oas.org/LinkClick.aspx?fileticket=UbyGRpAaPhY%3d&tabid=1168

West, D. M. (2007). Global e-government, 2007. United States: Center for Public Policy, Brown University; Retrieved from http://195.130.87.21:8080/dspace/handle/123456789/1028

Windley, P. J. (2002). eGovernment maturity. USA: Windleys' Technolometria. Retrieved from http://www.windley.com/docs/eGovernment%20Maturity.pdf

World Bank. (2005). Designing and Implementing e-Government: Key Issues, Best Practices and Lessons Learned. Retrieved from http://siteresources.worldbank.org/INTEDEVELOPMENT/Resources/559323-1114798035525/Workshop_Summary.pdf

World Bank. (2011). Definition of E-Government. Retrieved from http://web.worldbank.org/WBSITE/EXTERNAL/TOPICS/EXTINFORMATIONANDCOMMUNICATIONANDTECHNOLOGIES/EXTEGOVERNMENT/0,contentMDK:20507153~menuPK:702592~pagePK:148956~piPK:216618~theSitePK:702586,00.html

## KEY TERMS AND DEFINITIONS

**Customer Centricity:** Organizing e-government portals and services from a citizen perspective.

**Data Analytics:** Analyzing the data for insights.

**E-Government Maturity Model:** Set of stages (from basic to advanced ones) that can be used to determine the maturity stage of an e-government portal.

**E-Participation:** Involving the citizens in the e-government process.

**Ethnographic Work:** Grouping users according to some socio-cultural criteria like age and educational level.

**Eye-Tracking Techniques:** Observing users trying e-government services.

**One Stop Shop:** An e-government portal that offers a broad range of e-government services to the citizens.

# Chapter 9
# Challenges of Disinvestment in Public Sector Banks in India

**Sushil J. Lalwani**
*Sir Padampat Singhania University, India*

**Shweta Lalwani**
*Sir Padampat Singhania University, India*

## ABSTRACT

*Both Disinvestment and Privatization process in Public Sector Banks initiated by the then NDA Government came to an end soon after UPA Government took over. The Atal Bihari Vajpayee government had proposed to reduce government holding in state-run banks to 33% but the amendment could not be passed in Parliament as Congress, which was the main Opposition party, blocked the move. Later on Congress party with other partners came to power and even The Ministry of Disinvestment was closed .The recommendations of Disinvestment Commission could not be implemented. For last one decade disinvestment process came to a grinding halt, however, now again there are possibilities that Public Sector Banks may initiate the process again. Privatization process may seem to be a remote possibility at present, however, Disinvestment is on agenda of present government. The Government is now set to reduce shareholding to less than 52% while maintaining ownership but selling additional shares which will infuse more capital to fulfil capital adequacy norms as per Basel III. There are a number of challenges to this process and it is necessary to expedite the process. It is assumed that disinvestment process will make public sector banks more accountable and also efficiency may improve, ultimately pave way for privatization in near future.*

## INTRODUCTION: WHY DISINVESTMENT?

Disinvestment helps in mobilization of resources for rapid economic growth and makes banks more accountable to public which indirectly improves efficiency. More than 51% shares with public sector banks are said to be a potential source of capital formation in India. With an aim to help public sector banks raise capital, government is considering to reduce its stake up to 52% in a phased manner in these banks, Finance Minister Arun Jaitely in the Rajya Sabha, said that "A proposal for allowing public sector banks (PSBs) to raise capital from public market by diluting Government of India holding up to 52 per cent in phased manner is under consideration." (PTI, 2014)

DOI: 10.4018/978-1-4666-9908-3.ch009

World organizations have time and again warned inefficiency of state controlled banking in India and suggested to reduce shareholding. "The World Bank feels that Indian Banking system remains a massively inefficient state controlled system and not competitive. It has desired that public ownership in public sector banks be gradually reduced." (G., 2001)

The highest monetary authority in India, Reserve Bank Of India and its Dy. Governor opined that, "Unless the public sector banks are privatized, the Indian banking system will remain a public sector banking system. At the present time, public sector banking system operates like a Monolith, if the Indian system is to become modern efficient system, which is internationally competitive, it is essential that the Monolith should crack." (Tarapore. S.S, 1998). Accordingly, "The then Government had decided to accept the recommendations of the Narasimham Committee on Banking Sector Reforms for reducing the requirement of Minimum Shareholding by the nationalized banks to 33 per cent" (Rajeev, 2005)

Many Governments, particularly Congress led coalition had different opinion on issue of privatization or disinvestment of nationalized banks in India. The then Finance Minister (P.Chidambaram),rightly remarked in a statement that, while the government was willing to reduce its shareholding in public sector banks to 33 per cent, the basic public sector character of these banks would not be compromised. No single entity would be able to corner a major chunk of the shares. What we are saying is that earlier the then government thought of capitalization of the banks and we pumped in over Rs.200 billion to recapitalize these banks in 1993.But we also amended the Banking Nationalization Act to bring the equity so far as the State Bank of India is concerned. Now there are many banks that are coming to us for recapitalization. I have no hesitation in admitting that I am not in a position to give them any money today because I do not have the money to give. Then how do the banks recapitalize? They go to the market and recapitalize; they raise money from the market." (Nagraj, 1999)

The reduction of government share in equity capital of PSBs to 52 per cent will enable mobilisation of Rs 89,120 Crore approx. on the basis of current market price on November 21." There are about two dozen PSBs and government holding in them is from 56.26% to 88.63%. Public sector banks require equity capital of Rs 2.4 lakh crore by 2018 to meet Basel III norms.

Over the next five years, India's public sector banks could face a major shortage of capital. A recent Reserve Bank of India (RBI) committee looking into the governance of public sector banks has forecast that the state-owned banks require anywhere between Rs 2,10,000 crore and Rs 5,87,000 crore by 2018, depending on how fast their loans to corporates, individuals and farmers grow and to what extent those loans turn into non-performing assets, thus requiring them to be written off. Investment banks have their own estimates — Morgan Stanley, for instance, estimates that the banks will require about Rs 2,98,300 crore by 2019. (Celestine, 2014)

Banks will require the capital for reasons best known in financial circles. It is to fund growth in loans. For each loan they have to set aside a proportion of capital. An economic revival will bring in its wake strong demand for loans for investment, and it's in the government's own interest that banks are in a position to make those loans and have that enhanced amount of capital on hand. In fact public sector banks need more capital to write off non-performing assets also to ensure greater transparency in their financial statements.

Public sector banks, which have weaker internal controls and face political pressures to a greater degree than their private sector counterparts, consequently have steeper bad loan problems, too. Finally, banks will need greater funds to implement new norms relating to how to account for loans and how much capital they need to set aside for different categories of loans. Raising these funds, though, will require several steps, apart from legislative changes. Attracting private capital into public sector banks will need at least some governance and structural reform that need more thinking and debate. Reduce the government holding in PSEs to less than 50 per cent by transferring share to mutually complementary firms by creating Japanese style keiretsu, tied around a public sector bank or financial institution. (Nagraj, 1999)

*Public Sector Banks under financial crunch need disinvestment:* That is why a total capital of Rs. 12517 Crore was infused to ensure capital adequacy norms set for banks from the year 2007-08 to 2013-14.Disinvestment can bring about a boost in capital for Banks and therefore, this step is gaining momentum in the Indian economy. In Budget speech, Finance Minister Arun Jaitely had announced the government's intention to cut its stake in Banks so that present requirement of Rs.3 Lakh Crore for capital adequacy can be ensured. (PTI, www.articles.economictimes.indiatimes.com, 2014). The government decided to reduce the floor on its holding as it could only spare a little over Rs 11,000 crore for public sector banks. The rest of the funds need to be raised from the market. It has asked banks to sell non-core assets and initiate several other measures including disinvestment to meet the funding needs.

Disinvestment is looked upon as a source for economic development. In India, this tool has been used for this purpose, however the strategy used has not been sound. Banking sector as well as many other public sector enterprises have a great potential for raising funds, but it has to be used with a caution and with a long term perspective plan. Disinvestment, irrespective of the Banking sector, may have specific objectives:

1. Reduce burden on the Government
2. Improve public finances
3. Introduce Competition with market discipline
4. Encourage wide share in ownership
5. Depoliticize public services

To simplify, objectives are shown as per Figure 1:

*Figure 1. Objectives of Disinvestment*

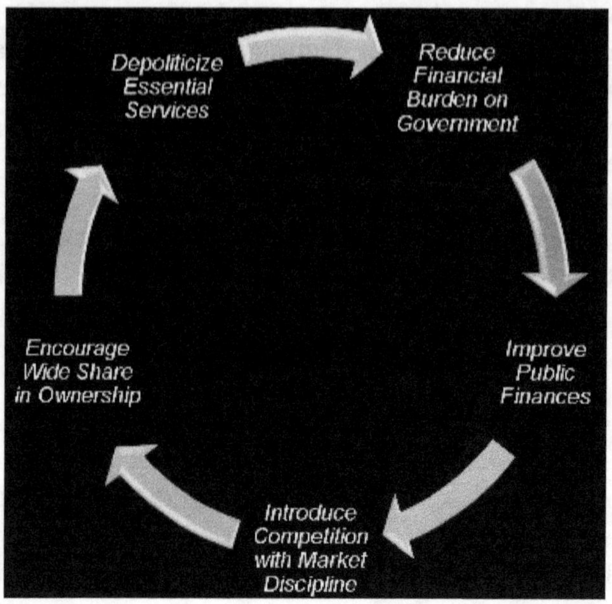

The Public Sector Banks have had an ad hoc disinvestment policy and therefore, raised capital in instalments without any sound policy. In context of statement by the Finance Minister, the public sector banks have more than 52% shareholding which could be utilized for raising more capital. (PTI, 2014). This additional capital raised through market may help PSBs to fulfil capital adequacy norms as per Basel agreements arrived at from time to time.

The objective of the paper is to analyze availability of funds with public sector banks though disinvestment to strengthen them to survive in global financial scenario and also to suggest that in the recent past an ad hoc policy was adopted to raise funds as per needs is not good for the economy. Even now there is a scope of selling shares by public sector banks and if taken up at a starch, may mobilize funds in huge amount for a better utilization.

Existing shareholding with public sector banks can give an idea about the scope for selling shares to public. The shareholding pattern is visible from Table 1:

*Table 1. PSUs Share Holding Pattern*[1]

| S.N. | Name of the Bank | % of Shareholding with Government of India |
|---|---|---|
| 1 | Allahabad Bank | 58.90 |
| 2 | Andhra Bank | 60.14 |
| 3 | Bank of Baroda | 56.26 |
| 4 | Bank of India | 66.70 |
| 5 | Bank of Maharashtra | 79.80 |
| 6 | Canara Bank | 69.00 |
| 7 | Central Bank of India | 88.63 |
| 8 | Corporation Bank | 63.33 |
| 9 | Dena Bank | 58.01 |
| 10 | Indian Bank | 81.51 |
| 11 | Indian Overseas Bank | 73.80 |
| 12 | Oriental Bank of Commerce | 59.13 |
| 13 | Punjab National Bank | 58.87 |
| 14 | Punjab &Sind Bank | 79.62 |
| 15 | Syndicate Bank | 67.39 |
| 16 | UCO Bank | 77.20 |
| 17 | Union Bank of India | 60.47 |
| 18 | United Bank of India | 78.92 |
| 19 | Vijaya Bank | 74.06 |
| 20 | State Bank of India | 59.87 |
| 21 | IDBI Bank Ltd. | 76.50 |

## DISINVESTMENT PROCESS IN INDIA

Banking sector has a long history of disinvestment. In 2008-09 the following banks raised Rs.1900 Crores through disinvestment: UCO 450,Central Bank of India 117, Central Bank of India 583,United Bank of India 250 and Vijaya Bank 500 Crores. Similarly, in the year 2009-10 Rs.1200 crores were mobilized through disinvestment by UCO Bank 450, Central Bank of India 450 and United Bank of India 300 crores. In the year 2010-11 again a sum of Rs.20117.23 Crores were mobilized through disinvestment and the share of banks was-UCO 300,Central Bank of India 250,United Bank of India 250,Vijaya Bank700,Bank of Maharashtra 588,Union Bank of India 111,again UCO Bank 373,IDBI Bank Ltd. 3119.04,again Central Bank of India 2003.19,Allahabad Bank 292 & 378,Andhra Bank 618 & 555,Bank of India 1010,again Bank of Maharashtra 352,Corporation Bank 309,Dena Bank 539,Indian Overseas Bank 1054,Syndicate Bank 633,again UCO Bank third time in the same year 940,Secodn time for United Bank of India 308,second time for Vijaya Bank 368,Bank of Baroda 2461,Oriental Bank of Commerce 1740,Punjab National Bank 184 and lastly Union Bank of India 682.

In the year 2011-12 disinvestment contributed to the economy a sum of Rs.12000 Crores through SBI 7900,Bank of Maharashtra 470,Central Bank of India 676,Indian Overseas Bank 1441,Punjab National Bank 655,UCO Bank 48 and IDBI Bank Ltd. 810 Crores.

In the year 2012-13 a sum of Rs. 12517 Crores were contributed by disinvestment through Bank of Baroda 850,Bank of India 809,Bank of Maharashtra 406,Central Bank of India 2406,Corporation Bank 204,IDBI Bank 555,Indian Overseas Bank 1000,PNB 1248,Punjab & Sind Bank 140,UCO Bank 681,Union Bank of India 1114,United Bank of India 100 and SBI 3004.

In instalments money was collected by sale of shares by the public sector banks which cannot be said to be a sound policy. There is a need for a final projection to use disinvestment as a source of capital formation or to put the same capital with the bank itself to fulfil capital adequacy norms required by the Basel agreements.

## ULTIMATE GOAL: PRIVATIZATION

Recently a Reserve Bank of India (RBI) panel headed by former Axis Bank Chairman PJ. Nayak had suggested that the government must cut its holding in public sector banks to under 50 per cent. It said that State-owned banks suffer due to ‘externally imposed constraints’ such as dual regulation by the RBI and the finance ministry and external vigilance by agencies such as the CVC and CAG, among others. The Nayak report said if the government’s stake in these banks were to reduce to less than 50 per cent, together with certain other executive measures, these external constraints and interventions will be removed. The panel said the Government should distance itself from several governance functions and all banks should be incorporated under the Companies Act. A bank investment company should be constituted and the government’s holding in all banks should then be transferred to this entity.

## METHODOLOGY

The present study has divided shareholding pattern of public sector banks into two parts, namely, Government Shareholding as a % of total number of shares and Public Shareholding as a % of total number of shares. Published data has been used and source of data is Annual reports and popular websites.[2] On the basis of data so collected, an analysis of public shareholding has been carried out to find out the possible mobilization of funds if disinvestment takes place. For this purpose it has been assumed that public sector banks will retail at least 51% shares to retail ownership and management of banks. Hence residual of Government shareholding beyond 51% has been calculated to find out funds availability with these banks.

The study is restricted to 21 public sector banks which exclude a few State Bank Group Banks for which separate data are not precise and some of them are in the process of merger.

The Research paper shall examine mobilization of resources under disinvestment process and also discuss possibilities of a popular move of privatization because the governments have no business to be in business. It is a matter of research analysis that these options will have limited impact with limited additional money in hand. The Disinvestment process itself may be inadequate and the only solution is for the government to reduce its holding below 50% or go for privatization, however, this research paper shall concentrate only on finances available to public sector banks under disinvestment process.

The RBI report on bank boards had suggested several radical moves, including the repealing of existing legislation governing public sector banks, and the creation of an independent bank holding company which would actually hold the government's equity stake in them.

The research analysis will reveal that one time disinvestment process be undertaken by Public Sector Banks so as to enable planners to raise more capital. Hence calculation has been made to calculate % of shareholding which can be disinvested by strategic sale method or other methods.

## Problems: Public vs. Private Banks

Public sector banks have all such problems which other PSUs in the country are confronted with. Needless to analyse, Public sector banks are facing number of problems and ultimately privatization is the only answer to existing problems and particularly the efficiency part.

As Rana Kapoor, founder and managing director of Yes Bank pointed out that public and private sector banks operate within the same environment and are subject to the same regulatory conditions, yet their performance is different. (Celestine, 2014). He advocates that an executive credit committee comprising the chairman and senior bank executives takes such decisions with any one such executive having a veto over the decision. "This way there is a spirit of collective decision making that exists," he says. He also suggests the removal of political appointees from bank boards and the splitting of the posts of the chairman and managing director. Notwithstanding, there are number of other problems which calls for a policy decision at apex level to go for disinvestment as well as privatization.

The British experience is a good experience of privatization .British public sector enterprises have been working extremely well after privatization. The then Prime Minister Mrs. Thatcher took bold and successful decision of privatizing several PSUs (1977) This phenomenon also calls for disinvestment or privatization process in the country to achieve such financial success. There are similarities between the two economies. (Mishra, 2002)

At present, if disinvestment is undertaken, then Public sector banks are likely to raise a good amount which is clear from table 2 given:

*Table 2. Showing Disinvestment potential of public sector banks*[3]

| S.N. | Name of the Bank | % of Shareholding with Government of India now available for disinvestment (Above 52%) |
|---|---|---|
| 1 | Allahabad Bank | 6.90 |
| 2 | Andhra Bank | 8.14 |
| 3 | Bank of Baroda | 4.26 |
| 4 | Bank of India | 14.70 |
| 5 | Bank of Maharashtra | 27.80 |
| 6 | Canara Bank | 17.00 |
| 7 | Central Bank of India | 32.63 |
| 8 | Corporation Bank | 11.33 |
| 9 | Dena Bank | 6.01 |
| 10 | Indian Bank | 29.51 |
| 11 | Indian Overseas Bank | 21.80 |
| 12 | Oriental Bank of Commerce | 7.13 |
| 13 | Punjab National Bank | 6.87 |
| 14 | Punjab &Sind Bank | 27.62 |
| 15 | Syndicate Bank | 15.39 |
| 16 | UCO Bank | 25.20 |
| 17 | Union Bank of India | 8.47 |
| 18 | United Bank of India | 26.92 |
| 19 | Vijaya Bank | 22.06 |
| 20 | State Bank of India | 7.87 |
| 21 | IDBI Bank Ltd. | 23.50 |

## Potential Disinvestment

In 21 Sample units of Banks, (See Table 2) 8 public sector banks have less than 10% of shareholding beyond 51% government holding to retain ownership and management. These 8 banks which have a small potential for disinvestment are Union Bank of India 9.47%, State Bank of India 8.87%, Andhra Bank 8.86%,Oriental Bank of Commerce 8.13%,Allahabad Bank 7.90%, Punjab National Bank 7.87%,, Dena Bank 7.01%, Bank of Baroda 5.26% of their total shareholding. What is the reason that these banks kept a meagre amount of shareholding beyond 51% is not clear in financial circles, however, one decision this way or that way has to be taken and these Banks must offload this surplus in the market immediately and hold required share only to be a PSB Bank. In principle decision must be taken now that all PSBs will offload shareholding beyond 51% and in that process all banks must have a deadline to offload. Similarly 9 Banks still have a large potential for disinvestment namely Central Bank of India 37.63%, Indian Bank 30.51%, Bank of Maharashtra 28.80, Punjab & Sind Bank 28.62%, United Bank of India 27.92%,UCO Banks 26.20%,IDBI 25.50%,Vijaya Bank 23.06 and IOB 22.80%.These 9 Banks can contribute a lot and decision has to be taken to offload this shareholding to mobilize more resources. Remaining 4 PSBs have shareholding between 11% to 20% of their total shareholding which should also be directed to offload surplus share in the market.

The RBI report points to several other constraints that public sector banks face as opposed to those from the private sector. These include dual regulation of such banks by the finance ministry and RBI, the short tenures of top executives, and the control exercised on banks by the Central Vigilance Commission, which impedes any attempt to take decisions.

The report does caution that "in private sector banks senior management is incentivized on the basis of bank profitability, and the compensation paid out — through stock options — is in substantial measure contingent on the stock price of the bank. However HN Sinor, a veteran banker who served on numerous RBI committees and headed the Indian Banks Association, says "the ultimate aim should be for government to divest its stake substantially from the state owned banks. India will need bigger banks. Now, to build bigger banks organically is very difficult. So to do it in an inorganic way by clubbing some of the banks will probably be the best route." Arundhati Bhattacharya, SBI Chairperson, in an interview to ET said "My personal opinion is that the government cannot keep pumping in cash into these banks year after year, they have to take the decision to reduce the stake below 51%. Any other measure will be temporary."

## CHALLENGES, CONCLUSION AND SUGGESTIONS

Disinvestment and Privatization in India have been controversial which has taken up as an economic and political problem ever since efforts for privatization/Disinvestment started in the country. The scheme had a half-hearted implementation. This process was recommended by a number of committees but end result is same and that is why it has emerged as a challenge in India.

It is concluded that entire process of disinvestment/privatization lacked professional approach. The Rangarajan Committee recommendations emphasised the need for substantial disinvestment. It stated that the percentage of equity to be disinvested could be up to 49% for industries explicitly reserved for the public sector. It recommended that in exceptional cases, such as the enterprises, which had a dominant market share or where separate identity had to be maintained for strategic reasons, the target public ownership level could be kept at 26%, i.e. disinvestment could take place to the extent of 74%. In other cases, it recommended 100% disinvestment of Government stake. Holding of 51% or more equity by the Government was recommended only for 6 Scheduled industries, namely: Coal and Lignite; Mineral oils; Arms, Ammunition and Defence equipment; Atomic Energy, Radioactive minerals & Railway transport. However, the Government did not take any decision on the recommendations of the Rangarajan Committee. Ritu (2015). Divestment Commission Recommendations in February 1997-October 1999 were not taken seriously. Similarly, G.V. Ramakrishna Commission in August 1996 recommended divestment/privatization of 58 different PSUs but only a few PSUs could be privatized, however, this was first major breakthrough .In the Budget Speech, 1998-99, the Finance Minister stated that ——Government has taken decision that shareholding in public sector enterprises will be reduced to 26 per cent. In Presidential address to Joint Session of Parliament, February 2001 it was stated thus: "The government's approach to PSUs has a threefold objective: revival of potentially viable enterprises; closing down of those PSUs that cannot be revived; and bringing down government equity in non-strategic PSUs to 26 per cent or lower. National Common Minimum Programme (NCMP) of the UPA coalition government was released on May 28, 2004. NCMP confirmed the commitment of the UPA government. On May 26, 2005, the Finance Minister declared to disinvest 10 per cent of government-owned equity in the Navratna company BHEL, however, after protests from the Left parties, this move came to a grinding halt.

The Finance Minister also ruled out the strategic sale route of disinvestment while keeping open the offer of sale route in13 profit-making PSEs identified by the earlier NDA government. In June 2006 another attempt was made, this time for the sale of 10 per cent stake each in two non-navratna profit-making companies — NALCO (National Aluminium Company) in Orissa and NLC (Neyveli Lignite Corporation) in Tamil Nadu.. On July 6, 2006, the Prime Minister decided to keep all disinvestment in abeyance till further orders.

In September 2012, then RBI governor D. Subbarao had said that the banking sector would need around Rs.5 trillion capital, of which equity capital would be Rs.1.75 trillion. Of this, between Rs.70,000 Crore and Rs.1 trillion can be raised from the market. This may not be a difficult task as between 2007 and 2012, banks had raised equity capital to the tune of Rs.52, 000 Crore from the primary markets.

Disinvestment in public sector banks is inevitable in view of completion of capital adequacy norms. Disinvestment of public sector banks has to be completed once for all and ad hoc policy should be avoided. It is suggested that a final policy for disinvestment should be announced.

Accordingly, disinvestment is of immediate necessity.

## REFERENCES

Celestine, A. (2014, June 15). *Shortage of capital: Should FM Arun Jaitley divest government's stake in PSU banks?* Retrieved from www.articles.economictimes.indiatimes.com: http://articles.economictimes.indiatimes.com/2014-06-15/news/50598272_1_public-sector-banks-psu-banks-loans

Disinvestment in PSBs in phased manner under consideration: FM Arun Jaitley. (2014, December 2). *The Economic Times.* Retrieved from http://articles.economictimes.indiatimes.com/2014-12-02/news/56648934_1_psbs-lakh-crore-bank-capitalisation

G., G. (2001). Privatization in India. In G. G., *Privatization* (pp. 213-214). Delhi: Mittal Publications.

Government to bring down stake in PSU banks to 52%. (2014, November 9). *The Economic Times.* Retrieved from [REMOVED HYPERLINK FIELD]http://articles.economictimes.indiatimes.com/2014-11-09/news/55917917_1_psu-banks-lakh-cror

Govt to bring down stake in PSU banks to 52%: Jaitley. (2014, November). *The Hindu Business Line.* Retrieved from [REMOVED HYPERLINK FIELD]http://www.thehindubusinessline.com/money-and-banking/govt-to-bring-down-stake-in-psu-banks-to-52-jaitley/article6580417.ece

Mishra, D. (2002). Privatization A Global Perspective. In *Disinvestment* (p. 73). Delhi: Vikas Publishing House.

Nagraj. (1999). Disinvestment and Privatization in India: Assessment and Options. *Indira Gandhi Institute of Development Research.* Mumbai.

Rajeev, D. (2005, July 26). *Business World.*

Tarapore.S.S (Composer). (1998). Speech. [D. G. RBI, Performer] India.

## ENDNOTES

1 Source: www.moneycontrol.com MARKETS SHAREHOLDING SCREENER as on 30th September 2014

2 www.moneycontrol.com Markets Shareholding Screener as on 30th September 2014

3 Source: www.moneycontrol.com MARKETS SHAREHOLDING SCREENER as on 30th September 2014

# Chapter 10
# Basel III:
## A Step Ahead in Banking Risk Management

**Shishir Kumar Gujrati**
*Union Bank of India, India*

## ABSTRACT

*Banking sector is considered as a backbone of any economy. It not only transacts money but also helps in promoting trade credit and various social welfare schemes of government. With the changing scenario of business, banking has also undergone a paradigm shift. From manual banking it has shifted to computerized core banking and moving fast towards paperless banking with the use of internet and mobile technology. With the expansion of banking activities, various types of risks associated with banking business have also expanded. To counter them, Basel I guidelines were issued in 1988, the loopholes of which were covered in improved guidelines issued in 1996 known as Basel II. The economic slowdown of 2008 revealed that risk containing measures were not enough to enable the banks in absorbing shocks arising from financial and economic stress. Thus, to improve the ability of banks to withstand the economic and financial stress, Basel III guidelines were issued in December 2010. The present paper attempts to explore the areas where Basel III supersedes its previous accord and how it strengthens the banks to face the periods of economic and financial adversaries.*

## INTRODUCTION

As banks no longer operate in a protected and regulated environment, there is an imperative need for them to develop and improve their capability to understand the changes in their economic environment and other circumstances having a critical bearing on their business activities. Risk is the potentiality of the events expected or unexpected to have an adverse affect on the earnings of the financial institution and the risk management is the process of identifying, measuring, monitoring and controlling risk. The risk arises due to uncertainties which in turn arise due to changes taking place in prevailing economic, social and political environment and due to lack of non-availability of the information concerning such changes. Globalization, privatization and liberalization have opened upon new methods of financial transaction where risk level is very high. Each transaction taken by bank changes the risk profile of the bank. Hence, providing real time risk information is one of the key challenges of the risk management exercise. In the process of financial intermediation, banks are exposed to severe competition and hence

DOI: 10.4018/978-1-4666-9908-3.ch010

are compelled to encounter various types of financial and non-financial risks. *Figure 1, 'Type of Risks'* shows a broad bifurcation of various types of risks.

1. **Credit Risk:** The risk that the borrower will not be able to meet the obligations under the terms of the original agreement. There is always a scope for the borrower to default from his commitments for one or the other reason resulting in the crystallization of credit risk to the bank. Such risks can also arrive from the reduction in the portfolio value arising from actual or perceived deterioration in credit quality. Thus, credit risk is a combined outcome of default risk and exposure risk (Indian Institute of Banking and Finance, 2009).
2. **Market Risk:** It is the risk of incurring losses on account of movement in the market prices on all the positions held by banks. It is the risk to the bank's earnings and capital due to changes in the market level of interest rates or price of securities, foreign exchange and equities as well as the volatilities of those prices. Liquidity risk is defined as the inability to obtain funds to meet cash flow obligations. It can be in the form of (i) funding risk which may arise from the need to replace net outflows due to unanticipated withdrawal or non-renewal of deposits (ii) time risk which arises from the need to compensate the change of performing assets into non performing one and (iii) call risk which arises due to crystallization of contingent liabilities. Interest rate risk refers to the potential impact on net interest income or net interest margin caused by unexpected changes in market interest rates. Forex (Foreign Exchange) risk is the risk of loss that bank may suffer on account of adverse exchange rate movements (Indian Institute of Banking and Finance, 2009).
3. **Operational Risk:** It is the risk of loss resulting from inadequate or failed internal processes, people and systems or from external events. Strategic risk is the risk arising from adverse business decisions, improper implementation of decisions or lack of responsiveness to industry changes (Indian Institute of Banking and Finance, 2009).

*Figure 1. Type of Risks*

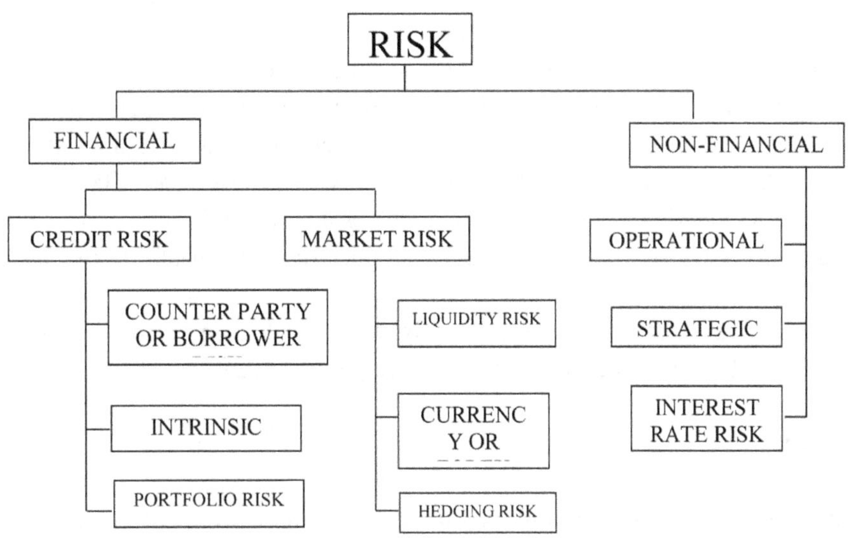

## Management of Risk

Risk management is a comprehensive process adopted by an organization that seeks to minimize the adverse effects it is exposed to due to various factors- economic, political or environmental, some of them inherent to the business, other unforeseen and unexpected. Present paper seeks to identify various risks faced by the banking industry and the process to identify and measure the risk and the provisions made to minimize them.

The asset liability management (ALM) is a part of the overall risk management system in the banks. It implies examination of all assets and liabilities simultaneously on a continuous basis with a view to ensuring a proper balance between fund mobilization and their deployment with respect to their (a) maturity profiles (b) cost (c) yield (d) risk exposure etc.

Management of risk involves the following process:

1. **Risk Identification**: It consists of identifying various risks associated with the risk taking at the transaction level and examining its impact on the portfolio and capital requirement.
2. **Risk Measurement:** It seeks to capture variations in the earnings, market value, losses due to default etc. arising out of uncertainties associated with various risk elements. Quantitative measures of risk can be classified into- based on sensitivity, based on volatility and based on downside potential.
3. **Risk Pricing:** Risk in banking transaction impact banks in two ways- (i) banks have to maintain necessary capital which is not without cost (ii) there is a probability of loss associated with all risk which needs to be factored into pricing. Risk pricing implies factoring risk into pricing through capital charge and loss possibilities. This would be in addition to the actual costs incurred in the transaction. Pricing takes following things into account- (i) cost of deployable funds (ii) operating expenses (iii) loss possibilities and (iv) capital charge.
4. **Risk Monitoring and Control:** The approach to risk management centres on facilitating implementation of risk and business policies simultaneously in a consistent manner. In order to achieve objective, banks put in place the following- (i) an organizational structure (ii) comprehensive risk measurement approach (iii)risk management policies adopted at corporate level and (iv) guidelines and other parameters used to govern risk taking. The banks should conduct periodic reviews of its risk management process to ensure its integrity, accuracy and reasonableness.
5. **Risk Mitigation:** Since risk arises from uncertainties associated with the risk elements, risk reduction is achieved by adopting strategies that eliminate or reduce the uncertainties associated with the risk elements. The techniques to investigate different types of risks are different. Risk mitigation measures aim to reduce downside variability in net cash flow but it also reduces upside potential simultaneously. In fact, risk mitigation measures reduce the risk variability in net cash flow.

Table 1, shows risk weighted assets and risk weighted provided on various types of advances. It ranges between twenty (20%) to hundred and twenty five percent (125%).

## Basel Approach

Towards the end of 1974, the Basel Committee on Banking Supervision (BCBS), under the auspices of the Bank of International Settlement comprising of Central Bank Governors from 10 participating countries was formed to set a minimal capital requirement for banks, first published in 1988 as Basel

*Table 1. Risk Weighted Assets*

| S. No. | Criteria of Categorization | Risk Weightage Provided |
|---|---|---|
| 1 | **Advance upto 5 crores or Turnover upto 50 crores** | **75%** |
| 2 | Advances greater than 5 crores linked to External Rating | |
| | AAA | 20% |
| | AA | 30% |
| | A | 50% |
| | BBB | 100% |
| | BB or Poor | 150% |
| | Unrated Advance | 100% |
| 3 | Investment in capital instruments of NBFC | 125% |
| 4 | Advance made to Real Estate firms irrespective of amount or rating | 100% |
| 5 | Capital market exposure | 125% |

Accord. The minimum capital requirement was linked to the credit exposure of the banks. As per the guidelines issued, all the banks were advised to have Capital Adequacy Ratio (CAR) at least 8%. Basel I provided only for a credit risk. However, the concept of market risk was implemented through an amendment in 1996. In Jan 1999, for dealing with the new era of challenges for the banking sector, the Basel Committee proposed a new capital accord which is known as Base II and the final draft of which was released in June 2004. (King & Terbert, 2011) H As per the guidelines of RBI, the Indian Banks have started following the provisions of Basel II from the financial year 2009-10. *Figure 2, 'Basel II Accord'* shows that, it is based on three pillars namely Minimum capital requirement, supervisory review and market discipline.

## Pillar I: Minimum Capital Requirement

It is set by the capital ratio which is defined as (Total Capital – (Tier I + Tier II + Tier III)/ Credit risk + Market risk + Operational risk). Core capital consists of paid up capital, free reserves and unallocated surplus less deduction. Tier II capital consists of debt of less than 5 year term, loan loss reserve, revaluation reserve, investment fluctuation reserve and redeemable preference shares. Tier II capital should not be more than 100% of Tier I and debt part of Tier II capital may not exceed 50% of Tier I capital. Tier III capital consists of short term debts having a maturity of at least two years. Tier III capital should not exceed 250% of Tier I capital (King & Terbert, 2011).

Total Risk Weighted Assets (RWA) = Risk Weighted Assets for Credit Risk+(12.5*Capital requirement for Market Risk)+(12.5* Capital requirement for Operational Risk)Capital Adequacy Ratio (CAR) = Regulatory Capital / Total RWA

*Figure 2.*

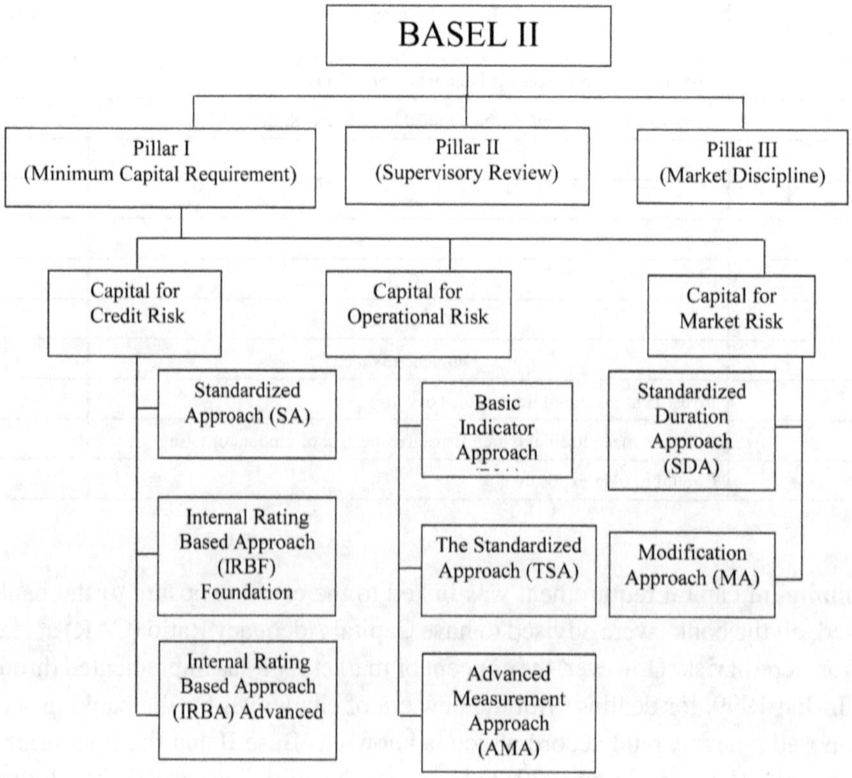


In case of credit risk, banks have to follow Standardized Approach and Internal Rating Based approach, either foundation or advanced. Capital charge for operational risk can be calculated using Basic Indicator Approach, Standardized Approach and Advanced Management Approach. The banks have to move from basic approach to advanced approach but cannot revert back.

Basic Indicator Approach (BIA) = K = $\sum$(GI 1,2,3… *$\alpha$)/3

where, GI= Gross Income positive (annual) of last 3 years and $\alpha$ = 15% as set by Basel

## Pillar II: Supervisory Review Process

The supervisor must ensure compliance of minimum standards and disclosure requirements of more advanced methods on a continuing basis (King & Terbert, 2011). Four key principles for supervisory review are-

1. Banks should have a process for assessing their capital adequacy in relation to their risk profile and a strategy for maintaining their capital levels.

2. Supervisors should review and evaluate bank's internal capital adequacy assessments and strategies as well as their ability to monitor and ensure their compliance with regulatory capital ratio.
3. Supervisors should expect banks to operate above the minimum regulatory capital ratios and should have the ability to require banks to hold capital in excess of the minimum.
4. Supervisors should seek to intervene at an early stage to prevent capital from falling below the minimum levels required to support the risk characteristics of a particular bank and should require rapid remedial action if capital is not maintained.

### Pillar III: Market Discipline

The purpose of Pillar III- Market Discipline is to complement the minimum capital requirement (P1) and the supervisory review process (P2). Pillar III provides disclosure requirements for banks. These disclosures will allow market participants to assess key information and thereby make informed decision about a bank. The disclosure is generally made on semi annual basis. However, qualitative disclosures related to policies, systems etc. are made on annual basis while critical information related to Tier I capital, capital ratios and their components may be published quarterly.

## BASEL III

The economic slowdown of 2008 revealed that risk containing measures were not enough to enable the banks in absorbing shocks arising from financial and economic stress. Thus, to improve the ability of banks to withstand the economic and financial stress, Basel III guidelines were issued in December 2010. BASEL III is only a continuation of effort initiated by the Basel Committee on Banking Supervision to enhance the banking regulatory framework under BASEL I and BASEL II. This latest Accord now seeks to improve the banking sector's ability to deal with financial and economic stress, improve risk management and strengthen the banks' transparency. The basic structure of BASEL III remains unchanged with three mutually reinforcing pillars. (http://www.iba.org.in/events/Event%20Report.pdf)

### Major Features of BASEL III

1. **Quality of capital:** The reforms of Basel III seek to ensure that the capital base of every internationally active bank is backed by a high-quality buffer that can absorb losses during periods of economic distress. Basel III aims to strengthen the fundamental definition of capital, with a focus on its overall quality, transparency and consistency.
2. **Capital & Counter Cyclical Buffers:** As part of Basel III reforms, two additional capital buffers intended to serve as further defenses against future losses: a capital conservation buffer and a countercyclical buffer. The common principle underlying both buffers is that banks should build up pools of capital during "good times," *i.e.*, periods of strong growth that can be drawn down during the inevitable "bad times" when unexpected losses may occur. The capital conservation buffer requires banks to hold an additional 2.5 percent of Total Capital. (https://rbi.org.in/scripts/NotificationUser.aspx?Mode=0&Id=9073)

3. **Leverage Ratio:** According to Basel Committee on Banking Supervision, Bank for International Settlements (2009). Strengthening the Resilience of the Banking Sector: Consultative Document 13. Basel III's "leverage ratio" is calculated by comparing Tier 1 capital with "total exposure," without reference to RWAs. The overall target is a leverage ratio of at least 3 percent (*i.e.*, Tier 1 capital should be at least three percent of total exposure). The Liquidity Coverage Ratio (LCR) is designed to ensure that an internationally active bank has sufficient unencumbered, high-quality liquid assets to offset the net cash outflows it could encounter under a month long acute stress scenario that includes both systemic and institution-specific shocks. The LCR requires that a bank's stock of high- quality liquid assets be at least equal to its total net cash outflows for the next 30 days, which is defined as the total expected cash outflows minus the total expected cash inflows in the stress scenario, up to a cap of 75 percent of expected outflows (http://www.bis.org/publ/bcbs164.pdf).

**LCR Formula:** $\frac{\text{Stock of high-quality liquid assets}}{\text{Total net cash outflows over the next 30 calendar days}} \geq 100\%$

The Net Stable Funding Ratio (NSFR) seeks to promote medium- and long-term funding by establishing minimum amounts of liquidity based on a bank's assets and activities, including those related to off-balance sheet (OBS) commitments—over a one-year period of extended stress. The NSFR requires that Available Stable Funding (ASF) exceed required Stable Funding (RSF) for assets and OBS exposures.

**NSFR Formula:** $\frac{\text{Available amount of stable funding}}{\text{Required amount of stable funding}} \geq 100\%$

4. **Systematically Important Financial Institutions (SIFI):** As a part of macro – prudential framework, systematically important banks will be expected to have loss-absorbing capability beyond the BASEL III requirements. Options for implementation include capital surcharges, contingent capital and bail-in-debt.

Table 2 exhibits a comparison of capital requirement under Basel II and Basel III. Minimum ratio of total capital to RWAs was eight percent (8%) as per Basel II whereas it has increased to 10.50% under Basel III. Similarly Minimum ratio of common equity to RWAs has also increased to 4.50 percent to 7 percent as per Basel III. Tier I capital to RWAs of Basel II was 4 percent which has increased to 6 percent as Basel III norms while Core Tier I Capital to RWAs has also increased form 2 percent to 5 percent as per Basel III norms. Other requirements have also introduced in Basel III which was not applicable under Basel II norms.

*Table 2. Comparison of Capital Requirements under BASEL II and BASEL III*

| Requirements | Under BASEL II | Under BASEL III |
|---|---|---|
| Minimum Ratio of Total Capital to RWAs | 8% | 10.50% |
| Minimum Ratio of Common Equity to RWAs | 2% | 4.50% to 7.00% |
| Tier I Capital to RWAs | 4% | 6% |
| Core Tier I Capital to RWAs | 2% | 5% |
| Capital Conservation Buffers to RWAs | None | 2.50% |
| Leverage Ratio | None | 3% |
| Counter Cyclical Buffer | None | 2.50% |
| Minimum Liquidity Coverage Ratio | None | To Be Decided by 2015 |
| Minimum Net Stable Funding Ratio | None | To Be Decided by 2018 |

(http://www.allbankingsolutions.com/Banking-data.shtml)

## CONCLUSION

Although guidelines under BASEL II were enough to secure the working of banks during normal course of business but when events like economic recessions emerged, it proved that there are certain loopholes in the guidelines issued for the smooth working of banks. To overcome these loopholes and to secure the banks from any further failure in the case of return of such economic crisis period, BASEL III guidelines were issued. These guidelines, however not implemented fully, will pave the way for efficient and smooth functioning of banks.

## REFERENCES


Basel Committee on Banking Supervision, Bank for International Settlements. (2009). Strengthening the Resilience of the Banking Sector: Consultative Document 13. Retrieved from http://www.bis.org/publ/bcbs164.pdf

Indian Institute of Banking and Finance. (2009). *Risk Management* (2nd Ed). New Delhi: McMillan India Ltd.

King, P., & Terbert, H. (2011). BASEL III: An Overview. Banking & Financial Services. *Policy Reports*, *30*(5), 1.

# Chapter 11
# Green Marketing in India:
## A Theoretical Perspective

**Ajit Kumar Shukla**
*Mahatma Gandhi Kashi Vidyapith, India*

## ABSTRACT

*Green marketing is the study of all efforts to consumer, produce, distribute, promote, package and reclaim products in a manner that is sensitive or responsive to ecological concerns. As consumers, we simply don't think about it on a day-to-day basis because the message does not surround us. Most of us did not grow up in a resource starved environment and so the implications of wastefulness have had no direct repercussions on our daily lives. We acknowledge the issue is out there and demonstrate concern for what is being done to improve our collective condition but beyond recycling or an interest in non-toxic HH cleaning products, we simply don't have access to green products or services, let alone do we have an understanding for how to evaluate their functionality or benefit- to us or the environment. In the present study narrows down on one specific area and that is to measure the awareness level of the customers with reference to the green marketing.*

## INTRODUCTION

The term green marketing generally sends shivers down to our spine. Still very much in its nascent years, the term has developed enough baggage to seemingly constrain it to a niche audience. However, all macro trends start in a micro-fashion and green marketing has both a global scientific grounding and non-debatable symbolic characteristics finding it. That is to say that green marketing has a clear and substantive role in driving forward the dialogue and demand for sustainable products and services, which ultimately will influence real change in the marketplace with long term implications for our resource consumption and environmental preservation. Green Marketing refers to holistic marketing concept. It comprises the planning, development and promotion of products or services that satisfy the needs of consumers for quality, output, accessible prices and service, without however a negative effect on the environment, with regard to the use of raw material, the consumption of energy etc.

Prothero & Fitchett (2000) argue that greater ecological enlightenment can be secured through capitalism by using the characteristics of commodity culture to further progress environmental goal. Marketing not only has the potential to contribute to the establishment of more sustainable forms of society but,

DOI: 10.4018/978-1-4666-9908-3.ch011

as a principle agent in the operation and proliferation of commodity discourse, also has a considerable responsibility to do so.

Karna, Hansen, & Juslin (2003) interpret that proactive marketers are the most genuine group in implementing environmental marketing voluntarily and seeking competitive advantage through environmental friendliness. The results also give evidence that green values, environmental marketing strategies, structures and functions are logically connected to each other as hypothesised according to the model of environmental marketing used to guide this study.

Sanjay K. Jain & Gurmeet Kaur (2004) in their study environmentalism have fast emerged as a worldwide phenomenon. Business firms too have risen to the occasion and have started responding to environmental challenges by practicing green marketing strategies. Green consumerism has played a catalytic role in ushering corporate environmentalism and making business firms green marketing oriented. Based on the data collected through a field survey, the paper makes an assessment of the extent of environmental awareness, attitudes and behavior prevalent among consumers in India.

Donaldson (2005) in his study realized in the Great Britain initially concluded that in general the ecological attitude of consumers changed positively. This study reported the strong faith of consumers in the known commercial brands and in the feeble behaviour referring to the "green" claims, which was the main cause behind the consuming failure to interpret their concerns beyond the environment in their behavior.

According to the American Marketing Association, green marketing is the marketing of products that are presumed to be environmentally safe. Thus green marketing incorporates a broad range of activities, including product modification, changes to the production process, packaging changes, as well as modifying advertising. Yet defining green marketing is not a simple task where several meanings intersect and contradict each other; an example of this will be the existence of varying social, environmental and retail definitions attached to this term.

William J. Stanton (1986) manifests, 'Green Marketing is any marketing activity of an institution that is intended to create a positive impact or to lessen the negative impact of a product on the environment in order to capitalize on consumer's concerns about environmental issues. It encompasses everything from using recycled material in making a product to claim on advertising or on package labels.'

Thus, Green Marketing is the movement by companies to develop and market environmentally responsible products. Other similar terms used are Environmental Marketing, Ecological (Eco) Marketing, Eco-centric Marketing, Environmentally Responsible Marketing, and Responsible Marketing.

## OBJECTIVE OF THE STUDY

The main objectives of the study are as following:

1. To throw light on the awareness levels of the customer in the various age groups regarding their understanding about green marketing in India particularly in Uttar Pradesh.
2. To elaborate the awareness levels of the customer in the various geographical areas regarding their understanding about green marketing in India particularly in Uttar Pradesh.

## RESEARCH HYPOTHESIS

The following Null hypothesis has been tested as a part of research:

**HO1:** There is significant difference in the awareness levels of the customers in the various age groups regarding the green marketing.

**HO2:** There is significant difference in the awareness levels of the customers in the various geographical areas regarding the green marketing.

## RESEARCH METHODOLOGY

The study has been exploratory in nature and a sample survey method has been employed for data collection. Primary data is used for the purpose of the study. Research design for this research is planned structure and strategy of investigation conceived so as to obtain answers to research question or objectives and also to control variances. The said study is conducted to understand the behaviour of the customers in Uttar Pradesh while purchasing an environment friendly car and also to understand their willingness to pay more in case the environment friendly car cost more. The scope of the research is limited to environment friendly car in Uttar Pradesh.

### Sampling Design

In the present study, all the cars owners or prospective car buyer in Uttar Pradesh is considered as the population. The prospective car owners could be all those people who intend to buy a car in near future or are visiting the car showroom for a test drive or for collecting the information of the cars.

### The Sample

The sampling plan used has been consistent with the methodological guidelines provided for conducting survey research in marketing. The stratified random sampling technique was used for the present work. A sample of 500 respondents was selected with the help of stratified random sampling method. The sample has been chosen at selected dealers of cars in big cities e.g. Varanasi, Lucknow, Kanpur, Ghaziabad, Aligarh, Meeruit, Allahabad, Jhansi, Gorakhpur etc. and few small cities i.e. Mirzapur, Gazipur, Ballia, Muradabad, Bareily, Sultanpur, Etawah, Saharnpur, Rampur, Faizabad, Jaunpur etc. in Uttar Pradesh. These included prospective car buyers and people who came to buy their next car. The sample consisted on the basis of demographical variables such as, qualification, and place of stay.

### Data Collection Tools

A non-disguised structured questionnaire has been used as the tools for collection of data from the field. It has been designed with utmost care so that accuracy of the work could be high. The five point Likert scale has been used for the research purposes. A pilot study was undertaken first in order to determine whether the questionnaire and the scale is easily understood and responded to by the respondents.

## Data Collection Process

A pilot study was also undertaken to pretest the questions in order to determine whether they are easily understood and responded to by the respondents. The automobile dealers were selected in both metros and non-metros as the ideal place for identifying the respondent who would be interested in buying a car. The people who had already owned cars or who are thinking of buying a car and have approached the showroom of a car dealer for buying a car have been considered as potential respondents. Data was collected with the help of the structured questionnaire has been tabulated, analyzed and interpreted using suitable statistical tools including the t test, and simple percentages. Tables have facilitated the representation of the data. The data was analyzed using the SPSS (Statistical Package for Social Sciences) While constructing the questionnaire researcher has made every effort to take the view of the prospective buyers towards the manufacturer. The flow of the questions is from the most general topic about the basic awareness on pollution by automobiles, carpooling, use of public transport etc. to set the flow of the respondent. Customer's expectation from the government is also being measured as a part of the study. Role of the regulator and legislation which can prompt customers to buy EFC is also explored in the questionnaire. The various factors which are important in buying a car have been carefully considered after discussing with the buyers and the sellers in the market place. Customers were expected to rank these factors in the order of their preference. Environment friendly design has also been considered as a factor to understand where this factor stands in the order of the preference while buying the EFC. The reliability of the scale was checked with the sample size as 100, which is 20 percent of the total sample size. All the filled up questionnaires have been screened for completeness and the ones in which responses of all the statements have been complete, were selected for analyses. The questionnaires incomplete in any respect were rejected.

## GREEN PRODUCTS AND ITS CHARACTERISTICS

The products those are manufactured through green technology and that caused no environmental hazards are called green products. Promotion of green technology and green products is necessary for conservation of natural resources and sustainable development. We can define green products by following measures:

- Products those are originally grown,
- Products those are recyclable, reusable and biodegradable,
- Products with natural ingredients,
- Products containing recycled contents, non-toxic chemical,
- Products contents under approved chemical,
- Products that do not harm or pollute the environment,
- Products that will not be tested on animals,
- Products that have eco-friendly packaging i.e. reusable, refillable containers etc.

## MARKETING MIX OF GREEN MARKETING

When companies come up with new innovations like eco friendly products, they can access new markets, enhance their market shares, and increase profits. Just as we have 4Ps- Product, Price, Promotion and

Place in marketing, we have 4ps in green marketing too, but they are a bit different. They are buttressed by additional Ps, namely People, Physical Evidence, Process, Probe, Politics, Penetration, Plan, Positive Implementation, Priority, Partition, Public Relations, Packaging, Performance, Power, Precedent, Perception, Participation, Profit, Position, Peerless, Productivity and Planet.

1. **Product:** The term is applied to systems and products that save energy directly or indirectly. It describes a product that meets on of these criteria: (1) It has qualities that will protect the environment. (2) It has replaced artificial ingredients with natural ingredients e.g. Organic products, Paperless transactions. The marketer's role in product management includes providing product designers with market-driven trends and customer requests for green product attributes such as energy saving, organic, green chemicals, local sourcing, etc., For example, Nike is the first among the shoe companies to market itself as green
2. **Price:** Green pricing refers to an optional utility service that enables customers of traditional utilities to support a greater level of utility investment in renewable energy by paying a premium on their products via electronics medium. Green pricing takes into consideration the people, planet and profit in a way that takes care of the health of employees and communities and ensures efficient productivity.
3. **Promotion:** A specific type of promotion that is centered around the factors having to do with the environment. Often times the companies that use green promotion also use very environmentally friendly operations and product packaging as well. Green promotion involves configuring the tools of promotion, such as advertising, marketing materials, signage, white papers, web sites, videos and presentations by keeping people, planet and profits in mind.
4. **Place:** Green Place practices and strategies that reduce the environmental and energy footprint of freight distribution. It focuses on material handling, waste management, packaging and transport Green place is about managing logistics to cut down on transportation emissions, thereby in effect aiming at reducing the carbon footprint.

## SIGNIFICANCE OF GREEN MARKETING:

Green marketing offers business bottom line incentives and top line growth possibilities. While modification of business or production processes may involve start-up costs, it will save money in the long term. For example the cost of installing solar energy is an investment in future energy cost savings. Companies that develop new and improved products and services with environmental impacts in mind give themselves access to new markets, substantially increase profits and enjoy competitive advantages over those marketing non environmental responsible alternatives. Issues like Global Warming and depletion of ozone umbrella are the main for the healthy survival. Every person rich or poor would be interested in quality life with full of health and vigor and so would the corporate class. Financial gain and economic profit is the main aim of any corporate business. But harm to environment cost by sustain business across the globe is realized now though off late. This sense is building corporate citizenship in the business class. So green marketing by the business class is still in the selfish anthological perspective of long term sustainable business and to please the consumer and obtain the license by the governing body. Industries in Asian countries are catching the need of green marketing from the developed countries but still there is a wide gap between their understanding and implementation.

## CHALLENGES IN GREEN MARKETING

### Need for Standardization

It is found that only 5% of the marketing messages from "Green" campaigns are entirely true and there is a lack of standardization to authenticate these claims. There is no standardization currently in place to certify a product as organic. Unless some regulatory bodies are involved in providing the certifications there will not be any verifiable means. A standard quality control board needs to be in place for such labeling and licensing.

### New Concept

Indian literate and urban consumer is getting more aware about the merits of Green products. But it is still a new concept for the masses. The consumer needs to be educated and made aware of the environmental threats. The new green movements need to reach the masses and that will take a lot of time and effort. By India's Ayurveda heritage, Indian consumers do appreciate the importance of using natural and herbal beauty products. Indian consumer is exposed to healthy living lifestyles such as yoga and natural food consumption. In those aspects the consumer is already aware and will be inclined to accept the green products.

### Patience and Perseverance

The investors and corporate need to view the environment as a major long-term investment opportunity, the marketers need to look at the long-term benefits from this new green movement. It will require a lot of patience and no immediate results. Since it is a new concept and idea, it will have its own acceptance period.

### Avoiding Green Myopia

The first rule of green marketing is focusing on customer benefits i.e. the primary reason why consumers buy certain products in the first place. Do this right, and motivate consumers to switch brands or even pay a premium for the greener alternative. It is not going to help if a product is developed which is absolutely green in various aspects but does not pass the customer satisfaction criteria. This will lead to green myopia. Also if the green products are priced very high then again it will lose its market acceptability.

## STRATEGY FOR GREEN MARKETING

Marketing Strategy decision plays a vital role in designing the low waste product systems that serve as pollution abatement mechanisms.

The marketing strategies for green marketing include:

- Marketing Audit (including internal and external situation analysis)
- Implement marketing strategies

- Develop a marketing plan outlining strategies with regard to 4Ps
- Plan results evaluation
- Challenges ahead
- Green products require renewable and recyclable material, which is costly
- Requires a technology, which requires huge investment in R&D
- Water treatment technology, which is too costly
- Majority of the people are not aware of green products and their uses
- Majority of the consumers are not willing to pay a premium for green products.

## PRESENT TRENDS IN GREEN MARKETING IN INDIA

Organizations believe they have a moral obligation to be more socially responsible. This is in keeping with the philosophy of CSR which has been successfully adopted by many business houses to improve their corporate image. Firms in this situation can take two approaches:

- Use the fact that they are environmentally responsible as a marketing tool.
- Become responsible without prompting this fact. Governmental Bodies are forcing Firms to become more responsible. In most cases the government forces the firm to adopt policy which protects the interests of the consumers. It does in following ways:
- Reduce production of harmful goods or by products
- Modify consumer and industry's use and /or consumption of harmful goods; or
- Ensure that all types of consumers have the ability to evaluate the environmental composition of goods.
- A Firm develops a technology for reducing waste and sells it to other firms.

There are many institutions/organizations which are busy to protect environment by various means. Some of them are following:

- **State Bank of India:** SBI is entered into green service known as "Green Channel Counter". SBI is providing many services like; paperless banking, no deposit slip, no withdrawal form, no checks, no money transactions form, All these transaction are done through SBI shopping & ATM cards.
- **Patanjali Ayurved Ltd.:** Patanjali Ayurved Ltd. uses maximum green vegetables and herbs in its medicines and also uses green colour in its packaging to make awareness among the people about environment.
- **McDonald's:** McDonald's restaurants use paper tray, paper glass, paper cup, paper bag during their services.
- **Indian Oil's Green Agenda Green Initiatives:** Indian Oil is fully geared to meet the target of reaching EURO-III compliant fuels to all parts of the country. Major cities will upgrade to Euro-IV compliant fuels by that time.
- **Wipro's Green Machines:** Wipro Infotech was India's first company to launch environment friendly computer peripherals. For the Indian market, Wipro has launched a new range of desktops and laptops called Wipro Greenware.

- **Going Green: Tata's new mantra:** Tata Motors is setting up an eco-friendly showroom using natural building material for its flooring and energy efficient lights. Tata Motors said the project is at a preliminary stage. The Indian Hotels Company, which runs the Taj chain, is in the process of creating eco rooms which will have energy efficient mini bars, organic bed linen and napkins made from recycled paper.
- **BSNL:** Bharat Sanchar Nigam Limited provides rebate to the customers who make payments via electronic mediums. Thus, BSNL encourages paperless activities.
- **Nike:** Nike is the first among the shoe companies to market itself as green. It is marketing its Air Jordan shoes as environment-friendly, as it has significantly reduced the usage of harmful glue adhesives.
- **CNG in Delhi:** Introduction of Compressed Natural Gas (CNG) in Delhi, was being polluted at a very fast pace until Supreme Court of India forced a change to alternative fuels. In 2002, a directive was issued to completely adopt CNG in all public transport systems to curb pollution.

## THE FUTURE OF GREEN MARKETING

There are many lessons to be learned to be learned to avoid green marketing myopia, the short version of all this is that effective green marketing requires applying good marketing principles to make green products desirable for consumers. The question that remains, however, is, what is green marketing's future? Business scholars have viewed it as a "fringe" topic, given that environmentalism's acceptance of limits and conservation does not mesh well with marketing's traditional axioms of "give customer what they want" and "sell as much as you can" .Evidence indicates that successful green products have avoided green marketing myopia by following three important principles:

### Consumer Value Positioning

- Design environmental products to perform as well as (or better than) alternatives.
- Promote and deliver the consumer desired value of environmental products and target relevant consumer market segments.
- Broaden mainstream appeal by bundling consumer desired value into environmental products.

### Calibration of Consumer Knowledge

- Educate consumers with marketing messages that connect environmental attributes with desired consumer value.
- Frame environmental product attributes as "solutions" for consumer needs.
- Create engaging and educational internet sites about environmental products desired consumer value.

### Credibility of Product Claim

- Employ environmental product and consumer benefit claims that are specific and meaningful.

- Procure product endorsements or eco-certifications from trustworthy third parties and educate consumers about the meaning behind those endorsements and eco certifications.
- Encourage consumer evangelism via consumers social and internet communication network with compelling, interesting and entertaining information about environmental products.

## DO THIS

We have to use the following activities in our daily routine of life.

- less use of polythene
- crush plastic bottle after use
- use disposable items
- love nature
- save water
- save fuel
- avoid smoking
- many more

## CONCLUSION

Green Marketing is a lifestyle change that will help in your business contribution . The study investigates the awareness levels of the customer in the various age groups regarding their understanding about eco-friendly car. The results of study indicate that there is no significant difference in the awareness of the respondents for environment friendly car with reference to the two age groups which was considered in the research. Study also examines the awareness levels of the customer in the various geographical areas regarding their understanding about eco-friendly activities. The results of the study show that customer who responded were either from the big cities or small cities in Uttar Pradesh. There is a significant difference in the awareness level of the customer in big cities and small cities. The results indicate that awareness level of the respondents is higher in big cities as compared to the small cities in Uttar Pradesh for environment friendly activities.

There is a need to increase the awareness levels in small cities metros of Uttar Pradesh by the marketers, media houses, and government. Population wise there exists a big potential in rural districts of the state and if one has to really make the impact of the pollution less than focus should be rural parts. Currently the scene is not very bad from the rural front but before it gets the same level of pollution in the rural Uttar Pradesh, it is suggested that preventive steps to be taken right from now to create the right level of awareness amongst the rural population about the protection of the environment. Marketers concerned with environmental impact may benefit from a better understanding of green marketing strategies and tactics to enable the firm to appeal to a greater extent to consumers with similar concerns.

## REFERENCES

Dahlstrom, R. (2011). *Green Marketing, Theory, Practice and Strategies*. Delhi: Cengage Learning India Private Ltd.

Donaldson, R. H. (2005). Green brands. *Greenleaf Publishing*, *24*(8), 14–17.

Hansen, A., & Machin, D. (2008). Visually Branding the Environment: Climate Change as Marketing Opportunities. *Discourse Studies*, *10*(6), 777–794. doi:10.1177/1461445608098200

Henion, K. E. (1976). *Ecological Marketing*. Grid Columbus Ohio.

Karna, J., Hansen, E., & Juslin, H. (2003). Social Responsibility in Environmental Marketing Planning. *European Journal of Marketing*, *37*(5/6), 848–873. doi:10.1108/03090560310465170

Kotler, P., Brown, J., & Makens, J. (2002). *Marketing for Hospitality and Tourism*. Delhi: Pearson Education.

Kotler, P., & Keller, K. L. (2013). *Marketing Management* (14th ed.). Delhi: Pearson.

McDaniel, S W., David H. R (1993). Strategic Green Marketing. *Journal of Consumer Marketing*, 10(3), 4-10.

Ottman, J. A. (2011). *The New Rules of Green Marketing, Strategies, Tools, and Inspiration for Sustainable Branding*. U.K.: Greenleaf Publishing.

Peattie, K., & Crane, A. (2005). Green Marketing: Legend, Myth, Farce or Prophesy? *Qualitative Market Research: An International Journal*, *8*(4), 357–370. doi:10.1108/13522750510619733

Prothero, A. (1998). Green Marketing: The 'Fad' That Won't Slip Slide Away. *Journal of Marketing Management*, *14*(6), 507–513. doi:10.1362/026725798784867680

Prothero, A., & Fitchett, J. A. (2000). Greening Capitalism: Opportunities for Green Community. *Journal of Macromarketing*, *20*(1), 46–56. doi:10.1177/0276146700201005

Sanjay, K.Jain & Gurmeet Kaur. (2004). Green Marketing: An Attitudinal and Behavioural *Analysis of Indian Consumers, Global. Business Review (Federal Reserve Bank of Philadelphia)*, *5*(2), 187–205.

Shukla, A. K. (2013). *Marketing Management* (2nd ed.). Varanasi: Vaibhav Laxmi Prakashan.

# Chapter 12
# Green Manufacturing:
## The Need of the Hour for Developing Nations – A Case Study

**Saurabh Sen**
*Sunbeam College for Women, India*

**Ruchi Sen**
*Sunbeam College for Women, India*

## ABSTRACT

*The manufacturing sector has greater responsibility for conducting and operating its business. The primary objective of every unit is to maximize profits. The manufacturing sector is the key driver of energy consumption and if an automobile consumes high fuel or if the resources are under-utilized, it is definitely the fault of the manufacturer. If we seriously need a solution to these problems, we need to change the way we design, manufacture, and sell the products. The manufacturing sector must use energy and resources efficiently. 'Green Manufacturing' or sustainable industrial activity is the need of the hour and the Government of India requires the manufacturing sector to play a bigger role in the country's economy. This paper focuses on the initiative taken by the industries to make the environment eco-friendly. The paper further will emphasize upon a case study of Hero MotoCop.*

## MEANING AND IMPORTANCE OF 'GREEN'

The term Green here refers to the ecological sustainability and encompasses elements like energy usage, efficiency and waste management and recycling. Green initiative aims to minimize the impact of human activities on the environment.

There are various factors which call for concerns for Green. They are:

1. **Rising emissions:** Greenhouse gas emissions have been increased rapidly in the recent past and are continuously accelerating. It is revealed by the scientists that it will increase by double by 2050. This means that there would be an exceptional negative change in the global eco-system, sea-level, crop production and relative activities.

DOI: 10.4018/978-1-4666-9908-3.ch012

2. **Fast depletion of scarce natural resources:** With growing population, the need for industrialization will increase and also the consumption of natural resources will rise. This will result in the imbalance between the demand and supply of products, rise in the price of goods and services. This problem could be solved by optimal utilization of natural resources and their alternate uses.
3. **Growing waste generation and pollution:** Rapid industrialization and urbanization has led to increase in industrial waste and chemical compositions. This results in environment pollution which can be dangerous to health of human beings.
4. **Growing Technological waste:** Another problem which is encountered by the nation is e-waste. With growing demand of technologies and gadgets, the problem of e-waste has emerged which again is a major source of environment pollution.

The above factors have persuaded the manufacturers to adopt Green manufacturing. A number of companies have started adopting Green initiatives as an integral part of their operations. These initiatives are driven by five factors:

- Rising energy and input costs
- Growing consumer pull for Green products
- Increasing regulatory pressures as policy makers introduce new and stricter environmental and waste management laws.
- Technological advances which open up new attractive business opportunities
- The need to enhance competitive differentiation, particularly for first movers or those who are able to break the compromise between short–term higher costs and numerous benefits (example: brand premium, new customer segments). (Bhattacharya, Jain & Choudhary 2011)

## Why Green Manufacturing?

The manufacturing companies produce goods which are not eco-friendly. So, they should focus on three major areas:

1. **Green energy:** Green energy basically includes the renewable energy sources like biomass, wind, solar, CNG etc. The manufacturing units should use these green energy sources to produce goods which are not only eco-friendly but also benefits the society as a whole.
2. **Green products:** Green products are the products which can be recycled, low in carbon, organic and are natural. These products are gaining popularity but are little costly. However, if the consumers demand these products and if these products are marketed well, the cost of developing these products will gradually decrease.
3. **Green processes in business operations:** The third and the last area on which the manufacturing units should focus is the business operations. This includes the use of appropriate technology which may increase the efficiency and decrease the cost.

## Green Manufacturing: The Need of the Hour for Developing Nations

Green manufacturing has the potential to achieve sustainable development and eradicate poverty on an unprecedented scale. A green manufacturing economy substitute's clean energy and low carbon technologies for fossil fuels, which addresses climate change, creates jobs, and reduces import dependencies. Adopting new technologies promote energy, resource efficiency and provide growth opportunities in new directions. If a developing economy moves towards green manufacturing, it will require the initiatives of leaders, civil society and leading businesses. It will require a sustained effort on the part of policy makers and their constituents to rethink and redefine traditional measures of wealth, prosperity and wellbeing. A developing economy can however, develop better opportunities for the people by adopting the concept of 'Green'. It can be self-reliant and thus can minimize its dependency on other countries for importing goods. Not only this, the countries can develop their quality 'green' goods and play the role of exporters. Thus, a developing economy need to move ahead and think in a different way to promote green manufacturing so as to preserve the environment, maximize their profits, play active role as exporters and provide better living to its citizens.

## India's Green Challenge

The rapid industrial, economic and demographic growth in India has resulted in high Greenhouse gas (GHG) emissions, rising demand of scarce resources and has generated wastes particularly in urban areas. Today, India is the fourth–largest economy and the fifth–largest GHG emitter in the world. During the 18 year period between 1990 and 2008, India's CO2 emissions increased more than 150 percent, placing it just behind China. Rapid urbanization and industrialization generate massive amounts of waste. For example, India generates close to 4 million tonnes of hazardous waste from industrial and biomedical sources. Apart from hazardous industrial waste and effluents which cause water and land pollution, e–waste is also becoming a major area of concern for India. Estimates suggest that only 3 percent of e–waste makes it to authorized recycling facilities, with the rest either going into landfills or being processed at informal recycling yards. (Digalwar Abhijeet, Tagalpallewar Ashok & Sunnapwar Vivek, (2013). The Indian e–waste market is expected to nearly double from 450 KT per annum currently to about 800 KT per annum by 2020.

## Green Business: An Integral Part

Green business is an important strategy to build a green brand that customers can trust. Though, developing such a brand is not an easy task and requires an integrated promotion campaign which consistently communicates the company's Green positioning and policies. Standard setting and labeling can be powerful tools used by companies to build the credibility as well as to help consumers make informed decisions. A survey conducted by CII-Ascon for the April-June quarter (2014) indicates positive growth in important sectors like consumer durables including the vehicle industry and white goods industry, which recorded a growth of 5-10 percent, leading to improvement in the overall industry growth. The CII-Ascon survey found that sub-sectors such as tablets, LEDs and LCDs, smartphones have achieved phenomenal growth of over 20 percent. The passenger car segment also for the first time in last two years has grown between 5 and 10 percent. Thus, it can be interpreted that, if, the companies adopt green business, it will benefit not only the business but the entire eco-system.

The success of companies adopting Green depends on the economic assessment which includes two basic elements, costs and profits. The companies then select their quantitative and qualitative Green initiatives- price strategy, cost strategy, employee recruitment strategy etc.

## Making Sense of Green: Hero MotoCorp

Environmental sustainability lies at the core of manufacturing practices of Hero MotoCorp and the company have been continuously introducing new steps in this regards. The company has proactively restricted the use of mercury and cadmium in painting and rubber compounding processes. All plastic parts come in a moulded form, which facilitates easy recyclability at the end of a vehicle's life cycle at the Hero MotoCorp. The company also installed a waste heat recovery system to utilize waste heat from its gas generator. This enables to save 4,000 Standard Cubic Metre (SCM) of natural gas and thereby, prevent 2,600 tonnes of CO2 emissions. The company also installed a vapour absorption machine, which enables to reduce 400 TR (340 KW) of electrical energy, thereby saving 524 tonnes of CO2 emissions annually. It also recycled paint sludge from its paint processes, which is 5-10 percent of the total volumes of paint sludge generated.

The products of the company once used to rely on asbestos based parts. However, they have now been replaced with non-asbestos based parts, which include brake liners, gaskets and other assembly parts. Similarly, lead was replaced by lead-free materials. Hazardous chemicals like hexavalent chromium were substituted in the plating process. The Green Vendor Development Programme is a landmark initiative that disseminates and embeds green practices among suppliers of the Hero MotoCorp. Around 130 suppliers are part of the Green Vendor Development Programme.

The Green Vendor Development Programme of Hero MotoCorp is the supply chain initiative drive taken to extend the corporate environment responsibility down the supply chain. As the production at Hero MotoCorp is increasing, the manufacturing activities at the vendor's are also increasing in the same proportion. This gives rise to the load on the environment. In order to improve the vendor environmental performance, Hero MotoCorp has developed exclusive vendor development program, which is a collaborative effort between the Hero MotoCorp Environmental group and the materials department, in order to influence the vendors to adopt pre-specified environmental requirements and undertake environmental initiatives.

In addition to the above steps taken, the concept of Hybrid Scooters was also unveiled in the 2012 Auto Expo in Delhi by the Hero MotoCorp. The concept of Series Hybrid is fuel productive and eco-friendly. The Hybrid Scooter launched by HeroCorp runs primarily on battery in urban conditions and will use range extender gasoline engine for long runs.

There are other areas in which the company is taking initiative to make the environment eco-friendly.

1. **Green Roof:** Hero's green roof, covering about 45000 sq meters, helps to conserve energy by moderating the temperature on the roof and within surrounding areas. The green roof can restore aesthetic and ecological value of open urban spaces. It addition to this, it protects conventional roofing systems by doubling the service life of the underlying waterproof membrane.
2. **Sewage Treatment Plant:** Hero ensures that sewage is biologically treated to attain efficacy. This treatment plant is designed to accommodate up to 6 hours of holding and ensuring effluent is 100% treated and recycled into soft water that is used in cooling towers.
3. **Effluent Treatment Plant:** To prevent water pollution, Hero has also invested in an Effluent Treatment Plant which is capable of treating waste water that contains degreasing chemicals, acidic/alkaline nature, plating waste, heavy metals and waste oil that is generated out of processes. The output parameter is maintained strictly with norms to ensure that 100% treated water is recycled back into the process while the sludge is safely disposed of at a secured landfill.

4. **Waste Food Recycling:** Hero ensures hygienic disposal of municipal waste through its organic waste converter, which in turn generates manure. This waste goes through 15 minutes of treatment and is then homogenized and odor free.
5. **Paint Conservation:** Along with preventing water pollution, Hero MotorCorp does its very best to prevent releasing pollutants in the air as well. On an annual average, the company recycles about 120 tons of paint sludge and additives and turns it into paint primer. It also has a Solvent Recovery Machine that helps to prevent 59 Kl of volatile organic compounds from getting released into the air on a yearly basis, thus ensuring cleaner air.
6. **Energy Conservation:** In January 2011, Hero initiated the Heat Recovery from Incineration project which has helped to save 1,258 tons of Co2 emissions and 16, 22, 400 units per annum. This process includes the recovery of waste heat from the incinerator through heat recovery coil. The waste heat is used for heating process water in engine component washing.

In October 2011, Hero introduced its Solar Power Project – 100 KW which has helped to save 1, 56, 000 units per annum, 121 tons of Co2 emissions and 37.96 tons on furnace oil. This is done through the solar energy that is captured by the photovoltaic cells during the day. This electrical energy is then connected to the main grid, to ensure optimum energy conservation.

In June 2012, Hero replaced its 400 ton air conditioner with a VAM chiller to reduce Co2 production and energy consumption. This machine produces chilled water by using heat from power generator sets or through heat sources such as oil, gas, hot water and steam.

Apart from these, Hero MotorCorp has also initiated other energy saving processes like:

- Substituting furnace oil with natural gas
- Replacing aluminum alloy fans by FRP fans of cooling towers
- Replacing copper ballast with electronic ballast in all lighting tasks
- Introducing power saving circuits in all machine panels of engine plants
- Installing power correction panels for loads running on state electricity for cost saving.

7. **Oil Conservation:** Hero MotorCorp has also initiated oil conservation through the installation of Chip Wringer which is capable of recovering neat cutting oil from chips that are generated from m/c operation. This has led to oil recovery of about 56 liters/ day per plant. The company also uses on line hydraulic oil filtration system on presses which has helped in saving 1200 liters/ year.
8. **Water Conservation:** Perhaps one of the biggest initiatives taken by Hero has worked consistently hard in conserving water through Water Management, Rain Water Harvesting and ETP Recycling Plant.
9. **Water Management:** Hero provides training and awareness on how to develop water balance. It also includes reducing water consumption at the source and recycling it back to process applications and other beneficial applications like cooling towers and irrigation after treatment. Water management also entails recharging rain water and regular monitoring to sustain savings.
10. **Rain Water Harvesting:** Hero has also introduced a rain water harvesting scheme that includes the collection and de-silting of rain water. The company has a catchment area in plants that measures about 2, 60, 000 square meters and has a potential recharge of about 1, 32, 600 cubic meters of rain water annually.

11. **ETP Recycling Plant:** This plant introduced by Hero has a capacity of recycling approximately 1400 Kld of treated effluent daily. It uses the modern technology of reverse osmosis and ultra filtration for purifying water. The recycled water is then supplied to the paint shop with desired parameters or used as Soft water/ DM as required.
12. **Green Supply Chain:** To complete the process of sustainable development, Hero MotorCorp has also included the company's supply chain in its green processes. It has put together a "Green Dealer Development Program" at the front end and a "Green Vendor Development Program" for the backend of the supply chain. Through these programs Hero makes it partners aware of the importance of caring for the environment. Dealers and vendors are also encouraged to manage their material resources, energy resources, industrial wastes, pollution and other effluents on the basis of a number of pre-determined parameters. Hero MotorCorp supports its partners in the Green Supply Chain venture by

- Developing required competencies
- Sharing knowledge
- Providing technical support

Through its Green Supply Chain, Hero MotorCorp aims at generating sufficient momentum in the industry and looks forward to the day when the entire automotive industry runs on a seamless green chain.

## CONCLUDING REMARKS

Green manufacturing is the core to manufacturing companies' competitive strategies. Though, the transformation journey to Green manufacturing has just started, yet the destination is far to reach. There are few early adopters like Hero MotoCorp to green manufacturing, yet other industries, manufacturers and the developing economies needs to develop comprehensive plans to address three basic areas — Green energy, Green products and Green processes. Hero MotoCorp has adopted numerous means and strategies to maintain and make the economy eco-friendly, but still it has to go a long way to make the economy a 'green' economy. The Government of these economies also has to play an effective role in this transformation with both stronger incentives on one hand and regulatory mechanisms on the other. Also, the industry associations can bring different stakeholders together and support the roll-out of a communication strategy. Thus, the chance for success is enormous for both manufacturing companies and the developing countries, what is required are the zeal to adopt 'Green Manufacturing'.

## REFERENCES

Annual Report of the Hero MotoCorp Ltd. (2013). Retrieved from www.heroMotoCorp.com/gvdp/green-vendor-development-program

Bhattacharya, A., Jain, R., & Choudhary, A. (2011). *Green Manufacturing, Energy, products and processes* (p. 8). The Boston Consulting Group.

Indian industry sees green shoots of manufacturing growth. (2014, August 11). Retrieved from http://articles.economictimes.indiatimes.com/2014-08-11/news/52687142_1_green-shoots-ficci-survey-april-june-quarter

India Greenhouse Emissions. (2007). Ministry of Environment and Forest, Government of India.

Pal, U. (2002). Identifying the path to successful green manufacturing. *Journal of the Minerals Metals & Materials Society*, *54*(5), 25. doi:10.1007/BF02701691

Research on India: Waste Management. (2009, August).

World Bank. (2008). Global Financial Crisis and Implications for Developing Countries. Paper for G-20 Finance Ministers' Meeting, São Paulo, Brazil.

## KEY TERMS AND DEFINITIONS

**Eco-Friendly:** It is referring to goods and services, laws, guidelines and policies that impose reduced, minimal, or no harm upon ecosystems or the environment.

**Environment:** The sum of all surroundings of a living organism, including natural forces and other living things, which provide conditions for development and growth as well danger and damage.

**Green Manufacturing:** It is a process of reducing pollution and waste by minimizing natural resource use, recycling and reusing what was considered waste, and reducing emissions by the industries.

**Manufacturing Sector:** Collection of industries engaged in chemical, mechanical, or otherwise or physical transformation of materials, substances, or components into consumer or industrial goods.

# Chapter 13
# Online Banking

**Marta Vidal**
*Complutense University, Spain*

**Javier Vidal-García**
*University of Valladolid, Spain*

## ABSTRACT

*Over recent years, technological developments in the Information and Communications Technology industry have ensured that the internet has become a significant part of man's way of life. For instance, there is tremendous popularity on the use of social sites, electronic commerce, and internet banking. Such use of the internet has created a global network in a cyberspace that connects everyone together regardless of one's geographical location, economic status, religion, or race. As a result, the trade sector, the finance sector, the media industry, and all other sectors that enable the world to run have had to depend on technology for normal function, and on the internet as a way of associating with the public. For instance, the fact that banks have stayed in the forefront of technological advances has led to significant value addition, and improvement of their products and services offered. Therefore, this paper discusses the use of technology in the finance sector, particularly internet banking in today's world, and the various factors associated with it.*

## INTRODUCTION

E-Banking also written as electronic banking refers to the usage of computers in carrying out bank transactions. Examples of such transactions include withdrawal of money through cash dispensers or engaging in funds transfer through a point of sale. Electronic banking is also known as internet banking or online banking (Ainin, Lim & Wee, 2005). Therefore, this illustrates the complex nature of the concept of financial services as there is not a universal definition of E-banking. However, it is significant to note that internet or E-banking refers to the use of various electronic services that allow a financial account holder with a particular bank to access all his or her information through a computer. Therefore, in the context of this discussion E-banking will be defined as a self-service activity that permits bank account holder to get access to their accounts, as well as their updated general information on a financial institution's products and services. In addition, these users have the liberty of conducting financial transactions

DOI: 10.4018/978-1-4666-9908-3.ch013

without time or geographical limitation by accessing the bank's website (Kallstrom, 2000, p. 20). There are different types of E-banking, for example, ATM transactions, phone banking transactions, home banking and internet transactions. The ATM banking transactions usually involves a process of access to funds as either a withdrawal or deposit of money into bank account through the automated teller machines (ATM). These machines work 24 hours every day, and they are found in different locations especially in densely populated areas. In order to operate an ATM, an individual needs to have an ATM card with its personal PIN. Services that a customer can access from an ATM machine include, deposit of money, withdrawals, bank statements, request check books and inquire about outstanding account balances

The next type of E-banking is telephone banking that essentially entails the use of a telephone to conduct financial transactions such as inquire account balance, transfer money or pay bills. Internet banking, on the other hand, involves the completion of bank transaction by simply accessing the financial institution's website through the internet. This type of online banking can be conducted by the use of either a computer or mobile phone internet enabled.

## BACKGROUND

Electronic banking is a precursor for home banking services the former entailing the use of the touch-tone telephones. In the late 1970's home banking was a common way of conducting financial services without the physical presence at a banking hall (Xu et al., 2006, p. 19). During this time, financial organizations referred to this service as home banking although the whole process depended on the use of phones. Financial services consumers were allowed to pay their bills, transfer money or check their account balances while at home via touch-tone telephones. Consequently, this important development in the financial industry led the invention of software that allowed customers to the bank to connect with their local bank through a dial-up connection. In the late 1980s, this service still unpopular because of a number of reasons. Firstly, the home banking service was only limited to allow certain transactions that the bank and the client had to agree initially. Secondly, this service required heavy investment in technology at the time, and only a few banks could manage to fund such costs. Finally, home banking was not popular after 1985 because the use of PCs was not extensively spread in many households (Laopodis, 2013, p. 26). Examples of banks that offered home banking services during this period include world's major bank that is Citibank, Manufacturers Hanover and Chase Manhattan. Noteworthy, all these financial institutions had roots of origin in America; therefore, illustrating the contribution of the United States in the e-banking services.

In the mid-1990's banks were starting to realize the need to move their financial services into the virtual realm. Apparently, e-banking was becoming an attractive concept as it helped banks diminish transaction costs; it was helpful in promoting easy integration of services as well as introduced interactive marketing capabilities. Additionally, online banking was instrumental towards boosting the bank's customer lists and profit margin faced by the businesses. Furthermore, internet banking allowed institutions to bundle their services into single packages; thus, attracting more customers at minimal overheads. The period of late 1990s saw the advent of the clicks and bricks euphoria; as a result, many banks realized that e-banking was a strategic and imperative innovation (Lassar et al., 2005, p. 15). More so, during this period there were a lot of mergers and acquisitions within the financial industry that resulted in expanding customer base Therefore, financial firms viewed the World Wide Web as the only channel that would help in maintaining customers, as well as build loyalty. However, in the wake of the banks realizing the potential of e-banking a lot of customers across the globe remained hesitant to conduct their financial transaction over the internet. For example, there was the Y2K scare that was a disambiguation about a world crisis by the year 2000. In this connection, many customers feared online transactions because of the fear that all computers would fail. Therefore, to avoid this problem a number of financial consumers were reluctant to move into the virtual world of financial service provision. Companies such as America Online, eBay and Amazon.com invested in marketing purchase of items through online platforms. For example, Bank of America took about 10 years to reach 2 million e-banking clients. In 2009 as per a report by Gartner Group, at least 47 percent of American adults were banking online.

## MAIN FOCUS OF THE CHAPTER

### 1. Growth of E-Banking

E-banking growth has been very encouraging considering the hurdles faced by financial institutions in marketing the provision of financial services over the internet. It can be traced back to the concept of home banking introduced in the 1970s (Liao et al., 1999). Notably, this type of virtual banking entailed making telephone calls to a financial firm through the use of a touch-tone telephone. Home banking had the limitations on the number of services that a customer could complete over the phone. In 1980s, there was the introduction of telephone banking as well as using the dial-up connection to access financial services in bank. This service had two categories that are operator attendance and automated service. Next, the introduction of internet banking that gained momentum in early 2000. Unlike home banking, the use of online banking allows customers to conduct various services without making physical presence at the bank offices. In addition, internet banking allows access to financial information through accessing internet over a computer or by use of mobile phone that has Internet connection. Finally, mobile banking is the latest revolution in virtual banking. Mobile banking involves conducting financial transactions via a mobile device; for example, a mobile phone or tablet. The introduction of mobile banking led to new methods of payments by using a mobile phone to pay for commodities or services remotely. The first form of mobile banking was referred to as SMS banking. However, the invention of smart phones has overtaken SMS banking and now users of the internet-enabled mobile phones can use various applications based on the operating system to carry out financial transactions. Internet banking is alluring especially considering the level of an e-banking usage now and 15 years ago. Evidently, there has been a remarkable growth in the number of households using virtual banking services. For example, currently internet hardware serves about 95 million households and out of this, at least 72,500,000 households are using internet hardware for online banking. Approximately, 47.5 million households are using the banks bill pay as compared to physically going to the bank's offices.

Population born between 1970 and 1990 also referred to as the generation Y embrace technology very fast once it comes to the market. Generation Y account for the highest number of users of online billing services to settle their account on student loans, credit cards and expenditures aimed at improving their lifestyle for example shopping online. Noteworthy, e-banking is highly entangled in every individual way of life without discriminating against age or those with disabilities. Looking into the future there is a forecast that by 2014 from 2009, the annual growth of e-banking will be four percent. Generation Y would be on the forefront of the main users of this financial service.

## 2. E-Banking Services

Internet banking offers various services depending on the bank of choice for each customer. However, the following are some of the e-banking services.

### a. Account Opening

Most banks that provide e-banking services allow their clients to open new accounts by accessing the bank's website. In order to complete this service, an individual logs in into the bank's website, fill an application online and submit the application. The submission of this application can be done either online or by handing in a printed copy of the online application form to a teller at the bank's branch.

### b. Access Account Information

An account holder with online banking services enjoys the opportunity of accessing financial information wherever they are as long they have Internet connection. Such information may include closing or opening accounts, checking updates as well as make inquiries captured in the account or even making payments.

### c. Electronic Check Conversion

Electronic check conversion allows customers to convert their paper check to a new electronic payment. Essentially, the benefit of electronic payment is that the account holder with a bank can withdraw money from their account and wait until the other party receives the check. In addition, this service is faster as the normal check takes longer duration to process.

### d. Transfer Funds

It is easy for customers to log into the online accounts request for their balances as well as transfer funds across personal accounts and to different users as a way of covering the shortage in some accounts.

### e. Request for Bank Statement

A bank statement is a financial institution document that is made available by the bank to the clients so that they keep track of their past transactions. It is important to go through this document because it allows one to check even the previous year transactions so as to make sure accounts are not compromised (Lassar et al., 2005, p. 24). In the event of complaint, users can save their bank statement either as word or as PDF on their computer, tablets or smartphone for future evidence.

### f. Buying of Bank Products

E-banking allows clients of the bank to buy products electronically. Examples of such products may include cars, land, silver, gold and mortgage. The bank products vary across different financial institutions.

## g. Payment of Bills

Users of online banking benefit from the ability to login into their accounts check outstanding balance either make payment to their credit card or pay other bills. In this age, it is easy to buy goods online safely and quickly or simply make enquiries; therefore, saving on travel costs and time.

## h. Order for a Check or Deposits Book

This is a booklet of blank checks that facilitates bank account holders to draw money from their account or deposit funds for the purpose of settling other company accounts or payment of bills (Lassar et al., 2005, p. 30). These checkbooks can be ordered online by e-banking service users, they receive the booklet through their mail.

## i. Conduct Reconciliation

It is important to undertake bank reconciliations in order to note any discrepancies between your accounting records and those held by the bank since this would enable swift and timely transactions. On the other hand, this service is a benefit to the commercial banks as it allows them to improve on customer's satisfaction by allowing their clients to conduct their reconciliations online.

## j. Make IRD Payments

IRD refers to the income that an individual is not entitled to receive during his or her lifetime. Such payments include IRA or other retirement schemes that an account holder cannot receive before death (Benjamin, 2000). The amount of IRD payments is not part of the final income tax return. This service is now available through internet banking, and it is easy to process all information an individual may need pertaining to IRD payments electronically.

## k. Changing of Passwords

Internet banking security is a fundamental factor customer considers when opening new bank accounts online. E-banking offers a service that allows the account holders to keep changing their passwords to protect their accounts from fraudsters or intruders. It is possible to change passwords as many times as possible. Therefore, to access this service one need to remember the security question and answer provided during account opening, as well as the old password. Thus, one completes setting a new password process after verifying the newly entered password.

## l. Alerts

An account holder with the access of internet banking can subscribe to receive alerts of every processed transaction by the financial institution. Consequently, the service will inform the customer about the existing bank account balance, and introduction of new products and transactions completed.

## m. Tax Information and Documents

Financial institutions assist their customers to complete several tasks such as offering tax documents online. Additionally, the banks help their clients to fill and submit the forms online. Overall, a financial firm helps in resolving tax related issues and usually this service is available to the customers free of charge.

## 3. Benefits of E-Banking

E-banking revolutionized provision of financial services around the world (Liao et al 66). Financial institutions as well as customers derive certain benefits from using e-banking as compared to the conventional method of banking.

## a. Benefits to the Banks

Internet banking contributes to a reduction of operational costs in the financial Institutions. In the long run commercial banks save on monies that would be paid to the tellers to manage the growing customer base in the bank. Therefore, it is relatively cheaper to conduct financial services over the internet for the banks. Virtual banking has allowed banks to acquire a greater customer base through reaching new target markets (Liao et al., 1999). Precisely, the use of internet surmounts any geographical boundaries that would be difficult and expensive to break when using traditional banking systems. Interestingly, the banks use internet to reach the well-off households as internet penetrates highly in households that have a sustainable income. E- Banking reduces the costs affiliated to marketing especially with the introduction of internet marketing, helping to create a similar playing field for small and big banks. Therefore, the upcoming financial institutions can fight for survival through competing for customer base in the same market with the successful banks (Liao et al., 1999). Otherwise, it would be impossible for the small financial firms to compete with the leading companies through the traditional systems of marketing because of capital and market power challenges enjoyed by the big banks.

There has been a significant change in the level of efficiency in commercial banks after the introduction of e-banking. Use of internet in banking facilities allows the firms to operate in a paperless environment. For example, it is easy to keep records within a single file for a huge number of clients. The level of customer service and satisfaction continues to improve remarkably with e-banking systems. Principally, this improvement is attributed by the levels of efficiency in banks. In addition, internet banking offers the customers services that would be difficult to access through bank's branches (Liao et al., 1999). For example, learning from tutorials uploaded on the banks' website about filing tax returns. More so, online banking contributes to a reduction of the number of people visiting the facilities daily; therefore, improving on customer service both online and offline. Using e-banking services helps a financial entity to improve its public image by giving a good impression to existing and prospective customers. Noteworthy, an account holder may not be willing to use e-banking system, but by providing such services a bank helps in promoting a good reputation to the prospective and current customers.

## b. Benefits of E-Banking to Customers

Online banking allows account users to make bill payments across accounts to just about anyone. For example, client of the bank can choose anybody or any company whom he or she wants to make payments to and the bill pay service will facilitate this transaction.

Customers enjoy other facilities that would be cumbersome to conduct from a banking hall at the same time. Internet banking gives the account holder the liberty to control almost every aspect of his or her account. Besides this control over personal or business bank accounts, the customer can access other services within the financial industry (Liao et al., 1999). For example, buy or sell interest-earning assets, keep an update on stock market and money market. It is imperative to mention that accessing internet banking services on the bank's website is free the only requirement is being an account holder with the entity and have access to the internet.

Customers enjoy the benefit of comparing best deals across banks and get access to the best special offers. Often individuals operate more than one bank account; therefore, it is easy using e-banking services to compare products offered by different banks. E-banking service allows bank account holders to access the financial institution on a 24 hours basis (Krantz, 2013, p. 19). Automated teller machines, and access to their bank account through the internet is convenient to the clients. Virtual banking is beneficial to customers because this system helps bank account holders to avoid queues common in banking facilities. Many of the customers who use online banking feel that this system saves time unlike when they spend time queuing in banks.

## 4. Challenges of E-Banking

Internet banking is beneficial to the stakeholders in the financial industry. Banks and customers enjoy extensive benefits by using this modern way of accessing financial information and products (Sarlak, 2011, p. 29). However, there are certain concerns or challenges that arise in the use of internet banking. Firstly, with the introduction of this new technology by the commercial banks there is a need to create a customer service support system that will provide support to the clients. Commercial banks face the challenge of maintaining a fast and reliable customer support system in a bid to protect their reputation as well as image in the market. Establishing such systems is costly but it is important towards getting the customers to trust internet banking as a way of undertaking financial transactions. Secondly, laws governing different countries present an interesting challenge to e-banking. Internet banking cannot be limited within a geographical location or borders (Lassar et al., 2005, p. 45). However, each country or state has different laws that are distinct and are not applicable in territories beyond where the laws are enacted. Therefore, there is a need to harmonize some laws pertaining to electronic banking worldwide so as to ensure access to financial information and products is not restricted. Thirdly, the issue of security over the internet is another challenge that continues to affect online banking. In fact, this is one of the challenges for banks as customers inquire know the level of security or protection that virtual technology offers to them before they proceed to open online banking accounts. Internet technology attracts online cyber-crimes, and often bank customers become victims of fraud or theft especially with the use of ATM's (Lassar et al., 2005, p. 45). Hacking and phishing of financial information is an emerging trend and a challenge that banks deal with every financial year. Fourthly, internet banking creates regulatory challenges because of globalization of the financial industry. Internet allows provision of services from any location in the world posing a danger in regulation of financial intermediaries by the central bank. Inherently, commercial banks will find ways to avoid any supervision or regulation by the relevant authorities. For example, it is mandatory for every business to acquire a license from the government; similarly, financial institutions have to establish a licensed branch before they are granted permission to venture into virtual banking (Marina, 2009, p. 4). Fifthly, internet banking has led to increased activities of money laundering. Anonymity is one of the features evident with electronic banking. A client opens an account in a bank, but it is difficult for the financial entity to identify the type of business the nominal account holder is undertaking or even the location of the transactions. Presently, many governments have put up guidelines to combat money laundering. For example, it is mandatory for every individual opening a bank account to verify their identity and notify the bank of their residential address (Marina, 2009, p. 6). Finally, online banking poses serious macroeconomic challenges to the country's economy. For instance, the technological revolution in the finance industry particularly the advancement of banking practices makes it difficult for central bank to implement monetary policy (Benjamin, 2000). Consequently, it is always a challenge for the central bank trying to control economic activities and inflation especially with the globalization of financial services. In essence, expansion of electronic banking leads to a significant decline in financial transaction costs. Consequently, this leads to cheap credit in the economy hence eroding the effectiveness of monetary policy (Benjamin, 2000). Tobin tax is an example of a tool used by many governments towards controlling availability of credit in the economy especially it helps to increase costs of accessing financial products from the banks by the borrowers.

## 5. Global Developments of E-Banking

The first worldwide development of electronic banking is SME finance. Over time, there has always been a need to solve financial constraints facing SME's around the world (Xu et al., 2006, p. 40). Small and medium enterprises (SME's) find it difficult to access finance especially whenever there is competition between SME's and leading businesses whereby the small firms find it difficult to sustain the competition. The loan size that SME's access is too small coupled with high costs of borrowing and low profitability of some businesses during the start-up period. Therefore, the introduction of internet banking plays a fundamental role in leveling the playing field between businesses in an attempts to borrow money from banks. Globally, there is enough evidence that SME's are now easily accessing credit compared to the period before the introduction of virtual banking. New bill payments methods were introduced immediately after the successful global growth of electronic banking. For example, internet payment service providers such as Paypal, dotbank and X.com contribute to easy bill payment services worldwide (Xu et al., 2006, p. 41). The ATMs also developed as a result of banks realizing that operating their services within the virtual realm will yield more benefits compared to the traditional way of banking. Thus, electronic banking contributed significantly to the morphing of credit cards into shopping portals. The dominance of credit cards as the leading method to conducting e-commerce payments led to many card companies to leverage of the existing market share and became shopping helpers. Therefore, finance services consumers have instant access to credit to use online as well as merchant guarantees globally. In brief, development of click and mortar business strategy continues to take the center stage in financial services provision (Xu et al., 2006, p. 41). Commercial banks realized that there is a need to blend their operation activities that are the brick and mortar delivery plus the online banking system. Consequently, even banks that were purely operating as virtual banks are now opening physical banks as a way of complementing their online brands.

## 6. Types of E-Banking Services

In general, Mittal (2000, p. 3) categorizes online banking services into three types (2). Firstly, there is the Basic Level Service (BSL) that defines how different banks use their websites to disseminate information regarding their array of products and services being offered to the public. BSL has the capacity to interact with customers via email.

Secondly, there are Simple Transactional Websites (STWs) that permit clients to submit their applications for preferred services and queries regarding balances on their accounts. However, STWs do not allow any fund-based transactions on personal accounts. The third type of online banking services are via Fully Transactional Websites (FTWs) that allow customers to transact funds in their accounts, pay bills, buy and sell securities, and subscribe to other products or services offered by the bank.

Conventional banks offer the stated forms of electronic banking services (Mittal 2000, p. 2). However, there are other types of banks known as "Internet banks" or "virtual banks" that deliver their services primarily via the internet. Some of such banks may not be physically present in a country. Customers, however, need access to relevant electronic devices in order to access e-banking services. The use of such devices represents different modes of internet banking.

There is the use of ATMs that allows customers to withdraw and deposit money in their banks accounts, request for bank statements and checks, and inquire about any outstanding balances in their accounts. Most ATMs run independently on a 24 hour basis and are found in urban locations depending on the availability of customers. All a customer needs is a personal ATM card with a secure pin number. Moreover, these ATM cards can range from VISA cards to Master cards depending on the technological sophistication of a certain bank.

Another mode of e-banking is the use of mobile phones to perform financial transactions such as balance inquiries, payment of bills, and money transfers. Nevertheless, others refer to this mode as mobile banking. Customers can get access to online banking services by use of SMS or via the internet when using an internet-enabled mobile phone.

## 7. Risks of E-Banking

According to Chavan (2013), internet banking is simply the delivery of traditional banking services through an electronic communication device or channel as the internet. However, in the process, e-banking has thrown open issues that have consequences beyond what a normal channel for delivery of banking services would normally envision. E-banking has created a new dimension to the numerous types of risks typically associated with the banking sector. As a result, malicious applications that target online financial transactions have increased dramatically in recent years. With regard to this, it has heightened some risks as well as creating new risk control challenges. For example, in the United States, such malicious applications have employed two kinds of attack vectors; remote cyber-attacks that redirect a victim to a remote site, and local attacks that take place on local computer networks.

The attack vectors eliminate geographical barriers in service delivery by being able to reach out to customers from diverse countries with different legal jurisdictions. Due to this, there remains the question of whether a universal supervisory system should be implemented to oversee such transactions. Furthermore, the authenticity of electronic contracts, security of financial transactions, and the privacy of customers have now showed different concerns due to the fact that the internet is not applicable for control by a single authority. It is a public domain that poses a risk of being hacked or malfunctioning. On the other hand, since online banking is the most cost effective and efficient mechanism of banking services, the banks that fail to adapt to new technological changes risk losing business by being edged out of competition (Chavan, 2013). In addition, it has created a new type of competition both from existing players as well as new players in the market who are not necessarily banks.

When accessing the internet, typical dangers come from third parties who may access, delete, or tamper with data under false pretenses. They achieve this through various mechanisms; for instance, hackers can use the internet to get unauthorized access to a customer's personal computer. They can also use viruses and worms, which are self-replicating programs that can be sent over the internet via e-mail and damage a customer's computer. Conversely, they can use Trojans, which are programs that compromise the security of a person's computer by intercepting passwords. Other ways include phishing, pharming, and use of rootkits. The latter is a malicious software that allows unauthorized administrator-level access to a personal computer without the knowledge of the real administrator. In addition, these rootkits share some features with Trojans. Phishing involves using a false address, website, or name for fraudulent purposes, whereas pharming involves redirecting computer users to a falsified server. In general, the systems that online banking customers use are exposed to risks beyond the control of the bank. Due to this, it is not realistic for banks to assume liability for such risks.

## 8. E-Banking Regulations

According to Williamson (2006), the regulatory concerns in online banking have mainly arisen out of the risks stated above. Legal and regulatory issues are those that relate to law jurisdictions and legality of electronic contracts on the basis of gaps in the regulatory environment governing electronic commerce. With regard to law jurisdiction, there have arisen questions on whether the law in effect should be for the area where the customer is accessing the internet or where the final transaction takes place. Still on this, there are questions regarding where the income will be generated and who will be responsible for taxing such income. According to Ahansanul, Ahmad, & Abu (2009), these issues do not have definite answers at the moment.

Regulators are concerned with the security of online banking transactions. The issues include how to adopt internationally accepted state-of-the art technological measures for access control, decryption and encryption, digital signature verification, firewalls, and public key infrastructure. In response, many financial regulations have been modified to ensure safety and viability of domestic banking, to protect customers' rights, to encourage market discipline, and to maintain the civic trust in the banking sector.

Regulatory thinking ensures that banks are aware of the involved risks and that they implement proper safeguarding systems and machinery to counter emerging risks. Nonetheless, having a system in place is not enough; the systems have to be regularly upgraded to changing technologies, which presents a much bigger challenge. Another solution is to formulate regulations that will allow for organized development of e-banking. Similarly, new instruments and methods for carrying out financial trades and the establishment of new service providers, will need legal recognition, definition, and permission. Essentially, it will be important to give an electronic signature an equal legal status as a handwritten signature. Moreover, existing legal permissions and definitions, like the legal perception of a national border and description of a bank, will also need to be modified (Benklifa & Olmstead, 2013, p. 23).

In the modern world, the Electronic Funds Transfer Act, EFTA, is a federal law that protects consumers involved in online banking transactions. The EFTA covers banking products and services such as computer banking, debit cards, and ATM cards. Under the act, a consumer must receive a written receipt when he or she uses an ATM card to deposit or withdraw funds, or when he or she uses a debit card to make purchases at a point-of-sale terminal. The receipt functions as a way of recording a consumer's electronic transactions. It gives information such as the date the transaction was made, the place the transaction was carried out, and the amount of the transaction.

## 9. Security in E-Banking

Several factors affect the safety of internet banking. These include regulatory body supervisions, customer awareness, and internet infrastructure. On the other hand, according to Chavan (2013), increased use of the internet and mobile services as a new channel for distribution of banking services requires more thought towards security against sham activities. However, this responsibility should not be left to banks alone; Lee states that customers and regulatory bodies also have a role in e-banking security. Furthermore, banks do not have any influence regarding the electronic devices and channels used by their customers to perform transactions.

The bank has the most roles. Firstly, it is supposed to formulate a secure online banking infrastructure. Then it should ensure the implementation of an appropriate information security policy. Thirdly, the bank should provide a robust monitoring system for fraudulent activities and notify its account holders of any high-risk transactions through SMS. Fourthly, the bank is supposed to offer a two-factor authentication (TFA) protocol for its account holders. The first factor is something like a PIN number, which the customer knows, whereas the second factor is something that the customer will own such as a smart card with a chip authentication (Lee, 2012, p. 8). On the other hand, the customers' responsibility is to ensure that they have enough knowledge regarding the safety tips required in e-banking. For instance, a customer should always stay alert in safeguarding his or her identity as well as limiting public access to personal computers. According to Lee, there are numerous tips for safely logging on and off to a computer (Lee, 2012, p. 10). For example, a customer should never use a public computer to access his or her internet banking website. Customers should also close any open tabs and windows in a browser before logging on into i-banking. Moreover, after using the online service, the customer should always remember to log off. In safeguarding their identity, customers should use unique passwords that are difficult to guess. According to Lee, a strong password should have at least six characters with a combination of numbers and letters. Furthermore, it is good for customers to often change their passwords and disable the 'Autocomplete' function in their browsers so that it does not remember previously input data.

Lee also advises that customers should never leave their TFA devices unattended (Lee, 2012, p.14). Other tips include disconnecting internet connections when not in use, backing up critical data on removable hard drives or Compact Discs, and installing internet security software for real-time detection of intrusions on a customer's computer. The roles of regulatory bodies in e-banking security are also several. According to Lee, regulatory bodies should develop adequate policies that promote customer protection and international cooperation among partners (Lee, 2012, p. 19).

## 10. Benefits of E-Banking

From a bank customer's perspective, the main benefit of internet banking is significant time management, elimination of queues due to the automation of most financial services and availability of easy maintenance tools for managing one's money. Other benefits include cheaper costs of attaining banking services and increased comfort. With regard to the latter, customers are able to make financial transactions any time of the day, and without physical interactions with the bank.

Fourthly, there is rapid and uninterrupted access to information. For example, business firms can enjoy easier access to information by checking on multiple accounts at the tick of a button. Fifthly, internet banking allows for better management of cash by speeding up cash cycles and increasing efficiency of business transactions since numerous cash management tools are available on the World Wide Web. For instance, it is possible to manage a firm's short-term cash through internet banks in money market funds, in commercial papers, in over-night deposits, or in bonds and equities (Appei, 2009, p.7).

In addition, e-banking allows a customer to enjoy the convenience of carrying out financial transactions from the comfort of his or her office or home. Sixthly, the fact that e-banking allows a rapid response enables customers to wait until the end of a financial transaction without any fuss about it. Finally, internet banking allows for effective management of funds. Customers are allowed to download their account history and fund analyses on their computers or mobile phones before carrying out any actual transaction (Chavan, 2013).

## 11. E-Banking Technologies

Online banking encompasses a wide array of established and emerging technologies. They range from products and services that customers opt for (like computer banking and ATM cards) to the technologies (like electronic check conversions) used by banks and merchants to process financial transactions. According to Anguelov et al. (2004, p.1), the availability of a variety of e-banking technologies in the marketplace has greatly advanced in recent years. In the financial sector, such technologies include automated teller machines, direct deposit, debit cards, and prepaid cards among others. These technologies have sped up processing of financial transactions, and have reduced costs of banking services.

### a. Automated Teller Machines (ATMs)

ATMs are electronic terminals that financial institutions provide to their customers so that they can withdraw money, make deposits, transfer funds, and check balances in their bank accounts. These terminals vary depending on the type of bank and the type of ATM card being used. However, in recent years, banks have formulated shared platforms that allow their customers to share their ATM machines regardless of the machine's location and brand name.

### b. Direct Deposit

Direct deposit describes a form of electronic payment by which a business firm or government institution pays funds. As a result, the funds are directly transferred into a customer's bank account without physical movement of either the sender or the recipient.

### c. Computer Banking

This represents the process by which consumers are able to access banking services via internet connection to a bank's website. The consumers are able to carry out financial transactions, pay bills, and receive money among many other banking services. However, according to Anguelov et al. (2004, p. 2), other financial services involve use of the internet but are not classified under computer banking. An example is the payment of credit card bills on the website owned by the credit card issuer.

### d. Electronic Fund Transfer (EFT)

EFT refers to the movement of funds from one bank account to another via an electronic medium.

### e. Check (Debit) Card

A debit card is used at a point-of-sale terminal or at an ATM to enable customers to have their funds debited directly from their bank account. However, other financial service providers, such as currency exchangers and check cashers, may use a debit card that acts as a stored-value card instead of tying it to a deposit account.

### f. Stored-Value Card

A stored-value card is a card on which money is stored, either through deposit or through prepayment by a customer. When the card issuer and acceptor are one entity, it is known as a single-purpose stored-value card, and the card represents prepayment for particular goods and services. An example is a phone card (Anguelov et al., 2004, p. 2). On the contrary, a limited-purpose stored-value card is constrained to specific points of sale in a particular location. An example is a vending machine found at a learning institution. On the other hand, there is the multi-purpose stored-value card that can be used for a wide array of purchases from multiple service providers. For instance, such a card may have a Visa or MasterCard logo.

### g. Payroll Card

A payroll card is a type of stored-value card that an employer issues to employees instead of the normal paycheck. This card enables the employees to access their funds at point-of-sale terminals or ATMs. The employer, on the other hand, uses online services to add the employee's pay to the card.

### h. Smart Card

A smart card is another type of stored-value card that has a chip or microprocessor embedded in it. The embedment allows the card to store data, carry out calculations, or conduct special-purpose processing to authorize purchases, authenticate personal identification numbers, store personal records, and verify account balances.

### i. Prepaid Card

A prepaid card represents a stored-value card that stores monetary values that the consumer has paid to the issuer in advance.

### j. Direct (Electronic Bill) Payment

This refers to a mode of payment that allows customers to pay their bills via electronic money transfers. The funds are transferred from the customer's account into the creditor's account via an electronic channel. A distinctive characteristic of direct payment is that the customer must initiate and approve each transaction.

### k. Electronic Check Conversion

This describes the process whereby information written on a check (account number, routing number, and transaction amount) undergoes electronic conversion in order to carry out a one-time transfer of funds from an account.

### l. Electronic Bill Presentment and Payment (EBPP)

EBPP refers to a type of payment of bills whereby the bills are presented to a customer electronically via e-mail or via a notice in a customer's electronic banking account. The customer may then decide to pay the bill electronically or physically depending on what is more convenient. In case of the former, the payment is deducted electronically from the customer's account.

## 12. Consumers and E-Banking

According to Chavan (2013), a sufficient level of human capacity building and infrastructure are required before third world countries can adopt universal technology for their domestic requirements. An example lies in the migration plan review for the Society for Worldwide Interbank Financial Telecommunications (SWIFT) that revealed that full migration has failed to occur due to many developing countries lacking adequate infrastructure, skilled technical expertise, and working capital. Another example is how many consumers in developing countries lack trust for broadly accepted electronic payment systems, whereas others cannot access the infrastructure required for processing electronic payments. Due to this, communication across the internet remains open and insecure for bank-client relations in developing countries.

The fact that there are a number of e-banking technologies to choose from means that a consumer can choose the one that is safest to use or the one that is easiest or cheapest to perform financial transactions. According to Anguelov et al. (2004, p. 1), consumer-use and acceptance of e-banking technologies appears to be determined by the demographic and socioeconomic characteristics of the consumer such as age and amount of income. Other factors that determine acceptance and use of these technologies include perceptions of certain technologies, ease of use, and personal consumer preferences.

Consequently, Anguelov et al. (2004, p.1) states more than ninety percent of all U.S households have a bank account, and almost all of these households have an electronic transfer associated with their account, such as direct deposit, computer banking, debit card, or ATM card. According to a survey conducted by Consumer Finances in 2001, approximately two-thirds of all U.S employers pay their workers by directly depositing funds into their bank accounts. Similarly, the department of Treasury deposits social security benefits to approximately four fifths of their recipients. On the other hand, statistics show that since the introduction of ATM cards in the 1960s, more than a billion ATM transactions were being carried out each month by 2003. Anguelov et al. (2004, p. 3) states that this number should keep on increasing year by year until it surpasses two billion monthly transactions.

On the contrary, consumers also use electronic products that store monetary value on a card or in a database related to their bank accounts. These products include military cards, college cards, payroll cards, prepaid cards, and insurance cards. Cards that store monetary values emerged in the 1970s and have become popular with about two million cardholders in the year 2000 (Anguelov et al., 2004, p. 3).

## CONCLUSION

The e-banking revolution has been the fastest invention to change the global business of banking. As a result, banks all over the world have reoriented their business strategies in order to encompass the new opportunities offered by online banking. In other words, the banking sector has led global electronic trade in recent years. Internet banking has enabled banks to change strategic behavior, scale borders, and create new possibilities as a result. Furthermore, internet banking has changed banking services towards the neoclassical economic theories of market functioning. Due to this, the market has become transparent and clients can easily compare banking services from different banks. For example, while using the internet, the customer is only one-click away from competitors. Thus, if a client is not satisfied with the products or services offered by one bank, he or she is able to change to a preferred banking partner faster and more easily.

Internet banking has tremendously reduced the physical costs of operating a bank. As Williamson (2006) stated, technological advancements in information technology have reduced the costs of processing financial information, whereas use of the internet facilitates transmission of financial information. In fact, this is why electronic banking services have gained popularity in recent years. In the future, this will ensure that banking rates are friendly as well as encouraging to more innovations regarding the current products and services being offered by banking institutions. In addition, electronic delivery of financial services has enabled banks to meet their clients' expectations and create close customer relationships (Williamson, 2006). Hence, as discussed by Chavan (2013), online banking will eventually triumph over traditional banking in the coming years as more developing nations are now building their economies with specific focus on e-learning, e-commerce, and e-banking.

## REFERENCES

Ainin, S., Lim, C. H., & Wee, A. (2005). Prospects and Challenges of E-Banking in Malaysia. *Electronic Journal of Information Systems in Developing Countries*, *22*, 1–110.

Appei, M. (2009). *Investing with Exchange Trade Funds Made Easy: A Start to Finish Plan to Reduce Costs and Achieve Higher Returns* (2nd ed.). Upper Saddle River, NJ: Pearson Education Inc.

Benklifa, M., & Olmstead, W. (2013). *Learn How to Trade Options (Collection)*. Upper Saddle River, NJ: Pearson Education.

Chavan, J. (2013). Internet Banking – Benefits and Challenges in an Emerging Economy. *International Journal of Research in Business Management*, *1*, 19–26.

Friedman, B. M. (2000). Decoupling at the Margin: The Threat to Monetary Policy from the Electronic Revolution in Banking. *International Finance*, *3*(2), 261–272. doi:10.1111/1468-2362.00051

Haque, A., Ismail, A. Z. H., & Daraz, A. H. (2009). Issues of E-Banking transaction: An Empirical Investigation on Malaysian Customers Perception. *Journal of Applied Sciences*, *9*(10), 1870–1879. doi:10.3923/jas.2009.1870.1879

Krantz, M. (2013). *Investing Online for Dummies*. Hoboken, NJ: John Wiley & Sons.

Laopodis, N. (2013). *Understanding Investments: Theories and Strategies*. New York, NY: Routledge.

Lassar, P., Lambert, L., Woodford, C., & Moschovitis, C. J. P. (2005). *The Internet: A historical encyclopedia*. Santa Barbara, Calif: ABC-CLIO.

Liao, S., Shao, Y. P., Wang, H., & Chen, A. (1999). The Adoption of Virtual Banking: An Empirical Study. *PERGAMON International Journal of Information Management*, *19*(1), 63–74. doi:10.1016/S0268-4012(98)00047-4

Marina, K. (2009). *Reference in the E-Banking*. Cairo: Publisher of the Universities.

Ozuru, H. N., Chikwe, J. E., & Idika, U. (2010). The Use of Traditional Payments And Electronic Payments Systems in Nigeria: A Discourse. *Proceedings of the 11th Annual Conference of International Academy of African Business and Development.*

Sarlak, M. A., & Astiani, A. A. (2011). *E-banking and emerging multidisciplinary processes: Social, economical, and organizational models*. Hershey, PA, USA: IGI Global. doi:10.4018/978-1-61520-635-3

Williamson, D. G. (2006). Enhanced authentication in online banking. *Journal of Economic Crime Management*, *4*, 1–42.

Xu, M. X., Wikes, S., & Shah, M. H. (2006). E-Banking Application and Issues. In *Abbey National PLC. E-Technologies. Encyclopedia of E-Commerce, E-Government, and Mobile Commerce*. Hershey, PA, USA: IGI Global. doi:10.4018/978-1-59140-799-7.ch042

## ADDITIONAL READING

Anguelov, C. E., Hilgert, M. A., & Hogarth, J. M. (2004). *U. S. Consumers and Electronic Banking 1995-2003*. Federal Reserve Working Paper.

Kallstrom, O. (2000). *Business Solution for Mobile E-Commerce* (Ericsson Review 2000-03-27).

Lee, S. (2012). *E-Banking Security*. Information Security (InfoSec), Government of Hong Kong Working Paper.

Mittal Shri, S. R. (2000). *Report on Internet Banking*. Reserve Bank of India Working Paper.

## KEY TERMS AND DEFINITIONS

**Automated Teller Machines (ATM):** Computing machine that allows bank clients to have access to their accounts with a card and a code number.

**E-Banking:** The performance of banking business through the internet. It is also known as “Internet banking” or “Online banking.”

**Electronic Commerce:** A business model that enables to conduct business over the internet.

**Financial Institutions:** An institution that provides financial services to potential clients.

**Online Security:** Computer security related to the internet involving browsing and network security. It is designed to establish measures to use against attacks through internet. Information Technology: It is the use of any computers, storage, networking and other processes to create, store and exchange electronic data.

**Phone Banking:** A service offered by a financial institution that enables clients to perform financial transactions over the phone.

# Chapter 14
# Human Resource Development in Globalized Era

**G.K. Sinha**
*Arya Mahila P.G. College, India*

## ABSTRACT

*Human resources development is the process of increasing the knowledge, the skills, and the capacities of all the people in a society. In economic terms, it could be described as the accumulation of human capital and its effective investment in the development of an economy. In political terms, human resources development prepares people for adult participation in political processes, particularly as citizens in a democracy. From the social and cultural points of view, the development of human resources helps people to lead fuller and richer lives, less bound by tradition. In short, the processes of human resources development unlock the door to modernization. Education is essential for all and is fundamental to their all-round development, material and spiritual. Education has continued to evolve, diversify and extend its reach and coverage since the dawn of human history. Even Alfred Marshall emphasized the importance of education as a national investment and in his view the most valuable of all capital is that invested in human beings. Every country develops its system of education to express and promote its unique socio-cultural identity and also to meet the growing challenges with the changing times. In this regard, major initiatives/programmes taken by the Central as well as State governments. This paper deals with the changes in our education structure and system after independence of country like increment of literacy rate, growth of educational institution, enrolment ratio of girls, pupil teacher ratio in educational institutions, government's expenditure on education, structural change of education and vocationalisation of education.*

## INTRODUCTION: CHALLENGES OF HUMAN RESOURCE DEVELOPMENT:

The current challenges facing India in respect of human resource development are to achieve full literacy rate for adults, upscale higher and technical education and expand opportunities for vocational training. In addition, the Government is also faced with the challenges of drawing up inclusive plans to bridge regional, social and gender disparities which would provide equal of opportunity as well as a productive and meaningful life.

DOI: 10.4018/978-1-4666-9908-3.ch014

To meet these challenges and achieve the ultimate goals of human resource development, special scheme have initiated by the Government of India to focus on specific segments of education system, by inter alia, promoting the participation of private sector.

In view of the fact that India has a federal system of governance and education is matter of concurrent list of Indian Constitution. Central government does not directly intervening in this matter. Therefore, implementation of Central Government policy involves close coordination with the state and local governments, particularly since the policy relating to education, except higher and technical education, is the responsibility of State Government.

## MAJOR INITIATIVES TAKEN BY GOVERNMENT

To meet these challenges and improve human resource development framework Government take some major initiatives:

## THE RIGHT OF CHILDREN TO FREE AND COMPULSORY EDUCATION (RTE)

The Constitution (Eighty-sixth Amendment) Act, 2002, inserted Article 21A in the Constitution provides for free and compulsory education of all children in the age group of six to fourteen years as a Fundamental Right in such manner as the State may, by law, determine. The RTE Act makes specific provisions for Special Training for age-appropriate admission for out-of-school children. The RTE Act also provides that such children shall continue to be provided free and compulsory elementary education even after they cross 14 years of age (*Govt. of India 2014).*

## KASTURBA GANDHI BALIKA VIDYALAYA

KGBV are residential upper primary schools for girls from SC, ST, OBC and Muslim communities. KGBVs are set up in areas of scattered habitations, where schools are at great distances and are a challenge to the security of girls. This often compels girls to discontinue their education. KGBV addresses this through setting up residential schools, in the block itself. KGBVs provide for a minimum reservation of 75% seats for girls from SC/ST/OBC and minorities communities and 25% to girls from families that live below the poverty line.

## MID-DAY-MEAL (MDM)

With a view to enhancing enrollment, retention and attendance and simultaneously improving nutritional levels among children, 'National Programme of Mid- Day Meal in Schools' is being implemented. Monitoring of the scheme is being made through Review Mission, Regional Workshop and National Review meetings.

## RASHTRIYA MADHYAMIK SHIKSHA ABHIYAN (RMSA)

This scheme is being implemented with the objective to enhance access to secondary education and improve its quality. The schemes envisages inter alia, to enhance the enrollment at secondary stage by providing a secondary school within a reasonable distance of habitation, with an aim to ensure GER of 100% by 2017 and universal retention by 2020. The other objectives include improving quality of education imparted at secondary level through making all secondary schools conform to prescribed norms, removing gender, socio-economic and disability barriers, etc.

## VOCATIONALISATION OF EDUCATION

"Vocationalisation of Secondary and Higher Secondary Education" is being implemented to address the issues of low esteem of vocational education in the country, weak synergy with industry in planning and execution, lack of vertical and horizontal mobility, induction courses and curricula as well as paucity of trained vocational education teachers. It is also envisaged that strengthening of vocational education at the secondary stage would contribute to the national target of 500million skilled manpower by 2022. The scheme has been revised and aligned with the National Vocational Education Qualification Framework (NVEQF) now assimilated in National Skills Qualifications Framework on the basis of learning's emerging from the pilot project in Haryana *(MHRD 2010)*.

## NATIONAL SCHEME OF INCENTIVE TO GIRLS FOR SECONDARY EDUCATION (NSIGSE)

The Centrally Sponsored Scheme "National Scheme of Incentive to Girls for Secondary Education" was launched in May 2008 with the objective to establish an enabling environment to reduce the drop-outs and to promote the enrolment of girl children belonging mainly to SC/ST communities in secondary schools. According to the scheme, a sum of Rs. 3000/- is deposited in the name of the unmarried eligible girls as fixed deposit, who are entitled to withdraw it along with interest on attaining 18 years of age and passing X class examination .

## RASHTRIYA UCHCHATAR SHIKSHA ABHIYAN (RUSA)

The Cabinet Committee on Economic Affairs (CCEA), in its meeting held on 3rd October, 2013 approved the Rashtriya Uchchatar Shiksha Abhiyan (RUSA), a Centrally Sponsored Scheme (CSS) for reforming the State Higher Education system. RUSA will be a new CSS spread over the 12th and 13th plan periods, for improving access, equity and quality in the state higher education system. RUSA is envisaged as the prime vehicle for strategic funding of State institutions so as to ensure that issues of access, equity and quality are addressed in an equitable manner. All funding under RUSA would be norm based and future grants would be performance based and outcome dependent. Commitment by States and institutions to certain academic, administrative and governance reforms will be a precondition for receiving funding under RUSA. Centre-State funding would be in the ratio of 90:10 for North-Eastern States, Sikkim, J&K,

Himachal Pradesh and Uttarakhand and 65:35 for other States and Union Territories. Support would be extended to only government and government aided institutions.

## CHANGING SCENARIO OF HUMAN RESOURCE DEVELOPMENT

The 12th Five Year Plan recognizes the importance of the development of capabilities that are needed to achieve the objective of faster, more inclusive and sustainable growth. The development of human capabilities is accorded high priority since these capabilities are considered as important instrumentalities that help raise the productive capacity of the economy and since proper development of human capabilities also help ensure that the growth is more inclusive by enabling the disadvantaged sections of the society access the opportunities provided by the growth process *(NUEPA 2014).*

One of the key implications of the 12th Five Year Plan goal of faster, more inclusive and sustainable growth for education development in the country is the need to create sufficient education and skill development opportunities for the younger population which would enable them to seek appropriate employment/ livelihood opportunities that are needed for improving their living standards (see table-1).

It is evident from the table-1 that the maximum persons were literate during 2011 census i.e.73.0 percent in which 80.9 percent male and 64.6 percent females. Whereas minimum percentage of literate persons i.e. 18.3 during 1951 in which 27.2 percent males and 8.9 percent females. The table also reveals that the percentage of literacy in females was increasing significantly during 1951 to 2011 it was 8.9 percent in 1951 and rose to 15.4 percent in 1961, and again increase to 22.0 percent, 29.8 percent, 39.3 percent, 53.7 percent and 64.6 percent in 1971, 1981, 1991, 2001 and 2011 respectively. Thus it is very significant change in an underdeveloped economy like India.

Table 2 shows that the highest number of educational institution in India was during 2013-14 in which 7906 lakh primary schools, 4011 lakh upper primary schools, 1313 secondary schools, 36671 colleges and 712 universities. Whereas lowest number of educational institutions was 2097 lakh primary schools, 136 upper primary schools, 74 senior secondary schools, 578 colleges and 27 universities during 1950-51. The number of colleges was increasing significantly during 1950-51 to 2013-14 i.e. 578 in 1950-51 and it was rose to 1819, in 1960-61 and again increased to 3277, 6963, in the year 1970-71 and 1980-81 respectively. While in the year 1990-91 it was declined i.e. 5748. And it was again increased during

*Table 1. Literacy Rates in India (in percentages)*

| Census Year | Persons | Males | Females |
|---|---|---|---|
| 1951 | 18.3 | 27.2 | 8.9 |
| 1961 | 28.3 | 40.4 | 15.4 |
| 1971 | 34.5 | 46.0 | 22.0 |
| 1981 | 43.6 | 56.4 | 29.8 |
| 1991 | 52.2 | 64.1 | 39.3 |
| 2001 | 34.8 | 75.3 | 53.7 |
| 2011 | 73.0 | 80.9 | 64.6 |

Source: GOI, MHRD, Educational Statistics at Glance -2014 p.14
Note: 1951-1971: Aged5+; 1981-2011: Aged7+

*Table 2. Numbers of Recognized Educational Institutions in India*

| | (in '00') | | | | (In absolute numbers) | |
|---|---|---|---|---|---|---|
| Level/Year | Primary | Upper Primary | Secondary | Senior Secondary | Colleges | University |
| 1950-51 | 2097 | 136 | NA | 74 | 578 | 27 |
| 1960-61 | 3304 | 497 | NA | 173 | 1819 | 45 |
| 1970-71 | 4084 | 906 | NA | 371 | 3277 | 82 |
| 1980-81 | 4945 | 1186 | NA | 516 | 6963 | 110 |
| 1990-91 | 5609 | 1515 | NA | 798 | 5748 | 184 |
| 2000-01 | 6387 | 2063 | 877 | 384 | 10152 | 254 |
| 2010-11 | 7485 | 4476 | 1312 | 720.46 | 32974 | 621 |
| 2013-14 | 7906 | 4011 | 1313 | 1026 | 36671 | 712 |

Source: GOI, MHRD, Educational Statistics at Glance -2014 p.14
Note: from 1950-51 to 1990-91, figures for Class XI-XII include Class IX-X

2000-01 i.e. 10152 and 32974, 36671 in the year 2010-11 and 2013-14 respectively. Similarly number of universities increased substantial it 27 in the year 1950-51 and rose to 45, 82, 110 and 184 in the year 1960-61, 1970-71, 1980-81 and 1990-91 respectively.

Table 3 delineates that the highest level wise enrolment of all categories of students was highest in the year 2012-13 i.e. 1321 lakhs in primary, 643 lakhs upper primary, 343 lakhs secondary, 198 lakhs senior secondary and 296 lakhs in higher education. Whereas lowest level wise enrolment of all categories of students was during 1950-51 i.e. 192 lakhs in primary level, 31 lakhs upper primary level, 15 lakhs senior secondary level and 4.0 lakhs in higher education. In the level of primary education there was slightly decline in enrolment of students during 2013-14 i.e. 1300 lakh. During 1950-51 to 2013-14 the overall trend has shown incremental in all level of education which is good sign for an underdeveloped country or emerging economies like India. It is also evident from above statistics that the government efforts are also materialized significantly.

*Table 3. Level wise Enrolment of All Categories of Students (in lakhs)*

| Level/Year | Primary (I-V) | Upper Primary (VI-VIII) | Secondary (IX-X) | Senior Secondary (XI-XII) | Higher Education |
|---|---|---|---|---|---|
| 1950-51 | 192 | 31 | NA | 15 | 4.0 |
| 1960-61 | 350 | 67 | NA | 34 | 10 |
| 1970-71 | 570 | 133 | NA | 76 | 33 |
| 1980-81 | 738 | 207 | NA | 110 | 48 |
| 1990-91 | 974 | 340 | NA | 191 | 49 |
| 2000-01 | 1138 | 428 | 190 | 99 | 86 |
| 2010-11 | 1348 | 619 | 319 | 195 | 275 |
| 2012-13 | 1321 | 643 | 343 | 198 | 296 |
| 2013-14 | 1300 | 657 | 370 | 222 | NA |

Source: GOI, MHRD, Educational Statistics at Glance -2014 p.16
Note: from 1950-51 to 1990-91, figures for Class XI-XII include Class IX-X

*Table 4. Number of Girls per hundred Boys Enrolled by Stages of Education*

| Level /Year | Primary (I-V) | Upper Primary (VI-VIII) | Secondary (IX-X) | Senior Secondary (XI-XII) | Higher Education |
|---|---|---|---|---|---|
| 1950-51 | 39 | 19 | NA | 15 | 13 |
| 1960-61 | 48 | 31 | NA | 26 | 21 |
| 1970-71 | 60 | 41 | NA | 33 | 28 |
| 1980-81 | 63 | 49 | NA | 45 | 36 |
| 1990-91 | 71 | 58 | NA | 49 | 46 |
| 2000-01 | 78 | 69 | 63 | 62 | 58 |
| 2010-11 | 92 | 89 | 82 | 79 | 78 |
| 2012-13 | 94 | 95 | 89 | 87 | 80 |
| 2013-14 | 93 | 95 | 90 | 89 | NA |

Source: GOI, MHRD, Educational Statistics at Glance -2014, p. 29
Note: from 1950-51 to 1990-91, figures for Class XI-XII include Class IX-X

The table-4 reveals that the number of girls' students per hundred boys' students enrolled by all stages of education from class I to XII and higher education was 39 in primary class, 19 upper primary classes, 15 senior secondary and 13 in higher education during 1950-51, while in 1960-61, there were 48 girls in primary classes, 31 in upper primary, 26 senior secondary level and 21 in higher education. The number of girls was increased again it was 60, 41, 33, in primary, upper primary and senior secondary classes respectively and 28 in higher education during 1970-71. In the year 1980-81 trend was shown again increasing i.e. 63 girls in primary, 49 in upper primary, 45 in senior secondary and 36 in higher education, similarly during 1990-91 it was rose to 71, 58, 49 in primary, upper primary and senior secondary classes respectively, whereas 46 in higher education. During 2000-01 it was again increased upto 78 in primary classes, 69 in upper primary classes, 63 in secondary classes, 62 in senior secondary classes and 58 in higher education. Likewise in the year 2012-13 the increasing trend was maintain it was 94 in primary, 95 in the upper primary, 89 in secondary, 87 in senior secondary classes while in higher education it was 80. The table depicted overall trend of girls per hundred boys since 1950-51 to 2013-14 from primary classes to higher education was increasing significantly, it is good gesture for Indian society as well as economy.

It is clear from table-5 that the highest pupil teacher ratio (PTR) was in India i.e. 24 in primary school, 20 in upper primary school, 21in senior secondary school and no data available in higher education during 1950-51. It was rose to 36 in primary, 31 upper primary and 25in senior secondary school in the year 1960-61. It was again increased upto 39 in primary, 32 upper primary and 25 in senior secondary school during 1970-71. Similarly in the year 1990-91 it was 43 in primary, 37 in upper primary and 31 in senior secondary school and there were no data available in higher education this period. While in the year 2010-11 the PTR in primary school was constant i.e. 43. Whereas in upper primary school and senior secondary school it was declined i.e. 33 and 34 respectively.

The table-6 reveals that the number of female teachers per hundred male teachers in India was highest in primary school, upper primary school, secondary school and senior secondary school i.e. 88, 83, 74 and 96 in the year 2013-14 respectively. Whereas lowest number of female teachers per hundred male teachers was in the year 1950-51 i.e. 20 in primary school, 18 in upper primary school and 19 in senior

*Table 5. Pupil Teacher Ratio (PTR) in India*

| Type of School / Year | Primary School | Upper Primary School | Secondary School | Senior Secondary School | Higher Education |
|---|---|---|---|---|---|
| 1950-51 | 24 | 20 | NA | 21 | NA |
| 1960-61 | 36 | 31 | NA | 25 | NA |
| 1970-71 | 39 | 32 | NA | 25 | NA |
| 1980-81 | 38 | 33 | NA | 27 | NA |
| 1990-91 | 43 | 37 | NA | 31 | NA |
| 2000-01 | 43 | 38 | 31 | 35 | NA |
| 2010-11 | 43 | 33 | 30 | 34 | 26 |
| 2012-13 | 30 | 30 | 30 | 40 | 23 |
| 2013-14 | 28 | 30 | 28 | 40 | NA |

Source: GOI, MHRD, Educational Statistics at Glance -2014 p.37
Note: from 1950-51 to 1990-91, figures for Senior Secondary include Secondary School

*Table 6. Number of Female Teachers per Hundred Male Teachers in India*

| Type of School /Year | Primary School | Upper Primary School | Secondary School | Senior Secondary School | Higher Education |
|---|---|---|---|---|---|
| 1950-51 | 20 | 18 | NA | 19 | NA |
| 1960-61 | 21 | 32 | NA | 26 | NA |
| 1970-71 | 27 | 38 | NA | 33 | NA |
| 1980-81 | 33 | 42 | NA | 38 | NA |
| 1990-91 | 41 | 50 | NA | 45 | NA |
| 2000-01 | 55 | 62 | 54 | 42 | NA |
| 2010-11 | 76 | 80 | 61 | 65 | 59 |
| 2012-13 | 87 | 80 | 69 | 92 | 64 |
| 2013-14 | 88 | 83 | 74 | 96 | NA |

Source: GOI, MHRD, Educational Statistics at Glance -2014 p.36
Note: from 1950-51 to 1990-91, figures for Senior Secondary include Secondary School

secondary school there was data available in higher education in this year. The trend shown in primary school was increasing i.e. 20 in the 1950-51 and 88 during 2013-14, similarly this trend was also maintain in upper primary school its 18 in the year 1950-51 and in the year 2013-14 it was 83. And in senior secondary school it was also shown increasing trend during 1950-51 to 2013-14 it was significant to our country. Apart from this data available in higher education was from 2012-13 to 2013-14 i.e. 59 and 64 respectively which is also shown satisfactory increment in this level.

Table 7 shown that the maximum amount of expenditure on education was Rs. 403236.51 crore during 2012-13 i.e. 4.29 percent of GDP. While minimum amount of total expenditure on by education and other department was Rs.64.46 crore in 1950-51 i.e. 0.64 percent of GDP. The table reveals that the overall trends of expenditure on education by education and other departments was increasing since 1950-51 to 2012-13, both in amount and as well as percent of GDP. It was also very significant that the

*Table 7. Public Expenditure on Education and Gross Domestic Product (GDP)*

| Year | GDP at Current Price (at Factor cost) (Rs. Crore) | Total Expenditure on Education by Education & Other Deptt. (Rs. Crore) | Expenditure on Education by Education & Other Deptt. as % of GDP |
|---|---|---|---|
| 1950-51 | 10080 | 64.46 | 0.64 |
| 1960-61 | 16220 | 239.56 | 1.48 |
| 1970-71 | 42222 | 892.36 | 2.11 |
| 1980-81 | 130178 | 3884.2 | 2.98 |
| 1990-91 | 510964 | 19615.85 | 3.84 |
| 2000-01 | 1925017 | 82486.48 | 4.28 |
| 2010-11 | 7248860 | 293478.23 | 4.05 |
| 2011-12 | 8391691 | 351145.78 | 4.18 |
| 2012-13 | 9388876 | 403236.51 | 4.29 |

Source: GOI, MHRD, Educational Statistics at Glance -2014, p.38

expenditure on education as percentage of GDP 0.64 per cent in the year 1950-51 which rose to more than double in the year 1960-61 i.e. 1.48 percent, while it was 2.98 percent during 1980-81 and after that it was again increased after two decades i.e. 4.28 percent in the year 2000-01. Whereas it was slightly decreasing during 2010-11 i.e. 4.05 percent and 4.18 percent in the year 2011-12. In the year 2013-14 it was slightly increasing i.e.4.29 percent.

## CONCLUSION AND SUGGESTION

The study divulges that the present scenario of human resource development India is changing significantly. The increment of literacy rate is remarkable because it was 18.3 percent persons (including males and females) during 1950-51 while it was rose to 73.0 percent in the 2011 Census in which 80.9 percent males and 64.6 percent females. It's shown very satisfactory trend. Number of recognized educational institutions was grown very substantial after independence only 578 colleges and 27 universities and 2307 thousand schools in our country. After sixty year of independence i.e. 2013-14 it was increased up to 712 universities, 36671 colleges and 11917 primary and upper schools and 2339 secondary and senior secondary school in our country. It is also notable that the number of girls per hundred boys enrolled by all stages of education was increased it was 13 and 15 in senior secondary school and higher education respectively per hundred of boys in the year 1950-51 whereas during 2012-13 it was rose to 87 and 81 which was shown sincere efforts of governments towards girls education and women empowerment.

In the globalization era that the private sector is plays very significantly there role in education system of country they also contributed in a very good amount of number of primary schools, secondary or senior secondary schools, colleges or technical institutes and universities. Today, the coexistence of both public sector and private sector in country's education structure perform remarkable role to improve and competent our academics and human resources to compete with challenges of globalization in current scenario.

Apart from this there is many deficiency and shortcomings emerging in education system. The regulatory bodies like University Grants Commission, All India Council for Technical Education, National Council for Teacher education etc. are not much effective on quality check of higher education. Government must take these issues seriously and reform the regulators. Besides uniform syllabus in higher and secondary education is also a serious problem in our education system so government must consider this issues.

## REFERENCES

Ahmad, S. M., & Mir, A. A. (2012). Need for Human Resource Development (HRD) Practices in Indian Universities: A Key for Educational Excellence. *Journal of Human Values*, *18*(2), 113–132. doi:10.1177/0971685812454481

All India Survey on Higher Education various issues. (n. d.). Govt. of India, MHRD.

Annual Report various issues. (n. d.). Govt. of India, MHRD.

de Silva, S. (1997). *Human Resources Development for Competitiveness: A Priority for Employers*. Italy: International Labour Organisation.

Dutt, M. (2010). Development and HRD in India. IDEAS 20th Anniversary, Tokyo.

Education for All towards Quality and Equity. (2014). India, NUEPA, New Delhi

Educational Statistics at Glance -2014. (n. d.). Govt. of India, MHRD.

Geetha Rani, P. (2002). *Financing Higher Education in India in the Post Reform Period: Focus on Access and Equity*. New Delhi: National Institute of Educational Planning and Administration.

Harbison, F., & Myers, C. A. (1964). *Education, Manpower and Economic Growth: Strategies of Human Resources Development*. USA: McGraw-Hill.

Kar, S., Roberts, M. A., & Ali, E. (2013). *Human Development in the New Millennium*. New Delhi: Regal Publications.

Marshall, A. (1930). *Principles of Economics* (8th ed.). London: Macmillan & Co. Ltd.

Sharma, D. (2009). *Human Resource Development in Schools*. New Delhi: APH Publishing.

Tyagi, R. S. (2011). *Academic Supervision in Secondary Schools: School-Based Approach for Quality Management*. New Delhi: NUEPA.

## KEY WORDS AND DEFINITIONS

**Gender Parity Index (GPI):** Is the ratio of Girls GER to Boys GER in a given level of education.

**Gross Enrolment Ratio (GER):** Is the total student enrolment in a given level of education, regardless of age expressed as percentage of the corresponding eligible official age group population in a given school year.

**Human Resource Development:** Is the process of increasing the capacity of the human resource through development. It is thus the process of adding value to individuals, teams or an organization as a human system.

**Literacy Rate:** Is the number of literates in the age group of 7 years and above expressed as percentage of the total corresponding population.

**Pupil Teacher Ratio (PTR):** Is the average number of pupils (students) per teacher at a specific level of education in a given school-year.

**Vocationalisation:** Is considered to be an important measure in improving the vocational relevance of education and in helping students to prepare for effective participation in any area of work. It is argued here that technology education is an example of best practice with regard to vocationalisation.

# Chapter 15
# Corporate Ethics and Social Responsibility

**Juhi Srivastava**
*Kashi Institute of Technology, India*

**Rakesh Kumar Pandey**
*United College of Engineering and Research, India*

## ABSTRACT

*Ethics and Social Responsibility in business and government today are very important subjects. These are talked about frequently and addressed in the news when unethical decisions are found. There needs to be an overall intent to be ethical and socially responsible in today's business environment in order to stay successful. Ethics are an individual belief system that consists of knowing what is right and wrong. Ethics can vary person to person. Ethics is in part analyzing decisions, beliefs, and actions. This paper is a study on ethics and social responsibility in today's organizations. This paper will explore the various aspects of how to establish ethics at the workplace, and responsibilities of the organization towards society. It also helps in knowing the importance of ethics and social responsibility in the organization.*

## INTRODUCTION

In the last twenty years, there has been a sea change in the nature of the triangular relationship between companies, the state and the society. No longer can firms continue to act as independent entities regardless of the interest of the general public. The evolution of the relationship between companies and society has been one of slow transformation from a philanthropic coexistence to one where the mutual interest of all the stakeholders is gaining paramount importance. Companies are beginning to realize the fact that in order to gain strategic initiative and to ensure continued existence, business practices may have to be molded from the normal practice of solely focusing on profits to factor in public goodwill and responsible business etiquettes.

Firms all over the world are beginning to grasp the importance of intangible assets, be it brand name or employee morale. Only firms that have gained the goodwill of the general public and are ideal corporate citizens will be to develop these intangible assets into strategic advantages. Many researchers have hypothesized that Social Responsibilities in emerging economies is still in a very nascent stage

DOI: 10.4018/978-1-4666-9908-3.ch015

and suitable mechanisms do not exist to ensure that companies practice Social Responsibilities with anything other than a charitable outlook.

In business today there are many instances of corporations that act from an ethical standard. In the wake of scandals it is more important than ever that company make an effort to push out improper behavior and practices. The importance of ethics in business is seen all the way into the structural natures of businesses. It is not just a notion that you have; it is in the way a business operates that can show the importance of ethics in your company. The dedication to ethics must come from the highest ranks of the organization. In order to have a principled company, you must have a principled leadership. (Berenbeim, 1992). "The Corporate Ethics Test". Business and Society Review, 31(1), 77-80).

The importance of ethics in business is seen all the way into the structural natures of businesses. The dedication to ethics must come from the highest ranks of the organization. In order to have a principled company, you must have a principled leadership.

## Define Ethics and Social Responsibility?

World Business Council for Sustainable Development (WBCSD) defines Social Responsibility as "The continuing commitment by business to behave ethically and contribute to economic development while improving the quality of life of the workforce and their families as well as of the local community and society at large."

The European Commission advocates Social Responsibility as "Being socially responsible means not only fulfilling legal expectations, but also going beyond compliance and investing more into human capital, the environment and relations with stakeholders."

Social responsibility has to do with the social conscious of an entity or corporation. It also deals with the citizenship and public spirit of the company. It is a common standard of justice. Ethics play an important role in social responsibility. The keys issues involved are the health and safety of every employee. It is a responsibility for every organization to offer the employee peace of mind. Social responsibility is an ethical ideology or theory that an entity, be it an organization or individual, has an obligation to act to benefit society at large. This responsibility can be passive, by avoiding engaging in socially harmful acts, or active, by performing activities that directly advance social goals. (Brenner 1992). "Ethics Programs and Their Dimensions". Journal of Business Ethics, 11,391-399).

Freescale company has been named one of the 2010 World's Most Ethical Companies by the Ethisphere Institute.

## Dimensions of Social Responsibility and Ethics

The Green Paper (2001) by the Commission of the European Communities identifies two main dimensions of Social Responsibility, an internal dimension relating to practices internal to the company and an external dimension involving the external stakeholders.

## Internal Dimension

This relates to practices internal to the company which need to be modified to incorporate social responsibility practices. The various components of the internal dimension of Social responsibility are shown in Figure 1.

*Figure 1. Components of Internal Dimension of Social Responsibility of Company*

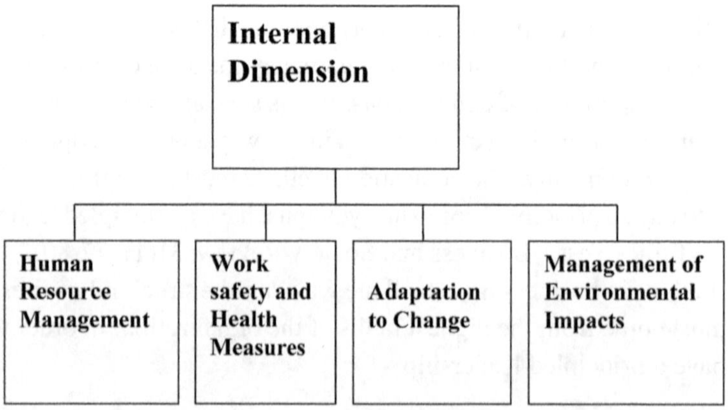


## a. Human Resources Management

Social Responsibility can be successfully implemented in an organization through precise management of its own work force. The internal dimension of Social Responsibility includes elements like providing an environment for life long learning for employees, employee empowerment, better information flow, improving the balance between work, family, and leisure, diversified work force, profit sharing and share ownership schemes, concern for employability as well as job security among others. Active follow up and management of employees who are off work due to disabilities or injuries have also been shown to result in cost savings for the companies. Molding of recruitment policies to include people from ethnic minorities, older workers, women and the long-term unemployed would be a significant step forward Gandz, & Bird (1989). "Designing Ethical Organizations" (Business Quarterly, p. 108-112).

## b. Work Safety and Health Measures

Worker safety and labour health have been documented to be having a direct impact on productivity of the labour force. Although legal measures exist in most nations on maintaining standards for ensuring worker safety and providing health benefits, recent trends have made it imperative for companies to adopt a proactive approach to this issue. The increased focus on safety standards and employee welfare has led to the development of standards across industries. Mechanisms are being designed especially in emerging markets for measuring, documenting and communicating these qualities thereby saving time, work and costs in the purchasing process.

## c. Adaptation to Change

A recent trend in the global business scenario has been the wide spread use of mergers and acquisitions for business expansion. Also downsizing has been used, often ineffectively, as a cost cutting measure by firms in their relentless push for profits. According to the Green Paper (2001) by the Commission of the European Communities "Restructuring in a socially responsible manner means to balance and take into consideration the interests and concerns of all those who are affected by the changes and decisions. In practice the process is often as important as the substance to the success of restructuring. In particular this involves seeking the participation and involvement of those affected through open information and consultation.

### d. Management of Environmental Impacts

The importance of this aspect of Social Responsibility cannot be over emphasized. Optimization of resource utilization and reducing environmentally damaging effluents can reduce the environmental impact. This will also enable the firms to affect significant cost savings in energy bills and pollution costs.

## External Dimension

This dimension relates to practices concerning external stakeholders. The significance of this dimension of CSR has come to the forefront with the advent of globalization leading to the development of international standards for business practices. External dimension of a company may have three basic elements as shown in figure 2.

### a. Local Communities

The development of positive relations with the local community and thereby the accumulation of social capital is particularly relevant for non-local companies. These relations are being increasingly used by multinational companies to support the integration of their subsidiaries. Deep understanding of the local community and social customs is an asset which can be utilized by the companies to gain strategic advantage.

*Figure 2. Components of External Dimension of Social Responsibility of Company*

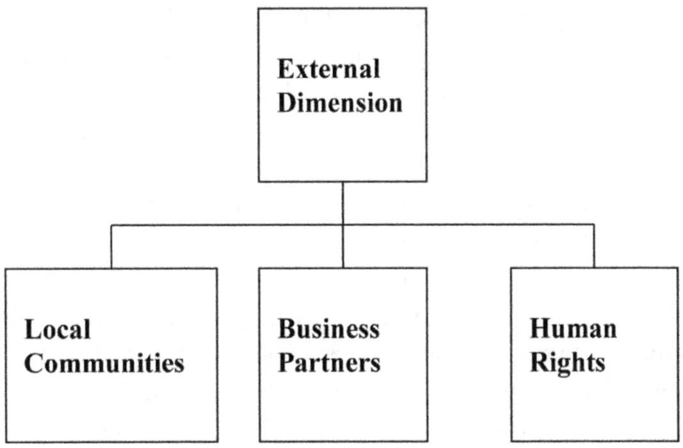

### b. Business Partners

Building long term relationships of sound ethical foundation with suppliers, customers (and even competitors in rare occasions) will enable companies to meet customer expectations better while reducing complexity and costs. Companies should realize their Social Responsibility practices will be judged taking into account the practices of their partners and suppliers throughout the supply chain.

### c. Human Rights

According to Robbins (2000), "Companies operating in countries where human rights are regularly violated may experience a climate of civil instability and corruption that makes for uneasy relations with government officials, employees, local communities and shareholders" (Francis, 1991). "Prevent Trouble by Improving Ethics" Christian Science Monitor, p. 9).

## BENEFITS OF MANAGING ETHICS IN THE WORKPLACE

The following list describes various types of benefits for managing ethics in the workplace.

1. **Attention to business ethics has substantially improved society.** Workers' limbs were torn off and disabled workers were condemned to poverty and often to starvation. Employees were terminated based on personalities. Influence was applied through intimidation and harassment. Then society reacted and demanded that businesses place high value on fairness and equal rights. Anti-trust laws were instituted. Government agencies were established. Unions were organized. Laws and regulations were established.
2. **Ethics programs help maintain a moral course in turbulent times.** During times of change, there is often no clear moral compass to guide leaders through complex conflicts about what is right or wrong. Continuing attention to ethics in the workplace sensitizes leaders and staff to how they want to act -- consistently.
3. **Ethics programs cultivate strong teamwork and productivity.** Ethics programs align employee behaviors with those top priority ethical values preferred by leaders of the organization. Usually, an organization finds surprising disparity between its preferred values and the values actually reflected by behaviors in the workplace. Ongoing attention and dialogue regarding values in the workplace builds openness, integrity and community -- critical ingredients of strong teams in the workplace. Employees feel strong alignment between their values and those of the organization. They react with strong motivation and performance.
4. **Ethics programs support employee growth and meaning.** Attention to ethics in the workplace helps employees face reality, both good and bad -- in the organization and themselves. Employees feel full confidence they can admit and deal with whatever comes their way.
5. **Ethics programs are an insurance policy -- they help ensure that policies are legal.** There is an increasing number of lawsuits in regard to personnel matters and to effects of an organization's services or products on stakeholders. Attention to ethics ensures highly ethical policies and procedures in the workplace. A major intent of well-designed personnel policies is to ensure ethical treatment of employees, e.g., in matters of hiring, evaluating, disciplining, firing, etc.

6. **Ethics programs help avoid criminal acts "of omission" and can lower fines.** Ethics programs tend to detect ethical issues and violations early on so they can be reported or addressed. In some cases, when an organization is aware of an actual or potential violation and does not report it to the appropriate authorities, this can be considered a criminal act, e.g., in business dealings with certain government agencies, such as the Defense Department. However, the guidelines potentially lower fines if an organization has clearly made an effort to operate ethically.
7. **Ethics programs help manage values associated with quality management, strategic planning and diversity management -- this benefit needs far more attention.** Ethics programs identify preferred values and ensuring organizational behaviors are aligned with those values. This effort includes recording the values, developing policies and procedures to align behaviors with preferred values, and then training all personnel about the policies and procedures. This overall effort is very useful for several other programs in the workplace that require behaviors to be aligned with values, including quality management, strategic planning and diversity management. Total Quality Management includes high priority on certain operating values, e.g., trust among stakeholders, performance, reliability, measurement, and feedback. Ethics management techniques are highly useful for managing strategic values, e.g., expand market share, reduce costs, etc. McDonnell Douglas integrates their ethics programs into their strategic planning process. Ethics management programs are also useful in managing diversity. Diversity programs require recognizing and applying diverse values and perspectives -- these activities are the basis of a sound ethics management program.
8. **Ethics programs promote a strong public image.** Attention to ethics is also strong public relations -- admittedly, managing ethics should not be done primarily for reasons of public relations. But, frankly, the fact that an organization regularly gives attention to its ethics can portray a strong positive to the public. People see those organizations as valuing people more than profit, as striving to operate with the utmost of integrity and honor. Aligning behavior with values is critical to effective marketing and public relations programs. (Genfan 1987). "Formalizing Business Ethics". Training and Development Journal, pp. 35-37).

## ROLES AND RESPONSIBILITIES IN ETHICS MANAGEMENT

Depending on the size of the organization, certain roles may prove useful in managing ethics in the workplace. These can be full-time roles or part-time functions assumed by someone already in the organization. Small organizations certainly will not have the resources to implement each the following roles using different people in the organization. However, the following functions points out responsibilities that should be included somewhere in the organization.

1. **The organization's chief executive must fully support the program.** If the chief executive isn't fully behind the program, employees will certainly notice -- and this apparent hypocrisy may cause such cynicism that the organization may be worse off than having no formal ethics program at all. Therefore, the chief executive should announce the program, and champion its development and implementation. Most important, the chief executive should consistently aspire to lead in an ethical manner. If a mistake is made, admit it.
2. **Consider establishing an ethics committee at the board level.** The committee would be charged to oversee development and operation of the ethics management program.

3. **Consider establishing an ethics management committee.** It would be charged with implementing and administrating an ethics management program, including administrating and training about policies and procedures, and resolving ethical dilemmas. The committee should be comprised of senior officers.
4. **Consider assigning/developing an ethics officer.** This role is becoming more common, particularly in larger and more progressive organizations. The ethics officer is usually trained about matters of ethics in the workplace, particularly about resolving ethical dilemmas.
5. **Consider establishing an ombudsperson.** The ombudsperson is responsible to help coordinate development of the policies and procedures to institutionalize moral values in the workplace. This position usually is directly responsible for resolving ethical dilemmas by interpreting policies and procedures (Raynard & Forstater, 2002).
6. One person must ultimately be responsible for managing the ethics management program.

## Developing Codes of Ethics

Consider the following guidelines when developing codes of ethics:

1. **Review any values need to adhere to relevant laws and regulations:** This ensures your organization is not (or is not near) breaking any of them. (If you are breaking any of them, you may be far better off to report this violation than to try hiding the problem. Often, a reported violation generates more leniency than outside detection of an unreported violation, particularly per the new Federal Sentencing Guidelines). Increase priority on values that will help your organization operate to avoid breaking these laws and to follow necessary regulations.
2. **Identify values needed to address current issues in your workplace:** Appoint one or two key people to interview key staff to collect descriptions of major issues in the workplace. Collect descriptions of behaviors that produce the issues. Consider which of these issues is ethical in nature, e.g.., issues in regard to respect, fairness and honesty. Identify the behaviors needed to resolve these issues. Identify which values would generate those preferred behaviors. There may be values included here that some people would not deem as moral or ethical values, e.g., team-building and promptness, but for managers, these practical values may add more relevance and utility to a code of ethics.
3. **Identify any values needed based on findings during strategic planning:** Review information from your SWOT analysis (identifying the organization's strengths, weaknesses, opportunities and threats). What behaviors are needed to build on strengths, shore up weaknesses, take advantage of opportunities and guard against threats?
4. **Consider any top ethical values that might be prized by stakeholders:** For example, consider expectations of employees, clients/customers, suppliers, members of the local community, etc.
5. **Examples of ethical values might include:** (The following list is the "Six Pillars of Character" developed by The Josephson Institute of Ethics, 310-306-1868):
    a. Trustworthiness: honesty, integrity, promise-keeping, loyalty
    b. Respect: autonomy, privacy, dignity, courtesy, tolerance, acceptance
    c. Responsibility: accountability, pursuit of excellence

   d. Caring: compassion, consideration, giving, sharing, kindness, loving
   e. Justice and fairness: procedural fairness, impartiality, consistency, equity, equality, due process.
   f. Civic virtue and citizenship: law abiding, community service, protection of environment
6. **Compose your code of ethics; attempt to associate with each value, two example behaviors which reflect each value:** Critics of codes of ethics assert that they seem vacuous because many only list ethical values and don't clarify these values by associating examples of behaviors.
7. **Include wording that indicates all employees are expected to conform to the values stated in the code of ethics:** Add wording that indicates where employees can go if they have any questions.
8. **Obtain review from key members of the organization:** Get input from as many members as possible.
9. **Announce and distribute the new code of ethics (unless you are waiting to announce it along with any new codes of conduct and associated policies and procedures):** Ensure each employee has a copy and post codes throughout the facility.
10. **Update the code at least once a year:** As stated several times in this document, the most important aspect of codes is developing them, not the code itself. Continued dialogue and reflection around ethical values produces ethical sensitivity and consensus. Therefore, revisit your codes at least once a year -- preferably two or three times a year. (Madsen & Shafritz, 1990).

## CONCLUSION

The lack of concern for the local community, the consumers and the environment by these corporations has created large scale public debate and action. It is important in this context to understand that the sustainable business growth is associated with care for the community. Organizations should develop and document a procedure for dealing with ethical and social responsibility dilemmas as they arise. Ideally, ethical and social responsibility dilemmas should be resolved by a group within the organization, e.g., a committee comprised of top leaders/managers and/or members of the board encourage voluntary commitment to social responsibility and this will lead to common guidance on concepts, definitions and methods of evaluation.

## REFERENCES

Berenbeim, R. E. (1992, Spring). The Corporate Ethics Test. *Business and Society Review*, *31*(1), 77–80.

Brenner, S. N. (1992). Ethics Programs and Their Dimensions. *Journal of Business Ethics*, *11*(5-6), 391–399. doi:10.1007/BF00870551

Francis, David R. (1991, June). Prevent Trouble by Improving Ethics. *Christian Science Monitor*, p. 9.

Gandz, J., & Bird, F. G. (1989, Autumn). Designing Ethical Organizations. *Business Quarterly*, *54*(2), 108–112.

Genfan, H. (1987, November). Formalizing Business Ethics. *Training and Development Journal*, 1987, 35–37.

Gray, R. (2001). *Social and Environmental Responsibility, Sustainability and Accountability, Can the Corporate Sector Deliver?* Glasgow, Centre for Social and Environmental Accounting Research, University of Glasgow. Retrieved from www.agenda-scotland.org/documents/ Can%20business%20 deliver%20Gray.pdf

Madsen, P., & Shafritz, J. M. (Eds.), (1990). Essentials of Business Ethics. New York: Penguin Books.

Raynard, P., & Forstater, M. (2002). *Corporate Social Responsibility: Implications for Small and Medium Enterprises in Developing Countries*. United Nations Industrial Development Organization.

Sims, R. R. (1991). Institutionalization of Organizational Ethics. *Journal of Business Ethics, 10*(7), 493–506. doi:10.1007/BF00383348

Thompson, T. (1991, Spring). Managing Business Ethics. *Canadian Public Administration, 34*(1), 153–157. doi:10.1111/j.1754-7121.1991.tb01449.x

Toffler, B. (1991, Winter). Doing Ethics: An Approach to Business Ethics Consulting. *Moral Education Forum*, 16(4), 14-20.

## KEY WORDS AND DEFINITIONS

**Community:** A community is a social unit of any size that shares common values, or that is situated in a given geographical area (e.g. a village or town). It is a group of people who are connected by durable relations that extend beyond immediate genealogical ties, and who mutually define that relationship as important to their social identity and practice. Although communities are usually small, community may also refer to large groups, such as national communities, international communities, and virtual communities.

**Ethics:** It is concerned with distinguishing between good and evil in the world, between right and wrong human actions, and between virtuous and nonvirtuous characteristics of people.

**Social Responsibility:** World Business Council for Sustainable Development (WBCSD) defines "The continuing commitment by business to behave ethically and contribute to economic development while improving the quality of life of the workforce and their families as well as of the local community and society at large."

# Chapter 16
# Self Help Groups:
## Bank Linkage Model in India

**Shruti Agrawal**
*Banaras Hindu University (BHU), India*

## ABSTRACT

*The chapter is based on the Self Help Group-Bank linkage Programme in India. The objective of the chapter is to assess the SHGs access to credit under SHG-Bank Linkage Programme, to know the progress of SHG-Bank Linkage Programme in India and to evaluate the impact of SHG-Bank Linkage Programme in India. Finally the chapter ends with suggestions to improve self help group-bank linkage programme and concludes that SHG-Bank Linkage Programme has provided a more favorable environment for enhancing India's potential for greater equitable growth with empowerment while considering the positive signs in their performance.*

## BACKGROUND

Banking Industry in India has made tremendous growth in the past few decades, but despite its improvements there are concerns that banks have not been able to reach the vast unbanked population of the country. To convert the unbanked population into banked population is a matter of great concern, or in other words we can say that to ensure financial inclusion of the poor and the underprivileged section and to find the out the causes of financial exclusion is the area of great concern as well.

In the light of the above concern, National Bank for Agriculture and Rural Development (NABARD) initiated systems and policies that would help in fulfilling the requirement and needs of the poor. Mr. A. Ramanathan emphasises on improving the access of the rural poor to an integrated microfinance services covering both savings and credit rather than providing just micro credit facilities. As a wide network of bank branches already existed, the strategy focus was not on creating alternate organizations, but on finding ways and means to improve the access and efficiency of the poor to the existing banking network, through design of new products and delivery mechanisms. So, to resolve the problem, banks found a solution that could be used by them for increasing the access of poor to reach the banks and that is the Self Help Group- Bank Linkage Model.

DOI: 10.4018/978-1-4666-9908-3.ch016

NABARD in the year 1992 in consultation with Reserve Bank of India, Commercial Banks and NGOs launched a pilot project for linking SHGs with Banks. Reserve bank of India had given directions to commercial banks to extend financial support to the SHGs as per NABARD guidelines. The project was further linked to Regional Rural Banks and Cooperatives.

In February 1992, NABARD promoted 500 SHGs with the pilot project programme. SHGs are basically originated by Prof. Mohammad Yunus, economist of Chittigong University of Bangladesh in the year 1975 to provide microfinance to rural women.

The SHGs in India were formed by Mysore Resettlement and Development Agency (MYRADA), a NGO in 1985 due to breakdown of the large cooperatives organized by MYRADA. By 1986–87, there were nearly 300 SHGs in MYRADA's projects. MYRADA then approached NABARD for an action research project on self-help groups which funded the research. Within the same timeline, Asian and Pacific Regional Agricultural Credit Association (APRACA) weighed options and agreed on further action for effectively increasing credit access for the poor. In India, NABARD and a member of APRACA, carried out an elaborate study which gave useful insights into the dynamics of group organization, saving potential and repayment ethics of the poor. Encouraged by the results of the study and action research project of MYRADA, NABARD then launched a pilot project linking SHGs with Banks.

## INTRODUCTION

SHG-Bank Linkage Programme is considered as a major strategy for providing financial services to the poor. It has its inception in 1990s and has made considerable and rapid strides exhibiting democratic functioning and group dynamism. It gathered momentum in the country during 1999-2000, as the credit linked during this period was more than twice the cumulative performance of the bank in credit linking of SHGs as on 31st March 1999.

The credit for such progress of Bank Linkage Programme in India is due to the active participation of NGOs, RBI, Commercial Banks, RRBs, Cooperative Banks, SIDBI, Private Banks, etc.

The National Bank continued to provide 100 per cent refinance assistance to banks for financing SHGs. The journey so far traversed by the Self Help Group – Bank Linkage Programme (SHG-BLP) crossed many milestones – from linking a pilot of 500 SHGs of rural poor two decades ago to cross 8 million groups a year ago. (https://www.nabard.org/english/shg_2.aspx)

Similarly from a total savings corpus of a few thousands of Indian Rupees in the early years to a whopping Rs. 27,000 crore today, from a few crore of bank credit to a credit outstanding of Rs. 40,000 crore and disbursements touching Rs. 20,000 crore during 2012-13. The geographical spread of the movement has also been quite impressive -from an essentially Andhra Pradesh – Karnataka phenomenon in the beginning now spreading to even the most remote corners of India. Over 95 million poor rural households are now part of this world's largest micro Credit initiative (Table 1).

The main objective of the programme has been financial inclusion by extending outreach to the poor households making available credit services at their doorstep with easy and self-managed assess to formal financial services on a sustainable basis and in a cost-effective manner.The SHG-Bank Linkage Programme was given a renewed thrust with the launch of SHG-2. The focus of SHG-2 would be on voluntary savings, cash credit as a preferred mode of lending, scope for multiple borrowings by SHG members in keeping with repaying capacity, avenues to meet higher credit requirements for livelihood

*Table 1. Grant Support to Partner Agencies (Rs. in lakh)*

| Agency | Cumulative Sanction up to 31.03.2013 | | Cumulative Achievement (31.3.2013) | |
|---|---|---|---|---|
| | Amount | SHG Nos. | Amount | SHG Nos. |
| NGOs | 19932.18 | 526699 | 6647.68 | 362803 |
| RRBs | 744.99 | 49250 | 185.43 | 45852 |
| Coop. Banks | 1046.23 | 73634 | 353.50 | 51266 |
| IRVs | 460.12 | 26883 | 77.04 | 11228 |
| Farmers Clubs | 40.63 | 2544 | 20.40 | 9832 |
| SHG Federation | 28.61 | 250 | 1.85 | 46 |
| PACS | 397.45 | 8533 | 4.28 | 85 |
| **Total** | **22650.21** | **687793** | **7290.18** | **481112** |

Source: NABAR D

creation, SHG Federations as non-financial intermediary, rating and audit of SHGs as part of risk mitigation system and strengthening monitoring mechanisms (https://www.nabard.org/english/shg_2.aspx)

The SHG-Bank Linkage Programme has the following objectives:

- To develop confidence between the weaker sections and banks.
- To mobilize the financial services with less transaction cost to the poor.
- To eliminate poverty.
- To empower women.
- To expand the flow of credit.
- To combine the flexibility of informal system with the financial resources of the formal financial institutions.

## REVIEW OF LITERATURE

- **Meyer R. (2002)** concluded that micro credit as form of financing firstly can have a large coverage of clients with a limited volume of loan. Secondly, in India SHG Bank linkage programme and micro credit financing has developed a cooperative work culture with team spirit and inculcate the efficiency and Ideas of the group members to give a success to small loans. Further it helps to shift from irregular low paid daily jobs to diversified source of earning or small business. Micro credit not only works as tool of income generation but also empowering poor people, more particularly women by helping them to access more education and health services
- **Srinivasan K. & Deo M. (2006)** concluded that eradication of poverty has become the main objective not only of public policy but also of operation of some NGOs, policy makers, and researchers in different countries. Though a number of factors and policies need to be developed to fight with poverty, the role of finance is crucial. Providing micro credit to poor for self employed income generating projects will definitely help to develop them.
- **Jasmine A. (2006)** concluded that SHG programme has a favourable impact on the living standards of its beneficiaries. It holds better promises for poverty alleviation and employment generation than the earlier programme due to its structure of easy credit, savings and peer monitoring.

- **Mulare and Mosley (1996)** concluded that the Government of Kerala state in India has introduced a novel scheme of poverty alleviation based on micro credit and self help grouping. Kudumbashree project in Kerela aim at improving living of poor women in rural and urban areas. It seeks to bring poor women folks together to form the grass root oganisation to help enhance their economic security. The project aims at removing poverty among rural women households through setting u of micro credit and productive enterprises.
- **Reddy (2005)** observes that the state of SHGs identifies key areas of weakness which undermine the sustainability of SHG movement. He identifies the major areas such as financial management, governance and human resource ranges from weak to average quality for a majority of SHGs. APMAS (2006) on the SHG-Bank-linkage programme in India, addressed a wide range of issues including cases of dropouts from SHGs, internal politics, issues of social harmony and social justice, community actions, book-keepings, equity, defaults and recoveries etc., and sustainability of SHGs.
- **Putnam (2000)** concluded that Self-Help Groups have been instrumental in empowerment by enabling women to work together in collective agency. Women's networks do not usually obtain business or political favours as they command few economic resources and frequently rely on time and non-monetized labour exchange. However, Self-Help Groups, when combined with savings and credit, have enabled women to benefit economically by monetizing their contributions and in the process have empowered them to become agents of change.
- **Sharma (2001)** stated that there is a copious literature on SHGs and their role in socio economic development of various sections in India. The studies generally report the significant changes in the living standards of SHG members is terms of increase in income level, assets, saving, borrowing, building capacity due ti income generating activities.
- **Puhazhendi and Satyasai (2001)** revealed the role of SHGs as institutional mechanism of economic and social empowerment of rural poor. SHGs help in increase in saving, Income generation, asset creation and standard of living.
- **Minimekalai and Rajaeswai (2001)** mentioned that the impact of Self Help Groups on empowerment of women from the perspectives of women's control over resources. Women's control over resources has been assessed in terms their share in the household assets, income, debt and saving.
- **Kurum. F. (2001)** concluded that providing credit access to members of poor households on a sustainable basis is the primary objective of self help group. A well conceived loan programme in a self help group will enhance its attractiveness to the members. These loans are often given for various purposes, without insistence on collateral but are available at a cost. There is no compulsion to avail of loan facility. SHG typically offer small, short term loans for meeting emergent and consumption requirements only to their members
- **Sacidananale (2006)** concluded that SHG emerged as a powerful tool that aimed at empowering women and eradicating poverty in a sustainable manner. It was thought that women's easy access to credit facilities and equal share in employment opportunities will ultimately lead to women empowerment.
- **Lalrintiana and Kanagaraj (2006)** concluded that self Help Groups are emerging as major mechanisms of development and empowerment of women in the third world. In India since ninth five year plan, most of the development programmes are channeled through SHGs. In all part parts of the country SHGs are organised by governmental and nongovernmental organisations. The

Government departments, banks and NGO facilitate them by providing revolving fund, organisational base, training, credit etc. It is worthwhile to call SHGs a mass movement on a national scale for development and empowerment of the poor and downtrodden in the country.

- **Karmakar (1999)** suggested that micro credit schemes using SHGs have enabled the poor to have easy and continued access to an easy source of credit without the scheme becoming a burden to the banking system.
- **Puhazhendhi (1999)** analyzed the functioning of SHGs, in performance, sustainability, empowerment of women, economic impact on the members, future potentials etc. He observed that SHGs in Tamil Nadu are performing well towards social change and transformation. The emerging trends are leading to positive direction of empowerment of members and promotion of micro finance.
- **Nagayya (2000)** maintains that an informal arrangement for credit supply to the poor through SHGs is fast emerging as a promising tool for promoting income-generating enterprises. He has reviewed the initiatives taken at the national level with a view of institutional arrangements to support this programme for alleviation of poverty among the poor, with focus on women. He maintained that NABARD and SIDBI are playing a prominent role at various stages of implementation of this programme. There are other national level bodies also supporting NGO's/VA/s, viz. Rastriya Mahila Kosh (RMK), Rashtriya Gramin Vikas Nidhi (RGVN) etc. He called for an imperative need to enlarge the coverage of SHGs in advance portfolio of banks as part of their corporate strategy, to recognize perceived benefits of SHGs financing in terms of reduced default risk and transaction costs.
- **Singh (2006)** conducted study about Peoples Education and Development Organisation"s SHGs programme and makes an attempt to evaluate social and economic impact on households of SHGs members. They observed that members involved in SHGs programme have increased involvement in decision making, awareness about various programmes and organisations. Moreover, the members get information about the different sources of credit and also reported that there are evidences of household income, food security and increased standard of living.
- **Kumar (2010)** while comparing the differences in quality of SHGs between SHGs under the umbrella of federations and other SHGs which are not part of federation observes that federation type SHGs are functioning well. He assesses the quality of SHGs by using NABARD CRI and also advised all banks to access the quality of SHGs using the CRI before every credit linkage. Sahu (2010) assessed the quality of SHG in Northwest India based on the 13 indicators of the 200 SHGs, 27 percent of the groups are found to be strong and stable. A majority of the groups (62.5%) are found to be moderately stable. 10.5 percent groups are found to be poor.

## OBJECTIVE OF THE STUDY

The following are the main objectives of the study:

1. To assess the SHGs access to credit under SHG-Bank Linkage Programme.
2. To know the progress of SHG-Bank Linkage Programme in India.
3. To evaluate the impact of SHG-Bank Linkage Programme in India.

## RESEARCH METHODOLOGY

The present article comprises of Secondary sources. Various articles, journals, magazines, newspapers and websites have been referred for it.

## CONCEPT OF SELF-HELP GROUPS

SHG-Banking is a programme that helps to promote financial transactions between the formal rural banking system in India comprising of public and private sector commercial banks, regional rural banks and cooperative banks with the informal Self Help Groups (SHGs) as clients. (SHGs are financial intermediaries owned by the poor). They usually start by making voluntary thrift on a regular -mostly fortnightly or monthly - basis (contractual savings). They use this pooled resource (as quasi-equity) together with the external bank loan to provide interest bearing loans to their members. Such loan provides additional liquidity or purchasing power for use in any of the borrower's production, investment, or consumption activities (Kropp & Suran, 2002).

Self Help Groups are voluntary associations of 10-20 people who come together for a common interest that is to achieve social and economic goals. Such groups are formed for mutual help and benefit and are formed democratically without any political interference. The members are encouraged to make voluntary thrift on regular basis. With the help of such savings, huge amount can be raised and can be given as small interest bearing loans to the members. The identification, formation, and nurturing of groups is carried out by NGOs, other development agencies or banks with the promoters inculcating habit of thrift among members. The training is provided to the members which helps them understand the essentials of financial intermediation which includes prioritization of needs, setting terms and conditions and accounts keeping. Banks after six months advances loans to the SHGs without any collateral security and the peer pressure enables timely repayment of loans to banks.

SHGs are playing a major role in removing poverty in the rural India today. The group-based model of self-help is widely practiced for rural development, poverty alleviation and empowerment of women. Self-help as a strategy for social development places emphasis on self-reliance, human agency and action. It aims to mobilize people, to give them voice and build people's organisations that will overcome barriers to participation and empowerment. Central to the idea of self-help is the formation of groups, concept of a community and the development of egalitarian relationships that will promote people's well being. SHGs serve as a medium of delivering micro credit to the members.(Das K Sanjay 2012)

Briefly, SHGs can be stated 'as a plan by the people, of the people for the people. It reflects the real people's participation in the process of development at micro level.

## FEATURES OF SELF HELP GROUPS

The following are the main features of self help groups

1. Small and fixed saving at frequent intervals
2. Self-Selection
3. Focus on Women

4. Savings first and credit later
5. Intra group appraisal systems and prioritization
6. Credit Rationing
7. Shorter repayment terms
8. Market rates of interest
9. Progressive lending
10. A multiple-eyed operation

## Objectives of Self-Help Groups

- To develop rural poor socially and economically, who live below the poverty line.
- To stop treating of women as slaves.
- To develop self-confidence among the rural poor.
- To bring out the potential in rural poor.
- To promote gender equality and equal rights.
- To promote unity among rural poor, learn to work together.
- To enhance community harmony.
- To promote education and make cent percent literacy for rural poor.
- To give importance to the differently disabled person and help them.
- To encourage women to take over village level administration.
- To take part in the political processes.
- To voluntarily save from their income and expenditure.
- To take small loans without having to pledge jewels with money lenders or pledge documents in the banks.
- To pay the school fees of children and meet emergency medical expenses from out of the savings.
- To understand about the economic, political situation and visit different places like government offices, banks etc.
- Creating awareness about the government and bank procedures.
- Developing the capability to manage a mini bank with ledgers and passbooks.
- Aiming at the total abolition of over interest rate
- Enhancing their knowledge and skills to undertake economic activities.
- Motivating them to increase their incomes by undertaking successfully, economic activities as individual or groups.
- Providing good marketing outlets for their products.
- Encouraging their participation in the Gram Sabhas, Panchayat Level Federation Clusters, Block Level Federations, Meetings of BLCC and DPCC held under the chairmanship of the District Collector.

## DIFFERENT MODELS OF SELF-HELP GROUP: BANK LINKAGE

The main aim of these models is to develop small and participative groups of the poor and to motivate them to save regularly and then to use these pooled savings as loans to the members with small interest bearing rate. SHG-Bank Linkage programme has gathered momentum due to its credit delivery system and also due to wide acceptance by Banks, NGOs, etc,

The three models of SHG-Bank Linkage programme in India are as follows:

## Model I: SHGs Formed and Financed by Banks

In this model, bank themselves takes the initiative of forming and nurturing the groups. Banks themselves open the saving accounts of groups and also provide them with loans once it is certain about the groups maturity to avail and utilize the credit facility. Up to March 2006, about 20% of the total number of SHGs financed was from this category. In this model bank also acts as SHGPL i. e, Self-Help Group Promoting Institution (Figure 1).

## Model II: SHGs Formed by NGOs and Formal Organisations but Directly Financed by the Banks

In this model, SHGs are formed and nurtured by NGOs, government agencies and other community based organizations. These agencies train the self help groups in thrift of savings and credit management. After observing groups operations and maturity to absorb credit, banks provides direct loan to the groups. About 70 percent of the total number of SHGs is financed under this model and it is the most popular amongst all three models and continues to have a major share. A large number of NGOs along with the State governments through their development agencies like the DRDA,

DWDA and some of the centrally sponsored social sector missions are also participating and are actively involving in it (Figure 2).

## Model III. SHGs Financed by Banks using NGOs and Other Agencies as Financial Intermediaries

In this model, SHGs are promoted and nurtured by other agencies. In this, the SHGS are financed by banks through NGOs and other agencies as financial intermediaries. . In such cases, the NGOs act as both facilitators and microfinance intermediaries. NGOs approach a suitable bank for bulk loan who in turn finance their member SHGs. Agencies like NBFCs are also playing significant role for promoting SHGs. NABARD provides refinance support to banks under the linkage project. This model is not so encouraging (Figure 3).

*Figure 1.*

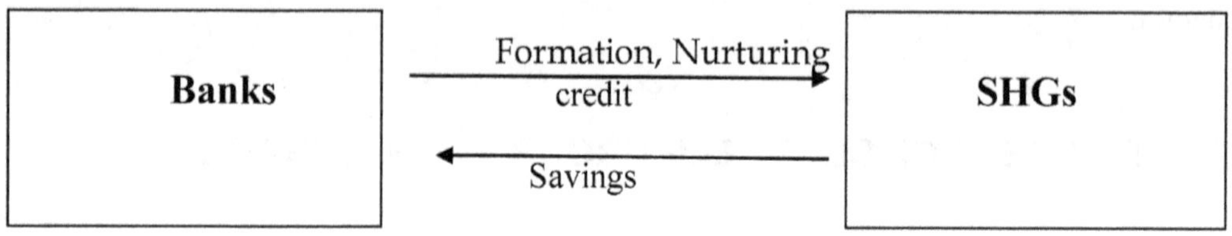

*Figure 2.*

*Figure 3.*

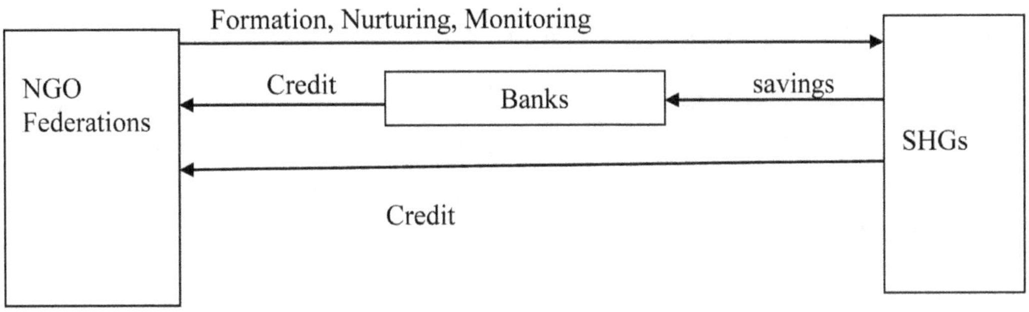


## ACCESS OF SHGS TO BANK

The Reserve Bank of India, the apex bank plays a vital role in the implementation of Bank linkage Programme. It gave guidelines and circulars to the banking system to initiate the programme. RBI gave permission to informal entities to open saving bank accounts in formal institutions. RBI also gave directions to the banks with regard to deregulating the lending conditions and interest rate to be fixed according to market conditions. RBI made SHG Banking as a priority sector lending for Commercial Banks, RRBs and Cooperative Banks.

According to National Rural Livelihood Mission as on June10, 2015 the following information has been gathered (Table 2):

So, from the above table it is evident that Banks are reaching households and encouraging them to form groups so as to enable them to lead a peaceful life. It is evident from the above table that no. of SHGs promoted is 22.5 lakh and the no. of households mobilized into SHGs is 269 lakh.

Further, Banks achievement Report for the year 2013-14, 2014-15 is as follows (Tables 3 and 4):

*Table 2.*

| | |
|---|---|
| No. of Households mobilized into SHGs (in lakh) | **269.0** |
| No. of SHGs promoted(in lakh) | **22.5** |
| No. of SHGs provided Revolving Fund | **366873.0** |
| Amount of Revolving Fund disbursed to SHGs(in Lakh) | **52311.6** |
| No. of SHGs provided community investment fund(CIF) | **279549.0** |
| Amount of CIF disbursed to SHGs(in Rs.lakh) | **168960.2** |

*Table 3. Bank Wise Achievement Report: April2013- March 2014 (Amount in Rs.Lakh)*

| Sr.No | Bank Name | Total SHGs | Total Amount |
|---|---|---|---|
| 1. | Public Sector Bank | 588273 | 1327374.34 |
| 2. | RRB | 259901 | 545849.77 |
| 3. | Private Sector bank | 43766 | 91317.66 |
| 4. | Cooperative Bank | 502 | 1029.84 |
| 5. | **Grand Total** | **892442** | **1965571.61** |

Source: NRLM

*Table 4. Bank Wise Achievement Report: April' 2014- March' 2015 (Amount in Rs.Lakh)*

| Sr.No. | Bank Name | Total SHGs | Total Amount |
|---|---|---|---|
| 1. | Public Sector Bank | 505482 | 1234901.15 |
| 2. | RRB | 269894 | 583113.45 |
| 3. | Private Sector bank | 53752 | 108770.94 |
| 4. | Cooperative Bank | 214998 | 220738.65 |
| 5. | **Grand Total** | **1044126** | **2147524.19** |

Source: NRLM

From Table 3 and Table 4, it is clear that no. of SHGs have increased from 892442 to 1044216. This shows an increment of 151764 SHGs by Banks. Also the total amount also increased from 1965571.61 lakh to 2147524.19 lakh i.e rs.181952.58 lakh is the increament in the the year 2014-15. Thus, it is clear that SHGs have accessed Banks in a significant manner.

## PROGRESS OF SHGS IN INDIA

The journey of SHG-Bank Linkage Programme started from a single step two decades ago from linking a pilot of 500 SHGs. But today it has become the world's largest microfinance activity with over 7.4 million SHGs representing 97 million rural households.

As per the reports of NABARD, In the current year there is a marginal increase of 1.53% with 74.30 lakh SHGs savings linked to Banks as on 31.03.2014 while the number of SHGs linked to Bank during the previous year was 73.18lakh.

Rural households access to regular savings linked to banks also increased from 95million to 96.6 million as on 31.03.2014. Another highlight is that 13.66lakh no. of SHGs were sanctioned fresh loans by Banks as on 31.03.2014 as against 12.20 SHGs during 2012-13.

The fresh loans issued by Banks rose by nearly 17%(rs.24017 crore) during the year 2013-14. However, there is a decline in the number of SHGs credit linked with banks by nearly 6%i. e from 44.51lakh in the year 2012-13 to 41.97lakh in the year 2013-14.But the amount of loan outstanding has gone up by 9%. The total loan outstanding by SHGs stood at rs.`42928 crore as on 31.3.2014. The average loan outstanding of SHGs with banks is rs.1,02,273 against rs.`88,500 a year back. The group formed under the NRLM/SGSY/Other Government sponsored programmes now constitutes 30% of the total number of groups (Table 5).

*Table 5. Overall progress under SHG Bank Linkage for last 3 years (Amount.in rs.crore/Numbers in lakhs)*

| Particulars | 2011-12 | | 2012-13 | | 2013-14 | |
|---|---|---|---|---|---|---|
| | No. of SHGs | Amount | No. of SHGs | Amount | No. of SHGs | Amount |
| SHGs Savings with Banks as on 31st March | 79.60 (6.7%) | 6551.41 (-6.7%) | 73.18 (-8.1%) | 8217.25 (25.4%) | 74.30 (1.53%) | 9897.42 (20.45%) |
| Loan disbursed to SHGs during the year | 11.48 (-4%) | 16534.77 (13.7%) | 12.20 (6.3%) | 20585.36 (24.5%) | 13.66 (12.02%) | 24017.36 (16.67%) |
| Loans outstanding against SHGs as on 31st March | 43.54 (-9%) | 36340 (16.4%) | 44.51 (2.2%) | 39375.30 (8.4%) | 41.97 (-5.71%) | 42927.52 (9.02%) |

Source: Status of microfinance in India,2013-14,NABARD

From the above table, it is been observed that there is a marginal increase of less than 2% in the no. of SHGs savings linked with Banks against the decline observed in the year 2012-13. However the savings by SHGs increased by 21% over the previous year.

In the year 2013-14, Banks have shown increased confidence by extending fresh loans to the SHGs. It increased by 12% which is just double from the previous year. The quantum of fresh loans extended to SHGs also showed an increase of nearly 17% during the year. The number of SHGs having loan outstanding with banks during the year declined by nearly 6% while the quantum of loans outstanding grew by little over 9%.

## STATE – WISE OUTREACH OF SHGS

The Region-wise number of SHGs having savings with banks as on 31stMarch 2014 is provided in Table – 6. As on 31st March 2014, a total of7429500 SHGs have saving bank accounts with the banking sector with Outstanding loan of Rs. 4252792.40 lakh.

The southern region accounted for the largest number of SHGs having savings with Bank as on 31st March 2014 followed by Eastern Region. Other regions have comparatively less no. of SHGs having bank account and least is the Northern Region with only 316299 SHGs savings linked with banks.

Again, Southern accounted for the highest loan disbursed by banks which amounts to Rs. 2061550.70 lakh followed by Eastern region. The lowest loan disbursed to North Eastern region.

Highest bank loan outstanding as on 31st March2014 is Southern Region with Rs.3179133 lakhs followed by central region and the lowest is for Eastern Region (Table 6).

## MILESTONES IN SHG-BANK LINKAGE PROGRAMME

**1992:** Launching of Pilot project of linking 500SHGs with the banking system.

**1993:** Introduction of bulk lending scheme to NGOs by NABARD, Studies on Transaction Cost conducted by external experts.

**1994:** Extension of policy Support by RBI – beyond the Pilot phase, Unleashing the concepts of banking with Poor, Extension of support for capacity building of NGOs by NABARD.

*Table 6. Progress under microfinance: Region Wise (Amount in Rs.Lakh)*

| Particulars | Northern Region | | North Eastern Region | | Eastern Region | | Central Region | | Western Region | | Southern Region | |
|---|---|---|---|---|---|---|---|---|---|---|---|---|
| | No. of SHGs | Amount | No.of SHGs | Amount | No.of SHGs | Amount | No.of SHGs | Amount | No.of SHGs | Amount | No.of SHGs | Amount |
| Savings of SHGs with Banks as on 31st March 2014 | 365208 | 28924.76 | 316299 | 12882.12 | 1468786 | 152655.56 | 685929 | 79055.81 | 89654 | 92990 | 3696324 | 623862.39 |
| Bank Loan disbursed during the year 2013-14 | 23918 | 28048.36 | 16201 | 12819.04 | 297478 | 151067019 | 66393 | 61806.90 | 87846 | 86443.65 | 874585 | 2061550.70 |
| Bank Loan Outstanding against SHGs as on 31st March 2014 | 103929 | 110063.55 | 124569 | 75379.91 | 978960 | 494463.10 | 419834 | 269666.48 | 269008 | 164046.06 | 2221038 | 3179133.30 |

(Source: NABARD, Mumbai)

**1995:** Setting up Credit and Financial Services Fund (CFSF) within NABARD - to support expansion of the programme, Setting up a working group on NGOs & SHGs- to assess ground realities and identify operational issues in implementation of the programme, Extension of Revolving Fund Assistance to Federations of SHGs by NABARD.

**1996:** Mainstreaming SHG-Bank Linkage bybanks - RBI and NABARD notifications, Tackling operational issues like Documentation, Defaulters, Size of group,Service Area etc

**1997:** Organizing National level Training consultation meet - thrust on trainers training, First experiment of RRB as Self Help Promoting Institution (SHPI), Up scaling training and awareness programmes by NABARD and the banking system, Emphasis on interventions winning in cooperative banks.

**1998:** Recognition of potential of government intervention, Extension RRB as SHPI to other10 other RRBs, Documentation of rating/grading practices for SHGs' appraisal.

**1999:** Recognition of potential of SHGs by GOI,Setting up task force on supportive regulatory & policy framework, Refinance requirements out grow CFSF -use of NABARD's normal resources. Extension of RRB-SHPI-experiment to 2more RRBs, Crystallization of NABARD's vision and Mission. Building partnerships with Governments. Deregulation of interest rates in SHG lending,Emphasis on studies documentation and Dissemination, Provision of promotional grants to NGOs for SHG promotion- development NGO appraisal tools.

**2000:** Thrust on widening the range of SHPIs, SHGs credit linked crosses 1,00,000. RBI advises banks to finance Microcredit organizations. Emphasis on flooding market with quality SHGs by NABARD. Thrust on expansion of the programme in Union Budget. Recognition ofpotential of Farmers Club as SHPIs. Roping in Rural Volunteers as potential SHPI, II National Consultation meet on training to redesign training modules, contents and methodologies. Collaboration with Indira Gandhi National Open University - for commencing a distance education programme on women's empowerment and SHGs. Introduction of State level Awards for best performance. Evaluation studies on impact on SHGs. Setting up a separate fund for scaling up the programme-microFinance Development Fund. Technical collaboration with GTZ, Germany commenced.

**2001:** Crossing 2,00,000 mark of credit linked SHGs. Thrust on backward States & districts. Extension of RRB-SHPI module to all RRBs. Launching of National Level newsletter. Diversifying capacity building approaches Videos, tools, visits. Accelerating promotional grant support to NGOs. Conceptualizing the use of technology in microFinance. Initiating efforts all developing a comprehensive Management Information System for SHG -Bank Linkage programme. Exposure visits to other mF initiatives for clients and banks. Launched studies to assess Savings pattern for the poor.

**2002:** Intensifying training interventions through exposure visits. Focus on backward states/provinces Encouraging and facilitating internalization of rating and self-rating techniques. Increasing role of Government in internalizing the concept. Launching a pilot in IT in microfinance. Launching studies to understanding the commercial prospects of SHG linkage. Closer look at saving products for the poor designing pilot project for savings product development through an RRB. Support by way of promotional grants to NGOs closes to 500 nos. About 50% of the 10-year mission covered. Diffusion of knowledge and experience with international mF practitioners. Redefining the role of banks in the programme as enhancing business opportunities not mere Service providers. (Source: NABARD)

## SELF HELP GROUPS AND ITS IMPACT

Self Help Groups (SHGs) have marked a great change in the social and economic lives of the poor. It helps the members to come together for some common objective and to be a helping hand for each other during the time of crisis. Such groups creates a relationship of mutual trust. The SHG is really a boon in the rural areas which gives financial autonomy to the rural women and make them economically independent (Laxman 2001). The SHGs have become a platform for exchange of experiences and ideas (Tilekar et al 2001). Micro financing through SHGs is contributing to the development of rural people in a meaningful manner. It is seen that significant changes in the living standards of SHG members have taken place in terms of increase in income levels, assets, savings, borrowing capacity and income generating activities. (Sharma 2001).

The most important Impact of SHGs is that it helps in eliminating poverty. Besides this, with the help of SHGs poor use credit for establishing micro enterprises rather than for consumption purpose and Living conditions as well as income levels also tends to rise. Another impact of SHGs is on social empowerment of the members of the group. The members acquire level of confidence, awareness and pride in themselves. Members also develop communication skill, enormous increase in self confidence and also learn to handle problem situations. The SHG programme also led to empowerment of women economically and socially as well. There has been drastic change in nutrition, health and hygiene, housing, sanitation, etc with the help of SHGs.

The economic impact of SHGs on poor are in terms of increased propensity to save, reduction in income inequalities, reduction of indebtedness with moneylenders, ensures additional employment and permits enhanced net incremental incomes.

## SUGGESTIONS FOR STRENGTHENING SHG-BANK LINKAGE PROGRAM

1. **Encouraging SHGs in Excluded Regions:** Some of the regions like North, Eastern and North-Eastern regions require promotion of SHGs. More NGOs and banking Network needs to be strengthened up these regions.
2. **Capacity building of Government functionaries:** Proper training should be provided to bank staff and NGOs on the self help group linkage program.
3. **Check on corruption/commission while sanctioning and upgrading the loan:** There should be a proper on the corruption and commission at grass root level. All such practices should be blocked initially so as to ensure smooth functioning of the group like revolving loan for money lending, luxurious consumption etc.
4. **Identification of poor by the NABARD**: NABARD should give due attention to those states where large population is poor. The SHG linkage programme is made for the weaker sections and it should be implemented as soon as possible.
5. **Incentive package for NGOs:** Certain incentives should be given to honest NGOs so as to encourage them for better performance and results.
6. **Transparency in maintenance of records:** Banks should keep a proper check of record of SHGs and it should be based on simple record keeping.
7. **SHGs to evolve norms for distribution of surplus:** There is a need to evolve norms for distribution of surplus (akin to dividend) especially at the time when a member drops out of the group.
8. **Identification of income/employment generating activities**: There is a great need to educate the groups on the identification of income generating activities so that the loans that they are availing should not result into vain (Reddy & Malik, 2011).

## CONCLUSION

From the above statement it can be concluded that Self help group Bank Linkage Programme is a boon to the weaker and marginalized section of the society. A group of 10-20 members has brought a vast change in the poverty level as the SHG-BLP is working very effectively. It is been observed that SHG-BLP is flexible, and imparts freedom of savings and borrowings according to the needs of the members. Self Help Group programme is expanding its outreach in various parts of the country where large population is poor or in those areas where there are less banking systems and NGOs. All such efforts are done with the pioneering initiative of NABARD, the monitoring and supervision of RBI, and the promotional policies of the government of India. At the grass root level the programme is being implemented by the commercial banks, cooperatives, and regional rural banks, with government agencies.

But there is a need to consider few things about the betterment of SHGs so that the flaws can be removed smoothly. First of all due consideration should be given to non-farm activities, i.e besides farming what are the other areas of economic activity. There is also a difficulty to find that economic activity which could yield that much of profit so that interest on loan could be covered up. So there is need to provide marketing facilities to the people who are involved in non farm activities so that goods can reach the market at right time and place. This will help in generating income and improved savings also. Thus SHG-BLP can do wonders to the rural poor living even in remote villages in improving their economic condition and protecting them from the clutches of the village moneylenders. Hence, it can be said that SHG-Bank Linkage Programme has provided a more favorable environment for enhancing India's potential for greater equitable growth with empowerment while considering the positive signs in their performance.

## REFERENCES

Das, S. K. (2012). Best practices of self help groups and women empowerment: A case of Barak Valley of Assam. *IDEAS, 7*(2).

Kropp, E. W., & Suran, B. S. (2002). *Linking Banks and (Financial) Self help Groups in India: An Assessment.* Paper presented at the Seminar on SHG-bank Linkage Programme at New Delhi on 25th and 26th November.

NABARD. (2012). *SHG2: Revisiting the SHG Bank Linkage Programme*. Mumbai, India: NABARD.

NABARD. (2014). *Status of Microfinance 2013-14.* Mumbai, India: NABARD.

National Rural Livelihood Mission. (2015). *Website.* Retrieved from http://aajeevika.gov.in/

Reddy, A. A., & Malik, D. P. (2011). A Review of SHG-Bank Linkage Programme in India. *Indian Journal of Industrial Economics and Development, 7*(2), 1–10.

## ADDITIONAL READING

Dasgupta, R. (2005). Microfinance in India: Empirical evidence, alternative models and policy imperatives. *Economic and Political Weekly*, *60*(12), 1229–1237.

Fisher, T., & Sriram, M. S. (2002). ). *Beyond micro-credit: Putting development back into micro-finance.* New Delhi, India:Vistaar Publications.

Moyle, D., Dollard, M., & Biswas, S. N. (2006). Personal and Economic empowerment in Rural Indian Women: A Self-help Group Approach. *International Journal of Rural Management*, 2(2), 245–266. doi:10.1177/097300520600200207

Reddy, A. A. (2006). Productivity Growth of Regional Rural Banks. *Economic and Political Weekly*, *41*(11), 1079–1086.

Srinivasan, N. (2008). *Microfinance India, State of the Sector Report, 2008.* India: Sage Publications Private Limited.

# Chapter 17
# Computational Investing

**Javier Vidal-García**
*University of Valladolid, Spain*

**Marta Vidal**
*Complutense University, Spain*

**Rafael Hernandez Barros**
*Complutense University, Spain*

## ABSTRACT

*Investing means using funds to start a venture or acquire part of an existing one in hopes that in time the business will accrue profits for the entrepreneur. Often, entrepreneurs opt to purchase companies' stocks. To be able to select the right – profitable – stocks to buy, one requires knowledge of modern portfolio theory, computational investing, stock brokerage, mutual funds, bonds, value investing, how capital gains are taxed, how to trade stocks and options online, and how to use diversification to allocate online investments.*

## INTRODUCTION

The Modern Portfolio Theory is a result of the ingenious efforts of Harry Markowitz. In 1952, Markowitz pioneered the concept by publishing an article, "Portfolio selection," in the *Journal of Finance*. Through the piece, he demonstrated how diversification of stock reduces portfolio risk (Strong, 2009, p. 156). In other words, a single investment is exposed to risk due to the fact that several factors create high uncertainty and, as a result, lower expected returns. Examples of such factors are time, resources, manpower, and so on. Thus, Markowitz proposed a model that ensures capital is spread across a variety of investments so as to cushion entrepreneurs against any unfavorable returns resulting from one or several securities.

To gain a better understanding of Modern Portfolio Theory, it is important to understand the key terms applicable in the model. Firstly, risk is the variability in outcomes based on the expected return. Hence, it is measured by calculating the standard deviation ($\sigma$) of a percentage of the return ($r_i$). Optionally, risk can be determined by computing variance ($\sigma^2$), which is the square of standard deviation. Secondly, expected returns ($E(r_i)$) is a function of probability ($p_i$) and percentage of the returns ($r_i$) expected from the security. In this case, the expected returns of a portfolio is a summation of individual returns ($\sum p_i$

DOI: 10.4018/978-1-4666-9908-3.ch017

$r_i$) of several securities. Thirdly, a security includes a finance lease, commercial loan, trade receivable, credit card, and so on. Fourthly, a portfolio is a collection of investment items such as bonds and stocks that require capital allocation. Fifthly, covariance ($\sigma_{ij}$) is a measure of the relationship that exists between variables (Francis and Kim). A positive covariance denotes that the variables progress in a similar direction. In other words, it shows positive correlation. Sixthly, an investment item's weight ($w_i$) is the ratio of the funds allocated to the stock to the total amount invested in the entire portfolio. Finally, portfolio risk ($\sigma_p$) is a logical expression that is based on the covariance and variance of securities in a portfolio.

Markowitz's diversification concept is useful in portfolio analysis. In this case, assets that have a positive correlation can be combined with an aim of reducing risk. Hence, that ensures that none of the returns of the portfolio is forfeited. In other words, the risk of the portfolio reaches its lowest value when the correlation between assets is at a minimum (Francis & Doncheol, 2013, p. 5). That remains the case even if the risk associated with individual assets is high.

According to Markowitz, diversification needs to be done strategically. In this case, an entrepreneur should invest in assets in different industries (Strong, 2009, p. 149). For instance, the investor should buy shares in manufacturing, mining, and service sectors. The reason for that is that companies that sell the same goods or services occasionally perform poorly and hence investors that diversify their portfolios by buying assets in the same industry stand to lose. Conversely, by investing in different sectors, poor performance in one industry does not affect the returns from other industries.

The significance of diversification can be illustrated using a portfolio containing two investment assets, A and B. Suppose the expected returns for asset A ($E(r_A)$) is 8%, while that of asset B ($E(r_B)$) is 24%. Also, suppose that the standard deviation for asset A ($\sigma_A$) is 22%, while that of B ($\sigma_B$) is 44%. Additionally, assume that the weight of asset A ($w_A$) is 2/3, while that of asset B ($w_B$) is 1/3. In this case, the expected return of the portfolio ($E(r_p)$) can be determined by the following calculations.

$$E(r_p) = w_A E(r_A) + w_B E(r_B)$$

$$E(r_p) = 2/3(8/100) + 1/3(24/100) = 0.0533 + 0.0800$$

$$E(r_p) = 0.1333 = 13.33\%$$

As shown in the example above, the expected return of the portfolio is a weighted average of the expected returns of the assets A and B (Graham & Smart, 2012, p. 219). This means that by investing in two different assets from different industries, the entrepreneur gains favorable returns from the portfolio. Thus, diversification of the portfolio improves the expected returns.

Markowitz also demonstrated the effect of diversification on portfolio risk. According to him, portfolio risk can be determined using the formula below.

$$\sigma_p = \sqrt{(w_A^2\sigma_A^2 + w_B^2\sigma_B^2 + 2w_A w_B \sigma_{AB})}$$

In this case, $\sigma_{AB}$ is the covariance of returns. For demonstrative purposes, let the values of $\sigma_{AB}$ be +0.095, -0.095, and 0 and the weighted values and standard deviations of the assets A and B remain as given in the previous example. Thus,

$$\sigma_p = \sqrt{(w_A^2\sigma_A^2 + w_B^2\sigma_B^2 + 2w_A w_B \sigma_{AB})}$$

$$\sigma_p = \sqrt{[(2/3)^2(0.22)^2 + (1/3)^2(0.44)^2 + (2*2/3*1/3*\sigma_{AB})]}$$

$$\sigma_p = \sqrt{[0.02151 + 0.02151 + 4/9*\sigma_{AB}]}$$

$$\sigma_p = \sqrt{[0.04302 + 4/9*\sigma_{AB}]}$$

If $\sigma_{AB} = +0.095$, then $\sigma_p = 0.6982$. Secondly, if $\sigma_{AB} = -0.095$, then $\sigma_p = 0.0282$. Lastly, if $\sigma_{AB} = 0$, then $\sigma_p = 0.2074$. Therefore, positive covariance increases portfolio risk, while a negative covariance reduces it. Thus, according to Markowitz's Modern Portfolio Theory, the diversification of stock results in the reduction of the risk of the portfolio, especially if the variables have negative covariance (Khan and Jain).

## BACKGROUND

Computational investing is another topic that provides insights on investing and stocks. It includes a collection of theories that have effectively been used as strategies for investing. For instance, John Bogle's passive investment approach recommends that entrepreneurs should allocate resources to assets that have minimum trading expenses. The reason for that is that active involvement in market-stock trade cannot match the returns of the market (Laopodis, 2013, p. 32). In other words, Bogle advocates for a long-term view approach to investing – one should pay attention to taxes and costs. Therefore, according to him, a well-diversified portfolio is an assortment of low-cost assets that have been in the market for a considerable number of years. That is, investors should adopt a buy-and-hold strategy.

Another theory of computation investing is value investing. According to Warren Buffet, who developed the idea, investors should exercise discipline, intelligence, and patience in relation to buying stock (Laopodis, 2013, p. 32). In other words, the entrepreneurs should purchase shares of reputable companies only.

Thirdly, computational investing includes active investing. The theory aids in analyzing the general proceeds obtained in the security market by engaging in regular trading. In this case, trading normally involves utilizing mutual funds to acquire certain securities. Unfortunately, the pricing models of market securities are not accurate and hence may cause losses (Voges & Pope, 2006, p. 432). The shortcomings of the models can be detected and resolved by experienced investors. Hence, active investing means one should consult a professional before buying stock.

Therefore, computation investing contains complex theories, which means that entrepreneurs should adopt the use of other tools to guide them in buying stock. Computer applications are instrumental in this regard. They make it easy to analyze and interpret information that is useful for decision making. For instance, Mathematica, which relies on the use of statistics, differential equations, calculus, and other mathematical functions, is utilized in market analysis. It can solve problems related stock options and thus is relevant to day traders (Wellin, Gaylord, & Kamin, 2005, p. 8).

Machine learning provides another means of managing information pertaining to investments. It entails the creation of structures and models that can provide useful information from raw data. The data is derived from a considerable number of securities that are influenced by a number of fundamental technical factors. In other words, the inputs are collected and then a model created to predict their future values. Thus, machine learning aids in the classification as well as regression analysis of the stock market (Balch).

The models used in machine learning may be linear in nature (Balch). Linear models can be described by the linear equation below.

$$y = m(x) + b$$

In this case *y* is the output, *x* is the input or independent variable, *m* is the gradient of the line, and b is a constant or y-intercept, which means that it is the value of *y* when *x* is zero. *m* is calculated by diving the change in output that occurs after a change in input. Thus, the linear equations can be applied in the pricing of stock, particularly in the Capital Asset Pricing Model (CAPM).

In the CAPM, the linear equation takes the form $E(R_i) = R_F + [\beta \times (E(R_M)\text{-}R_F)]$. In this case, $R_F$ is the risk free rate of return, $E(R_M)$ represents the proceeds from the market portfolio, β is the beta coefficient, and $[E(R_M)\text{-}R_F]$ is the market risk premium – an extra return for reimbursing investors for risks taken in clinging to a portfolio of assets in the market. When an asset yields expected returns, its beta coefficient is one (Kürschner 4). If the asset's returns exceed expectations, then its beta coefficient is greater than one. In that respect, if the returns are below market expectations, the asset's beta value is less than one. Hence, the CAPM has extensively been used by investment firms to measure financial performance.

Polynomial and data driven models can also be used in machine learning. The polynomial model consists of more than one parameter, each of which should be well identified. The model is non-linear in nature and hence quite fast in runtime. In comparison, data driven models are designed to function in query fashion and hence are multi-dimensional – allow users to add new input variables with time. To predict the future value of a stock, the mean of the dependent values must first be computed, which makes data driven models slow in runtime compared to polynomial models (Balch). The dependent variables that are typically used in the model include the profit/earnings (P/E) ratio.

## MAIN FOCUS OF THE CHAPTER

### Open a Stock Brokerage Account Online

Some of the concepts discussed in Modern Investment Theory and computational investing are useful to stock brokers, especially when opening an online account. A stock broker is an individual or company that trades in shares on behalf of a client. If the interaction between the client and the broker is through a website, the broker is referred to as an online broker. The online service allows the investor to allocate some funds to the brokerage firm for the purchase and sell of stock. Normally, the transactions occur on order basis, that is, the client must request the broker to buy or sell profitable shares. Apart from trading in shares, a significant number of online brokers also provide other support services such as tax reporting, creation of financial statements, and so on. Optionally, an investor may decide to do the online trading independently (Magliolo xvii). That means the entrepreneur will need to open an online stock brokerage account. To succeed in such a venture, the entrepreneur must consider several factors.

Firstly, the investor needs to acquire a portfolio tracking tool, which is a set of online tools that provide information on the trading of stock. Hence, the tool allows investors to keep a close eye on the performance of their stock while shopping for additional profitable investments. The portfolio tracking tool can be treated as an additional expense to the cost of opening an online brokerage. However, an effective method would be to treat portfolio tracking as a support service provided by an online broker (Hart, 2005, p. 36).

Secondly, transaction costs are incurred in operating the online brokerage account. Normally, the online broker that hosts the independent stockbrokerage account charges a specific amount for each transaction executed. In other words, an online broker may provide the portfolio tracking tool at a low cost, but charge the investor highly per transaction (Hart, 2005, p. 42).

Apart from that, some hosts charge for stop-sell order requests. Therefore, investors should take time to compare the charges of different hosts to ensure that they get value for their money.

Thirdly, the type of account matters. Often, investors have the option of opening either an individual retirement account (IRA) or retail account. Before opening an IRA, the entrepreneur should consult a tax advisor because some of the transactions done through the account are taxable. For instance, if a transfer of funds is done from the investor's IRA to an online broker's IRA, there are no tax penalties or consequences. However, taxes apply if the investor withdraws money from an online brokerage IRA. Conversely, transferring funds to a retail account has no tax implications. Similarly, the purchase of stock through the use of funds in the retail account has no tax implications. However, the income from the stocks sold through the account is taxable (Hart, 2005, p. 50).

Additionally, investors expect returns in form of dividends from companies in which they own shares. The dividends may be scrip dividends or dividend re-investment plans (DRIP). For the investors that subscribe to the scrip-dividend policy, the expected cash returns are automatically converted to new shares. Conversely, for those in DRIP, the cash dividends are first sent to a scheme administrator who then may use the funds to acquire the company's shares through the stock market or send the money to the stakeholders. Therefore, before opening an online account, the investor should consider the reinvestment service offered by the host (Hobson, 2012, p. 15).

Also, the investors need to determine the means through which they will fund their online brokerage accounts. Firstly, capital may be sourced from savings. In this case, keeping money in bank accounts yields low annual interest. Depositing the money into an online brokerage account will result in better cash benefits. Secondly, the IRA is also a source of funding. In this case, the funds can be transferred from an existing IRA to the online brokerage IRA mentioned earlier. Thirdly, the investors can opt to make direct deposits. In this regard, the cash-in-hand that they possess should be greater than or equal to the bare minimum required to open the online brokerage account. Given that the option will force the entrepreneurs to develop a working plan on how to make regular deposits into the account, discipline is required (Hart, 2005, p. 55). The investors can obtain additional hard cash from gifts, financial assets converted to money, extra income, refunds, and so on.

Therefore, before opening an online brokerage an account, one must consider several things. These include the type of account to be opened, transaction costs involved, and customer service. The investor should also take into account how the online brokerage shall be funded, the cost of the portfolio tracking tool, and the dividend re-investment policy provided. Once these queries have been addressed, the next step is to open an online brokerage account (Hart, 2005, p. 57). In reference to that, it is worth noting that managing a profitable stock investment portfolio requires thorough knowledge of ways of investing.

## Investing in Stocks

Equity investment – investing in stocks – refers to the value of assets and cash that an individual, company, or group puts into another entity. The amount of funds contributed determines the ownership or level of influence the investor has in the venture. This level of influence can also be referred to as shares. Thus, the more shares an entity purchases, the greater its equity stake. Equity investments are often handled by professional investors that administer large portions of money on behalf of amateur investors. The professional investors carry out such activities through private equity (PE) firms. Hence, private equity refers to the shares of individuals in a listed or unlisted company (Kumpf, 2013, p. 17). Equity investors benefit in two ways. Firstly, they make gains when the stock prices increase. Secondly, they receive dividends periodically. An increase in stock prices yields the most benefits and thus the entrepreneurs mainly buy shares of companies in hopes that the stock prices will rise. There are other aspects of private equity that must be addressed before one understands investing in stocks.

The private equity firms utilize three investment approaches that are based on maturity of portfolio entities and volume of equity purchased by the PE companies. Firstly, the firms allocate venture capital to young firms that have a potential of rapid growth. Normally, the venture capital is a small sum of money and hence the PE firms do not acquire a majority stake in the entity. Secondly, by providing growth capital, the companies acquire a minority stake in mature firms. Finally, the PE firms use buyouts to gain control of mature organizations (Kumpf, 2013, p. 17).

Buyouts can further be split into management buy-ins and management buy-outs. Management buy-ins are driven by outsiders, while management buy-outs are initiated by insiders. In a management buy-in, the private equity firm establishes its own management team, whereas in a management buy-out, the existing management is retained (Kumpf, 2013, p. 18).

Given that it is not easy to identify the best companies to invest in, investment tools are required. In this case, the Magnet Stock Selection Process (MSSP) is of great value. The MSSP is a technique designed to blend momentum, value, and growth to optimize long-term returns (Kimmel, 2009, p. 124). Magnet is an acronym that defines each of the factors considered in the selection process.

M stands for management and momentum. In this case, the entrepreneurs should invest in firms that have capable managers. The management should exemplify leadership, innovativeness, and success in the marketing of products. Additionally, whether or not the management owns a significant portion of the stock of the business, they should prove that they have always acted in the best interest of their shareholders. Momentum refers to the relationship between stock price and the market as a whole (Kimmel, 2009, p. 125). The entrepreneurs should conduct trend analysis of the share price performance for a few consecutive months and only invest in the venture if the evaluation shows strong performance.

A stands for acceleration of revenues and earnings. In this case, the PE firms should only buy shares of companies that regularly achieve at least a 15% increase in quarterly earnings and revenues (Kimmel, 2009, p. 125). This standard effectively eliminates big companies that dominate their industries, but fail to sustain quick growth rates. Acceleration of growth can also be shown by gross profit (GP) margin. The GP margins should continually rise each year (Kimmel, 2009, p. 126). A decline in GP margins shows that the firm is facing financial challenges.

G stands for growth at a discount, which is shown by the price/earnings (P/E) ratio. In this case, the growth of a company should be twice its P/E ratio (Kimmel, 2009, p. 126). This ensures that investors do not spend more than they should on stocks.

N stands for new product or management (Kimmel, 2009, p. 126). In this respect, the rapid rise of a company's share price shows that something innovative is happening. In other words, it indicates that the management is making strategic decisions that create growth prospects. Normally, if new products are not developed or no strategic decisions are implemented, the growth potential of an entity is constrained. Also, new management can be a source of novel ideas that may propel a company forward.

E stands for emerging products or industrial opportunities (Kimmel, 2009, p. 125). In this case, if new product lines are developed, then a company can look forward to growth. That is because new lines require capital, innovation, and personnel. A firm invests in new products to enhance its already existing lines. In this respect, opportunities are created and risks are taken to generate additional returns. Thus, investors should regard such changes as a sign of potential for growth for the company. In other words, investing in the stock of such firms may result significant returns in the long run.

Lastly, T stands for timing. The stock acquisition should be done at the right moment. In this case, the opportune time is when the share price declines. Investors should also invest in businesses during initial public offerings or when shares are sold at a discount. By acquiring the shares at such periods, the investors will reap significant rewards after the share prices appreciate in future (Kimmel, 2009, p. 125). In other words, as the companies grow, the entrepreneurs' equity also increases.

Thus, equity investment is an avenue for wealth generation. This is especially the case if approaches such as MSSP are effectively used in the selection process. One must also accept that private equity firms play a crucial role in identifying favorable investments. That is because the entities employ skilled personnel to identify successful businesses. Also, it is indisputable that the private equity managed by the PE firms aids upcoming and mature enterprises overcome financial limitations and hence ensure work is done properly (Loewen, 2008, p. 43). That said, to fully understand the subject of investing and stocks, one needs to consider other topics apart from equity. For instance, it is paramount to discuss bonds and mutual as well as exchange trade funds.

## Investing in Mutual Funds, Bonds and Exchange Traded Funds

It is important to have a diversified investment portfolio. The reason for that is that occasionally particular industries face challenges such as competition that reduce the anticipated returns. Apart from stocks, mutual funds, bonds, and exchange traded funds are viable investment options.

Mutual funds are created by a group of people who wish to invest in particular projects. There are benefits that arise from having such a pool of funds. Firstly, professional fund managers are employed to handle the invested funds. They diversify the holdings, thus reducing risk (Northcott, 2009, p. 12). The investors select the management and fund based on the anticipated risk and returns.

There are costs associated with mutual funds. These include operation and remuneration expenses. Normally, the expenses are covered by paying a regular fee, which is a percentage of the annual charge. The charge varies depending on size of the fund; larger funds have smaller expense ratios. However, different mechanisms may be employed by other funds (Northcott, 2009, p. 18). In this case, all expenses and costs are disclosed in a prospectus.

Mutual funds can be categorized into two types. Firstly, there are open-end funds. In this case, the sale of shares to investors is done without undue restraint. Also, the open-end fund managers decide how best to use the new money received. The options available in this regard include purchasing new securities or increasing the fund's shares in existing assets (Northcott, 2009, p. 27).

Secondly, there are closed-end funds, which have some restrictions. For instance, an investor may only be able to purchase shares in the concerned enterprise if some existing stakeholders of the entity are willing to sell theirs. This is due to the fact that the closed-end funds have a predetermined number of shares (Northcott, 2009, p. 28). Also, the entrepreneurs value their shares based on future price expectation. In contrast, the value of the shares of the open-end funds is determined by the market price of shares already sold and value of existing securities within the holding.

In this respect, mutual funds are used to invest in shares or bonds. In the case of shares, the companies targeted may be large, medium, or small cap. Cap means capitalization and thus the categories are based on market valuation. For instance, a medium cap firm is one that is valued from $2 billion to $10 billion. Therefore, a small cap company is one that is worth less than $2 billion (Northcott, 2009, p. 66). Large cap companies, those worth more than $10 billion, are considered less risky than small cap enterprises.

The mutual funds can also be used to purchase bonds. Bonds yield fixed returns. The amount of income generated depends on contractual requirements and solvency of the issuer of the bonds (Maeda, 2009, p. 15). Bonds may be provided by particular organizations or bond funds. In this case, the company bonds are considered risky due to the fact that in the past major companies exited the market after selling bonds.

In relation to investing in bonds, the entrepreneurs may opt to be active traders or buy-and-hold investors. Active trading is expensive because it involves regular transactions. Conversely, the buy-and-hold investors keep their bonds until they mature. As a result, the entrepreneurs earn interest.

There are other factors that should be considered in relation to investing in bonds. Firstly, the entrepreneurs should be aware of their risk tolerance. This can be determined by extensive analysis of the bond-returns. In this case, the volatility of returns is reduced by acquiring low yield bonds. Secondly, the bond maturity period is an important factor to keep in mind. For instance, some bonds may mature after 10 years, which means that the money will be unavailable for that long (Maeda, 2009, p. 17). In other words, purchasing a bond means lending your money to a corporation or government entity for a defined period in exchange for interest on the principal amount. Thus, it is imperative to conduct extensive research to identify high-yield bonds.

Besides the bonds and mutual funds, the entrepreneurs should consider investing in exchange trade funds (ETFs). ETFs are variations of mutual funds. However, unlike the case is with conventional mutual funds, the investors who put their money into the ETFs do not have to submit the money through financial agents. That is because the management of the funds is based on a fixed set of rules that determine the types of individual stocks held in a portfolio. In other words, the ETFs are passively managed and hence stock selection is updated on specified dates (Appei, 2009, p. 3). Another difference between the ETFs and regular mutual funds is that the individual investors can purchase the ETFs through the stock market, while mutual funds are managed by fund managers. In this respect, the investor is wholly responsible for transactions concerning the ETFs.

The ETFs have other characteristics. For instance, the value of shares traded is determined by the market price of the stock on the transaction date. Also, investors have to pay a broker's commission fee for the purchase of the ETFs. The cost of purchasing the ETF shares is low compared to the expenses incurred in acquiring regular stocks because of active competition. In reference to that, it is worth noting that all mutual funds, including the ETFs, attract sales charges.

Another advantage of the ETFs is that the sale and purchase of new shares is done on an investor-investor basis. This means that one investor sells shares to another entrepreneur in exchange for cash. Thus, updating the records is easy (Appei, 2009, p. 5).

Mutual funds, bonds, and exchange trade funds are all viable investments. However, each of the forms of investment bears its own risks. Additionally, the entrepreneurs must consider the costs associated with the investments among other factors before selecting one.

Investing and stocks is a wide subject. It covers the Modern Portfolio Theory, which advocates for diversification of investments to minimize portfolio risk. Secondly, it includes computational investing that provides several models used to analyze data for effective decision-making. Also, it addresses opening an online brokerage account. The subject provides information on the use of the portfolio tracking tool, transaction costs involved in the establishment of the account, and so on. Additionally, by studying the chapter, learners discover the significance of the MSSP approach to investing. Finally, the subtitle on mutual funds, bonds, and ETFs shows how pools of funds can be utilized to make investments.

## Value Investing

Another subject that needs to be addressed while discussing investing and stocks is value investing. Basically, it refers to the purchase of securities at a price that is lower than their intrinsic worth. That is, the cost of the shares is determined by the primary business value. This also means that the investor does not rely on the stock market to establish the true worth of a certain stock. Instead, the entrepreneur check's the firm's earnings. To gain a better understanding of the topic, one needs to review its fundamental aspects.

Generally, the investors who apply value investing opt to buy shares in companies that have declining stock prices, but are destined to experience greater returns in time. In this regard, such investors hope to make significant profits by selling the shares when the companies' earnings will force their share prices to rise (Browne, 2007, p. 25). For instance, in the 1950s, Berkshire Hathaway Inc., a textile company, was facing financial challenges. As a result, the price of its shares gradually declined. Warren Buffet, a former student of Columbia Business School, noted that previously the company showed great potential in terms of returns (Browne, 2007, p. 27). Thus, he prompted his father to acquire a considerable number of shares in the company to gain a controlling stake. At that time, the firm's shares traded for only eight dollars. Because of his father's stake in the business, Buffet was able to join Berkshire. By the 1960s, he had become part of the management and thus was able to influence decision-making. Buffet began remodeling Berkshire and hence in a short while the company's share value rose to $ 18. Decades later, the company sold its stocks at $90,000 per unit.

To be successful in value investing, one needs to be cognizant of several indicators. The investor needs to monitor the targeted firm's cash flow, profits, and sales. That is because doing so will enable the entrepreneur to identify the right time to acquire the stocks of a firm that trades at a discount for a lengthy period (Browne, 2007, p. 28).

The theory of value investing was introduced by Benjamin Graham. In 1934, while lecturing at Columbia Business School, Graham came up with a set of principles for guiding investors who wanted to engage in the venture (Greenwald et al., 2004, p. 38). According to him, stocks should be bought when they are trading on sale basis. That is, when a company is selling its shares at a discount. This is the principle that a considerable number of mutual fund managers apply. That is, the mangers use growth funds to invest in new fast growing firms and spend value funds in purchasing shares that are on sale (Browne, 2007, p. 43). As expected, with time, the investments made through value investing – value funds – yield greater returns. Secondly, the investors should first establish the true value of the target company. This can be done by calculating the total cash flows of the business. Given that future cash flows are included in the computations, the investor needs to make assumptions with respect to market conditions (Greenwald et al., 2004, p. 38). However, basing the value of a firm on probable factors may not reveal the true value of its assets or potential. Thus, the value investors prefer calculating a firm's worth using its intrinsic value.

The intrinsic value of the organization can be established by valuing the company's assets. In this case, the valuation is done using the business' financial statements. Firstly, some assets are adjusted to reflect their current prices. Thereafter, total liabilities are deducted from the sum of current assets/ inventory, cash, and receivables. The figure obtained is referred to as the reproduction cost (Greenwald et al., 2004, p. 14). A desirable security is a stock that retails at a price that is lower than the reproduction cost. Graham describes such a stock as net-net stock.

The intrinsic value of a firm can also be determined by assessing the organization's earnings power. In this case, the investors should first establish the company's inflow of earnings over a considerable number of previous years. Next, they should use the established trend to predict the firm's business cycle (Greenwald et al., 2004, p. 14). Then the figure obtained is compared to the reproduction cost. The company has earnings power if the value is greater than the intrinsic worth that was determined by assessing the organization's assets. That is, provided its corrected net worth is less than the reproduction cost. If that is the case, the firm's stocks become desirable.

Another thing that Graham suggests that investors should consider in relation to value investing is investment biases. The biases are influenced by legislative policy or size – number of investors who have confidence in the organization. Established laws may prevent an institution from acquiring stocks of particular businesses. Often, governments enact laws to prevent companies or individuals from investing in socially irresponsible ventures. In this case, an organization may be considered socially irresponsible because it violates environmental and safety policies among others (Greenwald et al., 2004, p. 21). Consequently, such firms experience a decline in their share prices. This forces the organizations to reform. A good time to invest in such organizations is when it becomes evident that the restructuring is progressing well.

In regard to size, the herd mentality determines investment into some entities. Generally, institutions do not make investment decisions. Rather, it is individuals – managers – who work for the organizations that decide the stocks to acquire. Normally, the institutional managers play safe. In other words, they purchase the stocks preferred by other organizational leaders. That is, they apply the principle of safety in numbers. A majority of the other managers make investments that are not risky to protect their jobs. In other words, the administrators sell the shares of companies that underperform and acquire the stocks of organization's that continuously increase their returns (Greenwald et al., 2004, p. 24). In this respect, one can see that the investors that rely on investment biases – the institutional managers– cannot engage in value investing. The entrepreneurs that engage in the venture need to know how to account for profits – capital gains.

## How Capital Gains are Taxed

The purchase and sale of stocks results in profits, also known as capital gains. Usually, the capital gains are taxable. Unfortunately, a significant number of online investors remain unaware of that fact because they do not have tax consultants. Thus, to avoid breaching the law, such entrepreneurs need to know the tax classes that they fall in and the methods they can use to account for the profits they make.

The type of taxation applied on the capital gains depends on whether the returns are long-term or short-term. Generally, the tax rates for long-term capital gains are lower than the rates applied to the short-term profits; the specific laws that established that policy came into effect between 2009 and 2012 (Krantz, 2013, p. 72). For the long-term capital gains, if an individual's ordinary tax rate is higher than or equal to25%, then the utmost capital gains tax (CGT) rate that can be applied on the profits the person makes is 15%. Otherwise, a maximum capital gain rate of 0% is charged if the individual's income tax rate is below that figure. For the short-term gains, the CGT rates that apply are shown in Table 1 below.

Additionally, the capital gains may be realized or unrealized. For investors that have a taxable brokerage account, a taxable event occurs as a result of capital appreciation. Capital appreciation basically refers

*Table 1. Income tax rates for short-term capital gains*

| Tax Rate | Married Filing Jointly or Qualified Widow(er) | Single | Head of Household | Married Filing Separately |
|---|---|---|---|---|
| 10% | $0 - $18,150 | $0 - $9,075 | $0 - $12,950 | $0 - $9,075 |
| 15% | $18,150 - $73,800 | $9,075 - $36,900 | $12,950 - $49,400 | $9,075 - $36,900 |
| 25% | $73,800 - $148,850 | $36,900 - $89,350 | $49,400 - $127,550 | $36,900 - $74,425 |
| 28% | $148,850 - $226,850 | $89,350 - $186,350 | $127,550 - $206,600 | $74,425 - $113,425 |
| 33% | $226,850 - $405,100 | $186,350 - $405,100 | $206,600 - $405,100 | $113,425 - $202,550 |
| 35% | $405,100 - $457,600 | $405,100 - $406,750 | $405,100 - $432,200 | $202,550 - $228,800 |
| 39.6% | over $457,600 | over $406,750 | over $432,200 | over $228,800 |

Source: Bankrate, *What is your tax bracket?* Bankrate, 2014, Web, 16 Sept. 2014.

to a rise in share prices. For instance, if an online investor acquires shares for $20 and the price of the stocks later rises to $80, then the capital appreciation would be $60. By selling the shares, the entrepreneur would realize capital gains, which are taxable. However, if the investor holds on to the shares, the capital appreciation is referred to as unrealized capital gains, which are not taxable (Krantz, 2013, p. 68).

It is not enough to know the tax class that one falls in. The online investors need to offset and keep track of the capital gains to evade penalties. Offsetting capital gains means deducting capital losses from the long-term plus short-term profits that result from the sale of shares. Evidently, if the capital losses exceed the gains, the investor would have made a net loss and thus the taxes would not apply. In this respect, tracking down the capital gains is essential. That is, the online investor should take note of the dates when the shares were bought and sold (Krantz, 2013, p. 75).

Still, the entrepreneur needs to fulfill another requirement. The Internal Revenue Service (IRS) requires one to have a reporting mechanism for capital gains. In this case, the online investor has several alternatives. To begin with, the entrepreneur can use personal finance software. For instance, Intuit developed Quicken is an application that can generate capital gains worksheets. The software presents the required data in accordance with the tax preparation guideline (Krantz, 2013, p. 76). Optionally, the online investor can provide the required information by using the portfolio-tracking tool. This web-based application compiles all information required to compute taxes.

Another alternative is to utilize an online brokers' website. Such sites keep information on the dates transactions were conducted, reveal whether the gains were realized or not, and so on (Krantz, 2013, p. 77). At the end of year, the online brokerage may mail the data to the investor. The investors can then forward the records to the IRS. This is a new development. Initially, it was the duty of brokers to get such data for their clients.

There are more options. For instance, the online investors may use web-based calculator sites to compute the capital gains. In this case, the entrepreneur keys in data on the sale and purchase of stocks and then the site automatically determines the net capital losses and gains. The online investor then downloads the summarized data for use in filing returns. Finally, the investor can use a dedicated online site that optimizes tax strategies. For instance, GainsKeeper is one of the reputed web-based sites that provide services for reducing taxes. Generally, such sites suit active traders who can afford to pay for the cost of the services (Krantz, 2013, p. 77).

## How to Trade in Stocks Online

Online stock trading is another important subtopic of investing and stocks. This type of trade is to some extent similar to regular transactions that involve one walking into a shop, picking the required items, paying for them, and leaving. That is, the online traders select the shares they prefer and electronically transfer the sum required for the purchase. Once the money is received, the sale is reflected. However, online trading has some complications because the prices of stocks are set in real time (Krantz, 2013, p. 129). Thus, the online investors have to use the following options in trading through the internet.

Firstly, the entrepreneurs can trade their stocks online through market orders. In this case, they have to instruct their stock brokers to sell their stock. Normally, the brokers are requested to sell the shares at the highest price that a willing customer is ready to pay. As a result, such orders are quickly executed (Krantz, 2013, p. 129). Given that it is easy to find such willing buyers, the online investors pay a small commission for the brokers' services.

Secondly, stocks can be traded online through limit orders. In this case, the online investors are allowed to set the prices at which they are willing to purchase or accept the sale of stock (Schwartz, 2010, p. 156). For instance, consider an entrepreneur who owns 40 shares, each valued at $100. Suppose the price of the stocks is declining and hence the investor estimates that soon the value of a share will plunge to $70. In this case, the online investor can sell the shares in two ways. The first option is through the market order, which was discussed above. However, that may not give the best returns since the buyers may momentarily offer lower prices than the projected minimum. Optionally, the online investor could set the lowest selling price at $85 to minimize losses. Thus, so long as the decline proceeds as expected, the limit order is the preferable alternative. When the shares' price falls to $85 per unit, the broker will sell all stocks if possible. Limit orders are not based on price alone. Some investors give a deadline within which to sell the stocks (Krantz, 2013, p. 129).

Sometimes, one may not obtain the returns expected after the sale of shares through the limit orders. This is because the shares' price may decline so rapidly that the seller is unable to place the stocks on sale at the agreed price. In this case, the broker may only sell a restricted number of stocks. The rest of the shares are kept in the investor's portfolio. Thus, the limit orders provide a false sense of security.

Online investors can also use stop market orders to trade online. This type of order is similar to a limit order in that a minimum buying or selling price is set. However, for the stop market orders, when shares' price reaches the designated value, the orders are converted into market orders (Krantz, 2013, p. 130). For instance, using the previous example, the broker may be instructed to execute a stop market order when the stocks' price reaches $85. In this case, if the value of shares suddenly plunges to $80 per unit, the online broker would still have to sell the shares at that price.

Fourthly, the shares can be traded through a stop limit order. This option is similar to a stop market order. However, once the defined price is exceeded, the stop limit order is converted into a limit order (Krantz, 2013, p. 130). Thus, the stop limit order prevents the sale of shares if the value of the stocks falls beneath the limit price. To elaborate further, still using the same example, suppose the activation price for selling stocks is $85 and the limit value is $75. When the shares' value falls below $85 per unit, the order becomes a limit order. Hence, when the price reaches $75, the broker is supposed to sell every available stock at that price (Krantz, 2013, p. 130). However, a further decline in price would result in no sale at all. That is, the remainder of stock is kept in the online investor's portfolio.

Lastly, the online stocks can be traded through a trailing stop. This type of order basically follows the market. For a favorable market, rising stock prices, the online investor instructs the broker to retain the shares until the value of the securities reaches a predetermined value. This order is referred to as a trailing sell stop. For a bearish market, the broker is expected to sell the shares as the stocks' price approaches a set minimum value (Pardo, 2008, p. 85). This order is known as an exit trailing stop. Thus, the online investors continuously search for positive yields during the stocks' transaction life.

## How to Trade in Options Online

Apart from stocks, options can also be traded online. An option is a financial instrument that gives one the right to sell or purchase a precise quantity of underlying stock at a prearranged price within a defined time period. The option seller is not legally obliged to carry out all the tasks stipulated in the contract when the financial instrument is handed over to a buyer. The online trading of options is done through screen-based or electronic methods. In the United States of America, there are several institutions – exchange companies – that specialize on options trading. They include the International Securities Exchange (ISE), Boston Options Exchange (BOX), and NASDAQ. The online trading of options has advantages as well as prerequisites that are worth discussing in details (Fontanills & Cawood, 2009, p.43). The online trading of options yields more benefits to the online investor than full-service or traditional brokerage. For example, for this type of trade, commission expenses are lower. That is, the traditional broker may charge $100 for a round turn, whereas an online brokerage charges only several dollars (Fontanills & Cawood, 2009, p. 45). In this case, a round turn refers to each deal or sale. Normally, a commission cost is charged on all orders. The charge applied varies depending on the service being offered. Also, the commission expenses decrease as the services offered to the investors increase. Another advantage of the online trading of options is that the online investors receive considerable support in terms of information as opposed to what happens in traditional brokerage. In other words, the entrepreneurs have access to applications that generate data on tax deductible costs and so on. However, the technique has some disadvantages. For instance, new traders need the services of online brokers that specialize in order-taking only. It is not easy to find such experts.

The online investors must fulfill other requirements to be able to successfully trade in options through the internet. Firstly, they need a computer, internet service provider, portfolio tracking tool, and an online brokerage account. Additionally, the investor should have knowledge on how to assess stocks. The valuation of shares is normally done through fundamental analysis of the equities. That is, the investor must review the targeted company's earnings, assets, changes in management, income statements, and so on (Fontanills & Cawood, 2009, p. 64). If the analysis shows that the market value of the stock is lower than its real worth, demand for the equity increases. Conversely, if the market price of the organization's stocks is higher that its calculated true value, demand decreases.

Also, the online option traders need to assess the extent of competition among firms that operate in the sector. For instance, high-tech firms operate in extremely competitive environments, which means the organizations can only survive by continuously unveiling new products. This makes investing in the companies risky as projects often fail, which results in significant losses. In this regard, the active online traders should study such industries in depth to be able to forecast the success of the companies they intend to invest in (Fontanills & Cawood, 2009, p 55). In this case, the necessary information about these types of firms is readily available; the online investors can find the data in investment websites such as Optionetics.

Besides that, the options investor should consider the type of broker to employ. There are three categories of brokers namely: discount, options specialty, and full-service brokers. The full-service brokers charge relatively high fees. This is because they conduct research on annuities, bonds, stocks, and other long-term investment options. In other words, they give advice on the best options to trade. The discount brokers charge relatively low fees since they rarely give recommendations on investment options (Benklifa & Olmstead, 2013, p. 33). As the name suggest, the option specialty brokers particularly cater to the needs of the online option investors. That is, they give advice on competition and so on. However, the differences among the brokers in terms of services provided are gradually diminishing. This is because internet tools are slowly integrating the services provided by the brokers and hence, eventually, one broker will be able to provide all the services.

Fourthly, a trading platform is crucial. A trading platform is an application that provides option and stock quotes in real time. Thus, an effective one allows the investor to transact directly. In addition, a good platform displays several option exchange firms and bid or ask prices of the companies. Thus, independent online traders use the platforms to identify favorable exit and entry option prices (Benklifa & Olmstead, 2013, p. 56).

Therefore, to be a successful online trader of options, one must have sufficient knowledge on several subjects. Firstly, the investors should know the types of brokers that exist and the services they offer. A broker can be a full-time, option specialty, or discount broker. Secondly, the online options trader should be aware of the commissions charged by the different types of brokers. Thirdly, a trading platform that provides information on the targeted stocks' prices is required. Lastly, before trading in options online, the investor should analyze the concerned company. Given that several types of online investment options exist, it is important to understand how to use diversification to reduce the risk involved in selecting each.

## How to Use Diversification to Allocate your Online Investments

The online investors, those who own portfolios that contain stocks that are traded through the internet, are at risk of facing fluctuating returns. They can prevent severe losses caused by market volatility through diversification. Diversification means that the investors should acquire stocks in companies that operate in different industries and have operations worldwide. Additionally, the entrepreneur should buy a variety of assets from companies of different sizes and obtain investment advice from several sources. If that is done, the investors can be certain that a deep plunge in the price of particular shares will not destroy their portfolios (Sindell, 2005, p. 318).

Each of the diversification approaches has specific benefits. To begin with, assets include stocks, bonds, mutual funds, exchange trade funds, options, and other financial instruments. Buying a variety of the assets allows the investor to benefit from the unique characteristics of each. For instance, mutual funds are managed by experts. Secondly, the purchasing of shares of companies that operate in different sectors safeguards a portfolio from unfavorable policy changes and so on (Sindell, 2005, p. 318). Thirdly, the buying of stocks of companies that conduct their business globally protects one from the challenges created by the weakening of the currency of particular country. For instance, if the US dollar declines in value, worldwide investments may be more profitable. Also, by investing across the world, the online investors reduce the impact of natural disasters and so on. Lastly, investing in firms of different sizes enables the entrepreneurs to take advantage of steady growth, which is associated with large organizations, the quick growth of small institutions, and the consistent returns of medium-sized corporations.

The online investors have access to several sources of information on diversification. Particularly, web-based institutions offer excellent advice on the subject. For instance, Fidelity provides online worksheets that aid the investors to select different assets according to the risk associated with each (Sindell,

2005, p. 318). NETirement.com provides an online calculator for use in assessing the assets' risks based on preset average returns of the investments.

## CONCLUSION

Investing and stocks is a wide subject. It covers the Modern Portfolio Theory, which advocates for diversification of investments to minimize portfolio risk. Secondly, it includes computational investing that provides information on the models used to analyze data for effective decision-making. Also, it addresses opening an online brokerage account. The subject provides information on the use of the portfolio tracking tool, transaction costs involved in the establishment of the account, and so on. Additionally, by studying the chapter, learners discover the significance of the MSSP approach to investing. Besides that, the subtitle on mutual funds, bonds, options, and ETFs shows how pools of funds can be utilized to make investments. In Apart from that, value investing shows how underpriced stocks can become significant. The subtitle on how capital gains are taxed enables the online investors to know the types of taxes that are applied on returns that result from the trading of shares online and methods they can use to report the profits. The chapter gives learners an opportunity to learn about other aspects of online investing including the trading of stocks and options through the internet and diversification of online investments, which reduces risk.

## REFERENCES


Appei, M. (2009). *Investing with Exchange Trade Funds Made Easy: A Start to Finish Plan to Reduce Costs and Achieve Higher Returns* (2nd ed.). Upper Saddle River, NJ: Pearson Education Inc.

Benklifa, M., & Olmstead, W. (2013). *Learn How to Trade Options (Collection)*. Upper Saddle River, NJ: Pearson Education Inc.

Browne, C. (2007). *The Little Book of Value Investing*. Hoboken, NJ: John Wiley & Sons, Inc.

Fontanills, G., & Cawood, R. (2009). *Trade Options Online*. Hoboken, NJ: John Wiley & Sons, Inc.

Francis, J., & Dongcheol, K. (2013). *Modern Portfolio Theory: Foundations, Analysis, and New Developments*. Hoboken, NJ: John Wiley & Sons, Inc.

Graham, J., & Smart, C. (2012). *Introduction to Corporate Finance: What Companies Do*. Mason, OH: South-Western Cengage Learning.

Greenwald, B., Kahn, J., Sonkin, P., & Van Biema, M. (2004). *Value Investing: From Graham to Buffett and Beyond*. Hoboken, NJ: John Wiley & Sons, Inc.

Hart, C. M. (2005). *I Want to Make Money in the Stock Market: Learn to Begin Investing Without Losing Your Life Savings*. Denver: Outskirts Press.

Hobson, R. (2012). *The Dividend Investor: A Practical Guide To Building A Share Portfolio Designed To Maximise Income*. Hampshire: Harriman House Ltd.

Khan, M. Y., & Jain, P. K. (2007). *Financial Management*. New Delhi: Tata McGraw-Hill Publishing Company Limited.

Kimmel, J. (2009). *The MAGNET Method of Investing: Find, Trade, and Profit from Exceptional Stocks*. Hoboken, NJ: John Wiley & Sons, Inc.

Krantz, M. (2013). *Investing Online for Dummies*. Hoboken, NJ: John Wiley & Sons, Inc.

Kumpf, S. (2013). *Listed Private Equity: Investment Strategies and Returns*. Hamburg, Germany: Diplomica Verlag GmbH.

Kürschner, M. (2008). *Limitations of the Capital Asset Pricing Model (CAPM)*. Norderstedt: GRIN Verlag.

Laopodis, N. (2013). *Understanding Investments: Theories and Strategies*. New York, NY: Routledge.

Loewen, J. B. (2008). *Money Magnet: How to Attract Investors to Your Business*. Mississauga, ON: John Wiley & Sons Canada, Ltd.

Maeda, M. (2009). *The Complete Guide to Investing in Bonds and Bond Funds: How to Earn High Rates of Return-Safely*. Ocala, Fla: Atlantic Publishing Group, Inc.

Magliolo, J. (2005). *Become Your Own Stockbroker: A Practical Guide to Trading in South Africa*. Cape Town, South Africa: Zebra Press.

Northcott, A. (2009). *The Mutual Funds Book: How to Invest in Mutual Funds and earn High Rates of Returns Safely*. Ocala, FL: Atlantic Publishing *Group*.

Pardo, R. (2008). *The Evaluation and Optimization of Trading Strategies*. Hoboken, NJ: John Wiley & Sons, Inc.

Schwartz, R. A. (2010). *Micro Markets: A Market Structure Approach to Microeconomic Analysis*. Hoboken, NJ: John Wiley & Sons, Inc. doi:10.1002/9781118268131

Sindell, K. (2005). *Investing Online For Dummies*. Hoboken, NJ: Wiley Publishing Inc.

Strong, R. (2009). *Portfolio Construction, Management, and Protection*. Ohio: South-Western Cengage Learning.

Voges, K. E., & Pope, N. (2006). Business Applications and Computational Intelligence. Hershey, PA, USA: IGI Global. doi:10.4018/978-1-59140-702-7

Wellin, P. R., Gaylord, R. J., & Kamin, S. N. (2005). *An Introduction to Programming with Mathematica*. Cambridge, MA: Cambridge University Press. doi:10.1017/CBO9780511801303

## ADDITIONAL READING

Balch, T. (2014, September 4). *Computational Investing, Part 1, 221: Machine Learning Preview* [YouTube video].

## KEY TERMS AND DEFINITIONS

**Bonds:** A debt investment in which an investor loans money to an entity which borrows the funds for a specified period of time at a fixed interest rate.

**Mutual Funds:** An investment vehicle that is made up of funds from many investors with the objective of investing in stocks, bonds, money market products and similar assets.

**Online Trading:** Individual investors buy and sell stocks over an electronic network through a brokerage company.

**Portfolio Management:** Professional asset management of different securities to reach investment goals.

**Stocks:** Defines the ownership certificate of any company. A share means the stock certificate of a particular company.

**Value Investing:** The strategy of selecting stocks that trade for less than their intrinsic value.

# Compilation of References


(2011). Reddy.Amarender A, Malik Pal Dharm 2011. *Indian Journal of Industrial Economics and Development*, *7*(2), 1–10.

Adner, R., & Helfat, C. E. (2003). Corporate effects and dynamic managerial capabilities. *Strategic Management Journal*, *24*(10), 1011–1025. doi:10.1002/smj.331

Agarwal, A. (2010). Financial Inclusion: Challenges and Opportunities. *Proceedings of the 23rd Skoch Summit.*

Agarwal, P. (2014). Financial Inclusion in India: a Review and Initiatives and Achievements. *IOSR Journal of Business and Management*, 16(6).

Aghion, P., & Howitt, P. (1998). *Endogenous growth theory*. Cambridge, MA: MIT Press.

Ahmad, S. M., & Mir, A. A. (2012). Need for Human Resource Development (HRD) Practices in Indian Universities: A Key for Educational Excellence. *Journal of Human Values*, *18*(2), 113–132. doi:10.1177/0971685812454481

Ahmed, A. D., Cheng, E., & Messinis, G. (2011). The role of exports, FDI and imports in development: Evidence from Sub-Saharan African countries. *Applied Economics*, *43*(26), 3719–3731. doi:10.1080/00036841003705303

Ahmed, K., & Chowdhury, T. A. (2009). Performance Evaluation of SMEs. *International Journal of Business and Management*, *4*(7), 126–133. doi:10.5539/ijbm.v4n7p126

Ainin, S., Lim, C. H., & Wee, A. (2005). Prospects and Challenges of E-Banking in Malaysia. *Electronic Journal of Information Systems in Developing Countries*, *22*, 1–110.

Alambath, M. (2008). Forest faces the evils of ecotourism. *Iftrac Tourism World*, *1*, 42–45.

Alasem, A. (2009). An overview of e-government metadata standards and initiatives based on Dublin Core. *Electronic Journal of E-Government*, *7*(1), 1–10.

Albanese, M. A., Mejicano, G., Mullan, P., Kokotailo, P., & Gruppen, L. (2008). Defining characteristics of educational competencies. *Medical Education*, *42*(3), 248–255. doi:10.1111/j.1365-2923.2007.02996.x PMID:18275412

Alhasant, S. (2008). *Socio-cultural Impacts of Tourism on the local community at Jordan*. Coventry University.

Al-Khouri, A. M. (2011). An Innovative Approach for E-Government Transformation. arXiv Preprint arXiv:1105.6358. Retrieved from http://arxiv.org/abs/1105.6358

All India Survey on Higher Education various issues. (n. d.). Govt. of India, MHRD.

Almazan, R. S., & Gil-Garcia, J. R. (2008). E-Government Portals in Mexico. Retrieved from http://www.igi-global.com/chapter/electronic-government-concepts-methodologies-tools/9818

Al-Qutaish, R. E., & Abran, A. (2011). A Maturity Model of Software Product Quality. *Journal of Research & Practice in Information Technology*, 43(4), 307-327. Retrieved from http://search.ebscohost.com/login.aspx?direct=true&profile=ehost&scope=site&authtype=crawler&jrnl=1443458X&AN=87525733&h=HZhdR3x4ibqL7aU3c%2B9zIsOv37eI%2Bbn5kDNyjOgdGWxtuF5WNSkG9PbkjezkKex8OnAfORK%2F4jx%2FA8ZsKNrW0w%3D%3D&crl=c

Alsmadi, I., Al-Kabi, M., & Wahbeh, A. (2012). A Conceptual Organization for Websites Metrics and E-Government Websites: A Case Study. *International Journal of Information Communication Technologies and Human Development*, *4*(1), 93–117. doi:10.4018/jicthd.2012010107

American Management Association. (2010). *Developing successful global leaders: A global study of challenges and opportunities*. New York, NY: American Management Association.

Andersen, M., & Skjoett-Larsen, T. (2009). Corporate Social Responsibility in Global Supply Chains. *Supply Chain Management: An International Journal*, *14*(2), 75–86. doi:10.1108/13598540910941948

Andreasson, K., Millard, J., & Snaprud, M. (2012). Evolving e-government benchmarking to better cover technology development and emerging societal needs. *Proceedings of the 6th International Conference on Theory and Practice of Electronic Governance* (pp. 430–439). Retrieved from http://dl.acm.org/citation.cfm?id=2463811

Anema, M. G., & McCoy, J. (2010). *Competency-based nursing education: Guide to achieving outstanding learner outcomes*. New York, NY: Springer–Verlag.

Ang, J. B., Madsen, J. B., & Rabiul Islam, M. (2011). The effects of human capital composition on technological convergence. *Journal of Macroeconomics*, *33*(3), 465–476. doi:10.1016/j.jmacro.2011.03.001

Anil, K. (2007). Tourism: Impact of Negative Factors On The Host Community-Case Of Kerala. *The Journal of Business Studies*, *4*(8), 39–43.

Annual Report of the Hero MotoCorp Ltd. (2013). Retrieved from www.heroMotoCorp.com/gvdp/green-vendor-development-program

Annual Report various issues. (n. d.). Govt. of India, MHRD.

Appei, M. (2009). *Investing with Exchange Trade Funds Made Easy: A Start to Finish Plan to Reduce Costs and Achieve Higher Returns* (2nd ed.). Upper Saddle River, NJ: Pearson Education Inc.

Arora, R.U. (2012). Gender inequality, economic development, and globalization: a state level analysis of India. *Journal of Developing Areas*, 41(1).

Arter, J. A., & McTighe, J. (2001). *Scoring rubrics in the classroom: Using performance criteria for assessing and improving student performance*. Thousand Oaks, CA: Corwin Press.

Arthur, W. Jr, & Bennett, W. Jr. (1995). The international assignee: The relative importance of factors perceived to contribute to success. *Personnel Psychology*, *48*(1), 99–114. doi:10.1111/j.1744-6570.1995.tb01748.x

Arunachalam, R.S. (2008, January). Scoping paper on Financial Inclusion: Considerations and recommendations for UNDP. The UNDP lasting solutions to development challenges.

Ashkanasy, N. M., Falkus, S., & Callan, V. J. (2000). Predictors of Ethical Code Use and Ethical Tolerance in the Public Sector. *Journal of Business Ethics*, *25*(3), 237–253. doi:10.1023/A:1006001722137

Ashley, C. (2000), The Impacts of Tourism on Livelihoods: Namibia's Experience. Overseas Development Institute. London: Portland House, Stag Place.

Ashley, C., & Jones, B. (1999). Joint ventures between communities and tourism investors: Experience in Southern Africa. *Presentation toFair Trade and Tourism Conference*, London.

Asiedu, E., & Lien, D. (2011). Democracy, Foreign Direct Investment and Natural Resources. *Journal of International Economics*, *84*(1), 99–111. doi:10.1016/j.jinteco.2010.12.001

Assar, S. (2011). *Practical studies in e-Government.* Springer. Retrieved from http://books.google.be/books?hl=fr&lr=&id=DzZk-Riel_MC&oi=fnd&pg=PR9&dq=Practical+Studies+in+E-Government&ots=twg6CbeZ3T&sig=J31HDADy1ndhCjGpZH3ycgcGmXY

Assar, S., Boughzala, I., & Isckia, T. (2011). eGovernment trends in the Web 2.0 era and the open innovation perspective: an exploratory field study. In *Electronic Government* (pp. 210–222). Springer. Retrieved from http://link.springer.com/chapter/10.1007/978-3-642-22878-0_18

Auerbach, A. J., Gokhale, J., & Kotlikoff, L. J. (1994). Generational accounting: A meaningful way to assess generational policy. *The Journal of Economic Perspectives*, *8*(1), 74–94. doi:10.1257/jep.8.1.73

Azagaiah, R., & Gejalakshmi, S. (2007). Working Capital Management – Efficiency Analysis. *Udyog Pragathi*, *31*(3), 15–90.

Backman, M. (2014). Human capital in firms and regions: Impact on firm productivity. *Papers in Regional Science*, *93*(3), 557–575. doi:10.1111/pirs.12005

Baliamoune-Lutz, M. (2006). Globalization and Gender: Is Africa Different? *Journal of African Economies*, *16*(2), 301–348. doi:10.1093/jae/ejl037

Banerjee, R., & Roy, S. S. (2014). Human capital, technological progress and trade: What explains India's long run growth? *Journal of Asian Economics*, *30*, 15–31. doi:10.1016/j.asieco.2013.12.003

Bansal, S. P. (2002). Ecotourism vis a vis Holistic Regional Development according to D.Singhai & Gautam. In Tourism in New Millennium (pp. 331-348). Chandigarh: Abhishek Publications.

Bansal, S. P. (2002). Socio-cultural impact of tourism in Himachal Pradesh according to Bansal and Garg. In Tourism in New Millennium (pp. 370-390). Chandigarh: Abhishek Publications.

Barney, J. B. (1991). Firm resources and sustained competitive advantage. *Journal of Management*, *17*(1), 99–120. doi:10.1177/014920639101700108

Barney, J. B., & Wright, P. M. (1988). On becoming the strategic partner: The role of human resources in gaining competitive advantage. *Human Resource Management*, *37*(1), 31–46. doi:10.1002/(SICI)1099-050X(199821)37:1<31::AID-HRM4>3.0.CO;2-W

Barrientos, S. W. (2002). Flexible Female Employment and Ethical Trade in the Global Economy. In P. Newell, S. Rai, & A. Scott (Eds.), *Development and the Challenge of Globalisation* (pp. 143–158). London: ITDG Publishing. doi:10.3362/9781780441108.010

Barro, R. J. (2013). Education and economic growth. *Annals of Economics and Finance*, *14*(2), 301–328.

Bartley, T. (2007). Institutional Emergence in an Era of Globalization: The Rise of Transnational Private Regulation of Labor and Environmental Conditions. *American Journal of Sociology*, *113*(2), 297–351. doi:10.1086/518871

Basel Committee on Banking Supervision, Bank for International Settlements. (2009). Strengthening the Resilience of the Banking Sector: Consultative Document 13. Retrieved from http://www.bis.org/publ/bcbs164.pdf

Bassanini, A., & Scarpetta, S. (2002). Does human capital matter for growth in OECD countries? A pooled mean-group approach. *Economics Letters*, *74*(3), 399–405. doi:10.1016/S0165-1765(01)00569-9

Beck, T., Demirguc-Kunt, A., & Peria, M.S.M. (2005). *Reaching Out: Access to and use of banking services across countries*. World Bank Policy Research (WPS 3754).

Becker, G. (1964). *Human capital: A theoretical and empirical analysis, with special reference to education*. New York, NY: Columbia University Press.

Beeler, B. G. (2000). *Opportunities and threat to local sustainable development: Introducing ecotourism to Venado Island, Costa Rica* [Thesis]. Lund University, Sweden.

Beerli, A., & Martin, J. D. (2004). Factors influencing destination image. *Annals of Tourism Research*, *31*(3), 657–681. doi:10.1016/j.annals.2004.01.010

Belderbos, R., Van Roy, V., & Duvivier, F. (2013). International and domestic technology transfers and productivity growth: Firm level evidence. *Industrial and Corporate Change*, *22*(1), 1–32. doi:10.1093/icc/dts012

Bellak, C. (2004). How domestic and foreign firms differ and why does it matter? *Journal of Economic Surveys*, *18*(4), 483–514. doi:10.1111/j.0950-0804.2004.00228.x

Benhabib, J., & Spiegel, M. (2005). Human capital and technology diffusion. In P. Aghion & S. Durlauf (Eds.), *Handbook of economic growth* (pp. 935–966). Amsterdam, The Netherlands: Elsevier.

Benklifa, M., & Olmstead, W. (2013). *Learn How to Trade Options (Collection)*. Upper Saddle River, NJ: Pearson Education.

Berchicci, L. (2013). Towards an open R&D system: Internal R&D investment, external knowledge acquisition and innovative performance. *Research Policy*, *42*(1), 117–127. doi:10.1016/j.respol.2012.04.017

Berenbeim, R. E. (1992, Spring). The Corporate Ethics Test. *Business and Society Review*, *31*(1), 77–80.

Berio, G., & Harzallah, M. (2005). Knowledge management for competence management. *Journal of Universal Knowledge Management*, *0*(1), 21–28.

Berntzen, L., & Olsen, M. G. (2009). Benchmarking e-government-a comparative review of three international benchmarking studies. *Proceedings of the Third International Conference on Digital Society ICDS '09* (pp. 77–82). Retrieved from http://ieeexplore.ieee.org/xpls/abs_all.jsp?arnumber=4782854

Bhaskarans, R. (2006). *Financial Inclusion: What needs to be done?* New Delhi: Reading on Financial Inclusion, IIBF & Taxman.

Bhattacharya, A., Jain, R., & Choudhary, A. (2011). *Green Manufacturing, Energy, products and processes* (p. 8). The Boston Consulting Group.

Bhattacharya, D., Gulla, U., & Gupta, M. P. (2012). E-service quality model for Indian government portals: Citizens' perspective. *Journal of Enterprise Information Management*, *25*(3), 246–271. doi:10.1108/17410391211224408

Bingley, P., & Westergaard-Nielsen, N. (2004). Personnel policy and profit. *Journal of Business Research*, *57*(5), 557–563. doi:10.1016/S0148-2963(02)00321-1

Birkinshaw, J. (1997). Entrepreneurship in multinational corporations: The characteristics of subsidiary initiative. *Strategic Management Journal*, *18*(3), 207–229. doi:10.1002/(SICI)1097-0266(199703)18:3<207::AID-SMJ864>3.0.CO;2-Q

Bizumic, B., Duckitt, J., Popadic, D., Dru, V., & Krauss, S. (2009). A cross-cultural investigation into a reconceptualization of ethnocentrism. *European Journal of Social Psychology*, *39*(6), 871–899. doi:10.1002/ejsp.589

Black, J. A., & Boal, K. B. (1994). Strategic resources: Traits, configurations and paths to sustainable competitive advantage. *Strategic Management Journal*, *15*(S2), 131–148. doi:10.1002/smj.4250151009

Black, S. (1990). The relationship of personal characteristics with the adjustment of Japanese. *Management International Review*, *30*(2), 119–134.

Bondy, K., Matten, D., & Moon, J. (2008). Multinational Corporation Codes of Conduct: Governance Tools for Corporate Social Responsibility? *Corporate Governance: An International Review*, *16*(4), 294–311. doi:10.1111/j.1467-8683.2008.00694.x

Boojihawon, D. K., Dimitratos, P., & Young, S. (2007). Characteristics and influences of multinational subsidiary entrepreneurial culture: The case of the advertising sector. *International Business Review*, *16*(5), 549–572. doi:10.1016/j.ibusrev.2007.06.003

Bornay-Barrachina, M., De la Rosa-Navarro, D., López-Cabrales, A., & Valle-Cabrera, R. (2012). Employment relationships and firm innovation: The double role of human capital. *British Journal of Management*, *23*(2), 223–240. doi:10.1111/j.1467-8551.2010.00735.x

Braungart, R. G., & Braungart, M. M. (2003). *Research in political sociology*. Greenwich, CT: JAI Press.

Brenner, S. N. (1992). Ethics Programs and Their Dimensions. *Journal of Business Ethics*, *11*(5-6), 391–399. doi:10.1007/BF00870551

Browne, C. (2007). *The Little Book of Value Investing*. Hoboken, NJ: John Wiley & Sons, Inc.

Brozova, H., & Subrt, T. (2008). Competency mapping and modelling in system design. *Scientia Agriculturae Bohemica*, *39*(2), 125–131.

Bruno, G. S. F., Crinò, R., & Falzoni, A. M. (2012). Foreign direct investment, trade, and skilled labour demand in Eastern Europe. *Labour*, *26*(4), 492–513. doi:10.1111/labr.12001

Buchholtz, A., Ribbens, B., & Houle, I. (2003). Takeover resistance and executive succession. *Academy of Management Journal*, *46*(4), 506–514. doi:10.2307/30040642

Bucovetsky, S. (2009). An Index of Capital Tax Competition. *International Tax and Public Finance*, *16*(6), 727–752. doi:10.1007/s10797-008-9093-9

Burke, K. (2006). *From standards to rubrics in 6 steps*. Heatherton, Victoria: Hawker Brownlow Education.

Čadil, J., Petkovová, L., & Blatná, D. (2014). Human capital, economic structure and growth. *Procedia Economics and Finance*, *12*, 85–92. doi:10.1016/S2212-5671(14)00323-2

Cağatay, N. (2001). *Trade, Gender and Poverty», Background Paper for UNDP"s Report on Trade and Sustainable Human Development*. UNDP.

Calantone, R. J., & Johar, J. S.Calatone & Johar. (1984). Seasonal segmentation of the tourism market using a benefit segmentation framework. *Journal of Travel Research*, *23*(2), 14–24. doi:10.1177/004728758402300203

Caligiuri, P., & Di Santo, V. (2001). Global competence: What is it and can it be developed through global assignments? *Human Resource Planning*, *24*(3), 27–35.

Caligiuri, P., & Tarique, I. (2012). Dynamic cross-cultural competencies and global leadership effectiveness. *Journal of World Business*, *47*(4), 612–622. doi:10.1016/j.jwb.2012.01.014

Calza, F., Aliane, N., & Cannavale, C. (2013). Cross-cultural bridges in European firms' internationalization to Islamic countries: The key role of cultural competence. *EuroMed Journal of Business*, *8*(2), 172–187. doi:10.1108/EMJB-07-2013-0038

Canary, H. E., & Jennings, M. M. (2008). Principles and Influences in Codes of Ethics: A Centering Resonance Analysis Comparing Pre- and Post-Sarbanes-Oxley Codes of Ethics. *Journal of Business Ethics*, *80*(2), 263–278. doi:10.1007/s10551-007-9417-1

Cañas, J., & Gilmer, R. W. (2009). The Maquiladora's Changing Geography. *The Federal Reserve Bank of Dallas: Second Quarter*, *2009*, 10–14.

Cantwell, J., & Mudambi, R. (2005). MNE competence-creating subsidiary mandates. *Strategic Management Journal*, *26*(12), 1109–1128. doi:10.1002/smj.497

Capelli, P. (1993). Are skill requirements rising? Evidence form production and clerical jobs. *Industrial & Labor Relations Review*, *46*(3), 515–530. doi:10.1177/001979399304600305

Carpenter, M. A., Sanders, W. G., & Gregersen, H. B. (2001). Bundling human capital with organizational context: The impact of international assignment experience on multinational firm performance and CEO pay. *Academy of Management Journal*, *44*(3), 493–512. doi:10.2307/3069366

Carroll, A., & Buchholtz, A. (2014). *Business and Society: Ethics, Sustainability, and Stakeholder Management*. Stamford, CT: Cengage Learning.

Carroll, A. B., & Shabana, K. M. (2010). The Business Case for Corporate Social Responsibility: A Review of Concepts, Research and Practice. *International Journal of Management Reviews*, *12*(1), 85–105. doi:10.1111/j.1468-2370.2009.00275.x

Caselli, F., & Coleman, J. W. II. (2006). The world technology frontier. *The American Economic Review*, *96*(3), 499–522. doi:10.1257/aer.96.3.499

Cassar, G. (2006). Entrepreneur opportunity costs and intended venture growth. *Journal of Business Venturing*, *21*(5), 610–632. doi:10.1016/j.jbusvent.2005.02.011

Cassiman, B., & Venugelers, R. (2006). In search of complementarity in innovation strategy: Internal R&D and external knowledge acquisition. *Management Science*, *52*(1), 68–82. doi:10.1287/mnsc.1050.0470

Castellacci, F. (2007). Technological regimes and sectoral differences in productivity growth. *Industrial and Corporate Change*, *16*(6), 1105–1145. doi:10.1093/icc/dtm033

Castellani, D., & Zanfei, A. (2003). Technology gaps, inward investments and productivity of European firms. *Economics of Innovation and New Technology*, *12*(6), 555–576. doi:10.1080/714933761

Celestine, A. (2014, June 15). *Shortage of capital: Should FM Arun Jaitley divest government's stake in PSU banks?* Retrieved from www.articles.economictimes.indiatimes.com: http://articles.economictimes.indiatimes.com/2014-06-15/news/50598272_1_public-sector-banks-psu-banks-loans

Cerrato, D., & Piva, M. (2012). The internationalization of small and medium-sized enterprises: The effect of family management, human capital and foreign ownership. *Journal of Management & Governance*, *16*(4), 617–644. doi:10.1007/s10997-010-9166-x

Chakrabarty, K.C. (2011, September). Financial Inclusion (Keynote address), Mumbai.

Chakrabarty, K.C. (2012, November).Financial Inclusion: Issues in Measurement and Analysis (Keynote address). *Proceedings of the BIS-BNM Workshop on Financial Inclusion Indicators*, Kuala Lumpur.

Chakraborty, K. (2008). Working Capital and Profitability: An Empirical Analysis of their Relationship with Reference to Selected Companies in the Indian Pharmaceutical Industry. *The Icfaian Journal of Management Research*, *VII*(12), 41–59.

Chani, M. I., Jan, S. A., Pervaiz, Z., & Chaudhary, A. R. (2014). Human capital inequality and income inequality: Testing for causality. *Quality & Quantity*, *48*(1), 149–156. doi:10.1007/s11135-012-9755-7

Chavan, J. (2013). Internet Banking – Benefits and Challenges in an Emerging Economy. *International Journal of Research in Business Management*, *1*, 19–26.

Chen, B. L., Chen, H. J., & Wang, P. (2011). Labor-market frictions, human capital accumulation, and long-run growth: Positive analysis and policy evaluation. *International Economic Review*, *52*(1), 131–160. doi:10.1111/j.1468-2354.2010.00622.x

Chen, C., & Huang, J. (2009). Strategic human resource practices and innovation performance: The mediating role of knowledge management capacity. *Journal of Business Research*, *62*(1), 104–114. doi:10.1016/j.jbusres.2007.11.016

Chen, H. J. (2012). Social status, human capital formation and the long-run effects of money. *Journal of Economics*, *105*(3), 225–246. doi:10.1007/s00712-011-0227-7

Chen, L. F., & Chien, C. F. (2011). Manufacturing intelligence for class prediction and rule generation to support human capital decisions for high-tech industries. *Flexible Services and Manufacturing Journal*, *23*(3), 263–289. doi:10.1007/s10696-010-9068-x

Cheshire, P., & Magrini, S. (2000). Endogenous processes in European regional growth: Convergence and policy. *Growth and Change*, *31*(4), 455–479. doi:10.1111/0017-4815.00140

Chonko, L. B., Wotruba, T. R., & Loe, T. W. (2003). Ethics Code Familiarity and Usefulness: Views on Idealist and Relativist Managers Under Varying Conditions of Turbulence. *Journal of Business Ethics*, *42*(3), 237–252. doi:10.1023/A:1022261006692

Choudrie, J., Ghinea, G., & Weerakkody, V. (2004). Evaluating global e-government sites: A view using Web diagnostics tools. *Electronic Journal of E-Government*, *2*(2), 105–114.

Chowdhury, S., Schulz, E., Milner, M., & Van de Voort, D. (2014). Core employee based human capital and revenue productivity in small firms: An empirical investigation. *Journal of Business Research*, *67*(11), 2473–2479. doi:10.1016/j.jbusres.2014.03.007

Clean Clothes Campaign. (2001, March) Controlling Corporate Wrongs: The Liability of Multinational Corporations, *Report of the IRENE Seminar*. Retrieved from http://www.cleanclothes.org/publications/corp-8.htm

Cleek, M. A., & Leonard, S. L. (1998). Can Corporate Codes of Ethics Influence Behavior? *Journal of Business Ethics*, *17*(6), 619–630.

Clement, M. B., Koonce, L., & Lopez, T. J. (2007). The roles of task-specific forecasting experience and innate ability in understanding analyst forecasting performance. *Journal of Accounting and Economics*, *44*(3), 378–398. doi:10.1016/j.jacceco.2007.04.002

Coates, T. T., & McDermott, C. M. (2002). An exploratory analysis of new competencies: A resource based view perspective. *Journal of Operations Management*, *20*(5), 435–450. doi:10.1016/S0272-6963(02)00023-2

Coff, R. W. (2002). Human capital, shared expertise, and the likelihood of impasse in corporate acquisitions. *Journal of Management*, *28*(1), 107–128. doi:10.1177/014920630202800107

Colley, R. H. (1961). *Defining advertising goals for measured advertising results*. New York: Association of National Advertisers.

Colombo, M. G., & Grilli, L. (2005). Founders' human capital and the growth of new technology-based firms: A competence-based view. *Research Policy, 34*(6), 795–816. doi:10.1016/j.respol.2005.03.010

Coltman, M. M. (1989). *Tourism Marketing*. New York: Van Nostrand Reinhold.

Commendatore, P., Currie, M., & Kubin, I. (2008). Footloose Entrepreneurs, Taxes and Subsidies. *Spatial Economic Analysis, 3*(1), 115–141. doi:10.1080/17421770701774914

Concept Note. (2015, March 6). Advancing Gender Equality and Empowerment of Women and Girls for a Transformative Post-2015 Development Agenda.

Crask, M. R. (1981). Segmenting the vacationer market: Identifying the vacation preferences, demographics and magazine readership of each group. *Journal of Travel Research, 20*(2), 29–34. doi:10.1177/004728758102000205

Crompton, J. L. (1979). Motivations for pleasure vacations. *Annals of Tourism Research, 6*(4), 408–424. doi:10.1016/0160-7383(79)90004-5

Crook, T. R., Todd, S. Y., Combs, J. G., Woehr, D. J., & Ketchen, D. J. (2011). Does human capital matter? A meta-analysis of the relationship between human capital and firm performance. *The Journal of Applied Psychology, 96*(3), 443–456. doi:10.1037/a0022147 PMID:21244126

Cruickshank, P., Edelmann, N., & Smith, C. (2010). Signing an e-Petition as a Transition from Lurking to Participation. In H. J. Scholl & M. Janssen (Eds.), *Electronic Government and Electronic Participation: Joint Proceedings of Ongoing Research and Projects of IFIP EGOV and IFIP ePart 2010* (pp. 275–282). Linz, Austria: Trauner Verlag.

Crujeiras, B., & Jiménez-Aleixandre, M. P. (2013). Challenges in the implementation of a competency-based curriculum in Spain. *Thinking Skills and Creativity, 10*, 208–220. doi:10.1016/j.tsc.2013.07.001

Czinkto, M. R., & Ronkainen, I. A. (2001). *International Marketing* (6th ed.). Orlando: Harcourt College Publishers.

Dahlstrom, R. (2011). *Green Marketing, Theory, Practice and Strategies*. Delhi: Cengage Learning India Private Ltd.

Dainty, A. R. J., Cheng, M. I., & Moore, D. R. (2005). Competency-based model for predicting construction project managers' performance. *Journal of Management Engineering, 21*(1), 2–9. doi:10.1061/(ASCE)0742-597X(2005)21:1(2)

Das k.Sanjay *2012,* BEST PRACTICES OF SELF HELP GROUPS AND WOMEN EMPOWERMENT: A CASE OF BARAK VALLEY OF ASSAM, Vol. 7 No. 2 May 2012

Davidson, K. (2009). Ethical Concerns at the Bottom of the Pyramid: Where CSR Meets BOP. *Journal of International Business Ethics, 2*(1), 22–32.

Davidsson, P., & Honig, B. (2003). The role of social and human capital among nascent entrepreneurs. *Journal of Business Venturing, 18*(3), 301–331. doi:10.1016/S0883-9026(02)00097-6

de Silva, S. (1997). *Human Resources Development for Competitiveness: A Priority for Employers*. Italy: International Labour Organisation.

Delone, W. H. (2003). The DeLone and McLean model of information systems success: A ten-year update. *Journal of Management Information Systems, 19*(4), 9–30.

DeLone, W. H., & McLean, E. R. (1992). Information systems success: The quest for the dependent variable. *Information Systems Research, 3*(1), 60–95. doi:10.1287/isre.3.1.60

Demirguc–Kunt, A., & Klapper, L. (2012, April). Measuring Financial Inclusion (Policy Research Working Paper 6025). *World Bank.*

Deshpande, A. P. (2014). Application of the competency modelling approach: Determining the ideal profile of the Orthopaedic surgeons. *Procedia: Social and Behavioral Sciences*, *133*, 12–19. doi:10.1016/j.sbspro.2014.04.164

Di Liberto, A. (2008). Education and Italian regional development. *Economics of Education Review*, *27*(1), 94–107. doi:10.1016/j.econedurev.2006.08.004

Díaz-Fernández, M., Lopez-Cabrales, A., & Valle-Cabrera, R. (2014). A contingent approach to the role of human capital and competencies on firm strategy. *BRQ Business Research Quarterly*, *17*(3), 205–222. doi:10.1016/j.brq.2014.01.002

Dickmann, M., & Doherty, N. (2010). Exploring organizational and individual career goals, interactions, and outcomes of developmental international assignments. *Thunderbird International Business Review*, *52*(4), 313–324. doi:10.1002/tie.20353

Diller, J. (1999). A Social Conscience in the Global Marketplace? Labour Dimensions of Codes of Conduct, Social Labelling and Investor Initiatives. *International Labour Review*, *138*(2), 99–129. doi:10.1111/j.1564-913X.1999.tb00062.x

Dimitratos, P., Liouka, I., & Young, S. (2014). A missing operationalization: Entrepreneurial competencies in multinational enterprise subsidiaries. *Long Range Planning*, *47*(1–2), 64–75. doi:10.1016/j.lrp.2013.10.004

Dimov, D. P., & Shepherd, D. A. (2005). Human capital theory and venture capital firms, exploring home runs and strike outs. *Journal of Business Venturing*, *20*(1), 1–21. doi:10.1016/j.jbusvent.2003.12.007

Dinopoulos, E., & Segerstrom, P. (2010). Intellectual Property Rights, Multinational Firms, and Economic Growth. *Journal of Development Economics*, *92*(1), 13–27. doi:10.1016/j.jdeveco.2009.01.007

Disinvestment in PSBs in phased manner under consideration: FM Arun Jaitley. (2014, December 2). *The Economic Times.* Retrieved fromhttp://articles.economictimes.indiatimes.com/2014-12-02/news/56648934_1_psbs-lakh-crore-bank-capitalisation

Diving Into the Rich Pool. (2011, September 24). *The Economist.*

Donaldson, R. H. (2005). Green brands. *Greenleaf Publishing*, *24*(8), 14–17.

Doremus, P., Keller, W. W., Pauly, L. W., & Reich, S. (1998). *The Myth of the Global Corporation.* Princeton, N.J.: Princeton University Press.

Downs, A. (1964). *Inside Bureaucracy.* Boston: Little Brown.

Draganidis, F., & Mentzas, G. (2006). Competency based management: A review of systems and approaches. *Information Management & Computer Security*, *14*(1), 51–64. doi:10.1108/09685220610648373

Dspace. (n. d.). Retrieved from www.dspace.iimk.ac.in

Dubois, D. D. (1998). *The competency casebook: Twelve studies in competency-based performance improvement.* Amherst, MA: Human Resource Development Press.

Dutt, M. (2010). Development and HRD in India. IDEAS 20th Anniversary, Tokyo.

Eckel, C., & Egger, H. (2009). Wage bargaining and Multinational Firms. *Journal of International Economics*, *77*(2), 206–214. doi:10.1016/j.jinteco.2009.01.004

Education for All towards Quality and Equity. (2014). India, NUEPA, New Delhi

Educational Statistics at Glance -2014. (n. d.). Govt. of India, MHRD.

Eiling, E. (2013). Industry-specific human capital, idiosyncratic risk, and the cross-section of expected stock returns. *The Journal of Finance*, *68*(1), 43–84. doi:10.1111/j.1540-6261.2012.01794.x

Etzel, M. J., & Wahlers, R. G. (1985). The use of request promotional material by pleasure travelers. *Journal of Travel Research*, *23*(4), 2–6.

European Commission. (2009). Benchmark Measurement of European eGovernment services, 8th Benchmark Measurement. Retrieved from http://www.capgemini.com/sites/default/files/resource/pdf/Benchmark_Measurement_of_European_eGovernment_services.pdf

European Commission. (2010). *Digitizing Public Services in Europe: Putting ambition into action, 9th Benchmark Measurement. Report Prepared by Capgemini* , IDC, Sogeti, IS-Practice and Indigov, RAND Europe and the Danish Technological Institute for the Directorate General for Communications Networks, Content and Technology.

European Commission. (2013). *Public Services Online 'Digital by Default or by Detour? Assessing User Centric eGovernment performance in Europe – eGovernment Benchmark 2012. Report Prepared by Capgemini* , IDC, Sogeti, IS-Practice and Indigov, RAND Europe and the Danish Technological Institute for the Directorate General for Communications Networks, Content and Technology.

Evald, M. R., Klyver, K., & Christensen, P. R. (2011). The effect of human capital, social capital, and perceptual values on nascent entrepreneurs' export intentions. *Journal of International Entrepreneurship*, *9*(1), 1–19. doi:10.1007/s10843-010-0069-3

Evans, P., Pucik, V., & Barsoux, J. (2002). *The global challenge: Frameworks for international human resource management*. Boston, MA: McGraw–Hill.

Eyben, R., et al. (2008). *Conceptualizing empowerment and the implications for pro-poor growth*. Brighton, Institute of Development Studies, University of Sussex.

Faggian, A., & McCann, P. (2009). Human capital and regional development. In R. Capello & P. Nijkamp (Eds.), *Handbook of regional growth and development theories* (pp. 133–152). Cheltenham, UK: Edward Elgar. doi:10.4337/9781848445987.00015

Fang, Z. (2002). E-government in digital era: concept, practice, and development. International Journal of the Computer, the Internet and Management, 10(2), 1–22.

Farrell, B. J., Cobbin, D. M., & Farrell, H. M. (2002). Codes of Ethics: Their Evolution, Development and Other Controversies. *Journal of Management Development*, *21*(2), 152–163. doi:10.1108/02621710210417448

Fath-Allah, A., Cheikhi, L., Al-Qutaish, R. E., & Idri, A. (2014a). *E-Government Maturity Models: A Comparative Study.*

Fath-Allah, A., Cheikhi, L., Al-Qutaish, R. E., & Idri, A. (2014b). E-Government Portals Best Practices: A Comprehensive Survey.

Fath-Allah, A., Cheikhi, L., Al-Qutaish, R. E., & Idri, A. (2015). E-Government Portals' Maturity Models: A Best Practices' Coverage Perspective. *Journal of Software*. Retrieved from http://www.jsoftware.us

Fath-Allah, A., Cheikhi, L., Al-Qutaish, R. E., & Idri, A. (2014c). *Towards a Measurement-Based E-Government Portals Maturity Model.*

Feeny, D. F., & Willcocks, L. P. (1998). Core IS capabilities for exploiting information technology. *MIT Sloan Management Review*, *39*(3), 9–21.

Fellner, K. (2008). *Wrestling With Starbucks: Conscience, Capital, Cappuccino*. New Brunswick, N.J.: Rutgers University Press.

Fisher, C., & Lovell, A. (2009). *Business Ethics and Values: Individual, Corporate, and International Perspectives* (3rd ed.). Harlow: Pearson Education.

Fontana, M., Joekes, S., & Masika, R. (1998). Global Trade Expansion and Liberalization: Gender Issue and Impact (Bridge Report no. 42). Brighton, UK, IDS.

Fontana, M., & Wood, A. (2000). Modeling the Effects of Trade on Women, at Work and at Home. *World Development*, *28*(7), 1173–1190. doi:10.1016/S0305-750X(00)00033-4

Fontanills, G., & Cawood, R. (2009). *Trade Options Online*. Hoboken, NJ: John Wiley & Sons, Inc.

Forfás. (2008). *eGovernment: International Best Practices*. Retrieved from http://www.forfas.com/media/forfas080916_eGovernment.pdf

Forstater, M. (2006). Green Jobs: Public Service Employment and Environmental Sustainability. *Challenge*, *49*(4), 58–72. doi:10.2753/CHA0577-5132490405

Forsythe, N., Korzeniewicz, R. P., Majid, N., Weathers, G., & Durrant, V. (2003). *Gender inequalities, economic growth and economic reform: A preliminary longitudinal evaluation, No. 2003/45*. Geneva: International Labour Office.

Foss, G. F., Janken, J. K., Langford, D. R., & Patton, M. M. (2004). Using professional specialty competencies to guide course development. *The Journal of Nursing Education*, *43*(8), 368–375. PMID:15344373

Francis, David R. (1991, June). Prevent Trouble by Improving Ethics. *Christian Science Monitor*, p. 9.

Francis, J., & Dongcheol, K. (2013). *Modern Portfolio Theory: Foundations, Analysis, and New Developments*. Hoboken, NJ: John Wiley & Sons, Inc.

Frankel, J. A., & Rose, A. K. (2005). Is Trade Good or Bad for the Environment? Sorting out the Causality. *The Review of Economics and Statistics*, *87*(1), 85–91. doi:10.1162/0034653053327577

Freachtling, D. C. (1987). Five issues in tourism marketing in the 1990s. *Tourism Management*, *8*(2), 177–178. doi:10.1016/0261-5177(87)90030-6

Friedman, B. M. (2000). Decoupling at the Margin: The Threat to Monetary Policy from the Electronic Revolution in Banking. *International Finance*, *3*(2), 261–272. doi:10.1111/1468-2362.00051

G., G. (2001). Privatization in India. In G. G., *Privatization* (pp. 213-214). Delhi: Mittal Publications.

Gancia, G., & Bonfiglioli, A. (2008). North–South Trade and Directed Technical Change. *Journal of International Economics*, *76*(2), 276–295. doi:10.1016/j.jinteco.2008.03.010

Gandz, J., & Bird, F. G. (1989, Autumn). Designing Ethical Organizations. *Business Quarterly*, *54*(2), 108–112.

Geetha Rani, P. (2002). *Financing Higher Education in India in the Post Reform Period: Focus on Access and Equity*. New Delhi: National Institute of Educational Planning and Administration.

Genfan, H. (1987, November). Formalizing Business Ethics. *Training and Development Journal*, 1987, 35–37.

Georgescu, M., & Georgescu, I. (2008). Do We Need a Powerful E-Government. *Communications of the IBIMA*, 5.

Ghere, G., King, J. A., Stevahn, L., & Minnema, J. (2006). A professional development unit for reflecting on program evaluator competencies. *The American Journal of Evaluation*, *27*(1), 108–123. doi:10.1177/1098214005284974

Ghosh, S.K., & Maji, S.G. (2004). Utilization of Current Assets and Operating Profitability: An Empirical Study on Cement and Tea Industries in India. *Indian Journal of Accounting*, December, 52-55.

Ghosh, S., & Mastromarco, C. (2013). Cross-border economic activities, human capital and efficiency: A stochastic frontier analysis for OECD countries. *World Economy*, *36*(6), 761–785. doi:10.1111/twec.12010

Gill, S. (2000). Toward a Postmodern Prince? The Battle in Seattle as a Moment in the New Politics of Globalisation. *Millennium*, *29*(1), 131–140. doi:10.1177/03058298000290010101

Giordano, A., & Pagano, A. (2013). Brazil in the transition towards knowledge economy: Between qualification and internationalization of human capital. *Transition Studies Review*, *20*(1), 19–31. doi:10.1007/s11300-013-0267-5

Girma, S., Gong, Y., & Görg, H. (2009). What determines innovation activity in Chinese state-owned enterprises? The role of foreign direct investment. *World Development*, *37*(4), 866–873. doi:10.1016/j.worlddev.2008.07.017

Glaeser, E. L. (1994). Why does schooling generate economic growth? *Economics Letters*, *44*(3), 333–337. doi:10.1016/0165-1765(94)90020-5

Glaeser, E. L., & Resseger, M. G. (2010). The complementarity between cities and skills. *Journal of Regional Science*, *50*(1), 221–244. doi:10.1111/j.1467-9787.2009.00635.x

Glaeser, E. L., Scheinkman, J., & Shleifer, A. (1995). Economic growth in a cross-section of cities. *Journal of Monetary Economics*, *36*(1), 117–143. doi:10.1016/0304-3932(95)01206-2

Glass, A. J., & Wu, X. (2007). Intellectual Property Rights and Quality Improvement. *Journal of Development Economics*, *82*(2), 393–415. doi:10.1016/j.jdeveco.2005.08.002

Global Monitor entrepreneurship Report. (2012).Women's Report.

Goetz, S. J., & Hu, D. (1996). Economic growth and human capital accumulation: Simultaneity and expanded convergence tests. *Economics Letters*, *51*(3), 355–362. doi:10.1016/0165-1765(96)00827-0

Goldin, C. (2001). The human capital century and American leadership: Virtues of the past. *The Journal of Economic History*, *61*(2), 263–292. doi:10.1017/S0022050701028017

Gordon, K., & Miyake, M. (2001). Business Approaches to Combating Bribery: A Study of Codes of Conduct. *Journal of Business Ethics*, *34*(3/4), 161–173. doi:10.1023/A:1012517622479

Government to bring down stake in PSU banks to 52%. (2014, November 9). *The Economic Times*. Retrieved from [REMOVED HYPERLINK FIELD]http://articles.economictimes.indiatimes.com/2014-11-09/news/55917917_1_psu-banks-lakh-cror

Govt to bring down stake in PSU banks to 52%: Jaitley. (2014, November). *The Hindu Business Line*. Retrieved from [REMOVED HYPERLINK FIELD]http://www.thehindubusinessline.com/money-and-banking/govt-to-bring-down-stake-in-psu-banks-to-52-jaitley/article6580417.ece

Grace, D., & Cohen, S. (2013). *Business Ethics* (5th ed.). Oxford: Oxford University Press.

Graham, E. M., & Wilkie, C. (1994). Multinationals and the Investment Provisions of the NAFTA. *The International Trade Journal*, *8*(1), 9–38. doi:10.1080/08853909408523791

Graham, J., & Smart, C. (2012). *Introduction to Corporate Finance: What Companies Do*. Mason, OH: South-Western Cengage Learning.

Grant, J. (2012). The Kimberly Process at Ten: Reflections on a Decade of Efforts to End the Trade in Conflict Diamonds. In P. Lujala & S. A. Rustad (Eds.), *High-Value Natural Resources and Peacebuilding* (pp. 151–179). London: Earthscan Press.

Gray, R. (2001). *Social and Environmental Responsibility, Sustainability and Accountability, Can the Corporate Sector Deliver?* Glasgow, Centre for Social and Environmental Accounting Research, University of Glasgow. Retrieved from www.agenda-scotland.org/documents/ Can%20business%20deliver%20Gray.pdf

Greenwald, B., Kahn, J., Sonkin, P., & Van Biema, M. (2004). *Value Investing: From Graham to Buffett and Beyond.* Hoboken, NJ: John Wiley & Sons, Inc.

Guillen, M. F., & Garcia-Canal, E. (2009). The American model of the multinational firm and the "new" multinationals from emerging economies. *The Academy of Management Perspectives*, *23*(2), 23–35. doi:10.5465/AMP.2009.39985538

Guo, W., Xiao, H., & Yang, X. (2012). An empirical research on the correlation between human capital and career success of knowledge workers in enterprise. *Physics Procedia*, *25*, 715–725. doi:10.1016/j.phpro.2012.03.148

Gupta, A., & Govindarajan, V. (2002). Cultivating a global mindset. *The Academy of Management Executive*, *16*(1), 116–126. doi:10.5465/AME.2002.6640211

Hamel, G. (1994). The concept of core competence. In G. Hamel & A. Henee (Eds.), *Competence based competition* (pp. 11–33). Chichester, UK: John Wiley & Sons.

Hansen, A., & Machin, D. (2008). Visually Branding the Environment: Climate Change as Marketing Opportunities. *Discourse Studies*, *10*(6), 777–794. doi:10.1177/1461445608098200

Haque, A., Ismail, A. Z. H., & Daraz, A. H. (2009). Issues of E-Banking transaction: An Empirical Investigation on Malaysian Customers Perception. *Journal of Applied Sciences*, *9*(10), 1870–1879. doi:10.3923/jas.2009.1870.1879

Harbison, F., & Myers, C. A. (1964). *Education, Manpower and Economic Growth: Strategies of Human Resources Development*. USA: McGraw-Hill.

Harpan, I., & Draghici, A. (2014). Debate on the multilevel model of the human capital measurement. *Procedia: Social and Behavioral Sciences*, *124*, 170–177. doi:10.1016/j.sbspro.2014.02.474

Harris, C. M., Pattie, M. W., & McMahan, G. C. (2015). Advancement along a career path: The influence of human capital and performance. *Human Resource Management Journal*, *25*(1), 102–115. doi:10.1111/1748-8583.12047

Harris, K. J., Kacmar, K. M., & Carlson, D. S. (2006). An examination of temporal variables and relationship quality on promotability ratings. *Group & Organization Management*, *31*(6), 677–699. doi:10.1177/1059601106286889

Hart, C. M. (2005). *I Want to Make Money in the Stock Market: Learn to Begin Investing Without Losing Your Life Savings*. Denver: Outskirts Press.

Harvey, M. G., & Novicevic, M. M. (2005). The challenges associated with the capitalization of managerial skills and competencies. *International Journal of Human Resource Management*, *16*(8), 1374–1398. doi:10.1080/09585190500220424

Hayton, J. C., & McEvoy, G. M. (2006). Guest editors' note. *Human Resource Management*, *45*(3), 291–294. doi:10.1002/hrm.20127

Heitor, M., Horta, H., & Mendonça, J. (2014). Developing human capital and research capacity: Science policies promoting brain gain. *Technological Forecasting and Social Change*, *82*(1), 6–22. doi:10.1016/j.techfore.2013.07.008

Held, D. (2013). *Global Covenant: The Social Democratic Alternative to the Washington Consensus*. Cambridge: Polity Press.

Henderson, H. (2000). Life Beyond Global Economic Warfare. In J. N. Pieterse (Ed.), *Global Futures: Shaping Globalisation* (pp. 63–82). London: Zed.

Henion, K. E. (1976). *Ecological Marketing*. Grid Columbus Ohio.

Hervas-Oliver, J. L., Sempere-Ripoll, F., & Boronat-Moll, C. (2014). Process innovation strategy in SMEs, organizational innovation and performance: A misleading debate? *Small Business Economics*, *43*(4), 873–886. doi:10.1007/s11187-014-9567-3

Hevey, D. (1997). The UK National (and Scottish) vocational qualification system: State of the art or in a state? *International Journal of Training and Development*, *1*(4), 242–258. doi:10.1111/1468-2419.00024

Higón, D. A., Antolín, M. M., & Manez, J. A. (2011). Multinationals, R&D, and productivity: Evidence for UK manufacturing firms. *Industrial and Corporate Change*, *20*(2), 641–659. doi:10.1093/icc/dtr007

Hitt, M. A., Bierman, L., Shimizu, K., & Kochhar, R. (2001). Direct and moderating effects of human capital on strategy and performance in professional service firms: A resource-based perspective. *Academy of Management Journal*, *44*(1), 13–29. doi:10.2307/3069334

Hobson, J. M., & Ramesh, M. (2002). Globalisation Makes of States What States Make of It: Between Agency and Structure in the State/Globalisation Debate. *New Political Economy*, *7*(1), 5–22. doi:10.1080/13563460120115499

Hobson, R. (2012). *The Dividend Investor: A Practical Guide To Building A Share Portfolio Designed To Maximise Income*. Hampshire: Harriman House Ltd.

Hong, Q., & Smart, M. (2010). In Praise of Tax Havens: International Tax Planning and Foreign Direct Investment. *European Economic Review*, *54*(1), 82–95. doi:10.1016/j.euroecorev.2009.06.006

Honjo, Y., Kato, M., & Okamuro, H. (2014). R&D investment of start-up firms: Does founders' human capital matter? *Small Business Economics*, *42*(2), 207–220. doi:10.1007/s11187-013-9476-x

Hopkins, M. (2003). *The Planetary Bargain – CSR Matters*. London: Earthscan.

Hsieh, S. I., & Hsu, L. L. (2013). An outcome-based evaluation of nursing competency of baccalaureate senior nursing students in Taiwan. *Nurse Education Today*, *33*(12), 1536–1545. doi:10.1016/j.nedt.2013.01.012 PMID:23428366

Huang, L., & Hsien-T, T. (2002). *The effects of electronic commerce on business management of travel agencies* [PhD Thesis]. Nation Chung San University.

Hughes, R. E. (2003). Skill or diploma? The potential influence of skill-based pay systems on sources of skills acquisition and degree programs. *Work Study*, *52*(4), 179–183. doi:10.1108/00438020310479018

Hunter, L. W., Bernhardt, A., Hughes, K. L., & Skuratowicz, E. (2001). It's not just the ATMs: Technology, firm strategies, jobs and earnings in retail banking. *Industrial & Labor Relations Review*, *54*(2), 402–424. doi:10.1177/001979390105400222

Huselid, M. A. (1995). The impact of human resource management practices on turnover, productivity, and corporate financial performance. *Academy of Management Journal*, *38*(3), 635–672. doi:10.2307/256741

Hussinger, K. (2010). On the importance of technological relatedness: SMEs versus large acquisition targets. *Technovation*, *30*(1), 57–64. doi:10.1016/j.technovation.2009.07.006

Incredible India. (n. d.). Retrieved from www.incredibleindia.org

India Greenhouse Emissions. (2007). Ministry of Environment and Forest, Government of India.

India Tourism. (n. d.). Retrieved from www.tourism.nic.in

Indian industry sees green shoots of manufacturing growth. (2014, August 11). Retrieved from http://articles.economictimes.indiatimes.com/2014-08-11/news/52687142_1_green-shoots-ficci-survey-april-june-quarter

Indian Institute of Banking and Finance. (2009). *Risk Management* (2nd Ed). New Delhi: McMillan India Ltd.

Intagliata, J., Ulrich, D., & Smallwood, N. (2000). Leveraging leadership competencies to produce leadership brand: Creating distinctiveness by focusing on strategy and results. *Human Resource Planning*, *23*(3), 12–23.

International Labour Organisation. (2013) *Codes of Conduct for Multinationals*. Retrieved from http://www.itcilo.it/english/actrav/telearn/global/ilo/guide/main.htm

International Labour Organisation. (2013). *Statistical Information and Monitoring Programme on Child Labour (2013)*. Retrieved from http://www.ilo.org/public/english/standards/ipec/simpoc/index.htm

Iranzo, S., & Peri, G. (2009). Schooling externalities, technology, and productivity: Theory and evidence from U.S. states. *The Review of Economics and Statistics*, *91*(2), 420–431. doi:10.1162/rest.91.2.420

Iribarren, M., Concha, G., Valdes, G., Solar, M., Villarroel, M. T., Gutiérrez, P., & Vásquez, Á. (2008). Capability maturity framework for eGovernment: A multi-dimensional model and assessing tool. In *Electronic Government* (pp. 136–147). Springer. Retrieved from http://link.springer.com/chapter/10.1007/978-3-540-85204-9_12

Islam, M. A., Khan, M. A., Obaidullah, A. Z. M., & Alam, M. S. (2011). Effect of Entrepreneur and Firm Characteristics on the Business: Success of Small and Medium Enterprises (SMEs) in Bangladesh. *International Journal of Business and Management*, *6*(3), 289–299.

Iyer, K. C., & Jha, K. N. (2006). Critical factors affecting schedule performance: Evidence from Indian construction projects. *Journal of Construction Engineering and Management*, *132*(8), 871–881. doi:10.1061/(ASCE)0733-9364(2006)132:8(871)

Jackson, S. E., & Schuler, R. S. (1995). Understanding human resource management in the context of organizations and their environments. *Annual Review of Psychology*, *46*(1), 237–264. doi:10.1146/annurev.ps.46.020195.001321 PMID:19245335

Jeffcott, B., & Yanz, L. (2013). Voluntary Codes of Conduct: Do They Strengthen or Undermine Government Regulation and Worker Organising? *Maquila Solidarity Network*. Retrieved from http://www.maquilasolidarity.org/resources/codes/volcodes99.htm

Jenkins, R. (2001). Corporate Codes of Conduct: Self Regulation in a Global Economy. *Technology, Business and Programme Paper # 2*, UNRISD. Retrieved from http://www.natural-resources.org/minerals/CD/docs/other/jenkins.pdf

Jenkins, R. (2013). *Transnational Corporations and Uneven Development: The Internalization of Capital and the Third World*. London: Routledge Press.

Judge, T., Thoresen, C., Pucik, V., & Welbourne, T. (1999). Managerial coping with organizational change: A dispositional perspective. *The Journal of Applied Psychology*, *92*(1), 107–127. doi:10.1037/0021-9010.84.1.107 PMID:17227155

Kabanoff, B., & Brown, S. (2008). Knowledge structures of prospector, analyzers, and defenders: Content, structure, stability, and performance. *Strategic Management Journal*, *29*(2), 149–171. doi:10.1002/smj.644

Karna, J., Hansen, E., & Juslin, H. (2003). Social Responsibility in Environmental Marketing Planning. *European Journal of Marketing*, *37*(5/6), 848–873. doi:10.1108/03090560310465170

Kar, S., Roberts, M. A., & Ali, E. (2013). *Human Development in the New Millennium*. New Delhi: Regal Publications.

Kasemsap, K. (2014a). Strategic innovation management: An integrative framework and causal model of knowledge management, strategic orientation, organizational innovation, and organizational performance. In P. Ordóñez de Pablos & R. Tennyson (Eds.), *Strategic approaches for human capital management and development in a turbulent economy* (pp. 102–116). Hershey, PA, USA: IGI Global. doi:10.4018/978-1-4666-4530-1.ch007

Kasemsap, K. (2014b). The role of knowledge sharing on organisational innovation: An integrated framework. In L. Al-Hakim & C. Jin (Eds.), *Quality innovation: Knowledge, theory, and practices* (pp. 247–271). Hershey, PA, USA: IGI Global. doi:10.4018/978-1-4666-4769-5.ch012

Kasemsap, K. (2015a). Developing a framework of human resource management, organizational learning, knowledge management capability, and organizational performance. In P. Ordoñez de Pablos, L. Turró, R. Tennyson, & J. Zhao (Eds.), *Knowledge management for competitive advantage during economic crisis* (pp. 164–193). Hershey, PA, USA: IGI Global. doi:10.4018/978-1-4666-6457-9.ch010

Kasemsap, K. (2015b). The role of data mining for business intelligence in knowledge management. In A. Azevedo & M. Santos (Eds.), *Integration of data mining in business intelligence systems* (pp. 12–33). Hershey, PA, USA: IGI Global. doi:10.4018/978-1-4666-6477-7.ch002

Kato, M., Okamuro, H., & Honjo, Y. (2015). Does founders' human capital matter for innovation? Evidence from Japanese start-ups. *Journal of Small Business Management*, *53*(1), 114–128. doi:10.1111/jsbm.12094

Kaul, R. N. (1985). *Dynamics of Tourism*. New Delhi: Starling Publishers.

Kayes, D. C., Kayes, A. B., & Yamazaki, Y. (2005). Essential competencies for cross-cultural knowledge absorption. *Journal of Managerial Psychology*, *20*(7), 578–589. doi:10.1108/02683940510623399

Kearsley, A., & Riddel, M. (2010). A Further Inquiry into the Pollution Haven Hypothesis and the Environmental Kuznets Curve. *Ecological Economics*, *69*(4), 905–919. doi:10.1016/j.ecolecon.2009.11.014

Khan, M. Y., & Jain, P. K. (2007). *Financial Management*. New Delhi: Tata McGraw-Hill Publishing Company Limited.

Khatick, S. K., & Singh, P. K. (2003). Liquidity Management in Eicher Ltd. – A Case Study. *The Management Accountant*, *38*(3), 217–220.

Kim, D.-Y., & Grant, G. (2010). E-government maturity model using the capability maturity model integration. *Journal of Systems and Information Technology*, *12*(3), 230–244. doi:10.1108/13287261011070858

Kimmel, J. (2009). *The MAGNET Method of Investing: Find, Trade, and Profit from Exceptional Stocks*. Hoboken, NJ: John Wiley & Sons, Inc.

Kim, T. (2015). Impacts of learning interventions on organizational human capital and performance. *Performance Improvement Quarterly*, *27*(4), 7–28. doi:10.1002/piq.21180

King, P., & Terbert, H. (2011). BASEL III: An Overview. Banking & Financial Services. *Policy Reports*, *30*(5), 1.

Kinoshita, Y., & Campos, N. F. (2003). Why Does FDI Go Where it Goes? New Evidence from the Transitional Economies (Working Paper). International Monetary Fund Press, Washington, D.C..

Klischewski, R., & Askar, E. (2010). Success factors of developing G2G services: the case of Egypt. *Proceedings of the 4th International Conference on Theory and Practice of Electronic Governance* (pp. 152–160). Retrieved from http://dl.acm.org/citation.cfm?id=1930354

Kotler, P. H., Armstrong, G., Saunders, J., & Wong, V. (2003). *Rinkodaros Principai*. Kaunas.

Kotler, P., Brown, J., & Makens, J. (2002). *Marketing for Hospitality and Tourism*. Delhi: Pearson Education.

Kotler, P., & Keller, K. L. (2013). *Marketing Management* (14th ed.). Delhi: Pearson.

Koziol, L., Koziol, W., Wojtowicz, A., & Pyrek, R. (2014). An outline of a compensation system based on human capital theory. *Procedia: Social and Behavioral Sciences*, *148*, 551–558. doi:10.1016/j.sbspro.2014.07.078

Krammer, S. M. S. (2010). International R&D spillovers in emerging markets: The impact of trade and foreign direct investment. *The Journal of International Trade & Economic Development*, *19*(4), 591–623. doi:10.1080/09638190902792464

Krantz, M. (2013). *Investing Online for Dummies*. Hoboken, NJ: John Wiley & Sons.

Kreng, V. B., & Huang, M. (2009). A discussion on international assignments performance and the constructing mechanism of career success development. *International Journal of Human Resource Management*, *20*(7), 1487–1502. doi:10.1080/09585190902983330

Kropp, D. W Erhard, Dr. Suran S. B.2002Linking Banks and (Financial) Self help Groups in India- An Assessment Paper presented at the Seminar on SHG-bank Linkage Programme at New Delhi on 25th and 26th November.

Kumar, V., Mukerji, B., Butt, I., & Persaud, A. (2007). Factors for successful e-government adoption: A conceptual framework. *Electronic Journal of E-Government*, *5*(1), 63–76.

Kumpf, S. (2013). *Listed Private Equity: Investment Strategies and Returns*. Hamburg, Germany: Diplomica Verlag GmbH.

Kürschner, M. (2008). *Limitations of the Capital Asset Pricing Model (CAPM)*. Norderstedt: GRIN Verlag.

Kwon, S., Wadholm, R. R., & Carmody, L. E. (2014). Assessing competencies: An evaluation of ASTD's Certified Professional in Learning and Performance (CPLP) designation. *Evaluation and Program Planning*, *44*, 48–58. doi:10.1016/j.evalprogplan.2014.01.002 PMID:24565949

LaDuke, S. (2002). Ethical issues in pain management. *Critical Care Nursing Clinics of North America*, *14*(2), 165–170. doi:10.1016/S0899-5885(01)00006-5 PMID:12038502

Lan, J., Kakinaka, M., & Huang, X. (2012). Foreign direct investment, human capital and environmental pollution in China. *Environmental and Resource Economics*, *51*(2), 255–275. doi:10.1007/s10640-011-9498-2

Lan, J., & Munro, A. (2013). Environmental compliance and human capital: Evidence from Chinese industrial firms. *Resource and Energy Economics*, *35*(4), 534–557. doi:10.1016/j.reseneeco.2013.05.003

Laopodis, N. (2013). *Understanding Investments: Theories and Strategies*. New York, NY: Routledge.

Lassar, P., Lambert, L., Woodford, C., & Moschovitis, C. J. P. (2005). *The Internet: A historical encyclopedia*. Santa Barbara, Calif: ABC-CLIO.

Lawler, E. E. I. (1994). From job-based to competency-based organizations. *Journal of Organizational Behavior*, *15*(1), 3–15. doi:10.1002/job.4030150103

Layne, K., & Lee, J. (2001). Developing fully functional E-government: A four stage model. *Government Information Quarterly*, *18*(2), 122–136. doi:10.1016/S0740-624X(01)00066-1

Lee, G., & Kwak, Y. H. (2012). *An Open Government Maturity Model for social media-based public engagement*. Government Information Quarterly. Retrieved from http://www.sciencedirect.com/science/article/pii/S0740624X1200086X

Legrain, P. (2002). *Open World: The Truth About Globalisation*. London: Abacus Press.

Leonard-Barton, D. A. (1992). Core capabilities and core rigidities: A paradox in managing new product development. *Strategic Management Journal*, *13*(S1), 111–125. doi:10.1002/smj.4250131009

Lepak, D. P., & Snell, S. A. (1999). The human resource architecture: Toward a theory of human allocation and development. *Academy of Management Review*, *24*(1), 31–48. doi: 10.2307/259035

Levinson, A., & Taylor, M. S. (2008). Unmasking the Pollution Haven Effect. *International Economic Review*, *49*(1), 223–254. doi:10.1111/j.1468-2354.2008.00478.x

Liao, S., Shao, Y. P., Wang, H., & Chen, A. (1999). The Adoption of Virtual Banking: An Empirical Study. *PERGAMON International Journal of Information Management*, *19*(1), 63–74. doi:10.1016/S0268-4012(98)00047-4

Libbee, M. (2001). Assessment as a diagnostic tool. *The Journal of Geography*, *100*(4), 175–178. doi:10.1080/00221340108978437

Li, H., Liu, Q., Li, B., Fraumeni, B., & Zhang, X. (2014). Human capital estimates in China: New panel data 1985–2010. *China Economic Review*, *30*(C), 397–418. doi:10.1016/j.chieco.2014.07.006

Lindberg, K., Wood, M.E., & Engeldrum, D. (1999). *Ecotourism a Guide for Planner and Managers* (Vol. 2). Dehradun: Natraj Publishers.

Lindberg, K. (1993). *Hawkins, D.E. Ecotourism: A Guide for Planners and Managers* (Vol. 1). North Bennington, VT: The Ecotourism Society.

Ling, F. Y. Y., & Ma, Y. (2014). Effect of competency and communication on project outcomes in cities in China. *Habitat International*, *44*, 324–331. doi:10.1016/j.habitatint.2014.07.002

Lin, J. Y. (2014). Effects on diversity of R&D sources and human capital on industrial performance. *Technological Forecasting and Social Change*, *85*(1), 168–184. doi:10.1016/j.techfore.2013.08.010

Lin, S. C., Kim, D. H., & Wu, Y. C. (2013). Foreign direct investment and income inequality: Human capital matters. *Journal of Regional Science*, *53*(5), 874–896. doi:10.1111/jors.12077

Lipsey, R. E. (2010). Measuring The Location Of Production In A World Of Intangible Productive Assets, FDI, And Intrafirm Trade. *Review of Income and Wealth. International Association for Research in Income and Wealth*, *56*(s1), S99–S110. doi:10.1111/j.1475-4991.2010.00385.x

Loewen, J. B. (2008). *Money Magnet: How to Attract Investors to Your Business*. Mississauga, ON: John Wiley & Sons Canada, Ltd.

Long, C. S. (2013). Success factors of human resource profession in Malaysia: A quantitative study. *New Horizons in Adult Education and Human Resource Development*, *25*(2), 49–61. doi:10.1002/nha.20016

Lucas, R. Jr. (1988). On the mechanics of economic development. *Journal of Monetary Economics*, *22*(1), 3–42. doi:10.1016/0304-3932(88)90168-7

Lundan, S. M. (2004). Multinationals, NGOs and Regulation: Greenpeace and the Global Phase-Out of Chlorine Bleaching. In S. M. Lundan (Ed.), Multinationals, Environment and Global Competition (pp.147– 170). Oxford: JAI (Elsevier) Press.

Maassen, G. F. (1999). *An International Comparison of Corporate Governance Models: A Study on the Formal independence and Convergence of One-Tier and Two-Tier Corporate Boards of Directors in the United States of America, the United Kingdom and the Netherlands. Ph.D. Series in General Management, Nr. 31*. N.L.: Rotterdam School of Management.

Madsen, P., & Shafritz, J. M. (Eds.), (1990). Essentials of Business Ethics. New York: Penguin Books.

Maeda, M. (2009). *The Complete Guide to Investing in Bonds and Bond Funds: How to Earn High Rates of Return-Safely*. Ocala, Fla: Atlantic Publishing Group, Inc.

Magliolo, J. (2005). *Become Your Own Stockbroker: A Practical Guide to Trading in South Africa*. Cape Town, South Africa: Zebra Press.

Mah, J. S. (2010). Foreign direct investment inflows and economic growth: The case of Korea. *Review of Development Economics*, *14*(4), 726–735. doi:10.1111/j.1467-9361.2010.00584.x

Makolm, J. (2002). Best practice in e-government. In *Electronic Government* (pp. 370–374). Springer. Retrieved from http://link.springer.com/chapter/10.1007/978-3-540-46138-8_60

Mallik, A. K., & Sur, D. (1998). Working Capital and Profitability: A Case Study in Interrelation. The Management Accountant, November, 805-809.

Malviya, S. (2005). Tourism, Environment and the Society (pp. 62-72). Delhi: Isha Books.

Manderson, E., & Kneller, R. (2012). Environmental Regulations, Outward FDI and Heterogeneous Firms: Are Countries Used as Pollution Havens? *Environmental and Resource Economics*, *51*(3), 317–352. doi:10.1007/s10640-011-9500-z

Mansfield, R. S. (1996). Building competency models: Approaches for HR professionals. *Human Resource Management*, *35*(1), 7–18. doi:10.1002/(SICI)1099-050X(199621)35:1<7::AID-HRM1>3.0.CO;2-2

Mareş, R. (2004). *Business and Human Rights: a Compilation of Documents (Vol. 13)*. Leiden: Martinus Nijhoff Publishers.

Margetts, H. Z., John, P., Escher, T., & Reissfelder, S. (2011). Social Information and Political Participation on the Internet: An Experiment. *European Political Science Review*, *3*(3), 321–344. doi:10.1017/S1755773911000129

Marina, K. (2009). *Reference in the E-Banking*. Cairo: Publisher of the Universities.

Marrelli, A. F. (1998). An introduction to competency analysis and modeling. *Performance Improvement*, *37*(5), 8–17. doi:10.1002/pfi.4140370505

Marshall, A. (1930). *Principles of Economics* (8th ed.). London: Macmillan & Co. Ltd.

Martin, B. C., McNally, J. J., & Kay, M. J. (2013). Examining the formation of human capital in entrepreneurship: A meta-analysis of entrepreneurship education outcomes. *Journal of Business Venturing*, *28*(2), 211–224. doi:10.1016/j.jbusvent.2012.03.002

Masters, J. K., & Miles, G. (2002). Predicting the use of external labor arrangements: A test of the transaction costs perspective. *Academy of Management Journal*, *45*(2), 431–442. doi:10.2307/3069357

Matten, D., & Crane, A. (2005). Corporate Citizenship: Toward an Extended Theoretical Conceptualization. *Academy of Management Review*, *30*(1), 166–179. doi:10.5465/AMR.2005.15281448

Maznevski, M. L., & DiStefano, J. J. (2000). Global leaders are team players: Developing global leaders through membership on global teams. *Human Resource Management*, *39*(2–3), 195–208. doi:10.1002/1099-050X(200022/23)39:2/3<195::AID-HRM9>3.0.CO;2-I

McCleary, K. W. (1987). A framework for national tourism marketing. *International of Hospitality Management*, *6*(3), 169–175. doi:10.1016/0278-4319(87)90051-X

McClintock, B. (1999). The Multinational Corporation and Social Justice: Experiments in Supranational Governance. *Review of Social Economy*, *57*(4), 507–522. doi:10.1080/00346769900000019

McDaniel, S W., David H. R (1993). Strategic Green Marketing. *Journal of Consumer Marketing*, 10(3), 4-10.

Mendenhall, M. E., & Oddou, G. (1985). The dimensions of expatriate acculturation: A review. *Academy of Management Review*, *10*(1), 39–47. doi: 10.2307/258210

Mendenhall, M. E., & Stahl, G. K. (2000). Expatriate training and development: Where do we go from here? *Human Resource Management*, *39*(2–3), 251–265. doi:10.1002/1099-050X(200022/23)39:2/3<251::AID-HRM13>3.0.CO;2-I

Mengistu, A. A., & Adhikary, B. K. (2011). Does good governance matter for FDI inflows? Evidence from Asian economies. *Asia Pacific Business Review*, *17*(3), 281–299. doi:10.1080/13602381003755765

Mezias, J. M., & Scandura, T. A. (2005). A needs-driven approach to expatriate adjustment and career development: A multiple mentoring perspective. *Journal of International Business Studies*, *36*(5), 519–538. doi:10.1057/palgrave.jibs.8400159

Middleton, V., & Clarke, J. (2001). *Marketing in Travel and Tourism* (3rd ed.). Roshester, Kent: MPG Books Ltd., Bodmin.

Mihaly, E. B. (1999). Multinational Companies and Wages in Low-Income Countries. *Journal of Small & Emerging Business Law*, *3*(1), 1–26.

Miles, R., & Snow, C. C. (1978). *Organizational strategy, structure and process*. New York, NY: McGraw–Hill.

Millennium development goals. (2014). UN.

Mirabile, R. J. (1997). Everything you wanted to know about competency modeling. *Training & Development*, *51*(8), 73–77.

Mishra, D. (2002). Privatization A Global Perspective. In *Disinvestment* (p. 73). Delhi: Vikas Publishing House.

Moav, O., & Neeman, Z. (2012). Saving rates and poverty: The role of conspicuous consumption and human capital. *The Economic Journal*, *122*(563), 933–956. doi:10.1111/j.1468-0297.2012.02516.x

Möller, K., Gamerschlag, R., & Guenther, F. (2011). Determinants and effects of human capital reporting and controlling. *Journal of Management Control*, *22*(3), 311–333. doi:10.1007/s00187-011-0138-3

Morena, E. (2013). The French *Confédération Paysanne* (CP) as Anti-Capitalist 'Peasant' Movement. In C. F. Fominaya & L. Cox (Eds.), *Understanding European Movements: New Social Movements, Global Justice Struggles, Anti-Austerity Protest* (pp. 94–108). London: Routledge Press.

Morris, M. H., Webb, J. W., Fu, J., & Singhal, S. (2013). A competency-based perspective on entrepreneurship education: Conceptual and empirical insights. *Journal of Small Business Management*, *51*(3), 352–369. doi:10.1111/jsbm.12023

Morrison, A., Raju, D., & Sinha, N. (2007). Gender Equality, Poverty and Economic Growth (Policy Research Working Paper No. WPS4349). Washington DC, World Bank.

Mudambi, R., Mudambi, S., & Navarra, P. (2007). Global Innovation in MNCs: The Effect of Subsidiary Innovation and Teamwork. *Journal of Product Innovation Management*, *24*(5), 442–455. doi:10.1111/j.1540-5885.2007.00262.x

N.A.O. (2002). Government on the Web II. Retrieved from http://www.nao.org.uk/publications/0102/government_on_the_web_ii.aspx

NABARD (2011-12), SHG2: Revisiting the SHG Bank Linkage Programme,Mumbai, NABARD .

NABARD (2013-14), Status of Microfinance 2013-14.Mumbai, NABARD .

Nagraj. (1999). Disinvestment and Privatization in India: Assessment and Options. *Indira Gandhi Institute of Development Research.* Mumbai.

Nahapiet, J., & Goshal, S. (1998). Social capital, intellectual capital, and the organizational advantage. *Academy of Management Review*, *23*(2), 242–266. doi: 10.2307/259373

National Rural Livelihood Mission 2015

Nigam, D. (2002). Tourism Environment and development of Garhwal Himalaya (pp. 43-48). New Delhi: Mittal Publications.

Nigam, S. C. (2002). Ecotourism and Sustainable Development (pp. 1-2). New Delhi: Rajat Publications.

Nigel, M. (2003). *Advertising in Tourism and Leisure: British Library Cataloguing in of National Advertiser*. New York Publication.

Noorbakhsh, F., Paloni, A., & Youssef, A. (2001). Human capital and FDI inflows to developing countries: New empirical evidence. *World Development*, *29*(9), 1593–1610. doi:10.1016/S0305-750X(01)00054-7

Northcott, A. (2009). *The Mutual Funds Book: How to Invest in Mutual Funds and earn High Rates of Returns Safely*. Ocala, FL: Atlantic Publishing *Group*.

O'Sullivan, L. (1999). The distinction between stable and dynamic cross-cultural competencies: Implications for expatriate trainability. *Journal of International Business Studies*, *30*(4), 709–725. doi:10.1057/palgrave.jibs.8490835

O'Connell, J., Gardner, G., & Coyer, F. (2014). Beyond competencies: Using a capability framework in developing practice standards for advanced practice nursing. *Journal of Advanced Nursing*, *70*(12), 2728–2735. doi:10.1111/jan.12475 PMID:25109608

Oddou, G., Mendenhall, M. E., & Ritchie, J. B. (2000). Leveraging travel as a tool for global leadership development. *Human Resource Management*, *39*(2–3), 159–172. doi:10.1002/1099-050X(200022/23)39:2/3<159::AID-HRM6>3.0.CO;2-J

O'Donnell, G. (1978). Reflections on the Patterns of Change in the Bureaucratic Authoritarian State. *Latin American Research Review*, *13*(1), 3–38.

O'Donohue, W., & Nelson, L. (2009). The Role of Ethical Values in an Expanded Psychological Contract. *Journal of Business Ethics*, *90*(2), 251–263. doi:10.1007/s10551-009-0040-1

Official Website: Corporate Social Responsibility Initiatives. (2013). Starbucks Coffee Company. Retrieved from http://www.starbucks.com/aboutus/csr.asp

Okali, C. (2011). *Integrating Social Difference, Gender and Social Analysis into Agricultural Development*. Brighton, UK: Future Agricultures.

Olfert, M. R., Jelinski, M., Zikos, D., & Campbell, J. (2012). Human capital drift up the urban hierarchy: Veterinarians in Western Canada. *The Annals of Regional Science*, *49*(2), 551–570. doi:10.1007/s00168-011-0448-2

Ordonez, B. (2014). Competency-based education: Changing the traditional college degree power, policy, and practice. *New Horizons in Adult Education and Human Resource Development*, *26*(4), 47–53. doi:10.1002/nha3.20085

Osana, H. P., & Seymour, J. R. (2004). Critical thinking in preservice teachers: A rubric for evaluating argumentation and statistical reasoning. *Educational Research and Evaluation*, *10*(4–6), 473–498. doi:10.1080/13803610512331383529

Ottman, J. A. (2011). *The New Rules of Green Marketing, Strategies, Tools, and Inspiration for Sustainable Branding*. U.K.: Greenleaf Publishing.

Ozuru, H. N., Chikwe, J. E., & Idika, U. (2010). The Use of Traditional Payments And Electronic Payments Systems in Nigeria: A Discourse.*Proceedings of the 11th Annual Conference of International Academy of African Business and Development*.

Pablo-Romero, M. P., & Gómez-Calero, M. P. (2013). A translog production function for the Spanish provinces: Impact of the human and physical capital in economic growth. *Economic Modelling*, *32*, 77–87. doi:10.1016/j.econmod.2013.01.040

Page, S. J. (2009). *Tourism Management and Managing Change* (3rd ed.). Elsevier Ltd.

Palacios-Marques, D., Gil-Pechuán, I., & Lim, S. (2011). Improving human capital through knowledge management practices in knowledge-intensive business services. *Service Business*, *5*(2), 99–112. doi:10.1007/s11628-011-0104-z

Pal, U. (2002). Identifying the path to successful green manufacturing. *Journal of the Minerals Metals & Materials Society*, *54*(5), 25. doi:10.1007/BF02701691

Pande, R. (2007). Gender, Poverty and Globalization in India. *Development*, *50*(2), 134–140. doi:10.1057/palgrave.development.1100367

Papadomichelaki, X., & Mentzas, G. (2012). e-GovQual: A multiple-item scale for assessing e-government service quality. *Government Information Quarterly*, *29*(1), 98–109. doi:10.1016/j.giq.2011.08.011

Pardo, R. (2008). *The Evaluation and Optimization of Trading Strategies*. Hoboken, NJ: John Wiley & Sons, Inc.

Payne, A. (2010). How many Gs are there in 'Global Governance' After the Crisis? The Perspectives of the 'Marginal Majority' of the World's States. *International Affairs*, *86*(3), 729–740. doi:10.1111/j.1468-2346.2010.00908.x

Pearson, R., & Seyfang, G. (2001). New Hope or False Dawn: Voluntary Codes of Conduct, Labour Regulation and Social Policy in a Globalising World. *Global Social Policy*, *1*(1), 48–78. doi:10.1177/146801810100100104

Peattie, K., & Crane, A. (2005). Green Marketing: Legend, Myth, Farce or Prophesy? *Qualitative Market Research: An International Journal*, *8*(4), 357–370. doi:10.1108/13522750510619733

Pehrsson, A. (2004). Strategy competence: A successful approach to international market entry. *Management Decision*, *42*(6), 758–768. doi:10.1108/00251740410542320

Peng, M. W., Sun, S. L., & Markóczy, L. (2015). Human capital and CEO compensation during institutional transitions. *Journal of Management Studies*, *52*(1), 117–147.

Pennings, J. M., Lee, K., & van Witteloostuijn, A. (1998). Human capital, social capital and firm dissolution. *Academy of Management Journal*, *41*(4), 425–440. doi:10.2307/257082

Peters, R. M., Janssen, M., & van Engers, T. M. (2004). Measuring e-government impact: existing practices and shortcomings. *Proceedings of the 6th international conference on Electronic commerce* (pp. 480–489). Retrieved from http://dl.acm.org/citation.cfm?id=1052281

Plain Language Action and Information Network (PLAIN). (2014). What is Plain Language? Retrieved from http://www.plainlanguage.gov/whatisPL/

Ployhart, R. E., & Moliterno, T. P. (2011). Emergence of the human capital resource: A multilevel model. *Academy of Management Review*, *36*(1), 127–150. doi:10.5465/AMR.2011.55662569

Ployhart, R. E., Weekley, J. A., & Baughman, K. (2006). The structure and function of human capital emergence: A multilevel examination of the attraction–selection–attrition model. *Academy of Management Journal*, *49*(4), 661–677. doi:10.5465/AMJ.2006.22083023

Pollak, A. (2013). Growth and convergence when technology and human capital are complements. *Economic Inquiry*, *51*(1), 31–45. doi:10.1111/j.1465-7295.2012.00454.x

Popham, W. J. (1997). What's wrong – and what's right – with rubrics. *Educational Leadership*, *55(2)*, 72–75. doi: 17239567

Porter, M. E. (1980). *Competitive strategy: Techniques for analyzing industries and competitors*. New York, NY: Free Press.

Posch, K. C., Posch, R., Tauber, A., Zefferer, T., & Zwattendorfer, B. (2011). Secure and Privacy-Preserving eGovernment—Best Practice Austria. In Rainbow of computer science (pp. 259–269). Springer; Retrieved from http://link.springer.com/chapter/10.1007/978-3-642-19391-0_19 doi:10.1007/978-3-642-19391-0_19

Pozzi, F., Bottino, R. M., & Persico, D. (2014). Enhancing human capital in TEL research: A case study from the STELLAR Network of Excellence. *Computers in Human Behavior*, *31*, 425–431. doi:10.1016/j.chb.2013.10.062

Prahalad, C. K. (2009). *The Fortune at the Bottom of the Pyramid, Revised and Updated 5th Anniversary Edition: Eradicating Poverty Through Profits*. New Jersey: Wharton School Publishing.

Prahalad, C. K., & Hamel, G. (1990). The core competence of the corporation. *Harvard Business Review*, *68*(3), 79–91.

Prothero, A. (1998). Green Marketing: The 'Fad' That Won't Slip Slide Away. *Journal of Marketing Management*, *14*(6), 507–513. doi:10.1362/026725798784867680

Prothero, A., & Fitchett, J. A. (2000). Greening Capitalism: Opportunities for Green Community. *Journal of Macromarketing*, *20*(1), 46–56. doi:10.1177/0276146700201005

Qadri, F., & Waheed, A. (2014). Human capital and economic growth: A macroeconomic model for Pakistan. *Economic Modelling*, *42*, 66–76. doi:10.1016/j.econmod.2014.05.021

Racela, O. C. (2014). Customer orientation, innovation competencies, and firm performance: A proposed conceptual model. *Procedia: Social and Behavioral Sciences*, *148*, 16–23. doi:10.1016/j.sbspro.2014.07.010

Rajeev, D. (2005, July 26). *Business World*.

Randriamano, Z. (2006). *Gender and trade: overview report, Bridge Report, Institute of development Studies. OCDE (2011). Women economic empowerment », Issues Paper, June 2011; OCDE and DAC Network on Gender Equality*. GENDERNET.

Rangarajan, C. (2008, January). Report of the committee on financial inclusion. *GOI*.

Ray, N., & Das, D. K. (2011). 3Hs Tourism, an Alternative Approach of Developing Tourism at Bishnupur: An Empirical Study. *South Asian Journal of Tourism and Heritage*, *4*(2).

Ray, N., Das, D. K., Sengupta, P., & Ghosh, S. (2012). Tourism and its Impact on Socio- Economic Condition: Evidence from West Bengal, India *Global. Journal of Business Research*, *6*(2).

Raynard, P., & Forstater, M. (2002). *Corporate Social Responsibility: Implications for Small and Medium Enterprises in Developing Countries*. United Nations Industrial Development Organization.

Ren, Y., Yuan, Y., & Zhang, Y. (2014). Human capital, household capital and asset returns. *Journal of Banking & Finance*, *42*, 11–22. doi:10.1016/j.jbankfin.2014.01.028

Research on India: Waste Management. (2009, August).

Rigby, D., & Zook, C. (2002). Open market innovation. *Harvard Business Review*, *80*(10), 80–89. PMID:12389463

Roberts, L., & Derek, H. (2004). Consuming the country side: Marketing for tourism. *Journal of Vacation Marketing*, *10*(3), 253–263. doi:10.1177/135676670401000305

Robinson, K. C., & McDougall, P. P. (2001). Entry barriers and new venture performance: A comparison of universal and contingency approaches. *Strategic Management Journal*, *22*(6–7), 659–685. doi:10.1002/smj.186

Rodríguez, R. A., Welicki, L., Giulianelli, D. A., & Vera, P. M. (2008). Measurement framework for evaluating e-governance on municipalities' websites. Proceedings of the 2nd international conference on Theory and practice of electronic governance (pp. 381–387). Retrieved from http://dl.acm.org/citation.cfm?id=1509176

Rodriguez-Dominguez, L., Gallego-Alvarez, I., & Garcia-Sanchez, I. M. (2009). Corporate Governance and Codes of Ethics. *Journal of Business Ethics*, *90*(2), 187–202. doi:10.1007/s10551-009-0035-y

Rodriguez, P., Patel, R., Bright, A., Gregory, D., & Gowing, M. (2002). Developing competency models to promote integrated HR practices. *Human Resource Management*, *41*(3), 309–324. doi:10.1002/hrm.10043

Rohleder, S. J., & Jupp, V. (2004). eGovernment leadership: High performance, maximum value. Accenture.

Rosell-Martinez, J., & Sanchez-Sellero, P. (2012). Foreign direct investment and technical progress in Spanish manufacturing. *Applied Economics*, *44*(19), 2473–2489. doi:10.1080/00036846.2011.564155

Rowley, J. (1998). Promotion and marketing communication in the information market place. *Journal of Library Review*, *47*(8), 383–387. doi:10.1108/00242539810239543

Rugman, A. M., & Verbeke, A. (2001). Subsidiary-specific advantages in multinational enterprises. *Strategic Management Journal*, *22*(3), 237–250. doi:10.1002/smj.153

Rugman, A. M., Verbeke, A., & Nguyen, Q. T. K. (2011). Fifty years of international business theory and beyond. *Management International Review*, *51*(6), 755–786. doi:10.1007/s11575-011-0102-3

Rychen, D. S. (2001). Introduction. In D. S. Rychen & L. H. Salganik (Eds.), *Defining and selecting key competencies* (pp. 1–15). Seattle, WA: Hogrefe and Huber.

Salvato, C., & Rerup, C. (2011). Beyond collective entities: Multilevel research on organizational routines and capabilities. *Journal of Management*, *37*(2), 468–490. doi:10.1177/0149206310371691

Salvendy, G. (2012). *Handbook of Human Factors and Ergonomics* (4th ed.). New Jersey: John Wiley and Sons. doi:10.1002/9781118131350

Sanjay, K.Jain & Gurmeet Kaur. (2004). Green Marketing: An Attitudinal and Behavioural *Analysis of Indian Consumers, Global. Business Review (Federal Reserve Bank of Philadelphia)*, *5*(2), 187–205.

Santarelli, E., & Tran, H. T. (2013). The interplay of human and social capital in shaping entrepreneurial performance: The case of Vietnam. *Small Business Economics*, *40*(2), 435–458. doi:10.1007/s11187-012-9427-y

Sarkar, J. B., & Saha, S. N. (1987). Profitability Crisis & Working Capital Management in the Public Sector in India: A Case Study.The Management Accountant, May, 328-333.

Sarlak, M. A., & Astiani, A. A. (2011). *E-banking and emerging multidisciplinary processes: Social, economical, and organizational models*. Hershey, PA, USA: IGI Global. doi:10.4018/978-1-61520-635-3

Schildt, H., Maula, M. V. J., & Keil, T. (2005). Explorative and exploitative learning from external corporate ventures. *Entrepreneurship Theory and Practice*, *29*(4), 493–515. doi:10.1111/j.1540-6520.2005.00095.x

Schlitte, F. (2012). Local human capital, segregation by skill, and skill-specific employment growth. *Papers in Regional Science*, *91*(1), 85–106. doi:10.1111/j.1435-5957.2011.00373.x

Schmidt, F. L., & Hunter, J. E. (1998). The validity and utility of selection methods in personnel psychology: Practical and theoretical implications of 85 years of research findings. *Psychological Bulletin*, *124*(2), 262–274. doi:10.1037/0033-2909.124.2.262

Schrage, E. J. (2004, January). *Promoting Worker Rights through Private Voluntary Initiatives: Public Relations or Public Policy? A Report to the US Department of State*. Retrieved from http://www.uichr.org/content/act/sponsored/gwri/report.pdf

Schulz, E., Chowdhury, S., & Van de Voort, D. (2013). Firm productivity moderated link between human capital and compensation: The significance of task-specific human capital. *Human Resource Management*, *52*(3), 423–439. doi:10.1002/hrm.21537

Schwartz, R. A. (2010). *Micro Markets: A Market Structure Approach to Microeconomic Analysis*. Hoboken, NJ: John Wiley & Sons, Inc. doi:10.1002/9781118268131

Seguino, S. (2006). The great equalizer: Globalization effects on gender equality in Latin America and the Caribbean (MPRA Paper No. 6509). Retrieved from http://mpra.ub.uni-muenchen.de/6509

Seifert, J. W., & McLoughlin, G. J. (2007). State e-government strategies: Identifying best practices and applications. Retrieved from http://oai.dtic.mil/oai/oai?verb=getRecord&metadataPrefix=html&identifier=ADA471212

Şener, F. (2006). *Intellectual Property Rights and Rent Protection in a North-South Product-Cycle Model. Manuscript*. Schenectady: Union College Press.

Sethi, S. P. (2003). *Setting Global Standards: Guidelines for Creating Codes of Conduct in Multinational Corporations*. Hoboken, N.J.: John Wiley & Sons.

Shaffer, M., Harrison, D., Gregersen, H., Black, J., & Ferzandi, L. (2006). You can take it with you: Individual differences and expatriate effectiveness. *The Journal of Applied Psychology*, *91*(1), 109–125. doi:10.1037/0021-9010.91.1.109 PMID:16435942

Shapiro, J. M. (2006). Smart cities: Quality of life, productivity, and the growth effects of human capital. *The Review of Economics and Statistics*, *88*(2), 324–335. doi:10.1162/rest.88.2.324

Sharma (2000), *Tourism Education Principle, Theories, Practices*. New Delhi: Kanishka Publisher.

Sharma, D. (2009). *Human Resource Development in Schools*. New Delhi: APH Publishing.

Sherer, P. D. (1995). Leveraging human assets in law firms: Human capital structures and organizational capabilities. *Industrial & Labor Relations Review*, *48*(4), 671–691. doi:10.1177/001979399504800405

Shin, H., Sok, S., Hyun, K. S., & Kim, M. J. (2015). Competency and an active learning program in undergraduate nursing education. *Journal of Advanced Nursing*, *71*(3), 591–598. doi:10.1111/jan.12564 PMID:25384709

Shultz, T. P. (2005). *Does the Liberalization of Trade Advance Gender Equality in Schooling and Health?* (Working Papers). Economic Growth Center, Yale University.

Siau, K., & Long, Y. (2005). Synthesizing e-government stage models–a meta-synthesis based on meta-ethnography approach. *Industrial Management & Data Systems*, *105*(4), 443–458. doi:10.1108/02635570510592352

Sigmund, P. E. (1974). The "Invisible Blockade" and the Overthrow of Allende. *Foreign Affairs*, *52*(2), 322–340. doi:10.2307/20038052

Simon, C. J. (2004). Industrial reallocation across US cities, 1977–1997. *Journal of Urban Economics*, *56*(1), 119–143. doi:10.1016/j.jue.2004.03.005

Simon, C. J., & Nardinelli, C. (2002). Human capital and the rise of American cities, 1900–1990. *Regional Science and Urban Economics*, *32*(1), 59–96. doi:10.1016/S0166-0462(00)00069-7

Sims, R. R. (1991). Institutionalization of Organizational Ethics. *Journal of Business Ethics, 10*(7), 493–506. doi:10.1007/BF00383348

Sindell, K. (2005). *Investing Online For Dummies*. Hoboken, NJ: Wiley Publishing Inc.

Smit, R., & Birri, T. (2014). Assuring the quality of standards-oriented classroom assessment with rubrics for complex competencies. *Studies in Educational Evaluation, 43*, 5–13. doi:10.1016/j.stueduc.2014.02.002

Snell, C. C., Youndt, M. A., & Wright, P. M. (1996). Establishing a framework for research in strategic human resource management: Merging resource theory and organizational learning. In G. R. Ferris (Ed.), *Research in personnel and human resource management* (pp. 61–90). Greenwich, CT: JAI Press.

Somers, M. J. (2001). Ethical Codes of Conduct and Organizational Context: A Study of the Relationship between Codes of Conduct, Employee Behaviour and Organizational Value. *Journal of Business Ethics, 30*(2), 185–195. doi:10.1023/A:1006457810654

Song, M., Nason, R. W., & Di Benedetto, C. A. (2008). Distinctive marketing and information technology capabilities and strategic types: A cross-national investigation. *Journal of International Marketing, 16*(1), 4–38. doi:10.1509/jimk.16.1.4

Soosay, C. A. (2005). An empirical study of individual competencies in distribution centers to enable continuous innovation. *Creativity and Innovation Management, 14*(3), 299–310. doi:10.1111/j.1467-8691.2005.00348.x

Sørum, H. (2011). An empirical investigation of user involvement, website quality and perceived user satisfaction in eGovernment environments. In Electronic Government and the Information Systems Perspective (pp. 122–134). Springer. Retrieved from http://link.springer.com/chapter/10.1007/978-3-642-22961-9_10 doi:10.1007/978-3-642-22961-9_10

Spar, D. L. (1998). The Spotlight and the Bottom Line: How Multinationals Export Human Rights. *Foreign Affairs, 77*(2), 7–12. doi:10.2307/20048784

Spencer, L. M., & Spencer, S. M. (1993). *Competence at work: Models for superior performance*. New York, NY: John Wiley & Sons.

Srikanth, R. (2013, September). A Study on - Financial Inclusion - Role of Indian Banks in Reaching Out to Unbanked and Backward Areas. *International Journal of Applied Research and Studies*, 2(9).

Stark, O., & Dorn, A. (2013). International migration, human capital formation, and saving. *Economics Letters, 118*(3), 411–414. doi:10.1016/j.econlet.2012.11.032

Stern, D. I. (2004). The Rise and Fall of the Environmental Kuznets Curve. *World Development, 32*(8), 1419–1439. doi:10.1016/j.worlddev.2004.03.004

Stevahn, L., King, J. A., Ghere, G., & Minnema, J. (2005). Establishing essential competencies for program evaluators. *The American Journal of Evaluation, 26*(1), 43–59. doi:10.1177/1098214004273180

Stevenson, H. H., & Jarillo, J. C. (1990). A paradigm of entrepreneurship: Entrepreneurial management. *Strategic Management Journal, 11*(4), 17–27.

Stohl, C., Stohl, M., & Popova, L. (2009). A New Generation of Corporate Codes of Ethics. *Journal of Business Ethics, 90*(4), 607–622. doi:10.1007/s10551-009-0064-6

Stotsky, J. G. (2006). *Gender and its Relevance to Macroeconomic Policy: A Survey (No. WP/06/233)*. Washington: Fiscal Affairs Department, International Monetary Fund.

Strong, R. (2009). *Portfolio Construction, Management, and Protection*. Ohio: South-Western Cengage Learning.

Subbiah, N. (2014). Role of banks in financial inclusion. *Research Journal of Commerce and Behavioural Science*, 1(4).

Subramaniam, M., & Youndt, M. (2005). The influence of intellectual capital on the types of innovative capabilities. *Academy of Management Journal*, *48*(3), 450–463. doi:10.5465/AMJ.2005.17407911

Succar, B., Sher, W., & Williams, A. (2013). An integrated approach to BIM competency assessment, acquisition and application. *Automation in Construction*, *35*, 174–189. doi:10.1016/j.autcon.2013.05.016

Sue, B. (2004). Tourism in Australia–Has the gaze altered? Tracking images through film and tourism promotion. *International Journal of Tourism Research*, *6*(3), 125–135. doi:10.1002/jtr.479

Sur, D., & Chakraborty, K. (2010). Efficiency of Working Capital Management in Indian Corporate Sector: An Empirical Analysis in the Post-liberalisation Era. *GITAM Journal of Management*, *8*(3), 119–138.

Sur, D., & Chakraborty, K. (2011). Evaluating Relationship of Working Capital and Profitability: A Study of Select Multinational Companies in the Indian Pharmaceutical Sector. *The IUP Journal of Management Research*, *X*(2), 7–22.

Sur, D., Chakraborty, K., & Das, S. (2007). Measuring Efficiency of Asset Management of Private Sector Enterprises in India during the Pre- and Post- liberalization Periods: A Study on Colgate-Palmolive (India) Ltd. *The Icfaian Journal of Management Research*, *6*(7), 25–36.

Survey Report of the Committee on Medium-term Path on Financial Inclusion (Year 2013-2014). (2014). Reserve Bank of India.

Svensson, G., Wood, G., & Callaghan, M. (2010). A Comparison of Business Ethics Commitment in Private and Public Sector Organizations in Sweden. *Business Ethics (Oxford, England)*, *19*(2), 213–232. doi:10.1111/j.1467-8608.2010.01585.x

Talaulicar, T. (2009). Barriers Against Globalizing Corporate Ethics: An Analysis of Legal Disputes on Implementing U.S. Codes of Ethics in Germany. *Journal of Business Ethics*, *84*(3), 349–360. doi:10.1007/s10551-009-0199-5

Tano, S. (2014). Regional clustering of human capital: School grades and migration of university graduates. *The Annals of Regional Science*, *52*(2), 561–581. doi:10.1007/s00168-014-0599-z

Tarapore.S.S (Composer). (1998). Speech. [D. G. RBI, Performer] India.

Tarzi, S. M. (2002). International Norms, Trade, and Human Rights: A Perspective on Norm Conformity. *The Journal of Social, Political, and Economic Studies*, *27*(2), 187–202.

Teece, D. J., Pisano, G., & Shuen, A. (1997). Dynamic capabilities and strategic management. *Strategic Management Journal*, *18*(7), 509–533. doi:10.1002/(SICI)1097-0266(199708)18:7<509::AID-SMJ882>3.0.CO;2-Z

Teixeira, A. A. C., & Fortuna, N. (2010). Human capital, R&D, trade, and long-run productivity. Testing the technological absorption hypothesis for the Portuguese economy, 1960–2001. *Research Policy*, *39*(3), 335–350. doi:10.1016/j.respol.2010.01.009

Teixeira, A. A. C., & Tavares-Lehmann, A. T. (2014). Human capital intensity in technology-based firms located in Portugal: Does foreign ownership matter? *Research Policy*, *43*(4), 737–748. doi:10.1016/j.respol.2014.01.001

Thai Labour Campaign. (2013). *Can Corporations Promote Labour Standards? Evidence from the Thai Footwear and Apparel Industry*. Retrieved from http://www.thailabour.org/docs/CodesReport

The European Centre for Total Quality Management. (2002, July). E-Government A Best Practice Perspective.

Thompson, T. (1991, Spring). Managing Business Ethics. *Canadian Public Administration*, *34*(1), 153–157. doi:10.1111/j.1754-7121.1991.tb01449.x

Toffler, B. (1991, Winter). Doing Ethics: An Approach to Business Ethics Consulting. *Moral Education Forum*, 16(4), 14-20.

Tomohara, A., & Yokota, K. (2011). Foreign direct investment and wage inequality: Is skill upgrading the culprit? *Applied Economics Letters*, *18*(8), 773–781. doi:10.1080/13504851.2010.491448

Trichet, F., & Leclère, M. (2003). A framework for building competency-based systems dedicated to human resource management. In N. Zhong, Z. Ras, S. Tsumoto, & E. Suzuki (Eds.), *Foundations of intelligent systems* (pp. 633–639). Heidelberg, Germany: Springer–Verlag.

Tyagi, R. S. (2011). *Academic Supervision in Secondary Schools: School-Based Approach for Quality Management.* New Delhi: NUEPA.

Tzeremes, N. G. (2014). The effect of human capital on countries' economic efficiency. *Economics Letters*, *124*(1), 127–131. doi:10.1016/j.econlet.2014.05.006

Ulrich, D., & Lake, D. (1991). Organizational capability: Creating a competitive advantage. *The Academy of Management Executive*, *5*(1), 77–92. doi:10.5465/AME.1991.4274728

UNCTAD. (2009). Mainstreaming gender in trade policy. Note by the UNCTAD secretariat TD/B/C.I/EM.2/2/Rev.1. Retrieved from http://www.unctad.org/en/docs/ciem2d2_en.pd

UNDESA. (2012). UN E-Government Survey 2012: E-Government for the People (United Nations). New York, United States. Retrieved from http://unpan1.un.org/intradoc/groups/public/documents/un/unpan048065.pdf

United Nations. (2008). Main Features Reviewed by the United Nations e-Government Survey. Retrieved from http://unpan1.un.org/intradoc/groups/public/documents/un/unpan029361.pdf

United Nations. (2012). Compendium of Innovative E-government Practices (Vol. IV). UN. Retrieved from http://books.google.com/books?hl=en&lr=&id=tX83tuHyv7AC&oi=fnd&pg=PA3&dq=Compendium+of+Innovative+E-government+Practices&ots=9nBmYhcl8r&sig=vxiObuDH_rwak-FkYYLxVZ1FS3g

Vandeveer, M., & Norton, B. (2005). From teaching to learning: Theoretical foundations. In D. Billings & J. Halstead (Eds.), *Teaching in nursing* (pp. 259–261). Philadelphia, PA: Saunders/Elsevier.

Verdin, P. J., & Williamson, P. J. (1994). Core competencies, competitive advantages and market analysis: Forging the links. In G. Hamel & A. Henee (Eds.), *Competence based competition* (pp. 77–110). Chichester, UK: John Wiley & Sons.

Vijayakumar, A., & Venkatachalam, A. (1995). Working Capital and Profitability- An Empirical Analysis.The Management Accountant, June, 748-750.

Virkar, S. (forthcoming). The Globalisation of the Media: Towards Cultural Homogeneity? In J. M. Alcántara-Pilar, S. del Barrio-García, E. Crespo-Almedros, & L. Porcu (Eds.), Analyzing the Cultural Diversity of Consumers in the Global Marketplace. Hershey, PA, USA: IGI Global.

Vitkienë, E. (1998). Paslaugø rinkodaros organizacinë sistema ir jos valdymas. In *Ekonomika ir vadyba-98* (pp. 454–458). Kaunas: Technologija.

Vogelsong, H. (2001). *Assessing the Economic Impact of Ecotourism Developments on the Albermarle/Pamlico Region.* Retrieved from www.cabi.org

Voges, K. E., & Pope, N. (2006). Business Applications and Computational Intelligence. Hershey, PA, USA: IGI Global. doi:10.4018/978-1-59140-702-7

W3C. (2012). Web Content Accessibility Guidelines. Retrieved from http://www.w3.org/WAI/intro/wcag

Wagner, U., & Timmins, C. D. (2009). Agglomeration Effects in Foreign Direct Investment and the Pollution Haven Hypothesis. *Environmental and Resource Economics*, *43*(2), 231–256. doi:10.1007/s10640-008-9236-6

Walker Orville, C., Boyd, H. W., Jmullins, J., & Larreche, C. (2001). *Marketing Strategy, translated by A. Rabi and Izadi*. Teheran: Cultural Research Bureau.

Wang, E. C. (2010). Determinants of R&D investment: The Extreme-Bounds-Analysis approach applied to 26 OECD countries. *Research Policy*, *39*(1), 103–116. doi:10.1016/j.respol.2009.11.010

Wang, H., Choi, J., & Li, J. (2008). Too Little or Too Much? Untangling the Relationship Between Corporate Philanthropy and Firm Financial Performance. *Organization Science*, *19*(1), 143–159. doi:10.1287/orsc.1070.0271

Wang, K. J., & Lestari, Y. D. (2013). Firm competencies on market entry success: Evidence from a high-tech industry in an emerging market. *Journal of Business Research*, *66*(12), 2444–2450. doi:10.1016/j.jbusres.2013.05.033

Ward, N.K. (1997). *Ecotourism: Reality or Rhetoric*. Retrieved from www.planeta.com

Wellin, P. R., Gaylord, R. J., & Kamin, S. N. (2005). *An Introduction to Programming with Mathematica*.Cambridge, MA: Cambridge University Press. doi:10.1017/CBO9780511801303

Wernerfelt, B. (1984). A resource based view of the firm. *Strategic Management Journal*, *5*(2), 171–180. doi:10.1002/smj.4250050207

West, D. M. (2007). Global e-government, 2007. United States: Center for Public Policy, Brown University; Retrieved from http://195.130.87.21:8080/dspace/handle/123456789/1028

West, D.M., & Deitch, A. (2004). Development of e-government strategies in Chile, Canada and Brazil. Retrieved from http://portal.oas.org/LinkClick.aspx?fileticket=UbyGRpAaPhY%3d&tabid=1168

West, D. M. (2004). E-Government and the Transformation of Service Delivery and Citizen Attitudes. *Public Administration Review*, *64*(1), 15–27. doi:10.1111/j.1540-6210.2004.00343.x

Williamson, D. G. (2006). Enhanced authentication in online banking. *Journal of Economic Crime Management*, *4*, 1–42.

Williamson, O. E. (1975). *Markets and hierarchies: Analysis and antitrust implications*. New York, NY: Free Press.

Windley, P. J. (2002). eGovernment maturity. USA: Windleys' Technolometria. Retrieved from http://www.windley.com/docs/eGovernment%20Maturity.pdf

Winston, M. E. (1999). Human rights and International Political Economy in Third World Nations: Multinational Corporations, Foreign Aid, and Repression. *Human Rights Quarterly*, *21*(3), 824–830. doi:10.1353/hrq.1999.0036

Winters, J. V. (2013). Human capital externalities and employment differences across metropolitan areas of the USA. *Journal of Economic Geography*, *13*(5), 799–822. doi:10.1093/jeg/lbs046

Women survey on the role of women in development 2014: gender equality and sustainable development. (2014). UN-Women, New York.

Woodside, A. G. & Jacobe. (1985). Steps two in benefit segmentation: Learning the benefits realized by major travel market. *Journal of Travel Research*, *26*(1), 2–7.

Woodside, A. G., & Motes, W. H. (1981). Sensitivity of market segments to separate advertising strategies. *Journal of Marketing*, *45*(1), 63–73. doi:10.2307/1251721

Worasinchai, L., & Bechina, A. A. A. (2010). The Role of Multinational Corporations (MNCs) in Developing R & D in Thailand: The Knowledge Flow Between MNCs and University. *Electronic Journal of Knowledge Management*, *8*(1), 171–180.

World Bank. (2005). Designing and Implementing e-Government: Key Issues, Best Practices and Lessons Learned. Retrieved from http://siteresources.worldbank.org/INTEDEVELOPMENT/Resources/559323-1114798035525/Workshop_Summary.pdf

World Bank. (2007). *Gender working towards greater equality, Gender equality as smart economics: A World Bank group action plan*. Washington, DC: World Bank.

World Bank. (2008). Global Financial Crisis and Implications for Developing Countries. Paper for G-20 Finance Ministers' Meeting, São Paulo, Brazil.

World Bank. (2011). Definition of E-Government. Retrieved from http://web.worldbank.org/WBSITE/EXTERNAL/TOPICS/EXTINFORMATIONANDCOMMUNICATIONANDTECHNOLOGIES/EXTEGOVERNMENT/0,contentMDK:20507153~menuPK:702592~pagePK:148956~piPK:216618~theSitePK:702586,00.html

Wright, P. M., & McMahan, G. C. (1992). Theoretical perspectives for strategic human resource management. *Journal of Management*, *18*(2), 295–320. doi:10.1177/014920639201800205

Wright, P. M., & McMahan, G. C. (2011). Exploring human capital: Putting 'human' back into strategic human resource management. *Human Resource Management Journal*, *21*(2), 93–104. doi:10.1111/j.1748-8583.2010.00165.x

Xu, M. X., Wikes, S., & Shah, M. H. (2006). E-Banking Application and Issues. In *Abbey National PLC. E-Technologies. Encyclopedia of E-Commerce, E-Government, and Mobile Commerce*. Hershey, PA, USA: IGI Global. doi:10.4018/978-1-59140-799-7.ch042

Yan, A., Guorong, Z., & Hall, D. T. (2002). International assignments for career building: A model of agency relationships and psychological contracts. *Academy of Management Review*, *27*(3), 373–391. doi: 10.5465/AMR.2002.7389910

Yanagihara, M., & Lu, C. (2013). Cash-in-advance constraint, optimal monetary policy, and human capital accumulation. *Research in Economics*, *67*(3), 278–288. doi:10.1016/j.rie.2013.06.001

Youndt, M. A., Subramaniam, M., & Snell, S. A. (2004). Intellectual capital profiles: An examination of investments and returns. *Journal of Management Studies*, *41*(2), 335–361. doi:10.1111/j.1467-6486.2004.00435.x

Young, S., & Tavares, A. T. (2004). Multilateral rules on FDI. Do we need them? Will we get them? A developing country perspective. *Transnational Corporations*, *13*(1), 1–30.

Yusuf, M. A., & Alam, Q. (2011). Empowering Role of the Village Phone Program in Bangladesh: In Retrospect, in Prospect. *Journal of Information Technology Impact*, *11*(1), 35–50.

Zadek, S. (2004). The Path to Corporate Responsibility. *Harvard Business Review*, *82*(12), 125–132. PMID:15605571

Zarutskie, R. (2010). The role of top management team human capital in venture capital markets: Evidence from first-time funds. *Journal of Business Venturing*, *25*(1), 155–172. doi:10.1016/j.jbusvent.2008.05.008

Zeithaml, V. A. (1988). Consumer perceptions of price, quality, and value: Ameans-end model and synthesis of evidence. *Journal of Marketing*, *52*(3), 2–22. doi:10.2307/1251446

Zingheim, P. K., & Schuster, J. R. (2003). Competencies and rewards: Substance or just style? *Compensation and Benefits Review*, *35*(5), 40–44. doi:10.1177/0886368703256932

# About the Contributors

**Saurabh Sen** was born to a traditional Indian middle class Bengali family in the oldest living city of the world, Varanasi (Kashi), on 25th October, 1978. He completed his Higher Secondary from a government school of the city. Dr. Sen, has always been inquisitive for rationales behind events in commercial world that led him to choose Commerce as his stream of education. After having acquired a Master's in Commerce with a specialization in Accounts and Finance his appetite for knowledge and excellence drove him to research. By virtue of his sincere effort and hard work he was awarded a Doctor of Philosophy of Commerce (PhD) by Banaras Hindu University (BHU). Dr. Sen has authored many research papers and articles in many reputed journals of national and international stature. He has also been participating in and presenting research papers in many national and international seminars and conferences. He is a life member of the Indian Accounting Association and the foundering member of its Varanasi Chamber. Dr. Sen is in the editorial board of two national journals of Commerce and Management where he imparts his thoughts and vision in the fields of Accounts and Finance. Dr. Sen was also nominated for a Bharat Jyoti award by the India International Friendship Society of New Delhi, during April 2013. He has been teaching Accounts and Finance for last eight years at Sunbeam College for Women, Varanasi.

**Anshuman Bhattacharya** secured his education from institutions of the city itself. Being a child of academic family, it was quite natural that he would be inborn studious; he has proved it correct. He earned all his degrees in the first division. Anshuman has been a student of Banaras Hindu University; and acquired his Doctorate in Commerce from the same university. Dr. Bhattacharya has contributed many research articles to number of renowned journals and has presented his scholarly research to national and international conferences and seminars. Presently, his academic intellect is devoted to Sunbeam College for Women; a reputed degree college of Varanasi and the state.

**Ruchi Sen**, a synonym of academic excellence, has always secured first division in all examinations that she has taken; obtaining second rank in the university merit list in Graduation added one more feather to her hat. Her inborn academic interest drove her to research and brought Doctor of Philosophy of Commerce (PhD) from Banaras Hindu University (BHU) to her. She has been teaching for the last seven years in Sunbeam College for Women, an affiliated institution to Mahatma Gandhi Kashi Vidyapith, Varanasi. Dr. Ruchi has been a devotee of intense study. Her intellectual literary works are published in journals of national and international repute; Dr. (Mrs) Sen has also authored a book on Business Statistics. She has been pro-active to attend and present her research papers in national and international seminars and conferences.

***

**Shruti Agrawal** is a research scholar from Banaras Hindu University. She is currently completing research for the faculty of commerce. Her topic for research is the 'role of microfinance institutions in empowering weaker sections in India--a case study.'

**Rafa E. Al-Qutaish** is an Associate Professor at École de Technologie Supérieure (ÉTS), University of Québec, Canada. He received a B.Sc. in Computer Science and a M.Sc. in Software Engineering degrees in 1993 and 1998, respectively. Also, he received a Ph.D. degree in Software Engineering from the School of Higher Technology (ÉTS), University of Québec, Canada in 2007. His research interests are in software measurement, software product quality, software engineering standardization, reverse engineering, software comprehension and maintenance, and compiler construction. Dr. Al-Qutaish is a senior member of the IEEE & IEEE-CS, and also a senior member of the IACSIT.

**Rafael Hernandez Barros** is a professor of Corporate Finance at the Universidad Complutense. His recent research work has been published in The Journal of Business Economics and Management, The Geneva Papers on Risk and Insurance or The Operational Risk Journal, among others. Rafael received his PhD in Finance from Universidad Autónoma de Madrid and earned his MBA at the IESE Business School. He has extensive practical experience in front and back office senior management roles in the insurance industry.

**Laila Cheikhi** is a Professor in the Computer Science and Systems Analysis School of ENSIAS, Rabat, Morocco. She received a M.Sc. (2004) from the University of Montréal and a Ph.D. (2008) from ETS, University of Quebec at Montreal, both in software engineering. She has over eight years of experience in computer engineering for the Ministry of Finance of Morocco. Her research interests include software quality models, software metrics, software engineering ISO standards, software product and process quality, software engineering principles, and data analysis.

**Dillip Kumar Das** is currently working as an Asst. Professor in the Department of Tourism, The University of Burdwan. He has been awarded a PhD in the year 2008 in Tourism from Utkal University, Bhubaneswar, Orissa, on the topic "Economic, Socio Cultural and Environmental Impact of Tourism: A case Study on Puri, Konark and Bhubaneswar". He has completed a Master's in Tourism Management (MTM) from IGNOU, and also twice Qualified UGC- NET (National Eligibility test for Lectureship) in December 2003 and in 2004. He has completed a master's degree in Economics, from Ravenshaw University, Cuttack, and also completed a diploma in Tourism Management, from the Indian Institute of Tourism and Travel Management, Bhubaneswar, Orissa. His areas of research interest are in ecotourism, tourism impact studies and travel agency management. He has altogether 15 years of academic experience in tourism education. Dillip is now currently associated with many different universities and institutes of repute in India, including: I.G.N.O.U, IITTM, Magadh University, Utkal University, etc.

**Abdoullah Fath-Allah** holds a bachelor degree in computer science (2005) and a master degree in computer networks with a minor in software engineering (2007) from Alakhawayn University in Ifrane, Morocco (AUI). Abdoullah has an 8 years' experience in industry, and he is an e-HR portals' consultant. He is currently a PhD student at ENSIAS (Morocco).

**Shishir Kumar Gujrati** is presently working as an assistant manager for the Union Bank of India at the regional office in Varanasi since 2012. Prior to that he worked as a lecturer in School of Management Sciences, Varanasi for about a year. He completed his PhD in 2011 from BHU. His professional qualification includes CAIIB & the AMFI-Mutual Fund exam.

**Ali Idri** is a Professor at Computer Science and Systems Analysis School (ENSIAS, Rabat, Morocco). He received a DEA (Master's 1994) and Doctorate of 3rd Cycle (1997) degrees in computer science, both from the University Mohamed V of Rabat. He has received his Ph.D. (2003) in cognitive computer sciences from ETS, University of Quebec at Montreal. His research interests include software cost estimation, software metrics, data mining, and ehealt.

**Kijpokin Kasemsap** received his BEng degree in Mechanical Engineering from King Mongkut's University of Technology Thonburi, his MBA degree from Ramkhamhaeng University, and his DBA degree in Human Resource Management from Suan Sunandha Rajabhat University. He is a Special Lecturer of the Faculty of Management Sciences, Suan Sunandha Rajabhat University, based in Bangkok, Thailand. He is a Member of the International Association of Engineers (IAENG), the International Association of Engineers and Scientists (IAEST), the International Economics Development and Research Center (IEDRC), the International Association of Computer Science and Information Technology (IACSIT), the International Foundation for Research and Development (IFRD), and the International Innovative Scientific and Research Organization (IISRO). He also serves on the International Advisory Committee (IAC) for the International Association of Academicians and Researchers (INAAR). He has numerous original research articles in top international journals, conference proceedings, and book chapters on the subjects of business management, human resource management, and knowledge management published internationally.

**jihène Malek** is a doctor in economics, graduated from the University of economic science and management, Tunis El Manar. She is writer for think-tanks, researcher, and expert with international networks.

**Rakesh Kumar Pandey** is an assistant professor at the United College of Engineering Research (UCER). He has immense knowledge in the field of research. He has participated in many national and international-level research papers and case studies. He has also attended many workshops on various management subjects. He has gained all his education from various renowned institutions, like schooling from St. Joseph's School, a BBA in IB with a Bachelor's Degree from Veer Bahadur Singh Purvanchal University (Jaunpur) and a MBA in Marketing and Human Resources with a Master's Degree from Mahamaya Technical University (Noida) along with all these qualifications he has a rich experience in the field of Customer delight process by working with Yebhi.com online shopping site for one year in Delhi. He has expertise and vibrant knowledge in marketing subjects. He has a very crisp knowledge and command over his subject. Workshop on (Brand Positioning) at XLRI Jamshedpur. Presented National research paper (Role of Nutritionist in Health Management) at Sunder Deep Collage of Hotel Management Ghaziabad. Presented and second runner up National Case Study competition (Success Story of Just Dial and its leaded named VSS Mani) at XLRI Jamshedpur. Continuing by sharing he came up with a new research paper titled "Growth Opportunities in Rural Market by changing techniques in supply chain management system" in which he shared the various aspects in the field of Retail and various techniques to enhance it. We all eagerly look forward for his many knowledge sharing research papers in future and wish him very best of luck for his bright future.

**Nilanjan Ray** is from Kolkata, India. He has obtained his PhD; M.Com (Mkt); MBA (Mkt), STC FMRM (IIT-Kgp). He has 9 years teaching experience in BBA, MBA, BCom and 6 years Research experience and guided around 56 Post Graduate students' project. Dr. Ray has contributed over 40 research papers in reputed National and International Referred, Peer Reviewed Journals , Proceedings and 4 Edited Research Hand Books from IGI-Global USA and 1 Research Hand Book from Apple Academic Publisher CRC Press A Taylor & Francis Group, USA . He has also associated himself as a reviewer of Tourism Management Elsevier, Journal of Service Marketing Emerald Group Publishing Limited, Journal of Business and Economics, Research Journal of Business and Management Accounting and as an Editorial Board Member of several referred Journals. He has also chaired in a technical session at IJAS Conference 2012, at Harvard University, Boston, USA. Dr. Ray is a life-member of the International Business Studies Academia.

**Ajit Kumar Shukla** is a professor of commerce, in the area of Marketing, dept. of Commerce, M.G. Kashi Vidyapith (University), Varanasi, India.

**Juhi Srivastava** is an assistant professor in Finance area in the Department of Management Studies, Kashi Institute of Technology, Varanasi. She has a Bachelor's in Commerce (B.Com) from the Sunbeam College for Women, Bhagwanpur (VBSPU University) and a Master's in Business Administration (MBA) with a specialisation in finance and human resources from the United Institute of Management, Allahabad (GBTU University). Her interest is in serving education in the field of financial studies to further grow as a better teacher. She has participated in various National seminars and Workshops. Her two research papers have been published in national journals.

**Marta Vidal** is Assistant Professor of Management at European University of Madrid. She received her BSc and MBA from ESADE Business School, she is a Phd student in Management at Complutense University of Madrid.

**Javier Vidal-García** is Assistant Professor of Finance, University of Valladolid, Spain. He graduated with a BSc in Management from Queen´s University Belfast, MSc in Finance from Aston Business School, MA in Economics from Autonomous University of Madrid, Phd in Financial Economics from Complutense University of Madrid and has been postdoctoral fellow at the Harvard Business School.

**Shefali Virkar** is currently part of the department of Politics and International Relations at the University of Oxford (UK). Shefali Virkar is a research student at the University of Oxford, UK, currently reading for a D.Phil. in Politics. Her doctoral research seeks to explore the growing use of Information and Communication Technologies (ICTs) to promote better governance in the developing world, with a special focus on the political and institutional impacts of ICTs on local public administration reform in India. Shefali holds an M.A. in Globalisation, Governance and Development from the University of Warwick, UK. Her Master's thesis analysed the concept of the Digital Divide in a globalising world, its impact developing countries and the ensuing policy implications. At Oxford, Shefali is a member of Keble College.

# Index

## I



## K



## L



## M



## O



## P



## R



## S



## T



## U



## V



## W

www.ingramcontent.com/pod-product-compliance
Lightning Source LLC
LaVergne TN
LVHW080525300926
849162LV00007B/1543